NATURAL LANGUAGE PROCESSING IN LISP

An Introduction to Computational Linguistics

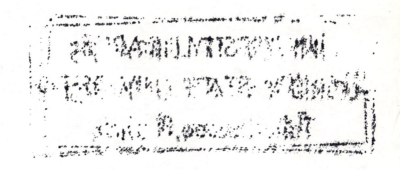

Natural Language Processing In LISP

An Introduction to Computational Linguistics

Gerald Gazdar
University of Sussex

Chris Mellish
University of Edinburgh

Addison-Wesley Publishing Company
Wokingham, England · Reading, Massachusetts · Menlo Park, California
New York · Don Mills, Ontario · Amsterdam · Bonn
Sydney · Singapore · Tokyo · Madrid · San Juan

The programs presented in this book have been included for their instructional
value. They have been tested with care but are not guaranteed for any particular
purpose. The publisher does not offer any warranties or representations, nor does
it accept any liabilities with respect to the programs.

Many of the designations used by manufacturers and sellers to distinguish their
products are claimed as trademarks. Addison-Wesley has made every attempt to
supply trademark information about manufacturers and their products mentioned
in this book. A list of the trademark designations and their owners appears on
page xvi.

Cover designed by Marshall Henrichs
and printed by The Riverside Printing Co. (Reading) Ltd.
Illustrations by Chartwell Illustrators.
Typeset by CRB Typesetting Services, Ely, Cambs.
Printed in Great Britain by Mackays of Chatham plc, Chatham, Kent.

First printed 1989.

British Library Cataloguing in Publication Data
Gazdar, Gerald
   Natural language processing in LISP : an
   introduction to computational linguistics.
   1. Natural language. Analysis of
   Applications of computer systems.
   Programming languages. LISP language
   I. Title   II. Mellish, C.S. (Christopher S.)
   1954–
   418

   ISBN 0-201-17825-7

Library of Congress Cataloguing in Publication Data
Gazdar, Gerald.
   Natural language processing in LISP.

   Bibliography: p.
   Includes index.
   1. Computational linguistics.   2. LISP (Computer
program language) I. Mellish, C.S. (Christopher S.),
1954–   . II. Title.
P98.G35   1989   410′.28′55133   88-16646
ISBN 0-201-17825-7

PREFACE

At the time of writing, almost every computing group and linguistics group in the world is urgently starting up courses in computational linguistics and natural language processing (NLP). In our view, the initiation of these courses is not a mere transitory whim of academic fashion: a 1985 industrial report predicted that the market for NLP products in the UK and US would expand by a factor of 100 over the ensuing decade. Many people with a training in NLP will be needed to develop, produce and maintain these products.

Audience

This book is aimed at computer scientists and linguists at undergraduate, postgraduate or faculty level, who have taken, or are concurrently taking, a programming course in LISP. However, a good proportion of the book will also be useful to people with an interest in linguistics or NLP but who do not have a computational background. The book is specifically intended to teach NLP and computational linguistics: it does not attempt to teach programming or computer science to linguists, or to provide more than an implicit introduction to linguistics for computer scientists. It is difficult to discuss a topic like NLP without assuming that one's readers have some familiarity with the rudiments of set theory (the notions of set, set membership, the subset relation, and so on), and likewise the rudiments of elementary logic (negation, conjunction, disjunction, the material conditional and biconditional, existential and universal quantification, and so on). So we make this assumption.

Coverage

The major focus of this book, as of the field to which it provides an introduction, is on the processing of the orthographic forms of natural language utterances and text. No attempt is made to provide serious coverage of issues in speech production and recognition, topics that deserve books to themselves, books that we would not be competent to write. Most of the book deals with the parsing and understanding of natural language, much less on the production of it. This bias reflects the present shape of the field, and of the state of knowledge. Although there is no chapter devoted to production (that is, language generation) as such, some discussion of it is interleaved with that on parsing and understanding.

The book is formally oriented and technical in character, and organized, for the most part, around formal techniques. The perspective adopted is that of computer science, not cognitive science. We have no claims to make about the way the human mind processes natural language. We concentrate on areas that are beginning to be well understood, and for which standard techniques (such as chart parsing) have begun to emerge. An inevitable consequence of this emphasis is that we spend a good deal more time on syntactic processing than on semantic or pragmatic processing.

Another consequence is that discussion of developments at the leading edge of NLP research, on such topics as parallel parsing algorithms, the new style categorial grammars, connectionist approaches or the emerging implementations of situation semantics and discourse representation theory, are excluded altogether or relegated to the further reading sections.

A less readily excusable omission is any consideration of the role of probabilistic techniques in NLP. Some of these techniques are reasonably well understood and offer valuable leverage on the ambiguity problems that confront virtually every aspect of NLP. But to use probabilities, one has to have access to them, or have access to data from which they can be extracted. Vast amounts of data are needed to get meaningful numbers out, and often the data has to be exhaustively and expensively hand-coded first – for example, by having each word tagged with its syntactic category. As a consequence, probabilistic NLP work is largely restricted, at present, to those few centres that have the necessary data and the resources to process it, notably IBM at Yorktown Heights in the US and Lancaster University in the UK.

Grammar formalism

Computational linguists have, over the years, adopted many different grammar formalisms for use by their parsers, sometimes borrowing them from linguistics, sometimes developing them from scratch for the purpose in hand. Even today, there are probably two dozen or more distinct grammar formalisms in use in various NLP projects across the world. Many of the current ones are 'unification based'. Rather than attempt to survey some subset of these, and devote space to the notations and technical niceties that distinguish them, we have simply adopted one, PATR, due to Stuart Shieber and his associates at SRI International, and used it throughout the book. PATR is relatively widely used in the NLP community, but that was not the primary reason for our choice. From the perspective of this book, it represents a very clean, uncluttered, basic unification grammar formalism that is sufficiently expressive that pretty much anything one might want to say in another grammar formalism can be readily translated into a PATR equivalent. It is also rather straightforward to implement an interpreter for PATR in LISP, and we show how to do this.

Contents

- **Chapter 1: Introduction** looks briefly at the origins of NLP, the emergence of structural notions in NLP, the ways in which researchers have attempted to represent meaning, the increasing appreciation of the role of real-world knowledge and the early indications that NLP is moving from academic research into commercial technology. The chapter concludes by considering the appropriateness of using LISP for NLP.

- **Chapter 2: Finite-state techniques** begins with finite-state transition networks and their implementation in LISP, moving on to the more interesting and useful finite-state transducers, and concludes with a brief look at the limitations of finite-state machines.

- **Chapter 3: Recursive and augmented transition networks** shows how the former can be used to model recursive phenomena in English, how they can be implemented in LISP and what their limitations are. After considering pushdown transducers, augmented transition networks are introduced, their implementation considered and their inherently procedural character noted.

- **Chapter 4: Grammars** considers the declarative representation of grammars, words, rules and structures, and introduces the PATR grammar formalism that is used throughout the rest of the book. Subcategorization, the use of features, encoding feature specifications in LISP, context-free, finite-state and indexed grammars and languages are among the topics discussed in some detail.

- **Chapter 5: Parsing, search and ambiguity** considers a simple parsing problem in minute detail, distinguishes bottom-up from top-down parsing, and breadth-first from depth-first search strategies, touches on the possibility of storing intermediate results, investigates the major sources of ambiguity, and explains determinism and look-ahead.

- **Chapter 6: Well-formed substring tables and charts** pursues the possibility of storing intermediate results in detail by introducing well-formed substring tables and charts. The fundamental rule of active chart parsing is discussed, as are such topics as chart initialization, rule invocation, search strategy, housekeeping, efficiency and alternative rule invocation strategies.

- **Chapter 7: Features and the lexicon** the longest chapter in the book, develops the feature–theoretic view of syntax and then goes on to look at the nature of the lexicon presupposed by feature-based language models. Feature structures are treated as graphs and implemented in LISP, subsumption and unification are defined, and a LISP realization of PATR is presented. Issues that arise in chart parsing with feature-based grammars, such as copying, duplication checking, indexing and the conflation of similar edges, are discussed. The rest of the chapter is devoted to the representation of lexical knowledge and the implementation of a lexicon in LISP.

- **Chapter 8: Semantics** moves from syntax to semantics via the notion of compositionality, and a look at meaning as reference. The issues that arise in translating English to a meaning representation language then take over, and a database query language DBQ is presented. Thinking of computational semantics as feature instantiation leads to consideration of transitive verbs and quantification, ambiguity, preferences and timing, and the possibility of building semantic checking into the grammar.

- **Chapter 9: Question answering and inference** includes such topics as the evaluation of DBQ formulae, standard logical inference, the implementation in LISP of backwards and forwards inference, the pathological nature of logical inference, primitives and canonical forms, inheritance and defaults. It concludes by presenting a simple semantic network in LISP.

- **Chapter 10: Pragmatics** shifts from semantics to pragmatics, initially by considering the semantic and pragmatic roles of noun phrases. The chapter goes on to present the contrast between given and new information, the notion of understanding by prediction and the use of discourse structure. It ends by presenting language generation as a goal-oriented process and language understanding as plan recognition.

Organization

After the introductory chapter, each chapter contains material of two types. The first type is a relatively self-contained treatment of some theoretical topic. Here, computational issues are discussed without reference to the details of LISP or any other programming language. A person without much computational background should be able to get a feel for the issues in NLP by just reading this material. The second type contains extracts of programs, notes on techniques and exercises in LISP. For our programs, we consistently use the Common LISP dialect of LISP, as implementations of Common LISP are readily available and Common LISP is emerging as a commercial standard. Partial solutions to a selection of the exercises are given at the back of the book. However, some exercises are relatively open ended or deal with interesting and important issues which we felt were too advanced to merit full discussion in the text. We anticipate that instructors may choose to develop their own solutions to some of these exercises and work through them in class. We have attempted to grade exercises as follows, to indicate their approximate level of difficulty:

- *easy* – an exercise that someone who has followed the text should be able to do fairly mechanically within half an hour.

- *intermediate* – an exercise that requires some thought – for instance, about a minor variation on a presented technique or about some limited linguistic phenomenon – but which does not require significant originality.

- *hard* – an exercise that requires substantial original thought or technical expertise.

- *project* – an exercise that could profitably be extended into a project.

It is extremely hard to be consistent or accurate in such a grading, especially when readers of the book may come from a variety of different backgrounds, but we hope that our crude classification does make the selection of relevant exercises easier.

Programming language

In our view, for a computational linguistics or NLP textbook to be maximally useful, it must commit itself to a particular choice of real programming language. However, the choice of language has to recognize the major regional language divisions in computing and artificial intelligence: in the US, almost all NLP is done in LISP, and LISP is widely used outside the US, as well.

We feel that the study of computational linguistics is only brought to life by actually writing and running programs. So, a textbook on the subject should provide a source of ideas and examples to stimulate the student's initial programming activity. It is much easier to follow a particular computational concept or algorithm, especially to those lacking a thorough computer science backgound, if it is expressed in a familiar programming language than if it is expressed (formally or informally) in some unfamiliar way. Thus, although we have had to introduce new notations for certain *declarative* notions, we have chosen to base our discussions of programming and algorithms around examples in an actual programming language, namely Common LISP.

As the programs presented in this book are intended to be as simple and self-explanatory as possible, rather than efficient, we have only used a small subset of LISP. The reader who has mastered one of the standard textbooks on the language should have no difficulty with the basic programming constructs used. The programs presented here are available on a 720K 3.5 inch MS-DOS disk for £12 (within the UK) or US$25 (outside the UK) from: Technical Reports, School of Cognitive and Computing Sciences, University of Sussex, Brighton BN1 9QN, UK. The programs are also available as part of the Sussex University POPLOG distribution (from Version 14). They are organized as a set of LISP library files and throughout the text we will refer to a program 'xxx' as lib xxx. A complete listing of all the examples presented in the main part of the text, together with other code relevant to the programming exercises, is to be found in the appendix.

Acknowledgements

We are grateful to ESRC and SERC for grant provision during the writing of this book; to Alex Franz and Karen Osborne for invaluable research assistance; to Margaret Mellish for her constant support and tolerance; to Roger Sinnhuber and his systems colleagues at Sussex for creating and maintaining the very agreeable computational environment in which this book came to be written and debugged; to the anonymous readers who made many useful comments on the original outline of the book, and on subsequent pre-final drafts; to our publishers Simon Plumtree, Debra Myson-Etherington and Stephen Bishop whose enthusiasm and determination to see us deliver kept us within months rather than years of our deadlines; and to Doug Arnold, Alan Black, Bob Carpenter, Richard Coates, Ben du Boulay, Lynne Cahill, Walter Daelemans, Jeff Dalton, Margaret Deuchar, Robert Duncan, Roger Evans, Jeff Goldberg, Ron Kaplan, Tom Khabaza, David Miller, Alison Mudd, Simon Nichols,

Hugh Noble, Geoff Pullum, Allan Ramsay, Graeme Ritchie, Louisa Sadler, Stuart Shieber, Aaron Sloman, Jasper Taylor, Peter Whitelock and Anna Zengteler for various kinds of help. Alan Black, in particular, played a major role in the realization of the example programs used to illustrate much of the text.

Gerald Gazdar

Chris Mellish

March 1989

CONTENTS

CHAPTER 1

INTRODUCTION

This is a textbook that aims to teach the reader about useful, well-understood techniques for natural language processing (NLP). In the chapters that follow, we will rarely have much to say about the history of the field, about approaches whose utility is doubtful or about techniques that are, as yet, poorly understood. Occasionally, the further reading sections that end each chapter will provide some pointers into the history, but that is not their primary function. Accordingly, this introductory chapter provides a thumbnail sketch of the history of NLP so that those new to the field can get some slight sense of what has gone on in the first three decades of work in computational linguistics.

We begin by looking at the origins of NLP on machines less powerful than the pocket calculators of today, at early applied computational linguistics and at early machine translation. We observe the move from numbers to strings and thence to structures, and at the parallel progress from procedural ways of thinking embodied in, for example, augmented transition networks, towards the declarative formalisms and data structures that have emerged in the 1980s. En route, we note how ambiguity has emerged as *the* problem for NLP and see the directions in which people have sought solutions to it.

Then we turn to the representation of meaning: classic procedural work from the 1970s, the emergence of network formalisms and the gradual resurgence of logicism in the 1980s after a decade in which it was deeply

1

unfashionable. Ambiguity rears its head again and we glance at a semantic technique for reducing it by imposing selectional restrictions. Such semantic techniques, it turns out, are insufficient for satisfactory NLP and so we look at the role of knowledge, especially real-world knowledge, and examine its relevance to participants' goals and beliefs, and hence also their speech acts, conversation and the structure of their discourse.

This is a book about NLP techniques, not about their application. However, after surveying the short history of the field in this introductory chapter, we take an even briefer look at the emergence of the new technology of current NLP applications and tools, including machine translation, database front ends, grammar development environments, intelligent text processing and articulate expert systems.

In subsequent chapters, our discussion will be illustrated with programming examples and exercises that use LISP. Although the program code used is intended to be straightforward, this book is not intended to teach the basics of programming, nor even the basics of LISP. It is assumed that readers already have some facility in LISP, or are being taught it in parallel with an NLP course based on this book. A bit more is said about the particular characteristics of LISP and its suitability for NLP in the penultimate section of this chapter.

This chapter concludes, in a final further reading section, by suggesting sources, some of which provide more information on the history of NLP than has been given here, and others of which survey current areas of application in detail. There are a number of good textbooks on LISP programming and these are also listed in this section.

1.1   The origins of natural language processing

The earliest computers were primarily number processors and the resources available on the first-generation programmable calculators are not dissimilar to the resources available on the early computers. If you try to imagine getting a cheap programmable calculator to do machine translation from Russian to English, then you may get a sense of the magnitude of the tasks that confronted the pioneers of natural language processing (NLP) in the 1950s and early 1960s. Even today, computers represent linguistic objects in non-linguistic ways. Consider the word GO. Many computers will represent this word as a sequence of two bytes; namely, 01000111 ($= 71$) and 01001111 ($= 79$), these being the ASCII codes for the letters G and O, respectively. If you give a computer a list of names and ask it to sort them, then George will precede Olga in the list that results, not because G precedes O in the alphabet, but because 71 is a smaller number than 79.

Three decades of computer science have given us programming languages that make it as easy to talk about linguistic objects like words and sentences as it is to talk about numbers and addition. But as recently as 30 years ago, things were very different, and the earliest work in NLP should be seen in the context of the resources that were available then.

As those who count sheep know well, counting is a very boring task. Even the very earliest computers counted fast and accurately, and they did not get bored. They could, for example, count how many times 'the' occurs in Hamlet. Some of the earliest work that came to be known as computational linguistics did exactly this kind of counting. A typical application was the attempted attribution of authorship to texts whose authorship was in doubt. In this kind of research, computers are used to compile statistics – for example, the frequency of occurrence of the word 'upon' – in texts whose origin is not in doubt. These figures are then compared with a corresponding set compiled from the disputed or unknown text and a case made that the text has, or has not, been written by the same author.

Other work once considered to be computational linguistics involved the use of computers to derive indexes and concordances from computer-readable texts. Nowadays, such work continues under the rubric of 'literary and linguistic computing', but no longer really counts as computational linguistics. And, of course, these days, even humble word-processing programs often come equipped with sophisticated indexing utilities that can be used to do certain tasks that once required serious computational effort.

One of the first linguistic applications of computers to be envisaged and funded was *machine translation (MT)*. The military and intelligence communities in the US and abroad, in particular, had great hopes in MT and invested accordingly. But, despite the level of funding, the first generation of work in MT was very disappointing. There was little appreciation of the fact that meaning was essentially involved, nor of the extent of ambiguity in ordinary text. The linguistic theories assumed, to the extent that any were assumed, were rudimentary. And even if they had not been, the computational resources necessary to support more sophisticated theories were simply not available. The first generation MT work amounted to little more than machine language programs for word-by-word substitution. With the wisdom of hindsight, it is unsurprising that the results were of no utility. By the mid-1960s this had become very apparent and US government agency funding for MT research dried up completely in the aftermath of a damning report on MT prepared by the National Academy of Sciences in 1966. No large commercial MT systems existed at the end of that decade. Two decades later, things had changed radically in this respect, as we shall see in the final section.

Many of the developments in NLP have arisen from a changing view of the nature of computers. For, although they are good at arithmetic, it is better to think of computers as very general symbol manipulation machines. The symbols that computers manipulate can represent numbers, or they can represent more complex objects like words, sentences, trees or networks. The machine code instructions that a computer executes perform very simple operations, like shunting information from one part of the machine's memory to another or adding together two numbers. The problem with many early programming languages, such as FORTRAN, was that they forced the programmer to think in terms of numbers and to specify algorithms at a level close to the actual machine code. The 'high-level' languages that have developed since then – for example, APL, Pascal and LISP – allow the programmer to specify instructions in terms of richer and more problem-oriented concepts. The existence of compilers for translating from this more abstract level to the primitive instructions that the machine actually executes relieves programmers of the burden of rephrasing every idea in these terms and leaves them free to concentrate on the problems they are really interested in.

A crucial landmark in the development of NLP as we know it today was the appearance in 1971 of Winograd's SHRDLU program. Winograd's program was written in LISP, the language of choice for most artificial intelligence (AI) researchers in the USA, and the language that we use in this book. One of Winograd's major contributions was to provide an 'existence proof' – to show that natural language understanding, albeit in restricted domains, was indeed possible for the computer. SHRDLU demonstrated in a primitive way a number of abilities – like being able to interpret questions, statements and commands, being able to draw inferences, explain its actions and learn new words – which had not been seen together before in a computer program. SHRDLU was a considerable achievement for one person, and one that would have been impossible without the availability of high-level programming languages.

Computer programming is the activity of giving a computer a precise and detailed set of instructions for how to perform some task. Certainly, a lot of knowledge that humans have seems to be represented in this *procedural* way. For instance, the chances are that you think of the knot in your shoelaces in terms of the sequence of actions that you would have to go through to create it. In fact, you may find it hard to describe the knot adequately without actually going through the motions. Other human knowledge, on the other hand, seems to be less dependent on how it is to be used. For instance, the knowledge that Paris is the capital of France could be used in a number of different ways in different contexts.

If we look at a computer program that performs some task involving natural language, we might well ask 'What knowledge does this program have of grammar? Of word meanings? Of the application domain it operates within?' The trouble is that this knowledge may well be implicit in the instructions that specify how to perform the specific task. The procedural representation suggested by computer implementation can thus get in the way of a theoretical characterization of the task and of what knowledge is required to perform it. A way out of this problem is to represent the rules and principles themselves *declaratively* as symbolic structures to be manipulated by a program.

The idea of having programs working with explicitly represented, inspectable rules has been very successful in applications of AI, where these rule-based systems have been developed for tasks like medical diagnosis and the interpretation of geological measurements. Programming languages such as Prolog and OPS5 have emerged which allow the programmer to simply specify the rules and to leave many of the actual processing decisions up to the machine. In NLP, an example of this might be a programmer specifying a grammar in much the same way as a descriptive linguist. With this representation, the computer would then be able both to generate example sentences allowed by the grammar and to determine whether given sentences were indeed grammatical. Even in a programming language like LISP, which is not inherently declarative, it is possible, and effective, to use declarative programming techniques by representing facts and rules as data structures and implementing various kinds of *interpreters* or *compilers* for using the information in particular tasks. This approach is widely regarded as the most appropriate for modern NLP and means that there can be a much closer dialogue than was previously possible, between NLP researchers, on the one hand, and those few theoretical linguists with an interest in grammar formalism design, on the other. It is also the approach that we will take with most of the programs in this book.

1.2 The imposition of structure

As subsequent chapters in this book make plain, linguistic objects are structured objects. But they do not make their structures manifest. A grasp of the meaning of a sentence depends crucially on an ability, which is likely to be unconscious for a native speaker of the language in question, to recover its structure. A computational device that infers structure from grammatical strings of words is known as a *parser*, and much of the history of NLP over the last 20 years has been occupied with the design of parsers.

A modern parser can be thought of as a device that takes a grammar and a string of words and gives either a grammatical structure imposed on that string of words, if the string of words is grammatical with respect to the grammar, or nothing, if it is not. Conceptually, the parser and the grammar are quite distinct kinds of things: a grammar is simply an abstract definition of a set of well-formed structured objects, whereas a parser is an algorithm – that is, a precise set of instructions – for arriving at such objects.

Whereas in early parsers the grammars employed were inextricably interwoven with the computer programs implementing the parsing algorithm, the trend towards declarative, as opposed to procedural, formalisms has led many modern computational linguists to separate clearly these two components. In spite of the fact that the grammar and the parsing algorithm are best seen as semi-independent components, the manner in which grammars are represented still plays a significant role in an overall parsing system, however.

Recursive transition networks (RTNs) are one way of specifying grammars. An RTN consists of a collection of networks, each of which is labelled with the name of some syntactic category, or 'part of speech' in traditional parlance. The networks themselves consist of a collection of states connected by directional arcs labelled with the names of syntactic categories. Each network has, in addition, an indication of its initial and final states (see Chapter 3 for a detailed discussion). The RTN can be interpreted as a collection of maps that permit us to find our way through the grammatical expressions of the language. To determine whether a given string of words is grammatical according to an RTN, it is necessary to find a route through the relevant maps, starting at initial states and ending up at final states. At each stage, progress can only be made by following the arcs in the network, whose labels tell which categories the successive words in the string must belong to. Only if all these conditions can be met has a successful path been found.

The RTN formalism used to appeal to NLP researchers precisely because of the naturally procedural interpretation suggested by it. In the 1980s, computational linguists shifted from procedural grammar representations to declarative ones (see Chapter 4 for examples). In part, this reflected analogous moves within linguistics itself, but it is also a consequence of the trends within AI and computer science discussed in Section 1.1.

RTNs themselves have been overshadowed in NLP by an elaborated version of the formalism known as the *augmented transition network (ATN)*. An ATN is simply an RTN that has been equipped with a memory and the ability to *augment* arcs with actions and conditions that make reference to that memory (see Chapter 3 for a detailed discussion of RTNs and ATNs). ATN-based parsers were probably the most common kind of parser employed by computational linguists in the 1970s, but they have begun to fall out of favour in recent years. This is largely because the 'augmentations' destroy the declarative nature of the formalism and because a parser using an ATN is limited in the search strategies it can employ (see Chapter 5 for a comprehensive account of the relation between parsing and search).

A much larger range of search strategies become practical once a data structure known as a *chart* is adopted for parsing, and chart parsers have now become one of the basic tools of modern NLP. A chart is basically a data structure in which the parser records its successful attempts to parse subconstituents of the string of words. Once the parser has recorded the presence of a constituent in one part of the string, it never needs to look for the same kind of constituent there again. This represents a significant improvement on the backtracking algorithms used in most ATN systems. The ability of the chart to record, in addition, the current goals of the parser leads to the possibility of implementing very sophisticated algorithms (see Chapter 6 for a detailed discussion of chart-based parsers).

Ambiguity is arguably the single most important problem in NLP (see Chapter 5). Natural languages are riddled with ambiguities at every level of description, from the phonetic to the sociological, and in this respect they differ radically from formal languages, such as the propositional calculus or LISP. Yet, as users of natural languages, we are blithely unaware of this pervasive ambiguity – it only comes to our attention in the guise of such linguistically marginal phenomena as puns, misunderstandings and contested libel suits.

Consider the possible readings of the sentence:

Flying planes made her duck.

One reading is distinctly improbable: it requires us to imagine a female person intermittently lowering her head to avoid a projectile whenever she is engaged in the activity of flying an airplane. Two other readings are semantically quite bizarre: they involve aquatic birds being constructed in improbable ways. So, only one reading remains; namely, that in which she ducks to avoid airplanes that are flying overhead. We will examine later some of the semantic mechanisms used by computational linguists to tackle the problem of ambiguity. This example is a *globally ambiguous* sentence; that is, the entire string of words has more than one structure associated with it. Much of the ambiguity problem in NLP arises, however, from *local ambiguities*; that is, ambiguities that exist only in some subpart of the whole. Consider the following example:

The company that bought Scicon sold VIM.

This sentence is not globally ambiguous and it says nothing at all about whether or not Scicon sold VIM. But if you restrict your attention simply to the last three words, then you might well hypothesize the existence of a sentential subconstituent made up of 'Scicon sold VIM'. This is a local ambiguity, and such local ambiguities can sidetrack natural language parsers into many time-wasting investigations of possibilities that do not work out in the end. Marcus initiated a line of research into so-called deterministic parsers, which are parsers that are not fooled into pointless activity by local ambiguities of this kind (see Chapter 5 for some further discussion). The human parser seems to be adept at overcoming most, but not all, cases of local ambiguity. Work on deterministic parsers seeks to explain why garden path sentences such as (1) below cause such perceptual problems, whereas sentences like (2) do not:

(1)   The metal blocks the tube supports disintegrated.
(2)   The metal block the tube supports disintegrated.

This issue is further discussed in Chapter 5.

1.3   The representation of meaning

Language understanding involves relating linguistic forms to meanings; language generation involves the opposite. We can certainly represent linguistic forms in the computer, but what about meanings? A computer manipulates only formal symbols. How can we say that one symbolic structure correctly represents the meaning of a sentence, whereas another does not?

There have been many different ideas about how meaning can be represented in humans and machines. One possibility involved considering the meaning of an utterance to be a procedure; that is, a set of instructions to achieve what the speaker wants. Such an idea fitted in naturally with the AI concept of the mind as a computational device following rules and instructions of some kind. The competent hearer would be able to construct this procedure and could then decide whether or not to actually run it.

According to the simplest versions of what came to be known as 'procedural semantics', the meaning of a command is a procedure to carry out the required action, the meaning of a question is a procedure to find the answer, the meaning of a statement is a procedure to add the new information conveyed to the hearer's model of the world, and so on. However, there are profound philosophical problems with any simple form of procedural semantics, not the least of which is the problem of defining exactly what is, and what is not, a procedure. If a procedure is a representation that can *only* be run, and whose internal structure cannot be analyzed in any way, then procedural semantics alone cannot account for the fact that a hearer may refuse to obey a command, because it seems impossible or dangerous. On the other hand, if the internal structure of a procedure is something that can be reasoned about, then it is not clear what distinguishes a procedural representation from any other representation that can sometimes be interpreted as a set of instructions.

Given the difficulty of accounting for all possible language uses in the same formalism, most logicians and AI workers have concentrated on representing the meanings of simple statements about the world. It is at least arguable that other uses of language (such as asking questions or issuing commands) involve statement meanings as a component of their meaning. The problem of representing the meanings of statements about the world merges into that of knowledge representation in general, and this is a central concern for AI research.

Some early formalisms for knowledge representation, based on the idea of networks, were motivated by intuitive psychological considerations. Intuitively, it seems, we think of the world in terms of concepts; when we hear something new, we may discover new concepts, or we may discover new relationships between existing concepts. Thus, we can think of representing knowledge in terms of a graph, where the nodes represent the concepts and the links between them represent the relationships that are known. Such 'semantic net' systems, as they are known, are designed to facilitate certain restricted kinds of inference, such as inheritance of properties from node to node (see Chapter 9 for further discussion).

One network-based notation that has provoked a lot of attention is Schank's Conceptual Dependency. This was explicitly intended as a psychological model of how people represent the meaning of sentences. In 1963, the philosophers Katz and Fodor had promulgated the idea of having a fixed set of primitives out of which all meanings were to be constructed. Schank continued in this tradition by proposing a set of (about) 11 primitive actions – for instance, PROPEL (apply a force to) and MTRANS (mental transfer of information). The idea was that these could be combined to express any event in the world. Conceptual dependency was designed to be independent of its use with any particular natural language, to allow it to act, for example, as an 'interlingua' for translating between languages. Associated with each of Schank's primitive actions was a set of underlying argument positions, which could be filled differently for each instance of the action. For example, every time an instance of PROPEL is represented, there has to be an 'actor' (the performer of the action), an 'object' (the thing the force acts on) and a 'direction' (where the activity is coming from and going to).

Nowadays, many of the ideas in the early network-based systems have been subsumed in systems with more structure. Unadorned semantic networks have no way of expressing the fact that certain concepts and relationships should be grouped together into larger chunks. Thus, they cannot explain how a participant might 'focus' on a particular group of things in a discourse or how a reader might have sensible expectations about what is coming next, after recognizing a familiar situation. Some of the systems that have emerged in response to this need are partitioned semantic networks, the knowledge representation language KL-ONE and various systems based on Minsky's 'frames'. One of the latter, scripts, will be discussed in Section 1.4.

The network-based systems of the 1970s have been criticized by a number of researchers for being semantically ill defined and for failing to capture certain distinctions that critics have taken to be important – for example, the distinction between type and token, or that between the membership and subset relations. Indeed, until recently, little effort was spent on producing formal theories of what these networks actually meant and how exactly we should go about expressing any given knowledge in them. A rival class of knowledge representation languages, which has received a great deal of formal attention of this kind, is that of logics – in particular, first-order logic (see Chapter 9).

First-order logic has been used as a representation language in AI right from the beginnings of the subject. Thus, Woods's LUNAR program for answering questions about lunar rock samples, which was produced at roughly the same time as SHRDLU, used a logical representation for the meanings of questions. The current interest in logic programming systems is just one symptom of the growing realization of the importance of logic. Indeed, some researchers argue that many existing network notations, insofar as they are well defined, are equivalent to, or weaker than, first-order logic, and that we should therefore dispense with them. On the other hand, others argue that logic is too neutral a representation language, not tuned to the kinds of meanings that natural language conveys.

The idea of representing natural language meanings in logic is one aspect of a vein of 'logicism' that is present in much of the recent work on NLP. The aim of this enterprise is to produce a formal account of how natural language conveys meaning by drawing on work in formal semantics and the philosophy of language. Almost all computer models of language understanding make use of some concepts from this work – for example, the idea that meaning can be obtained *compositionally*, an idea that goes back to the work of Frege in the 1890s.

The compositionality principle, also known as Frege's principle, maintains that the meaning of any phrase can be obtained by some operation on the meanings of its parts. So, given a structural description of a sentence, it is possible to work out what the sentence means by first finding the meanings of the individual words, then combining these together to construct the meanings of small phrases, then combining these to construct the meanings of larger phrases, and so on until the meaning of the whole sentence is formed. There is no necessity for things to work this way: we can readily imagine (artificial) languages in which, say, the meaning of an expression is determined, in part, by its linear position in the string – for example, a language in which 'one hundred and seven' denotes 93 if it occurs sentence-initially, 107 if it occurs sentence-medially, and 700 if it occurs sentence-finally. The semantics of such languages would not be stateable compositionally – at least, not in any straightforward way. The work of the philosophical logician Montague is taken by many as an important demonstration of the utility of the compositionality principle in the analysis of natural language. Montague showed that many previously problematic, semantic phenomena in natural language were amenable to formal treatment within a strictly compositional regime. Montague's account was not computational in form and left important computational issues, such as the role of inference and the representation of word meanings, untouched. Nevertheless, his methodology has proved an inspiration to many workers in NLP.

As we have seen, a processing account of language comprehension must provide some explanation of how ambiguity is resolved. This involves specifying extra mechanisms for filtering out syntactic or semantic analyzes that are inappropriate. Many computer programs for manipulating natural language have made use of *selectional restrictions*, originally proposed by Katz and Fodor in the early 1960s. Selectional restrictions were introduced as a way of accounting for the fact that, for instance, a sentence as a whole can be unambiguous even though individual words may have several alternative possible senses. The theory was based on the idea that with each sense of a word it is possible to associate semantic markers, specifying features of the meaning as well as conditions on the features of word senses that could combine with it. So, for instance, one possible sense of the word 'spirit' (alcoholic fluid) would have the marker 'physical object', whereas another sense (vital principle) would not. The adjective 'yellow', when describing a colour, requires that the noun it qualifies has the marker 'physical object'. Another sense of 'yellow' (cowardly) requires the noun to have the marker 'animate', but neither of the senses for 'spirit' considered here has this marker. Thus, the phrase 'yellow spirit' can be shown quite formally to have only one possible sense here (yellow-coloured alcoholic fluid), rather than four – to keep things simple, we ignore the other possible senses of 'yellow' and 'spirit'.

Within a processing framework, it is possible to extend the basic Katz and Fodor ideas in a number of ways. For instance, it is possible to ensure that semantic marker analysis causes a syntactic analysis to be rejected if no corresponding semantic readings can be found. The semantic tests can be applied to the referents of phrases, rather than simply the word senses. And a notion of 'preference' can be introduced and dispreferred readings allowed to succeed when no highly ranked reading is available (cf., 'Cowardice is a yellow spirit that haunts the field of battle').

The use of semantic markers and selectional restrictions is a crude technique that can, nevertheless, be computationally effective, especially within restricted domains. It is, however, only the tip of a very large iceberg of possible ways in which knowledge can resolve ambiguity. This is well illustrated by considering an example due to Winograd. If somebody says 'The city councillors refused the demonstrators a permit because they feared violence', most people will understand without apparent difficulty that 'they' refers to the councillors. If instead somebody says 'The city councillors refused the demonstrators a permit because they advocated revolution', most people will decide that 'they' means the demonstrators. Knowledge of some kind is enabling people to resolve this ambiguity, and yet this is considerably more subtle than anything that could be readily expressed by semantic markers and selectional restrictions.

1.4 The role of knowledge

We have seen that resolving ambiguity in sentences requires an understander to have a general knowledge of the world. Understanding the significance of a vague utterance expressed in context also requires knowledge. Thus, a theoretical model of language understanding is not complete without a model of knowledge representation and retrieval, and we cannot construct a robust understanding computer without providing it with an encyclopaedic knowledge of the world. These are rather pessimistic conclusions, but they need not prevent us from continuing with the theoretical study of language or indeed from constructing useful computer programs that operate in limited domains. They do, however, suggest that we must try to classify in a rigorous way the kinds of knowledge that guide a language user and codify enough of it to ensure that our overall models are realistic.

How can knowledge of the world guide a reader to correctly interpret a partially ambiguous piece of natural language encountered in context? Where a sentence is ambiguous, world knowledge must indicate that some possible readings are to be preferred over others. At the simplest, it may allow some readings to be rejected because they presuppose physically impossible situations, but even this will be inadequate if the writer is using metaphor or has established a context where the normal physical laws do not apply. Another idea is to exploit the potential a text has to create expectations in the mind of a reader and to think of the reader as preferring readings that are in accord with these expectations. One such model of expectation-based understanding is provided by Schank's script applier mechanism (discussed in Chapter 10). This works on the principle that many events in the world – especially those involving humans, such as going to a restaurant or using public transport – proceed in a stereotyped way. Therefore, when we read about them, at any point there is a limited number of things that we expect to happen next. We can represent knowledge of prototypical events as sequences of expected actions in 'scripts' for the events. To come up with sensible expectations, a robust natural language understander will need to have a large number of such scripts. This introduces many questions: How can an understander decide which script is appropriate for a given situation? Whether the current script is no longer adequate? How to handle deviations from expected behaviour? The more interesting stories about human beings frequently cannot be understood in terms of stereotyped situations. Rather, it is necessary to reason at a lower level about the goals and plans of the participants to generate expectations.

If we are reading a story, we will be more successful if we can understand the goals and plans of the various characters. We must also, however, bear in mind to some extent the objectives of the writer. Knowledge of the other participant in a communicative exchange is even more important if the medium is speech, as spoken utterances are frequently abbreviated, elliptical, oblique and subject to context-peculiar interpretation. Consider, for example, the following:

    A :   Excuse me, do you know if there is a newsagent near here?

    B :   It's early closing today.

    A :   What about Brighton?

    B :   Johnson's in Ship Street is open until 5.

It is hard, if not impossible, to come up with any sensible interpretation of this exchange between two people if we ignore the fact that the people are communicating and cooperating. Likewise, a hearer who can ask 'Why is she telling me this?' and come up with a reasonable hypothesis is going to be in a better position to understand than someone who cannot. An intelligent hearer must regard utterances in the same way as any other actions performed by an intelligent being. That is, an utterance is an action that, given certain preconditions, will achieve effects planned for by the speaker.

The notion of *planning* has always been of great interest to AI workers and there is now the possibility that planning work in other domains, such as the movement of robot arms, will be applicable to natural language understanding and production (see Chapter 10).

Unfortunately for NLP, the plan associated with an utterance is rarely, if ever, transparently marked in the syntax. Often, the intention is conveyed in a form of words that superficially suggests a different intention. A classic example is an utterance like:

    Can you pass the salt?

which looks as if it ought to be a question but which is normally intended as a request, or an utterance like:

    It is rather cold in here.

which looks like a simple assertion of fact but may well convey intentions having to do with getting a window or door closed by the addressee. NLP researchers now hope that these so-called 'indirect speech acts' can be explained in a unified framework that treats utterances as actions involving the beliefs and goals of the participants, and that assumes principles of cooperative behaviour on behalf of the speaker and the addressee. That is, a successful utterance will cause a change in the addressee's beliefs or goals. The cooperative addressee will attempt to understand the relevance of this change for the speaker's overall plan and will hence establish a suitable cooperative response. To adequately appreciate the effects of utterances, then, it is necessary to be able to reason about beliefs.

In general, it is necessary to reason not only about the speaker's beliefs and the addressee's beliefs, but also about the speaker's beliefs about the addressee's beliefs, the addressee's beliefs about the speaker's beliefs about the addressee, and so on. For instance, to be successfully ironic, the speaker must be expressing some proposition that he or she believes to be false. However, if that is all that is required, then simple lies would be instances of irony. But they are not. In addition, the speaker must believe that the addressee believes it is false and the speaker must believe that the addressee believes that the speaker believes it is false.

Once we start to consider either natural language conversations of more than one utterance or extended discourses, such as this introductory chapter, it becomes clear that there is more structure to be found than that in the sum of the utterances, even taking into account the goals of the participants. That is, people adhere to certain rules and conventions about how conversations and discourses should be organized – for example, when turn-taking should happen in the former.

From a computational point of view, the identification of these rules and conventions can serve not only to enable computers to produce more acceptable conversational behaviour, but also to control the inferences that must be made for successful understanding. For instance, if specific linguistic devices are used in a language for indicating the beginning – for example, 'by the way' – and the end – for example, 'anyway' – of a digression, or for indicating how the speaker or writer is shifting the focus from one topic to another, this is information that a computer program should pick up.

An example from the work of Grosz serves to illustrate the point. Early computational approaches to the interpretation of pronouns used simple heuristics based on recency. So, such a program, on encountering a pronoun, would prefer to interpret it as referring to an item in the previous sentence rather than the one before that, and so on. One of the naturally occurring dialogues that Grosz recorded, however, contained an example of what appears to be a pronoun referring back to something last mentioned 60 utterances (30 minutes) previously. Grosz accounts for this in terms of the discourse having an implicit structure that is tree shaped, rather than linear. Thus, although the reference is back to an object that is chronologically *distant*, it is to something relatively *close* in the implicit discourse structure.

1.5   The emergence of a new technology

There is a sense in which MT, that dream of the 1950s, is now a reality, and there is a sense in which it works. It is a reality because there are commercial software houses selling MT programs and customers in the marketplace buying those programs. Current MT programs work in the following sense: some of the companies that use them save money on translation. They do not 'work' when that is taken to mean 'consistently produce translations from raw text that are indistinguishable from those produced by skilled human translators with unlimited time on their hands.' They all require either pre-editing of the input into some form they can accept, or post-editing to revise or replace the passages that they cannot handle, or both. However, translation by humans is a very expensive and time-consuming enterprise, and, in practice, it also invariably requires post-editing. Anything that speeds up the process and reduces the number of hours that a skilled translator or post-editor has to spend with the material stands a chance of saving money. One example of such a 'working' MT program is METEO, which has translated weather forecasts from English to French on a regular basis in Canada since 1977. More than three-quarters of what it translates is done correctly, without any intervention from human translators.

Another growing application of NLP research is in the field of natural language front ends to databases. A computer database is a store of information about some domain. Thus, a company might have a database listing all employees, their age, their current job, the date they were hired, the number of their office, their home address, the equipment they have at their disposal, the name of their immediate superior, and so on. Given such a store of information, a way of accessing it is needed, and, until recently, this has been done in one of two ways:

(1)   The system interrogates you, the user, usually via a menu of options, to find out what you want to know.

(2)   You interrogate the system by asking it questions in a database query language (see Chapter 9 for an example).

The first strategy is simple and does not require that users have any special training or knowledge of the structure of the database. But it is slow and, more importantly, very inflexible. The second strategy is fast and flexible, but requires users to become familiar with the database and to learn a formal language that is usually as complex as a programming language. Programs that translate a (very restricted subset of a) natural language into a database query language are known as *natural language front ends*. They promise to provide the best of both strategies via the familiarity and flexibility of a natural language (see Chapter 9 which provides an example). A number of such front ends are now available commercially.

The future of MT depends, minimally, on the availability of formal grammars for both the source and target languages. Likewise, the spread of natural language front ends beyond the confines of the English-speaking world depends on the availability of grammars for languages other than English. In these circumstances, there is a need for computational tools that will permit people with some linguistic training to develop formal grammars for a range of different languages. The first generation of such tools has already emerged. They allow linguists to build up a large grammar gradually, testing the consequences of each rule as they go along, experimentally parsing test sentences, checking if the grammar correctly excludes ungrammatical strings, and examining the semantics to see what ambiguities, if any, have been detected, and what meanings have been assigned.

Even with such tools, a formal grammar for even a fragment of a natural language represents a massive investment of skilled labour. This cost could be radically reduced if grammars could be constructed in a largely automatic fashion on the basis of written texts; that is, by *grammar acquisition* programs. This is an area fraught with profound theoretical problems: under one idealization, it is possible to demonstrate mathematically that no such programs could ever achieve their goal. On the other hand, in at least one very circumscribed domain (numeral systems), there has been demonstrable progress. At the very least, we can soon expect to see the appearance of programs that induce the grammatical idiosyncrasies of particular words on the basis of large corpora. And if, as many theoretical linguists of different persuasions now suppose, languages differ much less in their syntax than they do in their lexicons, then there are some grounds for cautious optimism in this area.

Readers familiar with the current generation of word-processing software know that these indispensable devices allow you to issue commands, albeit usually in a very terse notation, that correspond to, for example, 'find all instances of *competant*' or 'copy lines 15 through 72 to another file.' But these programs do not allow you to issue commands like, for example, 'find all references to contemporary politicians' or 'copy all the material on Ireland to another file' or even 'correct all the misspellings.' And yet such instructions are routinely given to secretaries. However, even to correct spelling as intelligently as a human being, it is necessary to understand the meaning of the text, and sometimes understanding will be needed even to detect the misspelling in the first place. We can expect soon to see syntax-based spelling correctors replacing the word-based systems that are currently available. Spelling correctors based on a real understanding of the texts they work on are still, however, a long way off.

Explanation generation for expert systems is another area where NLP techniques are beginning to be applied. An expert system is a computer program that offers advice. It may assist or even replace a human expert. The advice itself may require almost nothing in the way of NLP; thus, a medical expert system for disease diagnosis might just produce the name of a disease, together with the probability that the patient has that disease. As this example may illustrate, however, humans are not, in general, satisfied merely with advice, no matter what degree of confidence they have in the expert – and with computerized experts, this may not be high. They want to know what the basis of the advice is; in other words, they want an explanation of how the expert arrived at the advice given. For any class of problems that are hard enough to make it worth constructing an expert system, there will typically be a vast number of bases for the advice given, and so an articulate expert system must be able to express itself in a correspondingly vast number of different ways. This makes the incorporation of potted scripts for each of the possible explanations quite impractical. The program needs to be able to synthesize a comprehensible explanation from scratch on the basis of the particular chain of inferences that led it to the advice it gave. To be able to do this, it needs to have a very good grasp of the syntax and semantics of the fragment of a natural language that will be used in its explanations. As expert systems become more common, explanation generation is becoming an increasingly import-ant application area for NLP. Many of those working in the area of expert systems regard the explanation-giving facility as the key to public accept-ance of expert systems. The explanations also have an educational value, of course – for junior doctors who consult an expert system for diagnostic purposes can learn from it in much the same way that they might learn from a consultant.

1.6   Using LISP for natural language processing

LISP is an expressive language for stating algorithms in computational linguistics and Common LISP, the version used in this book, is a widely available and carefully designed representative of the large class of LISP dialects that are available. In NLP, we are frequently interested in manip-ulating symbols (words, phonemes, parts of speech) and structured objects (sequences, trees, graphs) made from them. LISP is a high-level language in which we can directly express operations on symbols (represented by symbols, strings, numbers, for instance) and structures (represented by lists, vectors, records, for instance) without having to worry about how these high-level concepts are actually represented in the machine. The concept of *recursion* plays a fundamental role in NLP. Linguistic objects are described by recursive data structures and operations on these data structures are naturally expressed as recursive algorithms. Unlike some programming languages, LISP places no restrictions on procedures calling themselves (directly or indirectly), and so can express such algorithms directly.

Although the programs presented in this book are primarily designed to be clear and explanatory, rather than efficient, it should be pointed out that LISP is a language for writing 'serious' NLP programs too. In this book, extensive use is made of lists, but LISP provides many other kinds of complex data structures – for instance, arrays, hash tables and vectors. The LISP programmer is therefore presented with a wide range of possible ways of implementing the objects manipulated by a program. According to the characteristics of the task at hand, one or other of these might suggest itself as the most efficient – for instance, to achieve an appropriate indexing behaviour. The provision of a *garbage collector* in LISP means that the programmer can write programs that freely create and discard data structures, confident that unused storage will be recycled and that there will be no artificial limits on the sizes or numbers of data structures.

SUMMARY

- The earliest computers were quite unsuitable for NLP.
- Early attempts at machine translation failed.
- Winograd's SHRDLU was a turning point in NLP.
- Modern NLP has increasingly adopted declarative formalisms.
- Ambiguity is the single most important problem in NLP.
- First-order logic has been widely used to represent meanings.
- Interpreting an utterance depends on knowledge of the context.
- Commercial applications of NLP are becoming practical.
- LISP is an appropriate programming language for NLP.

Further reading

SHRDLU is described in Winograd (1972) and LUNAR in Woods (1973). Marcus's approach to parsing is presented in Marcus (1980). Katz and Fodor's influential early approach to semantics is to be found in Katz and Fodor (1963), while Minsky's equally influential 'frames' paper was eventually published as Minsky (1981). Schank (1972) introduces his notion of Conceptual Dependency, while Schank and Abelson (1977) does the same for scripts. Partitioned semantic networks first appear in Hendrix (1975), Brachman and Schmolze (1985) provide an overview of KL-ONE, and Sondheimer, Weischedel and Bobrow (1984) indicate its relevance to NLP. The role of discourse structure in resolving pronominal reference is the subject of Grosz (1977). Procedural semantics gets careful critical discussion in Woods (1981). Montague's work can be found in his posthumous 1974 collection, but readers are advised to approach it via the Dowty *et al.* (1981) textbook.

The seminal work on automatic induction of grammars is Gold (1967), Power and Longuet-Higgins (1978) report results in one very specific domain, and Selfridge (1986) offers a rather different perspective on language learning. Tsujii (1986) and King (1987) look at the prospects for MT, the history of MT is engagingly told by Slocum (1985) and Hutchins (1986), and more material on the history of NLP in general can be gleaned from Barr and Feigenbaum (1981, Sections IV.A and V.A.), Tennant (1981), Sparck Jones and Wilks (1983, Section I), Ritchie and Thompson (1984), Grosz *et al.* (1986, especially the introduction), Ballard and Jones (1987), and Lehnert (1988). Gazdar *et al.* (1987) provides a near-exhaustive listing of NLP work done in the 1980–7 period. Johnson (1985), Wahlster (1986) and Schwartz (1987) are relevant reading for anyone with an interest in the commercial applications of NLP products, while Pullum (1987) sounds a cautionary note in respect of military applications. Two important and difficult problems, neither addressed in this book, which need solutions if NLP products are to become widespread, are (a) how to deal with ill-formed input (Weischedel and Sondheimer 1983) and (b) the evaluation of the performance of NLP systems (Guida and Mauri 1986). Winograd (1983), Grishman (1986) and Allen (1987) provide textbook introductions to NLP that are not tied to specific programming languages. Unusually, more than one-half of Allen's book is devoted to semantic and pragmatic issues in NLP, and is thus somewhat complementary to the present book.

The standard reference on Common LISP is Steele (1984), but Wilensky (1986) is more approachable as a textbook, and also includes reference material on the whole of the language. Winston and Horn (1989) is an excellent introduction to LISP for those wishing to go on to write AI programs – whereas its coverage of the language is not so complete, it develops a number of interesting example programs. Touretzky (1984) is a textbook especially aimed at those with a non-mathematical background. It goes slowly and carefully over the fundamentals of LISP, but does not keep completely to the Common LISP standard and is rather limited in coverage. Yuasa and Hagiya (1987) and Yuasa (1988) may also prove useful to the LISP beginner. The start of the appendix (p. 408) briefly documents any standard LISP functions and special forms needed in this book, but which are not found in all of these textbooks.

CHAPTER 2

FINITE-STATE TECHNIQUES

Finite-state automata (FSAs) are among the simplest computing machines that can be envisaged. They are well understood mathematically, easy to implement and efficient at doing what they do. If an NLP problem can be conveniently solved with a finite-state automaton, then it is probably a good idea to solve it that way. However, FSAs are subject to certain formal limitations that render them ill suited to certain computational linguistic tasks. This chapter provides a fairly comprehensive introduction to these machines and their implementation, indicates possible areas of application and gives some concrete examples of their use, and examines their limitations.

We begin this chapter by presenting finite-state transition networks (FSTNs). An FSTN can be regarded as a neutral description of a language (a set of sequences of symbols), but it can also be interpreted, for instance, as a specification of an FSA to recognize elements of the language or as a specification of an FSA to generate elements of the language. We move on to consider a simple extension to the basic FSTN notation, which then allows networks to be interpreted as finite-state transducers, which are FSAs that can recognize elements of one language, while generating elements of another. We conclude the chapter with a look at what FSAs can and cannot do.

2.1   Finite-state transition networks

Czestawa Szymanowska leaves the house of her relatives in San Francisco and takes the bus to the airport. Although her relatives left Poland in the 1960s, they continue to speak Polish at home, so the fact that Czestawa can speak hardly a word of English has caused her no problems whatsoever. But she is alone at the airport and she needs to know if she can reroute her return flight via London, so she can visit a cousin who her relatives have told her now lives there. There are long queues at the check-in desks so Czestawa goes over to one of the public terminals in the foyer and types her question in, in Polish – actually only an approximation to Polish, since the terminal has an ASCII keyboard and she is forced to omit diacritics. The machine duly replies, in Polish.

Putting aside for the moment all questions about how such a machine could have understood her query and constructed an answer, let us simply consider the question of how such a machine might infer that her query was expressed in Polish, rather than Spanish, Russian, English or any of the other dozen or so languages that it is equipped to handle.

Here are a couple of strawman solutions. Firstly, different languages employ the letters of the Roman alphabet with different frequencies. The letter 'j', for example, is much more commonly used in Dutch than it is in English. So, one possibility is to compile letter frequency tables for the various languages and then use these to compare against the frequency profiles of pieces of unknown text. The problem with this solution, which might be very satisfactory for books or newspapers, in the present context is that the sample of text is likely to be very small, perhaps only two or three words, and thus will not have any meaningful letter frequency profile.

A second candidate solution is suggested by the fact that in order to be made available for its presumed function, such a machine must, presumably, contain a parser for Spanish, a parser for Arabic, a parser for English, and so on. So, presented with the input in a language of unknown identity, we run the Spanish parser on it; if that fails to arrive at a parse, then we run the Arabic parser, and so on. Eventually, we try the Polish parser and succeed. The obvious problem with this solution, at least in a world of serial machines and relatively slow parsers, is that by the time that it realizes that the query was in Polish, the traveller Czestawa will have missed her plane. It is a case of using a sledgehammer to crack a nut.

Suppose this was what Czestawa typed in:

Czy pasazer jadacy do Warszawy moze jechac przez Londyn?

Now, the authors of this book do not speak a word of Polish, nor a word of Spanish, but if they are told that what Czestawa typed in is either Polish or Spanish, then they can tell right away that it is Polish – told that it was

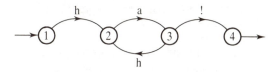

Figure 2.1   A laughing machine.

either Polish or Serbo-Croat, they might be less confident in their judge-
ment. Indeed, if you were to put your hand over all but the first word, they
would still guess confidently that they were dealing with Polish, not Spanish. So, the authors are willing to make a decision here based on exposure
to less than a half-dozen letters in a language none of whose words are
known to them.

The reasoning used is something like this:

- 'Czy' could not be a Spanish word but it could be a Polish word.

- If the first word is Polish rather than Spanish, then the chances are
  extremely high that the whole utterance will be in Polish, not a
  mixture of Polish and Spanish.

But how can we be so sure that 'czy' is not a word of Spanish? We cannot
read, utter or understand any Spanish, and we have not bothered to look
up 'czy' in a Spanish dictionary. Well, we cannot be absolutely sure, of
course. But we have naive theories about the possible orthography (written
form) of Spanish words and Polish words. These naive graphotactic theories are consistent with 'czy' being a Polish word, but not consistent with it
being a Spanish word. If we could articulate theories of this kind, improve
them in the light of the way Polish and Spanish graphotactics really work,
and encode them in a manner that a computer could understand, then we
would be a long way towards solving the problem that Czestawa's inter-
locutor solves in our scenario above.

However, before we tackle the problem posed by our airport advice
unit, let us turn to a much more trivial problem, one which is apparently
quite unrelated: getting a computer to laugh. Laughing, for present purposes, consists of displaying the sequences of characters 'ha!', 'haha!',
'hahaha!', and so on. Figure 2.1 is a diagram of an abstract machine, TO-
LAUGH-1, that will do just that.

This diagram, a *finite-state transition network (FSTN)* is a conventional illustration of a very simple *finite-state automaton (FSA)* with four
states, 1, 2, 3 and 4, state 1 being an *initial state*, signalled by the '→'
pointing into it, and state 4 being a *final state*, signalled by the '→'

emerging from it. The four nodes of the graph representing these states are linked by four directed *arcs*:

- one, which starts from state 1 and goes to state 2, is labelled 'h';
- another, which starts from state 2 and goes to state 3, is labelled 'a';
- another, which starts from state 3 and goes to state 2, is labelled 'h'; and
- the final one, which is labelled '!', which goes from state 3 to state 4.

In machines of this kind, we will also make use of unlabelled arcs, which are referred to as 'jump' arcs for reasons that will become apparent.

How is this diagram to be understood? Well, the machine must start in an initial state, which can only be state 1 in this instance. If the initial state is also a final state, then it can simply do nothing, but that does not apply in the present case. If the state it finds itself in is not a final state, then it must change state by traversing an arc that starts from the state it is in and changing into the state to which the arc points. In traversing the arc, the machine must follow the instruction that labels the arc. Here, and for the present, we will interpret a label like 'h' as an instruction to print the letter 'h' – on a VDU, a printer, a paper tape or whatever. Since only one arc leaves state 1, our machine has no choices open to it: it has to change state to state 2 and print an 'h'. State 2 is not a final state, and like 1, it has but a single arc leaving it. So, the machine must follow this arc, print an 'a', and find itself in state 3. Now, for the first time, our machine is faced with a choice: it can move to state 4 or back to state 2. If it moves on to state 4, generating a '!', then it will have reached a final state. Now although an FSA, for that is what our diagram depicts, is not *required* to halt when it reaches a final state, unless the latter has no arcs leaving it, it is *permitted* to halt in final states. In this case, however, there is nowhere else to go and the machine will halt, leaving the string 'ha!' on the VDU as a trace of its activity. State 3 has another arc leaving it, labelled with 'h' and leading back to state 2. The machine may choose to traverse this arc. If it does so, then it will find itself faced with exactly the same sequence of arcs, actions and choices as it was when it was last in that state. And so we may see 'haha!' printed, or 'hahahaha!', or any such sequence.

We are interpreting this FSTN as a machine for *producing* laughter and it is important to appreciate that the choice that needs to be made when the machine finds itself in state 3, whether to move to state 4 or back to state 2, is a choice that is outside the machine's own competence. If we were to program a laughing machine based on this automaton, then our program would need to consult some outside authority, such as a random number generator, the time of day or the user, at this point.

But this 'production' or 'generation' interpretation of our FSTN is not the only possible interpretation, nor even the only useful one. Imagine a video game that tells the user jokes. When the user has got the joke, he or she is supposed to type in 'haha!' or 'hahaha!' or the like. So, we see dialogues like this:

Game: \<joke\>

User: haha!

Game: You liked my joke. I will tell you another.

Game: \<joke\>

User: That was awful.

Game: You are not laughing. You did not like that joke. Never mind, perhaps this will amuse you.

Game: \<another joke\>

User: hohoho!

Game: You are not laughing. You did not like that joke. Never mind, perhaps this will amuse you.

Game: \<yet another joke\>

Putting on one side reservations we might have about the plausibility of any human user bothering to interact with a program as obviously dim as this one, let us consider how we could press our FSTN into service to check whether the user is 'laughing'. It turns out that we can, simply by changing our interpretation of the labels on the arcs. In the new interpretation, the game prints out its joke and then positions itself in an initial state corresponding to the initial node (1) of the network. It begins to inspect the user's input. If the first letter of that input is an 'h', then it traverses the arc that connects state 1 to state 2 and moves over the letter 'h' in the string that forms the user's input. Then it has to attempt to match the next letter in the string with the letter that labels one of the arcs leaving its current state; if there is a match, then it proceeds as before. If there is another letter in the string, but no match with an arc, then the machine fails to recognize the string. Likewise, if there are no further letters in the string and the machine finds itself in a non-final state. But if there are no further letters and the machine is in a final state, then it has succeeded in recognizing the string and so can print out its little message 'You liked my joke' and so on.

Notice that, in this dialogue, the game has failed to recognize 'hohoho!' as an instance of laughter. The reader should elaborate the machine in Figure 2.1 so as to permit the recognition of 'hohoho!', 'hoho!', 'hehe!', 'hehehehe!' and the like as laughter, but exclude 'hoha!', 'hehoha!' and other mixed cases.

In illustrating two different interpretations of our FSTN as machines, we have shown that the FSTN is actually quite a neutral description of the possible sequences of symbols that count as laughing. Because of this neutrality, we were able to interpret it both as a specification of a machine to *recognize* laughter and as a machine to *generate* laughter. To be

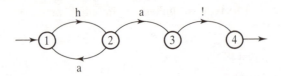

Figure 2.2   Non-deterministic laughing machine.

precise, we should distinguish clearly between the abstract description of laughing (the FSTN) and the different interpretations of it (the FSAs). For instance, there is a conceptual difference between the nodes in the graph and the possible states of a machine that the graph might represent. In practice, however, it is common to blur such distinctions, and so we will talk about FSTNs and the FSAs they could represent interchangeably, only making the distinction when it is important.

Recognition with an FSA so far seems very simple. But suppose we now consider a variant of our network, TO-LAUGH-2, shown in Figure 2.2. There is an important distinction between FSTNs like that in Figure 2.1 and that in Figure 2.2. The first specifies a *deterministic* automaton which, as its name suggests, is one whose behaviour (during recognition) is fully determined by the state it is in and the symbol it is looking at. Our second machine is *not* deterministic because if it finds itself in state 2 and looking at an 'a', then it can either return to state 1 and attempt to find a following 'h', or it can move to state 3 in the hope that the 'a' is the penultimate symbol in the string (since 3 leads to a final state in one transition). As this description is intended to imply, an implementation of a non-deterministic machine can follow false paths. Such an implementation will either need the ability to explore more than one path through the network of arcs simultaneously or else have the ability to backtrack to an earlier choice point when it discovers that it has been on a wild goose chase.

It was mentioned previously that unlabelled arcs can also appear in FSTNs. When the machine is generating, it can traverse such an arc, a 'jump' arc, without generating any symbol. When it is recognizing, it can likewise traverse such an arc without consuming any symbols from the input string. Jump arcs are an important source of non-determinism, because when an ordinary labelled arc leaves a state as well as a jump arc, the machine always has the option of taking the jump, even if the next symbol is the one required by the labelled arc. Figure 2.3 shows another non-deterministic laughing machine, TO-LAUGH-3, where the non-determinism arises at state 3.

The distinction between deterministic and non-deterministic automata is an important one, and we shall return to it from time to time in the course of this book. In the present context, that provided by finite-state machines, the distinction is one of style rather than substance: for every

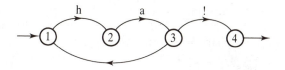

Figure 2.3   Laughing machine with 'jump' arc.

non-deterministic FSTN, there is an equivalent deterministic FSTN that describes exactly the same set of strings of symbols. We will not attempt to prove this here but the reader's attention is drawn to the fact that the deterministic FSTN in Figure 2.1 is exactly equivalent to the non-deterministic FSTN in Figure 2.2 in terms of the strings of symbols that it describes.

At this point, the link between our laughing machine and the Polish tourist in San Francisco airport may be beginning to become apparent. If we can encode our knowledge of possible English/French/Polish... words in FSTNs, there can be a relatively simple mechanism for determining in which languages a given sequence of words might be acceptable. Before we return to Czestawa, however, we will step back from the examples and consider an alternative way of talking about FSTNs. The graphic state diagram used in Figure 2.1 is perspicuous, at least for simple machines, but it does not lend itself to ready communication with computers, certainly not with those that are restricted to character and keyboard input. Nor does it lend itself readily to mathematical or logical analysis. Besides, a single notation provides only one perspective on a class of formal objects. Different notations, although all ultimately equivalent, can provide different perspectives and different ways of thinking about the formal objects, and how to use them and implement them. Accordingly, we will now define an intendedly perspicuous formal language for FSTNs.

2.2   A notation for networks

An FSTN description has three components:

(1)   A name for the network.
(2)   A collection of declarations.
(3)   A collection of arc descriptions.

The first component, the name, is only of mnemonic value when we are discussing FSTNs, since no other component makes reference to it. However, as we shall see in Chapter 3, the name of a network plays an absolutely crucial role in the definition of RTNs. It is introduced here for consistency and for completeness. The relevant statement of our language simply consists of the word Name followed by a name for the network (any string of one or more characters), followed by a colon. For example:

Name TO-LAUGH:

The second component, the declarations, consists of a single obligatory initial states declaration and a single obligatory final states declaration. Each declaration consists of a word indicating what is being declared and a list of the terms being declared, separated by commas. Thus, for instance:

Final 1, 2, 3

declares 1, 2 and 3 to be final states. So, a set of declarations for the FSTN in Figure 2.1 would look like this:

Initial 1
Final 4

It is often very convenient to be able to employ a single expression to abbreviate some subset of symbols and so we will introduce a type of declaration explicitly for this purpose. An abbreviation declaration consists of the abbreviatory expression, which must be distinct from any symbol, followed by the word abbreviates, followed by a colon and a list of symbols, separated by commas and terminated by a period. The use of this type of declaration will be clearer in the light of some examples:

V abbreviates:
  a, e, i, o, u.
C abbreviates:
  b, c, d, f, g, h, j, k, l, m, n, p, q, r, s, t, v, w, x, y, z.

We will put no orthographic restrictions on symbols, states or abbreviations: any character or string of characters, upper or lowercase, may appear in any role. When other things are equal, we will adhere to a convention of using integers for states, lowercase (strings of) letters for symbols and uppercase (strings of) letters for abbreviations. But this is merely the convention used here – it is not to be thought of as part of our definition of the formal language.

The third major component of our FSTN description consists of a set of one or more arc descriptions, each of which has exactly the same form. An arc description consists of the word From followed by a state, followed by the word to, followed by another state (not necessarily distinct from the first state), followed by the word by, followed by a single item. In this context, an item can be a symbol, an abbreviation (declared elsewhere) or the hash symbol (#, pronounced 'jumping' in this context).

This sounds much more cumbersome than it looks. Here, to illustrate, are the arc descriptions that would be needed to describe Figure 2.1:

> From 1 to 2 by h
> From 2 to 3 by a
> From 3 to 2 by h
> From 3 to 4 by !

And here is the complete description of the FSTN in Figure 2.3:

> Name TO-LAUGH-3:
>   Initial 1
>   Final 4
>   From 1 to 2 by h
>   From 2 to 3 by a
>   From 3 to 1 by #
>   From 3 to 4 by !.

Notice that our choice of symbols so far has always been restricted to single letters and !. But nothing in the theory of FSTNs restricts us in this way, and, in fact, we can define an even simpler laughing machine by using a single multi-character symbol:

> Name TO-LAUGH-4:
>   Initial 1
>   Final 2
>   From 1 to 1 by ha
>   From 1 to 2 by !.

This FSTN illustrates another aspect of FSTNs that we have not explicitly mentioned up to this point; namely, the possibility of an arc looping back to the state that it started out from. This is very useful when we wish to allow for unrestricted repetition of a symbol. The following FSTN, ENGLISH-1, uses such loops to good effect in a machine that will produce or recognize simple English sentences.

EXAMPLE: English-1 FSTN

> Name ENGLISH-1:
>   Initial 1
>   Final 9
>   From 1 to 3 by NP
>   From 1 to 2 by DET
>   From 2 to 3 by N

From 3 to 4 by BV
From 4 to 5 by ADV
From 4 to 5 by #
From 5 to 6 by DET
From 5 to 7 by DET
From 5 to 8 by #
From 6 to 6 by MOD
From 6 to 7 by ADJ
From 7 to 9 by N
From 8 to 8 by MOD
From 8 to 9 by ADJ
From 9 to 4 by CNJ
From 9 to 1 by CNJ.

NP abbreviates:
   kim, sandy, lee.
DET abbreviates:
   a, the, her.
N abbreviates:
   consumer, man, woman.
BV abbreviates:
   is, was.
CNJ abbreviates:
   and, or.
ADJ abbreviates:
   happy, stupid.
MOD abbreviates:
   very.
ADV abbreviates:
   often, always, sometimes.

This network uses some abbreviations corresponding to basic syntactic categories used in the description of English syntax. What is a syntactic category? Well, at its simplest, a *syntactic category* is the name we give to collections of expressions of the language that have the same distribution. So, for example, 'Sandy' and 'the person you spoke to' are both noun phrases: they may or may not refer to the same person, but regardless of that, they have exactly the same syntactic privileges of occurrence. Construct any English sentence you like using the proper name 'Sandy' and you will be able to construct another perfectly grammatical English sentence by substituting 'the person you spoke to' for 'Sandy' in the sentence you first constructed. The two sentences may mean different things, but they will both be grammatical. Examples of syntactic categories that linguists commonly make use of are noun phrase (NP), sentence (S), verb phrase (VP), verb (V), and so on. We can also think of more detailed descriptions, such as plural noun phrase, interrogative sentence, passive verb phrase and tensed verb, as examples of more specified syntactic categories. Notice that in our example, the two noun phrases that we claimed to be intersubstitutable were actually both singular noun phrases. Although a singular noun phrase can sometimes be substituted for a plural one (or conversely) while preserving grammaticality, this is not always the case.

For the purposes of our illustrative example, a word is an NP (noun phrase) if it can stand alone as the subject of a sentence. By N we mean common noun, as distinct from proper noun. Determiners (DET) are words that can come before (common) nouns, as in 'the woman', but adjectives (ADJ) like 'stupid' can interpose. The category BV is used here for parts of the verb 'to be' which can be optionally followed by an adverb (ADV) such as 'often'. A word of category MOD is used to modify adjectives, changing 'stupid' into 'very stupid', for instance. Finally, the category CNJ (conjunction) is used for words that can join two sentences into a single larger sentence. Here are some example strings that can be recognized by this network:

Kim was happy.

Lee is a consumer and often very very stupid.

Sandy was sometimes a stupid man and Kim is always the happy woman.

Our indentation is conventional, not part of the language definition, but adhering to it will make some of the complex networks exhibited in the next chapter a good deal easier to read. It will be convenient to have a name for this formal language in the course of this chapter and the next, and we shall refer to it as *NATR* (*network and transducer representation*).

We have not, as yet, said anything explicitly about what exactly it is that NATR means. For the most part, this is too obvious to need saying, but in the case of abbreviations we have a bit of notation that does not map one to one into our existing graphic representation. However, our abbreviations are exactly what their name suggests. Thus, for example:

From 1 to 2 by A.
A abbreviates:
a, b, c.

is wholly synonymous with:

From 1 to 2 by a
From 1 to 2 by b
From 1 to 2 by c.

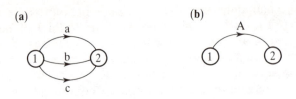

Figure 2.4   Abbreviating multiple arcs.

and thus corresponds to the FSTN fragment shown in Figure 2.4(a). Since fragments like this get to look very messy when more than two or three arcs join a given pair of states, we shall, henceforth, import our abbreviations into the graphic representation whenever it is convenient to do so. So, we may exhibit the fragment of Figure 2.4(b) in place of the unabbreviated fragment in Figure 2.4(a).

Restricting ourselves to the deterministic type of FSTN for the moment, we can introduce another formalism for (partially) representing (deterministic) FSAs used for recognition. This is the state-transition table, a matrix that exhibits the transition function of an FSA in a very clear and readily implemented manner. The vertical axis lists the states and the horizontal axis lists the symbols. The states in the matrix represent the state the machine moves into if it starts in the state given by the vertical coordinate and consumes the symbol given by the horizontal coordinate. Here is the state-transition table that corresponds to Figure 2.1:

	h	a	!
1	2	0	0
2	0	3	0
3	2	0	4
4	0	0	0

A zero indicates that the automaton cannot proceed, and will thus be unable to accept an input string that would have the effect of forcing it into that position in the matrix. So, for instance, the first row of the matrix shows that if the machine is in state 1, the only possibility is a transition to state 2, which requires the consumption of the symbol 'h'. Similarly the third row shows that from state 3 there are two possibilities, corresponding to the symbols 'h' and '!'. Bear in mind that, as it stands, the state-transition table is an incomplete representation of the automaton, since it does not indicate which states are initial and which are final.

Now, at last, we are in a position to directly address the problem with which we started, that of natural language graphotactics (the definition of possible words in terms of permissible letter sequences). One graphotactic constraint that is familiar to most users of English is that the letter 'q' must be followed by a 'u'. Another example from English is the requirement that a word-initial 'st' only be followed by a vowel, a 'y' or an 'r' (we ignore the word 'sthenic' on the grounds that no self-respecting native speaker of English would dream of using it). Constraints of this kind are easy to code up in an FSTN. ENG-MONOSYL is a first attempt at an FSTN for the orthographic forms of possible one syllable English words.

EXAMPLE: FSTN for possible monosyllabic English words

```
Name ENG-MONOSYL:
  Initial 1, 2
  Final 3, 4, 5
  From 1 to 2 by C0
  From 2 to 3 by V
  From 3 to 4 by C8
  From 4 to 5 by s
  From 1 to 7 by C3
  From 7 to 2 by w
  From 1 to 6 by C2
  From 6 to 2 by l
  From 6 to 5 by #
  From 1 to 5 by C1
  From 5 to 2 by r
  From 1 to 8 by s
  From 8 to 5 by C4
  From 8 to 2 by C5
  From 3 to 9 by l
  From 3 to 10 by s
  From 3 to 11 by C7
  From 9 to 4 by C6
  From 10 to 4 by C4
  From 11 to 4 by th.

V abbreviates:
  a, ae, ai, au, e, ea, ee, ei, eu, i, ia, ie, o, oa, oe, oi, oo, ou, ue, ui.
C0 abbreviates:
  b, c, ch, d, f, g, h, j, k, l, m, n, p, qu, r, s, sh, t, th, v, w, x
C1 abbreviates:
  d, sh, th.
C2 abbreviates:
  b, c, f, g, k.
C3 abbreviates:
  d, g, h, t, th.
C4 abbreviates:
```

c, k, p, t.

C5 abbreviates:

c, k, l, m, n, p, pl, qu, t, w.

C6 abbreviates:

b, f, m.

C7 abbreviates:

d, f, l, n, x.

C8 abbreviates:

b, c, ch, ck, d, f, g, h, k, l, m, mp, mph, n, ng, p, que, r, s, sh, th, v, w, x, y, z.

It is important to remember that FSTNs such as the one just presented only attempt to define *possible* English (or Polish or Spanish) words, not *actual* English (or Polish or Spanish) words. In the case of Polish and Spanish, it is rather likely that an FSTN for the actual words could be defined, but it would be a massive undertaking to attempt to construct it by hand. And there are languages, such as Bambara, for whose actual word set it seems that no FSTN could be given. But for many practical purposes, an FSTN for possible words is more use than one for the actual words. Speakers make words up constantly, but their neologisms are always possible words of the language in question. Thus, an English speaker will hardly notice the neologism in 'her secretary nixonized the tapes' but will immediately react to the third item in 'her secretary nxioniezd the tapes.'

We have been discussing graphotactics, but FSTNs are not restricted in their application to this, linguistically rather barren, level of description. For most languages, although not all, it makes sense to postulate a unit of syntactic organization between the letter and the word. This unit is known as a *morpheme* (roughly speaking, the minimal meaningful unit). Here, as elsewhere in this book, we restrict our attention to the written form of languages (In the spoken form, we have individual sounds, known as *phones*, rather than letters of an alphabet, and these sounds typically group into higher level sound units such as syllables.) Rather than attempt to define the notion of a morpheme, we will simply exhibit the component morphemes of some English words:

print-s
print-ed
print-ing
re-print
im-print
slow-ly
in-de-cipher-able

English does not have a rich morphological structure but many languages allow the speaker to express in a single word something that an English speaker would require a whole sentence to say. For example, the Swahili word 'wametulipa' translates into English as 'they have paid us', while 'unamsumbua' translates as 'you are annoying him.' It is often possible to capture the permissible morpheme sequences of a language, or of part of a language, by means of an FSTN. SWAHILI-1 is an FSTN for a subset of Swahili words.

EXAMPLE: Swahili-1 FSTN

Name SWAHILI-1:
  Initial 1
  Final 5
  From 1 to 2 by SUBJ
  From 2 to 3 by TENSE
  From 3 to 4 by OBJ
  From 4 to 5 by STEM.

SUBJ abbreviates:
  ni, u, a, tu, wa.
OBJ abbreviates:
  ni, ku, m, tu, wa.
TENSE abbreviates:
  ta, na, me, li.
STEM abbreviates:
  penda, piga, sumbua, lipa.

This FSTN will recognize each of 100 morphological variants of four Swahili verbs. This is pleasing, but is it useful? The answer is probably no. After all, if we are concerned with Swahili words at this kind of level of detail, as opposed to wondering whether some string of characters was a possible Swahili word, then we are almost certain to want more than the yes or no that an FSTN can provide. To get more information, we need a parser or a transducer, not a recognizer. We will look at finite-state transducers in some detail in a subsequent section of this chapter.

At this point, let us take stock and recapitulate with some practical rules of thumb for the specification of FSAs by FSTNs:

- If we want to get from state i to state j without moving across a symbol in the input, or putting a symbol on the output, then we connect i and j with a jump arc.

- If we want to get from state i to state j while having the option to move across, or print, a symbol s, then we connect i and j with two arcs, one a jump arc and the other labelled with s.

- If we are in state i and wish to move across, or print, zero or more occurrences of a symbol s, then we connect i to itself with an arc labelled with s.

- If we are in state i and wish to move across, or print, one or more occurrences of a symbol s, then we connect i to a new node j with an arc labelled with s, and then we connect j back to i with a jump arc.

- If we are in state i and wish to move across, or print, one or more occurrences of a string S that can be reached between states i and j, then we connect j back to i with a jump arc.

- If the presence of even one occurrence of the string is optional in the latter case, then i should also be connected to j with a jump arc, pointing in the opposite direction to the one already introduced.

These are simply heuristics: they may not have the intended effect if they interact with other features of the FSTN, most obviously if any of the named states, or intermediate states, are also final states.

Exercise 2.1   Draw out the graphic representation for the ENGLISH-1 FSTN.   [*easy*]

Exercise 2.2   Design an FSTN that will recognize well-formed English number names – for example, 'four thousand seven hundred and one', etc.   [*easy*]

Exercise 2.3   Design an FSTN that will recognize well-formed time of day expressions – for example, 'five fifteen', 'quarter to four', etc., in either British or American English.   [*easy*]

Exercise 2.4   Investigate the problem that the jump arc gives rise to in converting Figure 2.3 into a state-transition table.   [*intermediate*]

Exercise 2.5   Devise a variant of the state-transition table that will allow general non-deterministic FSTNs to be represented. Use it to represent the FSTN in Figure 2.2 and the ENGLISH-1 network.   [*intermediate*]

Exercise 2.6 Investigate the adequacy of the ENG-MONOSYL FSTN for its intended domain:

(a) What, if any, monosyllabic English words does it fail to accept?

(b) What, if any, impossible (in English) letter sequences does it accept?

Modify it to correct any inadequacies you uncover. [*intermediate*]

Exercise 2.7 Extend the ENG-MONOSYL FSTN to handle English words that may have several syllables. [*intermediate*]

Exercise 2.8 Design a comparable FSTN for a language such as Polish or Spanish, using your own knowledge of the language, a patient informant or a dictionary. [*intermediate project*]

Exercise 2.9 Write a program that will read a (possibly very large) file of words and construct a letter sequence FSTN on the basis of those words. What theoretical issues does such a project pose? How might you evaluate the result? [*hard project*]

2.3 Deterministic FSTNs in LISP

If a transition network is deterministic, it can be translated into a single LISP function for recognition quite straightforwardly. In this function, the nodes of the network give rise to tags, while transitions between nodes are implemented by go. Here is such a function for the TO-LAUGH-1 network (Figure 2.1):

```
(defun to_laugh (tape)
  (prog ((newtape tape))
    label_1
    (case (car newtape)
      (h (setq newtape (cdr newtape)) (go label_2))
      (otherwise (return nil)))
    label_2
    (case (car newtape)
      (a (setq newtape (cdr newtape)) (go label_3))
      (otherwise (return nil)))
    label_3
    (case (car newtape)
      (! (setq newtape (cdr newtape)) (go label_4))
      (h (setq newtape (cdr newtape)) (go label_2))
      (otherwise (return nil)))
```

```
label_4
(if (null newtape)
  (return t)
  (return nil))
))
```

This function takes as argument a list of symbols representing a tape, such as:

```
(h a h h a ! !)
```

and returns t or nil, according to whether the sequence of words is accepted by the TO-LAUGH-1 network.

Although this approach works, it uses a pathological programming style and the resulting program is almost completely unstructured. Apart from the fact that such a simple method of translation will not work when the network is non-deterministic, there are other reasons why this approach is not to be preferred:

- First of all, the size of the code that has to be written is significantly greater than that of the original network specification.

- Secondly, the code will only support one task – recognition. If we wish to use the network for some other purpose, such as random generation, we must produce completely new code. So our approach here will be, instead of representing a network *procedurally*, to represent a network *declaratively* as a LISP data structure that can be examined and manipulated. We will then write general-purpose recognition and generation programs that will work on any network represented as a data structure in the approved way.

Exercise 2.10   What would happen if we tried to translate the TO-LAUGH-2 network (Figure 2.2) into LISP in the same way as we translated TO-LAUGH-1?   [*intermediate*]

2.4   Non-deterministic FSTNs in LISP

Before we start writing general network traversal programs, we need to consider how we are going to represent transition networks as LISP data structures. If we ignore abbreviations for now, we will need to know the following about a network:

- What its initial nodes are.
- What its final nodes are.
- What its arcs are.

Thus, we will represent a network as a list structure with components for the initial nodes, the final nodes and the transitions (arcs). These components will be represented by lists in a format that is easy to remember and to type. So here are some example networks:

```
(setq swahili_1
 '((Initial (1))
   (Final (5))
   (From 1 to 2 by subj)
   (From 2 to 3 by tense)
   (From 3 to 4 by obj)
   (From 4 to 5 by stem))
```

```
(setq english1
 '((Initial (1))
   (Final (9))
   (From 1 to 3 by NP)
   (From 1 to 2 by DET)
   (From 2 to 3 by N)
   (From 3 to 4 by BV)
   (From 4 to 5 by ADV)
   (From 4 to 5 by |#|)
   (From 5 to 6 by DET)
   (From 5 to 7 by DET)
   (From 5 to 8 by |#|)
   (From 6 to 6 by MOD)
   (From 6 to 7 by ADJ)
   (From 7 to 9 by N)
   (From 8 to 8 by MOD)
   (From 8 to 9 by ADJ)
   (From 9 to 4 by CNJ)
   (From 9 to 1 by CNJ)))
```

Note that we have to write # inside '|'s in LISP, to avoid it being interpreted as a macro character. Also, we enclose the lists of initial states and final states in an extra level of list structure. Although this is not necessary now, it will be helpful to adopt this convention when we are dealing with more complex kinds of networks. Here are the basic procedures for accessing the components of a network:

```
(defun initial_nodes (network)
  (nth 1 (assoc 'Initial network)))

(defun final_nodes (network)
  (nth 1 (assoc 'Final network)))

(defun transitions (network)
  (cddr network))
```

Notice that we have made use here of the fact that a network is in the form of an association list, the first two elements having the keys Initial and Final. Since the assoc function returns the entire list element, including the key, we need to use nth 1 to extract the bare list of node names. We will also need some basic procedures for accessing the components of a transition. A transition is always a list of the form:

```
(From <node> to <newnode> by <label>)
```

and we need to be able to extract the (starting) node, the (destination) new node and the label from such a data structure. In this, we can make use of the fact that such a list is in the form of a property list:

```
(defun trans_node (transition)
  (getf transition 'From))

(defun trans_newnode (transition)
  (getf transition 'to))

(defun trans_label (transition)
  (getf transition 'by))
```

For abbreviations, we will introduce a global variable abbreviations whose value will be a list of lists such as the following:

```
(defvar abbreviations)

(setq abbreviations
  '((NP kim sandy lee)
    (DET a the her)
    (N consumer man woman)
    (BV is was)
    (CNJ and or)
    (ADJ happy stupid)
    (MOD very)
    (ADV often always sometimes)))
```

2.5   Traversing FSTNs

The various interpretations of FSTNs as FSAs all involve FSAs that go from state to state in a way that echoes a traversal of the network. We thus turn now to the question of how to set about getting a computer to traverse networks of the kind we have been examining. One way to imagine the traversal of a network is to think of a kangaroo that jumps from node to node but which is constrained to take jumps only where there are arcs. As the kangaroo jumps about, portions of the input string are consumed, if the network is being used for recognition, or portions of the output string are produced, if the network is being used for generation. During recognition, we can think of the input string being displayed in large letters on the wall, with some kind of pointing device indicating which symbols remain to be processed. In a finite-state network, the kangaroo is only allowed to make a jump if:

(1)   The arc is labelled by a symbol that is the same as the next symbol in the input.

(2)   The arc is labelled by an abbreviation and the next symbol in the input is one of the symbols covered by that abbreviation.

(3)   The arc is labelled '#'.

In the first two cases, the kangaroo moves the input pointer forward one word and makes the jump. In the latter, it simply jumps across without changing the input pointer.

The kangaroo model is a useful way to think about the information that needs to be kept during the traversal of a network. If we wish to translate this into computer programs, we must think carefully about what the kangaroo needs to remember and what information is available to it. In doing recognition, our kangaroo needs to keep track of its own current location (which node it is at) and the pointer into the input string. More-over, it is capable of moving that pointer. In summary, at any moment in the traversal of an FSTN, the state of the computation can be characterized by the following items:

- R1. a node name (the kangaroo's location).
- R2. the remaining input string.

When the network is being used for generation, we will have to replace these items with the following:

- P1. a node name (the kangaroo's location).
- P2. the output string generated so far.

Note that both R1 and R2 influence the future behaviour of the automaton in recognition mode, whereas P2 is irrelevant to future behaviour in generation mode.

Apart from our reference to the distinction between deterministic and non-deterministic FSTNs, we have not really addressed the issue of making choices in this discussion so far. In general, successful traversal of an FSTN involves choice and hence search. Given that R1, R2 characterize the complete current state of the traversal, this is precisely the information that we will need to keep if we wish to record different possibilities that need to be investigated. Following standard terminology, we shall call a collection of items R1, R2 that characterizes a complete (intermediate) state of a traversal a *state*, even though this word is also used to refer to a state of an FSA. (Woods uses the term *configuration* for a complete intermediate state of a parser, and this might be a more appropriate term to use here.) We will show a state as a sequence of two items, as follows:

<2, a h a !>

R2. remaining input (symbols to be processed)

R1. current node

This state represents the intermediate point of a traversal where the kangaroo has got to node 2 and still has to deal with the symbols 'a', 'h', 'a' and '!' (in that order).

When we are traversing a network, we need to keep track of both the *current state*, which expresses where we are now, and *alternative states*, which express other possibilities that could be tried as well as the current one. Consider what happens, for instance, if we are using the network of Figure 2.2 and get into the state just described. In the network of Figure 2.2, there are two arcs leaving state 2: if the next symbol in the input is an 'a', then any of them could be traversed, leading to the following possible *next states*:

<1, h a !>
<3, h a !>

In general, we might expect each of these to yield several next states, and each one of these to yield several next states, and so on, giving rise to a whole tree of possibilities, as shown in Figure 2.5.

In practice, the *search tree* arising from this example is not very complex, as most branches quickly lead to states from which no further progress can be made. Nevertheless, only one of the possible states can be investigated at a time – the *current state*. As the tree is generated, the new states need to be remembered somehow so that they can be investigated if necessary – they need to be added to some representation of the *alternative states* there are so far. One way of organizing the search is to keep a 'pool' of alternative states to be investigated. At each stage in the traversal, one

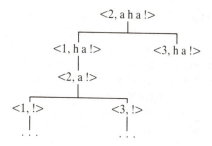

Figure 2.5 Search tree.

of these alternatives is selected and made the current state. The valid next states from this state are worked out and added to the pool. Then another alternative is selected from the pool, and so on. We start off with a state in the set of alternatives for each initial node of the network. For instance, if s1 and s2 were the two initial nodes, s2 and s9 were the two final nodes, and the string was 'a b c d e', the initial set of alternative states would be:

<s1, a b c d e>
<s2, a b c d e>

And the set of legitimate final states would be:

<s2, >
<s9, >

If our machine winds up in either of these two states then it has succeeded in recognizing the string.

Here is an informal description of our algorithm:

(1)   Create the set of alternative initial states (the initial pool).

(2)   Do the following repeatedly:

    (2.1) Select one of the alternative states (removing it from the pool).

    (2.2) If it is a final state, stop and announce success.

        Otherwise,

        (2.2.1) Calculate the valid next states that could follow from it.

        (2.2.2) Add these to the pool of alternatives.

(3)   If the pool of alternatives ever becomes empty, stop and announce failure.

This is obviously not a complete description of what to do, because it does not specify how to decide which alternative to select at each stage. Two main approaches to this problem are *depth-first* and *breadth-first* search. In terms of the search tree, depth-first search follows a path deeper and deeper in the search tree and only moves up the tree to consider an alternative if all the possibilities below its current state have been tried. On the other hand, breadth-first search investigates states roughly in order of their depth in the tree. Intuitively, depth-first search involves preferring to investigate alternatives that have been added to the pool recently, whereas breadth-first search attempts to be fair by avoiding any alternative remaining too long in the pool before being investigated. We will see a lot more of these basic strategies later in this book. Note also that this is a general search algorithm which can be used for any search task that can be characterized as an exploration of states of some kind.

How do we calculate the valid next states that follow from a given state <NODE, INPUT>? For each arc (with label L and destination D) leaving node NODE, we must include states in the set as follows:

(SYM) if L is a symbol and the first symbol of INPUT is the same, include <D, ... rest of INPUT ...>

(ABB) if L is an abbreviation and the first symbol of INPUT is covered by the abbreviation, include <D, ... rest of INPUT ...>

(JMP) if L is '#', include <D, INPUT>

2.6   Traversing FSTNs in LISP

In this chapter and the next, we will develop a number of programs for performing useful tasks with various kinds of networks. These programs will have a certain 'family resemblance' but will differ in their details. The first task we will consider is using a network for *recognition* (the task 'recognize'). The function recognize, given a network and a 'tape' (list of items), will return t or nil, according to whether the list is accepted by the network. Here is its definition:

```
(defun recognize (network tape)
  ;; returns t if sucessfully recognizes tape – nil otherwise
  (catch
    'stop
    (dolist (initialnode (initial_nodes network))
      (recognize_next initialnode tape network))
    nil))   ; failed to recognize
```

Although the initial function called is recognize, the bulk of the work in this program is done by the function recognize_next. recognize_next is given a node in the network and a tape (list of remaining words). Its job is to explore all the ways the network can be traversed, starting at the given node and using up precisely the words that are on the tape. So, initially, we have to call recognize_next repeatedly, once with each initial node of the network. This ensures that all possible paths are explored:

```
(defun recognize_next (node tape network)
   ;; throws t or returns nil
   (if (and (null tape) (member node (final_nodes network)))
      (throw 'stop t)                              ; success
      (dolist (transition (transitions network))
         ;; try each transition of the network
         (if (equal node (trans_node transition))    ; if it starts at the right node
            (dolist (newtape (recognize_move (trans_label transition) tape))
               ;; try each possible new value of tape
               (recognize_next (trans_newnode transition) newtape network))))))
```

Looking first at the last part of the definition, we can see that recognize_next goes through the network transitions that originate from the node it is given. For each transition, it attempts to 'move the tape' as directed by the label on the arc. recognize_move returns all the possible new values of the tape in a list. In fact, for recognition there is always either one new value, if the required item is at the front of the tape or if there is no required item, or no new value, if a required value is not at the front of the tape. Then, for each of these possible new versions of the tape, recognize_next is called recursively, with the destination of the arc and the new tape. Thus, recognize_next finds all the possible ways of moving one step further in the network and, with each of these, delegates the problem of looking further to another call of recognize_next.

In terms of our previous discussion, each call of recognize_next is in charge of a single state, whose node and tape are given by the first two arguments. recognize_next works out what new states immediately follow from this and calls recognize_next on each of these in turn. Figure 2.6 shows the pattern of calls that results if we look at the sequence:

(kim was a consumer and lee was stupid)

using the ENGLISH-1 network. In this tree, a function call is shown above the function calls that it invokes. Notice that the call tree mirrors the search tree exactly. It is readily seen from the figure that in this case there was hardly any search – each of the first three calls of recognize_next only produced a single new state. The calls marked with Xs produced no new states and yet were not successful final states. In investigating all the possibilities, our program tries all the states that arise from a given alternative before trying alternatives to it, traversing the tree from left to right. This means that it is doing a depth-first search. However, the program improves on the general search algorithm, in that it represents most of the pool of alternatives

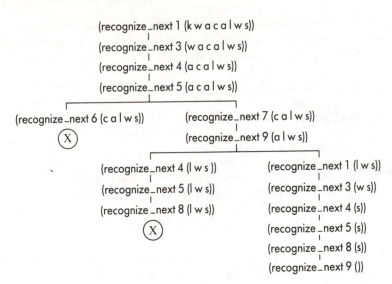

Figure 2.6   Call tree.

implicitly rather than explicitly. When a given call of recognize_next is generated, the next alternative at that level in the call tree is only actually
computed when the first call returns – that is, it indicates failure.

Given that every call of recognize_next can end up calling another
recognize_next, how does the program terminate? If the network can indeed be
traversed, we can hope that eventually a call of recognize_next will be
generated where the node is a final node of the network and the tape is
empty. This is the case tested for by the outer if. If the test succeeds, it is
now known that the network can be traversed, and no more searching
needs to be done. In general, we will be quite deep in recursive calls of
recognize_next when this happens, and so we need to stop any further work
being done in any of them. So, we use throw to make the program abandon
all of these. This use of throw will bring us back to the original call of recognize,
making the catch construct there return the value t. This is then returned as
the result of recognize. What if the network cannot be traversed using the
given tape? In this case, all the calls to recognize_next will eventually peter out,
reaching states from which no further progress can be made. Once the
whole set of possibilities has been searched and all calls of recognize_next have
returned, we are back in the function recognize and can return the result nil.
There is only one problem remaining. If there could be infinitely many
potential paths through the network, we will not be able to search through
all of them before announcing nil. Indeed, we might spend so much time
looking at infinite parts of the search space that we might never find a
successful traversal, if it exists. Fortunately, the only way this could happen
would be through the network having cycles consisting of arcs labelled '#'.

For instance, the network only needs to have a transition of the form:

```
(From n to n by |#|)
```

for the search among all possible traversals to be infinite in some cases. But it is not a serious problem to avoid introducing cases like this into our networks.

With a definition of recognize_move, our program will be complete. recognize_move returns a list of new tapes, which will have one element or none, depending on the label and the existing tape. If the first word in the tape is the same as the label (the SYM case), then the rest of the tape is returned as the single new tape. Similarly, if the next word is abbreviated by the label (case ABB). Finally, if the label is '#' (the JMP case), the tape is returned unchanged as the single new tape. In all other cases, no new tapes are returned – we cannot take this arc in the network. Here is the definition of recognize_move:

```
(defun recognize_move (label tape)
  (if (equal label (car tape))
    (list (cdr tape))
    (if (member (car tape) (assoc label abbreviations))
      (list (cdr tape))
      (if (equal label '|#|)
        (list tape)
        '()))))
```

Let us consider now what has to be done if we wish to adapt this program for the exhaustive generation of all the sequences that are allowed by a transition network. We still need to search all possible paths through the network, but now we are not constrained to traverse arcs that are compatible with an input tape. For generation, we will use the tape to record the words generated so far. Thus, the tape will start as the empty list and will get longer as we progress through the network. Here is the function for generating possible new tapes (corresponding roughly to the function recognize_move):

```
(defun generate_move (label tape)
  (if (equal label '|#|)
    (list tape)
    (if (assoc label abbreviations)
      (let ((results '()))
        (dolist (word (cdr (assoc label abbreviations)) results)
          (setq results (cons (append tape (list word)) results))))
      (list (append tape (list label))))))
```

Note that generate_move can produce a list of several results. When the label on the network arc is an abbreviation, any of the words abbreviated can appear in the output tape. The procedures generate and generate_next used for exhaustive generation are very similar to the procedures recognize and recognize_next used for recognition. Here are their definitions:

```
(defun generate_next (node tape network)
  ;; prints out sentences
  (if (member node (final_nodes network))
    (print tape)
    (dolist (transition (transitions network))
      (if (equal node (trans_node transition))
        (dolist (newtape (generate_move (trans_label transition) tape))
          (generate_next (trans_newnode transition) newtape network))
        '()))))  ; transition from the wrong node


(defun generate (network)
  ;; generates valid sentences of the given network
  (dolist (initialnode (initial_nodes network))
    (generate_next initialnode nil network))
  t)
```

Note how the initial calls to generate_next have nil as the tape argument and that the test for termination in generate_next does not have to specify anything about the tape. In addition, since we are generating *all* the legal sequences, we do not want to exit back to the top function when we find a solution. Instead, the program prints out the successful tape and keeps going.

One trouble with exhaustive generation is that it cannot be allowed to run to completion if the network allows an infinite number of different strings. Nevertheless, it can still be useful to run such a system for a while, to get an idea of the range of the strings allowed by a network. If we try generating from the ENGLISH-1 network, however, we do not get any solutions and the program gets into an infinite loop. The trouble is that there are places in the network that allow certain constructions to be iterated indefinitely in the language. As the generate program makes choices in a fixed order, if it ever chooses to repeat a particular type of phrase it will *always* choose to do this and so will try to produce an infinitely long sentence.

If the transitions of a network are reordered to avoid non-productive infinite loops, there is still a problem in that the program does not produce a 'representative sample' of the strings allowed. This is because, once the program has made a decision about part of the string, it is happy to go on investigating other decisions that it encounters later. Only if for some reason all future possibilities fail to work out will it remake this decision. Because of the way one call of generate_next has to return (exhaust all its possibilities) before another can run, the program will always focus on one alternative and further developments from it before it tries other alternatives.

Exercise 2.11   Run the recognition program (lib fsrecog) with various networks and look at the search spaces (use trace). The ENGLISH-1 network is in the library file lib english1.   [*easy*]

Exercise 2.12   Prove, informally but in more detail than given in the text, that, if the network contains no #-cycles, the recognition program will find an existing traversal if there is one; otherwise it will return nil in finite time.   [*hard*]

Exercise 2.13   Find the point in the ENGLISH-1 network where the generation program loops. Reorder the transitions so that the program does actually produce some solutions.   [*intermediate*]

Exercise 2.14   Write a spelling check program that reads in words, checks whether they can be recognized by an FSTN describing 'possible' words of the language and prints them out if not.   [*intermediate*]

Exercise 2.15   Write a program that conducts the search *breadth-first* instead. In breadth-first search, each possible state is taken in turn and the new states that immediately arise from it are derived. Then all these new states are taken in turn and the next states immediately arising from them are derived. The idea is to spend time evenly in the different parts of the search space. For this program, you will need to represent a state explicitly by a data structure; for instance, a list of the form:

```
(<node> <tape>)
```

The top level of your generation program could look like this:

```
(defun generate (network)
   (let ((agenda (generate_initial_states network)))
     (do () ((null agenda))   ; do until agenda empty
       (setq agenda (generate_next_states_list agenda network)))))

(defun generate_next_states_list (agenda network)
   (if (null agenda)
      '()
      (append
        (generate_next_states (car agenda) network)
        (generate_next_states_list (cdr agenda) network))))
```

[*hard*]

Exercise 2.16   Our recognition program does just that – it recognizes whether or not a string is accepted by a given FSTN. But although it discovers quite a lot about the string in the course of a successful recognition, this information is lost. All we get by way of result is a truth value.

Alter the recognize program to return the path taken through the network, represented as a list of node names, instead of the value t. One way of thinking about what this program does is simply in terms of it recording the history of its successful arc transitions in a list. But another, equally good, way of thinking about it is as a program that maps one string of symbols (the sentence) into another string of symbols (the path); in other words, as a program that *transduces* one string into another.   [*intermediate*]

2.7   Finite-state transducers

An FSA of the kind we have discussed, used to analyze some existing input, is a recognizer, not a parser or a transducer, so all it can do is decide on the well-formedness of a string. If it can reach the end of the string in a final state, then the string is well formed; if it cannot reach the end of the string, or if cannot reach the end of the string and simultaneously be in a final state, then the string is not well formed. That is all the information it provides. To get more information, we need a parser or a transducer, not a recognizer.

Although we can interpret an FSTN as a machine that produces a simple yes or no output for any input, with some small extensions to the notation, we can interpret one as a *finite-state transducer (FST)*. An FST is a more interesting kind of FSA that allows a string of output symbols to be produced as an input string is recognized.

One way to think of an FST is as a special kind of FSA that inspects two (or more) symbols at a time and proceeds accordingly. To put some intuitive flesh on this rather barren statement, we describe a family of hypothetical children's games. Imagine a long, straight pavement made up of coloured, square paving stones set two abreast. At any given time, apart from when a player actually makes a move forwards, the player must have his or her left foot on a left-side paving stone and his or her right foot on the right-side paving stone that is immediately adjacent to it. And, at any given time, the player must be in one of a (finite) number of states. For simplicity, we will assume just two states: that of having your hand in your pocket, and that of not having it there. Each variant of the game consists of a collection of rules, of which the following are examples:

- If your left foot is on a red paving stone and your right foot is on a green paving stone and your hand is in your pocket, then you can advance to the next pair of stones and keep your hand in your pocket.
- If your left foot is on a blue paving stone and your right foot is on a blue paving stone and your hand is not in your pocket, then you can advance to the next pair of stones and put your hand in your pocket.

Given such a collection of rules, the player's goal is to move from the beginning of the pavement to the end, without making any move that is not expressly permitted by the rules. A child playing this game will be implementing an FST.

As we have just presented it, an FST is a kind of inspector that runs along checking if two strings of symbols stand in an appropriate correspondence. As such, it seems very little different, and hardly more useful, than an FSA running as a recognizer. But just as an FSTN can be interpreted as both a string recognizer and a string generator, so a network representing an FST can be interpreted, for instance, both as a string correspondence checker and as a machine that reads one string while writing another. We will use the term FST to refer to any such finite-state machine that makes use of multiple tapes, even though it is the latter interpretation that is of most interest and utility in the natural language domain. How, then, are we to conceive of an FST applying to a linguistic domain? Here is an example of the kind of rule that we might use in a linguistic application:

- If your current English word is 'fish' and you are in state 13, then you may print 'poisson' and advance to the next English word and shift into state 7.

But before we get overambitious and attempt English–French machine translation with an FST, let us step back and equip ourselves with a notation for talking about FSTs.

An FST can be specified by an FSTN whose arcs are labelled with pairs of symbols, as opposed to single symbols, and as before we will blur the distinction between the abstract notation, which describes sets of pairs of strings, and the possible machines that it might specify. To specify an FST, then, the simplest thing to do is just to augment the NATR language we already have for defining FSTNs. Let us imagine that the symbols we are dealing with are being read from, or printed on to, tapes. There is no need to make any changes in our formalism for expressing initial and final states. But we do need to allow our arc description statements to specify pairs of symbols as labels. We will use expressions like A_a, where A is a tape 1 symbol and a is a tape 2 symbol, for such symbol pairs. In fact, there is no need to restrict ourselves to two tapes. Both our syntax for transducer symbol declarations and our notation for symbol pairs are designed to generalize to the n-tape situation, for n greater than 2. Hence, A_a_α could be used for a symbol triple in a three-tape situation, for example. However, in what follows, we will restrict ourselves to two-tape machines.

An arc description statement for an FST will appear thus:

From 1 to 2 by A_a

What about cases where we wish to read, or write, a symbol on one tape, but do nothing on the other? Here, we can use our jumping symbol; so, #_a and A_# will be well-formed pairs. (Thus, the hash remains a special symbol, part of our language for talking about FSTs. If you want to have the FST manipulate the real hash symbol, then it will need to be set off in quotes.)

This minor generalization from single symbols to pairs – or, more generally, n-tuples – of symbols is all we really need to define FSTs. Here is an example of an abbreviation for an FST:

DIGIT abbreviates:
one_un, two_deux, three_trois, four_quatre, five_cinq, six_six,
seven_sept, eight_huit, nine_neuf, ten_dix.

Having introduced these additions to our existing FSTN language, we can consider ENG_FRE-1, which is an example of a complete FST specified in this augmented NATR notation.

EXAMPLE: Eng_fre-1 FST

Name ENG_FRE-1:
Initial 1
Final 5
From 1 to 2 by WHERE
From 2 to 3 by BV
From 3 to 4 by DET
From 4 to 5 by NOUN.

WHERE abbreviates:
where_ou.
BV abbreviates:
is_est.
DET abbreviates:
the_#.
NOUN abbreviates:
exit_la sortie, policeman_le gendarme, shop_la boutique, toilet_la toilette.

The little FST described in ENG_FRE-1 would be completely trivial were it not for one wrinkle: in French the form of the determiner or definite article varies with the gender of the noun it accompanies, whereas English shows no such variation. This FST gets round the problem by letting the English 'the' map into nothing, and then requiring English nouns to map into the relevant French noun preceded by a determiner marked for the appropriate gender. Thus, la sortie and le gendarme, for example, are single symbols as far as this FST is concerned. This is not a very elegant solution to the problem since it obfuscates the correspondence that holds between the English 'the' and French 'la/le'.

An alternative FST for this English–French translation task, one that is arguably more perspicuous, despite the introduction of an additional state and two additional arcs, is given in ENG_FRE-2.

EXAMPLE: Eng_fre-2 FST

Name ENG_FRE-2:
  Initial 1
  Final 5
  From 1 to 2 by WHERE
  From 2 to 3 by BV
  From 3 to 4 by DET-FEMN
  From 4 to 5 by N-FEMN
  From 3 to 6 by DET-MASC
  From 6 to 5 by N-MASC.

WHERE abbreviates:
  where_ou.
BV abbreviates:
  is_est.
DET-FEMN abbreviates:
  the_la.
DET-MASC abbreviates:
  the_le.
N-FEMN abbreviates:
  exit_sortie, shop_boutique, toilet_toilette.
N-MASC abbreviates:
  policeman_gendarme.

Notice in ENG_FRE-2 how the gender distinction has been, in effect, encoded into the states: if we traverse the net via state 4, then we must have a feminine determiner and a feminine noun, whereas if we go via state 6, then we must have a masculine determiner and a masculine noun. There are no other possibilities.

Notice also that if we use this transducer to translate from French to English, then it will operate deterministically – it will never need to make a choice. But if we use it to translate from English to French, its operation will not be deterministic: in translating 'Where is the policeman?' it will be faced with a choice when it reaches the determiner. It can either traverse the DET-MASC arc or the DET-FEMN arc and it has no basis for deciding which. If it goes the DET-FEMN route, then it will fail when it reaches the N-FEMN arc, since policeman has no French counterpart in N-FEMN. So, any algorithm that we devise to employ FSTs that exhibit such non-determinism will need to incorporate either an ability to backtrack or an ability to explore multiple arcs in parallel. It is worth noting that our earlier and uglier English–French FST was deterministic in both directions.

The examples of FSTs that we have just been playing with are misleading in that nobody nowadays would dream of attempting to do serious English–French machine translation with an FST, for reasons that will begin to emerge in the final section of this chapter and which should be self-evident by the time you have reached the end of this book. But FSTs are potentially well suited to providing efficient solutions to certain small self-contained areas of linguistic analysis. Examples that spring to mind are the translation or interpretation of number names and time of day expressions (although not in all languages), text to speech transduction in languages with fairly well-behaved orthographies and the inflectional analysis of word forms. We will look briefly at the latter here, returning to our earlier Swahili example, reconstructed as an FST mapping between the Swahili morphemes and reasonably perspicuous representations of their syntactic and semantic content (SWAHILI-2).

EXAMPLE: Swahili-2 FST

Name SWAHILI-2:
  Initial 10
  Final 90
  From 10 to 21 by Subj_ni
  From 10 to 22 by Subj_u
  From 10 to 23 by Subj_a
  From 10 to 24 by Subj_tu
  From 10 to 25 by Subj_wa
  From 21 to 31 by 1ST
  From 22 to 31 by 2ND
  From 23 to 31 by 3RD
  From 24 to 32 by 1ST
  From 25 to 32 by 3RD
  From 31 to 40 by SING
  From 32 to 40 by PLUR
  From 40 to 50 by TENSE
  From 50 to 61 by Obj_ni

From 50 to 62 by Obj_ku
From 50 to 63 by Obj_m
From 50 to 64 by Obj_tu
From 50 to 65 by Obj_wa
From 61 to 71 by 1ST
From 62 to 71 by 2ND
From 63 to 71 by 3RD
From 64 to 72 by 1ST
From 65 to 72 by 3RD
From 71 to 80 by SING
From 72 to 80 by PLUR
From 80 to 90 by STEM.

1ST abbreviates:
  1st_#.

2ND abbreviates:
  2nd_#.

3RD abbreviates:
  3rd_#.

SING abbreviates:
  Sing_#.

PLUR abbreviates:
  Plur_#.

TENSE abbreviates:
  Future_ta, Present_na, Perfect_me, Past_li.

STEM abbreviates:
  LIKE_penda, BEAT_piga, ANNOY_sumbua, PAY_lipa.

This network will map a Swahili expression like 'wa-me-ni-sumbua' (on the second tape) into Subj-3rd-Plur-Perfect-Obj-1st-Sing-ANNOY (on the first tape), or conversely, and it can be seen why this might well be a useful thing to do in a system designed to analyze or synthesize inflected Swahili words. Notice that the FST given is deterministic when we use it to map from Swahili into our analysis expressions, but not when we go in the opposite direction. Notice also that we have been cheating in our discussion so far: real Swahili words come to us as 'wamenisumbua' not as 'wa-me-ni-sumbua' with all the morpheme breaks conveniently marked. But we can solve this problem with the FST machinery that we already have: we simply need to transduce 'w a m e n i s u m b u a' into 'wa me ni sumbua'.

An FST is an FSTN that deals with two tapes. Thus, we can amend our programs to deal with FSTs, mainly by changing the tape-handling procedures. Let us represent the object characterized by a transducer as a list of two tapes, each of which is a normal list of symbols. Now the label on a network arc will need to specify constraints on the next symbol on both tapes. We can show this by providing a pair of labels (list of two labels) or an abbreviation that stands for such a pair. For instance, here is the network and abbreviations for the ENG_FRE-1 example:

```
(setq eng_fre1
 '((Initial (1))
   (Final (5))
   (From 1 to 2 by WH)
   (From 2 to 3 by BE)
   (From 3 to 4 by DET)
   (From 4 to 5 by NOUN)))

(setq abbreviations
 '((WH (where ou))
   (BE (is est))
   (DET (the |#|))
   (NOUN (exit la_sortie) (policeman le_gendarme)
         (shop la_boutique) (toilet la_toilette))))
```

As before, the tape-handling procedures will depend on whether we wish to do recognition or generation. With transducers, there are in fact more possibilities, as we may wish to recognize inputs on both tapes, generate output on both tapes or recognize input on one and produce output on the other. Here is the tape-handling function for the case where we wish to recognize input on the first tape and produce output on the second:

```
(defun transduce_move (label tape)
  ;; returns a list of tapes
  (if (listp label)   ; a pair
    (let ((results '()))
      (dolist (newinput (recognize_move (car label) (car tape)))
        (dolist (newoutput (generate_move (cadr label) (cadr tape)))
          (setq results (cons (list newinput newoutput) results))))
      results)
    (if (equal label '|#|)
      (list tape)
      (if (assoc label abbreviations)
        (transduce_move_list (cdr (assoc label abbreviations)) tape)))))

(defun transduce_move_list (labels tape)
  (if (null labels)
    '()
    (append
      (transduce_move (car labels) tape)
      (transduce_move_list (cdr labels) tape))))
```

We have made use here of the recognize_move and generate_move procedures previously developed for finite-state machines that are recognizing and generating (these appear in lib fstape). In a network for an FST, a label on an arc will be (possibly an abbreviation for) a pair of labels. We need to attempt to move the first (input) tape in accordance with the first label (this is what recognize_move does). If this is successful, we need to produce output on the second tape in accordance with what the second label dictates (this is what generate_move does). If all goes well, we finally glue together the new input tape with each output tape in turn to give the list of new tapes.

Here is the rest of the program. As before, we have a main function and a next function. The initial double-tape consists of the words to be analyzed (the input tape) and an empty list (the output tape so far). The terminating condition on the double tape is that the first component must be empty. In this case, the second component is the complete sequence generated on the second tape. This program stops as soon as one successful network traversal has occurred (as in the recognize case).

```
(defun transduce_next (node tape network)
   ;; returns nil or throws an output tape
   (if (and (null (car tape)) (member node (final_nodes network)))
      (throw 'stop (cadr tape))
      (dolist (transition (transitions network))
         (if (equal node (trans_node transition))
            (dolist (newtape (transduce_move (trans_label transition) tape))
               (transduce_next (trans_newnode transition) newtape network))
            nil))))    ; transition from wrong node

(defun transduce (network tape)
   (catch
      'stop
      (dolist (initialnode (initial_nodes network))
         (transduce_next initialnode (list tape nil) network))
      nil))
```

Exercise 2.17 Draw a diagram of the SWAHILI-2 network. [*easy*]

Exercise 2.18 Design an equivalent FST that will run deterministically from the analysis expressions to the Swahili words. [*intermediate*]

Exercise 2.19 Elaborate the ENG_FRE-1 FST to cover a small but useful subset of the phrases that you might need in a foreign airport. [*easy*]

Exercise 2.20 Design an FST that will transduce well-formed English number names, such as 'twenty two', into the corresponding Arabic numerals – that is, '22'. [*easy*]

Exercise 2.21   Design an FST that will transduce well-formed English time-of-day expressions into their French counterparts, or those of some other language. Thus, for example, it should map 'seven minutes past noon' into 'midi sept'.   [*intermediate*]

Exercise 2.22   Design an FST that will transduce well-formed English number names into well-formed French number names, or those of some other language. Thus, for example, it should map 'ninety four' into 'quatre vingt quatorze'.   [*easy*]

Exercise 2.23   Design an FST to transduce 'w a m e n i s u m b u a' into 'wa me ni sumbua', etc., for all the Swahili data.   [*easy*]

Exercise 2.24   Imagine two parallel sequences of phonemes and phones set side by side so that each phoneme is paired with a phone (ignoring null elements, for the sake of simplicity). An FST can crawl down this sequence of phoneme–phone pairs obeying rules such as the following:

● If your current phoneme is /d/ and your current phone is [t] and you are in state 17, then you may advance to the next pair and shift into state 11.

In this example, state 17 might well be the state that the automaton gets into as it emerges from an unvoiced consonant, say. If the FST is able to reach the end of the sequence of pairs in an approved final state, then the phone sequence is a well-formed realization of the phoneme sequence according to the rules that the FST embodies (and conversely). We can reformulate the inspection rule as one of transduction:

● If your current phoneme is /d/ and you are in state 17, then you may print [t] and advance to the next phoneme and shift into state 11.

Devise a small FST incorporating such phoneme–phone matching rules and show how it can handle some standard phonological problems.   [*intermediate, requiring knowledge of phonology*]

Exercise 2.25   Design an FST that will translate three-character strings consisting of any letter of the alphabet, a mid-string marker character, say '^', and any letter of the alphabet into its mirror image. So, for instance, the string 'a^h' would be mapped into the string 'h^a'. Roughly how many states would you need for a similar FST that reversed strings like 'ak^yp' consisting of four alphabetic characters with a mid-string marker in the middle?   [*intermediate*]

Exercise 2.26   Deterministic FSTs, like deterministic FSTNs, can be (partially) represented by state-transition tables. The difference is that whereas the state-transition table for an FSTN is a two-dimensional object, that for a two-tape transducer is a three-dimensional object, with one dimension for the states and one dimension for each of the symbol sets associated with the tapes. This is illustrated here with a two-dimensional slice of the three-dimensional matrix for the FST that we used as an example in the text:

est	1	2	3	4	5
where	0	0	0	0	0
is	0	3	0	0	0
the	0	0	0	0	0
exit	0	0	0	0	0
policeman	0	0	0	0	0
shop	0	0	0	0	0
toilet	0	0	0	0	0

This can be interpreted as saying that if you are in state 2 and the next word on your input tape is 'est', then you can print 'is' on your output tape and change into state 3. Otherwise, you are stuck. The full matrix would require five more of these two-dimensional slices, one for each word from the symbols vocabulary of the second tape. (An alternative to this three-dimensional approach would be to use a two-dimensional table with one dimension for the states and the other dimension for symbol pairs.) Write a program that will compile deterministic two-tape FST descriptions given in our formal language into three-dimensional state-transition matrices. Now write a program that will use these matrices, and information about initial and final states, to translate from the language used on one tape to that used on the other. What happens if your compiler is given a non-deterministic FST to compile? [*hard*]

Exercise 2.27   Run the finite-state transduction program lib fstrans using the ENG_FRE-1 network (which appears in lib eng_fre1). Make some extensions of your own to this network. [*easy*]

Exercise 2.28   Write the tape-handling procedures for the case where we wish to produce output on both tapes in a transducer. Test this with the ENG_FRE-1 network. [*intermediate*]

2.8   Limitations of finite-state machines

One recent natural language application of finite-state devices has been in the recognition of inflected words in languages that make heavy use of inflectional morphology. Such a language is Finnish: nouns have 2000 odd distinct forms and verbs some 12 000. To the relief of Finnish newborns, these forms mostly result from simple regular concatenation of morphemes, which linguists refer to as *agglutination*, but there is enough irregularity to make an accurate description non-trivial. For Finnish, we can define a grammar for inflected words which is essentially just an FSTN. Each morpheme, including the stem, is associated in the lexicon with:

- its (underlying) form,
- its syntactic/semantic properties, and
- a pointer to the items that may follow it.

An (underlying) inflected word form is well formed, roughly speaking, if and only if it consists of the concatenation of a sequence of forms, beginning with a root and ending with some conventional marker, arrived at by following pointers through the lexicon.

The interest of the work we have just described, from the perspective of computational linguistics, is that FSTNs and FSTs, especially if deterministic, allow for extremely efficient implementations. FSTs also have the advantage of being bidirectional: once we have the FST, we can get from, say, phone to phoneme just as easily as we can get from phoneme to phone. This makes FSTs attractive for a number of applications, ranging from spelling checking to machine translation in restricted domains. But finite-state devices have their limitations for NLP purposes, and we conclude this chapter by taking a look at some of them.

In evaluating such devices, there are two relevant notions of adequacy that need to be kept in mind, which we shall call 'mathematical' and 'notational', respectively.

Mathematical adequacy is concerned with whether the formal objects characterized by the notation, under the intended semantics, have the properties manifested in the real-world objects that the notation and its interpretation is intended to model. Although FSTNs can recognize non-finite languages, languages that contain an infinite set of strings, there are many non-finite languages that they cannot recognize. Thus, it is easy to build an FSTN to recognize the language of strings consisting of any number n of as (known as the language a^n) or the language of strings consisting of any number m of as followed by any number n of bs (the language, $a^m b^n$), but quite impossible to build an FSTN to recognize the language of strings consisting of some number n of as followed by the same number of bs (the language $a^n b^n$), unless an upper bound is put on the size of n, in which case we cease to have a non-finite language. This is a failure of mathematical adequacy. Strings of the general form $a^n b^n$ arise in a language when the language permits one string to be embedded inside another and puts no limit on such embedding. A lexicon of the sort described in the opening paragraph of this section can only define sets of strings that are finite-state languages: a natural language whose word-set involved constructions like $a^n b^n$ would show that kind of account of the lexicon to be mathematically inadequate as a theory of natural language lexicons in general.

Notational adequacy is to do with how elegantly the notation describes the real-world objects. In general, a short description is preferable to a longer one, repetition and long windedness increasing the possibility of errors in the use of the notation. An ideal notation allows one to exploit the similarities between different structures and state general properties when they exist. Looking at the SWAHILI-2 network we can detect some notational inadequacy by observing the similarity between the arcs following the rewriting of the symbol Subj and those following the rewriting of the symbol Obj. For instance, the arc with label Subj_ni is immediately followed by one labelled 1ST, as is the arc with label Obj_ni. The notation does not allow us to 'factor out' the similarities between these sets of arcs. Similarly, if we wished to describe English sentences of the form subject–verb–object using a FSTN, we would find that we would have to separately describe possible subjects and objects, even though almost all phrases that can appear as one can equally appear as the other. We will return to this problem in Chapter 3.

Exercise 2.29   Readers unfamiliar with the fact that no FSTN can recognize the language $a^n b^n$ are encouraged to attempt to provide an informal proof of it.   [*hard*]

SUMMARY

- FSTNs are the simplest approach to NLP.
- FSTNs are of very little use by themselves.
- FSTs map one string of symbols into another.
- FSTs can be used for sublanguage translation.
- FSTs can be used for morphological processing.
- FSAs are easy to implement.
- FSAs do not suffice for NLP.

Further reading

For technical introductions to FSTNs and discussion of some of their formal properties, see Aho and Ullman (1972, Sections 2.2 and 2.3), Aho and Ullman (1977, Chapter 3), Hopcroft and Ullman (1979, Chapter 2) or Gersting (1982, Chapters 7 and 8). Relevant accounts of directed graphs and graph traversal algorithms are to be found in Aho et al.(1982, Chapter 6) and Sedgewick (1983, Chapters 29–30). Technical presentations of FSTs are available in Lynch and Pierson (1968), Lewis and Stearns (1968), and Aho and Ullman (1972, Sections 3.1 and 3.3). Useful background reading on NLP uses of transition networks and pattern matching is provided by Winograd (1983, Chapter 2). Some researchers have continued to take an interest in finite-state devices for syntactic parsing: Blank (1985), Brodda (1986), Ejerhed (1982), Ejerhed and Church (1983), Langendoen and Langsam (1984), and Pulman (1986), for example.

The formal properties of the morphology of Bambara, mentioned earlier, are the subject of Culy (1985). Other work relevant to the question of the adequacy of finite-state machinery for phonological and morphological processing purposes includes Langendoen (1981), Carden (1983), Church (1983b, pp. 116–17), and Gazdar and Pullum (1985). Further details of the morphology of Swahili are to be found in Perrott (1951). ENG-MONOSYL is loosely based on the English phonotactics to be found in Whorf (1940).

The applicability of FSTs in phonology was noticed almost immediately. Johnson (1972) proved that a phonology that permitted only simultaneous rule application, as opposed to iterative derivational application, was equivalent to an FST. A decade later, Kaplan and Kay presented a paper in which they showed how the iteratively applied rules of standard generative phonology could, individually, be algorithmically compiled into FSTs. The closest thing to a published account of this work can be found in Kay (1983, pp. 100–4). Kaplan and Kay's work directly influenced that of Koskenniemi (1983a, 1983b, 1984) which, in turn, led to that of Karttunen and his students on the KIMMO system (Gajek et al. 1983, Khan et al. 1983, and Karttunen 1983). The Koskenniemi-style approach is described and evaluated in Gazdar (1985). Finite-state phonology or morphology fragments exist for Arabic (Kay 1987), Japanese (Alam 1983), Rumanian (Khan 1983), French (Lun 1983), German (Görz and Paulus 1988), Semitic (Kataja and Koskenniemi 1988), Spanish (Meya 1987), Old Church Slavonic (Lindstedt 1984), Swedish (Blåberg 1985), Turkish (Hankamer 1986) and English (Karttunen and Wittenburg 1983, Russell et al. 1986, Black et al. 1987). Some interesting complexity results relevant to this approach are presented in Barton et al.(1987, Chapters 5 and 6), to which Koskenniemi and Church (1988) replies. Further theoretical developments are reported in Bear (1988), Carson (1988), and Reape and Thompson (1988). The potential role of finite-state parsing in speech recognition is the subject of Church (1983a), while Gibbon (1987) proposes its use for the processing of tone systems.

Good introductions to the notion of search spaces and search techniques are given by Raphael (1976), Nilsson (1980, Chapter 1), Barr and Feigenbaum (1981, Chapter II), Rich (1983, Chapters 2–4), Charniak and McDermott (1985, Chapter 5), and Winston (1984, Chapter 4). Pearl (1984) provides a definitive reference on the topic.

CHAPTER 3

RECURSIVE AND AUGMENTED TRANSITION NETWORKS

We saw in the last chapter how FSTNs and FSTs can capture patterns of language and be used for responding to and producing language. We also implied, however, that FSTNs cannot capture, or cannot capture elegantly, some aspects of natural languages that we would like to be able to handle in NLP. For instance, FSTNs are not mathematically adequate for the description of certain kinds of embedded structures. There are also questions of notational adequacy, to which we return in this chapter, as we investigate how the network metaphor can be taken further to allow for the description of recursive structures in natural languages. Recursive transition networks and pushdown transducers are introduced as the recursive analogue of FSTNs and FSTs. The development of network-based machines for language processing has culminated in the design of various kinds of augmented transition networks, which essentially provide us with specialized programming languages for writing language processing applications.

3.1   Recursive transition networks

If you have access to computer mail facilities, you may occasionally get
annoyed with people who besiege you with irrelevant messages and seem
to expect a sensible reply each time. You may have speculated that, for
people whose messages are particularly predictable and uninteresting, the
process of producing replies might be automated in some way. Such an
automated reply generator would not have to be very sophisticated, but it
would have to respond robustly to any of a large number of potential
natural language inputs, and the responses would have to be fairly plausible. Thus, such a system might be designed to respond to particular
patterns in the input and produce responses that are related to them. For
instance, a general rule like:

> I have discovered a new bug in ... .
> ⇒ Yes, I found that one last week.
>   But I do not have time to fix ... just now.

would enable the system to respond to a number of different inputs. So if
the input was 'I have discovered a new bug in *the operating system*,' the
response would be 'Yes, ... but I do not have time to fix *the operating
system* just now.' A simple program along these lines, called ELIZA, was
written by Joseph Weizenbaum in the 1960s. ELIZA was an attempt to
reproduce some of the conversational abilities of a non-directive psycho-
logist. It is reputed to have fooled some of its conversational partners into
thinking that they were interacting with another human being.

Given the machinery of FSTs developed in the last chapter, a
strategy for implementing our reply generator immediately suggests itself.
We simply encode the different stimulus–response rules in one giant FST
that transduces possible input sentences into possible outputs. Once we
start to build an FST with the kind of complexity required by a system like
ELIZA, however, we encounter certain problems. To be able to copy
arbitrary parts of the input into the output – for instance, the name of the
computer program in the foregoing rule – we need to be able to specify an
abbreviation that stands for any pair of identical legal symbols. Thus:

> EQUAL abbreviates:
> a_a, about_about, acorn_acorn, ...

for each possible word in the English language. While it would be tedious
to specify such an abbreviation in our current notation, it would be simple
to make our recognition programs deal with this identity mapping spe-
cially.

Less tractable are problems to do with producing patterns, which
have the right degree of specificity without having the size of the FST
explode drastically. Let us concentrate for the moment purely on the

problem of recognizing instances of patterns for which certain responses are plausible. We will come back to the general transduction issues later. Consider, for instance, the problem for someone who wishes to write an ELIZA program that will give the following responses:

> everyone hates me
> ⇒ who do you think hates you?

> everyone dismisses me when i ask a question
> ⇒ who do you think dismisses you?

but will not produce the following:

> everyone with me is so stupid
> ⇒ who do you think with you?

> everyone except me is happy
> ⇒ who do you think except you?

The desired responses seem to be appropriate when the input is of the form 'everyone ... me ...', but only when the first slot is filled with an English verb, such as hates or dismisses. We can account for the fact that the second two responses are inappropriate by the fact that 'with' and 'except' are not verbs. In an FSTN to recognize this pattern, this regularity appears as follows:

```
Name EVERYONE-ME:
   Initial 1
   Final 4
   From 1 to 2 by everyone
   From 2 to 3 by VERB
   From 3 to 4 by me
   From 4 to 4 by ANYWORD.


VERB abbreviates:
   hates, dismisses, likes, ... .
ANYWORD abbreviates:
   a, about, acorn, ... .
```

where ANYWORD is an abbreviation that covers every English word. Now let us try to generalize this. For, actually, in the pattern 'everyone ... me ...', we ought to allow for the first slot to be filled with more than one word, as the following examples show:

> everyone will punish me
> ⇒ who do you think will punish you?

> everyone has forgotten me
> ⇒ who do you think has forgotten you?

The obvious solution is to include a whole bunch of connected arcs between 2 and 3, instead of the single verb arc. This will encode the notion of 'valid sequence of verbs'. A fairly simple-minded version might involve the following arcs in the bunch:

> From 2 to 21 by has
> From 21 to 3 by V-PERF
> From 2 to 22 by will
> From 22 to 3 by V-BASE
> From 2 to 3 by V-PRES

where:

> V-PERF abbreviates:
>   forgotten, punished, loved, ...
> V-BASE abbreviates:
>   forget, punish, love, ...
> V-PRES abbreviates:
>   forgets, punishes, loves ... .

This seems quite reasonable, but consider what happens when we want to allow our program to respond to other patterns such as the following:

> everyone will love you
>   ⇒ who do you think will love me?

Because the pattern for 'everyone ... you ...' also involves sequences of verbs, when we encode it as a network we will have to go through the construction of a bunch of arcs that looks just like the ones we have just developed for the first pattern. Indeed, we may need to have a copy of these arcs in many places in a complete ELIZA system. The FSTN notation is not being as useful here as it might be. Quite apart from forcing us to develop networks that are quite large for relatively uncomplicated patterns, it has not given us any way to think about the 'verb sequence' bunch of arcs as a single object. In particular, if we subsequently decide to refine our notion of valid sequence of verbs, we will have to make changes in all the places where this bundle of arcs appears in the networks. In our ELIZA program, we are thus encountering in a much more serious way the problem of notational inadequacy, which we noted briefly in connection with our transducer SWAHILI-2 at the end of Chapter 2.

A fundamental advance is made by using *recursive transition networks (RTNs)* instead of FSTNs. Basically, RTNs are just like FSTNs except that they introduce the extra concept of a named subnetwork. That is, it is possible for an arc to name a subnetwork to be traversed, instead of a specific word (or class of words) that is to appear. The idea is that if we have a commonly used bunch of arcs, we can express this abstraction by making it into a self-contained, named network. This network can then be referenced *by its name* in a network that needs it, rather than having to appear expanded out in every place. Note that we have not used the names of networks at all so far. In contrast to the practice in this book, some authors name a subnetwork by the initial node that the traversal is to start from. This allows the network writer to choose one of several initial nodes as being appropriate for a particular use of a network, but has the disadvantage that node names have to be globally accessible.

Just as an FSTN can be regarded as a specification of an FSA, so an RTN can be regarded as a specification of a machine, a *pushdown automaton (PA)*. Informally, in an RTN, to traverse an arc that is labelled with a subnetwork name instead of a word, it is necessary to traverse the subnetwork named, but remembering where to resume when that has been done. A pushdown automaton is an FSA that is equipped with an extra memory, a *stack*, that can be used for this purpose. We will examine the role of a stack in RTN traversal later in this chapter. For an RTN, network traversal is defined partially in terms of itself. This is the reason for the word 'recursive' in recursive transition network. We will see in a later section that, although this informal definition looks dangerously circular, it is possible to make computational sense of it.

Here is how our earlier finite-state ELIZA network fragments could be reconceived in RTN terms:

Name EVERYONE-ME:
  Initial 1
  Final 4
  From 1 to 2 by everyone
  From 2 to 3 by VERB-GROUP
  From 3 to 4 by me
  From 4 to 4 by ANYWORD.
Name VERB-GROUP:
  Initial 1
  Final 2
  From 1 to 11 by has
  From 11 to 2 by V-PERF
  From 1 to 12 by will
  From 12 to 2 by V-BASE
  From 1 to 2 by V-PRES.

ANYWORD abbreviates:
  a, about, acorn, ...
V-PERF abbreviates:
  forgotten, punished, loved, ...
V-BASE abbreviates:
  forget, punish, love, ...
V-PRES abbreviates:
  forgets, punishes, loves ... .

Having the VERB-GROUP network mentioned in patterns like EVERYONE-ME is an asset because it allows several words to appear between the 'everyone' and the 'me', but eliminates the problems otherwise caused by strings like:

> everyone who Mayumi saw me with ...

Note that we could absorb our convention for abbreviations into the more general notion of named subnetworks. But, in computational practice, we want a better way of dealing with abbreviations than thinking of them as networks, whether explicitly or implicitly present.

In RTNs, as we have defined them, a (sub)network is only referred to outside of itself by its name, and therefore it does not matter if a node name that is used in one network is also used in another. For instance, there is a node '1' in each of the two networks shown.

Exercise 3.1 Produce an improved VERB-GROUP subnetwork, which accepts strings like 'has been seen', 'will not eat', 'is still waiting', 'will have been seen', and so on. [*easy*]

3.2   Modelling recursion in English grammar

The model of English usage suggested by our computer mail answerer is a very piecemeal and *ad hoc* one. It suggests that often the way we use language is simply by responding to particular, special-purpose patterns with stereotyped responses. Although this may sometimes be true, it gives us little information about how people understand and respond to sentences that they have never seen before or the basic principles that lie behind efficient language use. In this section, we will begin to develop a more general RTN for a small fragment of English. This will be unsatisfactory in a number of ways, but will be useful as a running example in the discussions to follow. To keep things simple, we will ignore the intricacies of verb groups suggested by our previous examples.

To start with, we need some abbreviations corresponding to some basic lexical categories used in the description of English syntax. We have seen N, NP and DET in the ENGLISH-1 network of Chapter 2. The symbol V is used here to stand for English verbs and the symbol WH for English relative pronouns like 'who' and 'which'. Secondly, we need to define some larger networks in terms of these categories.

EXAMPLE: RTN for a fragment of English

Name S:
  Initial 0
  Final 2
  From 0 to 1 by NP
  From 1 to 2 by VP.
Name NP:
  Initial 0
  Final 2
  From 0 to 1 by DET
  From 1 to 2 by N
  From 2 to 3 by WH
  From 3 to 2 by VP.
Name VP:
  Initial 0
  Final 1, 2
  From 0 to 1 by V
  From 1 to 2 by NP
  From 1 to 3 by that
  From 3 to 2 by S.

N abbreviates:
  woman, house, table, mouse, man, ...
NP abbreviates:
  Mayumi, Maria, Washington, John, Mary, ...
DET abbreviates:
  a, the, that, ...
V abbreviates:
  sees, hits, sings, lacks, saw, ...
WH abbreviates:
  who, which, that.

In this RTN, S is the network for English sentences. A sentence can be recognized by finding first a noun phrase (NP) and then a verb phrase (VP). The noun phrase at the beginning of a sentence – for example, a phrase like 'Mayumi' or 'the woman' – is the subject of the sentence. A noun phrase can include a relative pronoun (WH) introducing a qualifying verb phrase, which is a rather simple type of relative clause, as in 'the man who sings'. The verb phrase is sometimes known as the predicate of the sentence and this contains a verb and possibly a noun phrase (the object of the verb). It is also possible for certain verbs to be followed by the word 'that' and a sentential complement, as in 'thinks that Maria sings'. Thus, the above S network will recognize sentences like:

> Mayumi sees the house.
>
> Maria sings.
>
> The table hits Washington.
>
> Mayumi sees that Maria sings.
>
> The table that lacks a leg hits Washington.

and also various other, less natural sounding, sequences of words. Note finally that the arc labels now have a dual status: they may simply stand for a set of items in the lexicon, as previously, they may just name a subnetwork, or they may do both. Thus, we can have items in the lexicon, such as 'Mayumi', listed as members of the category NP, or we can have an NP network, or we can have both.

This fragment demonstrates that English syntax is fundamentally recursive. For instance, it is easy to construct an English sentence that contains an English sentence, an English sentence that contains an English sentence that contains an English sentence ... and so on for as long as we like. But, of course, such sentences will become increasingly hard to understand as they get longer:

> Mayumi says that Maria is a genius.
>
> Mayumi says that Mayumi says that Maria is a genius.
>
> Mayumi says that Mayumi says that Mayumi says that Maria is a genius.

The recursiveness of English, and most other natural languages, means that RTNs are a natural tool for expressing its regularities.

In our network, one way of traversing the S network involves traversing the VP network, which in turn involves traversing the S network again as a subtask. Once we have networks that display 'genuine' recursion in this way, we can see that RTNs are indeed more powerful than FSTNs with an abbreviatory convention for word categories. We could imagine a reference in an arc to a subnetwork as a shorthand for having a copy of that network in that position instead of the arc. This would explain why traversing the arc involves traversing the whole subnetwork. This shorthand model works nicely for examples like the VERB-GROUP subnetwork, but will not work when the definition of a phrase (directly or indirectly) includes itself. When this happens, the model would claim, in effect, that the finitely stated RTN is shorthand for an *infinite* network (Figure 3.1).

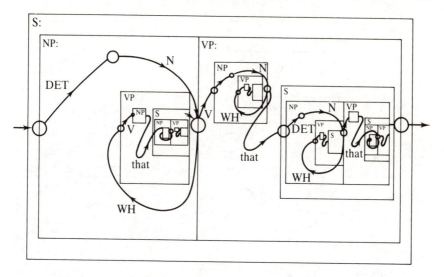

Figure 3.1   Expanded RTN for English.

Exercise 3.2   Write an FSTN that accepts all the 'Mayumi says' sentences in the infinite sequence described in the text. Can you write an FSTN that accepts all the sentences in the following sequence:

> The man chants.
> The man who the woman sees chants.
> The man who the man who the woman sees sees chants.

but which does not accept 'unbalanced' strings like:

> *The man who the man who the woman sees sees
> *The man who the man who the woman sees sees sees chants

Note the use of '*' to signal ungrammaticality.   [*intermediate*]

Exercise 3.3   Extend the example RTN so that it accepts the following sentences:

> Lee knew Kim appointed the chairman.
> Lee presented the prize to the author.
> The chairman died.

but so that it does not accept the following:

> *Lee knew Kim to the author
> *Lee presented
> *Lee died Kim appointed the chairman

[*easy*]

Figure 3.2 Kangaroos traversing an RTN.

3.3 Traversing RTNs

Although introducing named subnetworks seems conceptually like a small change to make to FSTNs, it does introduce significant complexity in the procedure for traversing a network. The basic problem is that, to traverse one arc, it may be necessary to traverse a whole subnetwork. While that subnetwork is being traversed, the position of the original arc must be remembered, so that the traversal can resume there afterwards. Our kangaroo model of network traversal, introduced in Chapter 2, needs to be embellished somewhat to account for this.

In a recursive network, a kangaroo may come across a subnetwork name on an arc, instead of a word. In this case, we can think of it as recruiting another kangaroo (from a large labour pool) to traverse the subnetwork for it. As this second kangaroo jumps through the subnetwork, it is allowed to move the pointing device along the input string. It is also allowed to recruit other kangaroos to traverse sub-subnetworks for it (and the levels of delegation may go arbitrarily deep). When any kangaroo has finished, it reports success to the kangaroo that recruited it, who waits patiently until this happens. So, when the second kangaroo has finished jumping through its subnetwork it reports back to the first kangaroo. The first kangaroo wakes up again, noticing that the pointer has been moved on, finishes jumping along the arc mentioning the subnetwork and continues from the new node as before.

In the kangaroo model, at any time, there is one kangaroo jumping through a network and a line of other kangaroos, each remembering a place in a network and waiting to resume work once its subordinate has finished, as illustrated in Figure 3.2. The first of the waiting kangaroos (the one who joined the line last) is waiting for the currently active kangaroo, the second waiting kangaroo is waiting for the first, the third waiting kangaroo is waiting for the second, and so on. If the active kangaroo gets to the end of its network, it wakes up the first waiting kangaroo and then rejoins the labour pool. This first waiting kangaroo leaves the line and resumes work. When it finishes, it wakes up the first kangaroo in the line (who was previously the second) and itself goes back to the labour pool. On the other hand, if the active kangaroo finds a subnetwork that needs traversing, it recruits a new kangaroo from the labour pool (*not* the waiting line), sets this kangaroo off on the subnetwork and itself joins the waiting line, at the front, waiting for the subcontracted work to be complete.

The main innovation here is the line of waiting kangaroos. How are we to represent this computationally? In fact, the line of waiting kangaroos corresponds to the computational device of a *pushdown stack*. A pushdown stack is a device for storing information that can be manipulated by two basic operations:

(1)   A piece of information can be PUSHed (added) on to the stack. This corresponds to a kangaroo joining the line at the front.

(2)   The most recently added piece of information can be POPped (removed) from the stack. This corresponds to the first kangaroo in the line being woken up, leaving the line and resuming work.

When we need to indicate the contents of a pushdown stack, we will simply separate the items with colons, the first (most recently added) item being on the left. We will denote the empty stack by empty space. So here is how we would denote the stack that results from 'pushing' the symbols a, b and c on to the empty stack in that order:

c : b : a :

While a kangaroo is waiting in the line, it only needs to remember its place in a network, so that it can resume there afterwards. All other information can be picked up when it starts work again – the networks themselves will not have changed, and the pointer will have changed in ways completely outside its control. Thus, the pieces of information to be stored in the pushdown stack are simply positions in the networks. We can represent a position in a network by the name of the node where the kangaroo will resume work (the destination of the arc that requires the traversal of the subnetwork). In general, if we allow the same node name to be used in different networks, we require the name of the network containing the node as well. Where it is necessary to distinguish which network a node belongs to, we will qualify the name in the following fashion:

S/3

which denotes the node named 3 in the network S.

If we wish to extend our previous account of network traversal to RTNs, the notion of 'state' will have to be extended now to include a third component:

- R3. a pushdown stack of positions (node names).

Here, then, is a fully specified example state describing a point in an RTN traversal (recognition, not generation):

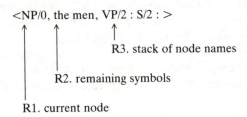

<NP/0, the men, VP/2 : S/2 : >

R3. stack of node names

R2. remaining symbols

R1. current node

This state represents the intermediate state of a traversal where the remaining words to be considered are 'the men' and the active kangaroo is sitting on node 0 in the network NP. The line of waiting kangaroos contains kangaroos waiting to continue moving from node 2 in network VP (at the front of the line) and node 2 in network S (at the back of the line).

Given this modified notion of 'state', the basic search algorithm for network traversal does not need to be different from the finite-state case. This time each of the initial set of states needs to have an empty stack. Thus, since 0 is the only initial node in the top-level network for English sentences, the only initial state for traversing this network would be:

<S/0, ..., >

where '...' is the input string. What are the valid final states that indicate successful traversal? To be successful, we must have reached a final node in the top-level network, we must have an empty line of waiting kangaroos and we must have used all the symbols in the input. Thus, if we were using our networks for English sentences, the only possible final state would be:

<S/2, , >

How do we calculate the valid next states that follow from a given state <NODE, INPUT, STACK>. For each arc (with label L and destination

D) leaving node NODE, we must include states in the set according to the following rules. We illustrate these with examples from the foregoing example networks:

>   (POP) if NODE is a final node,
>   the top of STACK is H and
>   the rest of STACK is T,
>   include <H, INPUT, T>
>
>   e.g., from <NP/2, sings, S/1 : > we can get
>   <S/1, sings, >
>
>   (SYM′) if L is a symbol and
>   the first symbol of INPUT is the same,
>   include <D, ... rest of INPUT ..., STACK>
>
>   e.g., from <VP/1, that John, S/2 : > we can get
>   <VP/3, John, S/2 : >
>
>   (ABB′) if L is an abbreviation
>   which covers the first symbol of INPUT,
>   include <D, ... rest of INPUT ..., STACK>
>
>   e.g., from <NP/1, man sings, S/1: > we can get
>   <NP/2, sings, S/1 : >, since 'man' is an N
>
>   (PUSH) if L is a network name,
>   for each initial node INIT of that network
>   include <INIT, INPUT, D : STACK>
>
>   e.g., from <VP/1, the man, S/2 : > we can get
>   <NP/0, the man, VP/2 : S/2: >
>
>   (JMP′) if L is #, include <D, INPUT, STACK>

Of these principles, two are new and correspond to entering and leaving subnetworks (PUSH and POP). The others are essentially the same as in the finite-state network case.

Here is an example of recognition using our initial English networks and the sentence 'Mary sees that man.' We will show the stages of the recognition by a sequence of 'snapshots', each time showing the set of alternative states under consideration. Initially, we just have one state:

>   <S/0, Mary sees that man, >

Removing this from the set, only the PUSH rule is applicable and so we get:

>   <NP/0, Mary sees that man, S/1 : >

Selecting this, only the ABB' rule applies (the first word is an NP):

<NP/2, sees that man, S/1 : >

From NP/2, the only arc requires a WH word, and 'sees' is not of this category. Since NP/2 is a final node, the only option is then to POP to:

<S/1, sees that man, >

From S/1, there is no choice but to PUSH, looking for a VP:

<VP/0, sees that man, S/2 : >

Once again, there is no choice but to recognize the V and proceed (by ABB') to VP/1:

<VP/1, that man, S/2 : >

From VP/1, there are now three possibilities. Since VP/1 is a final node, we can POP back to the S network. Alternatively, we can proceed to VP/3 by consuming the word 'that' (SYM'). Finally, we can try to PUSH for an NP. Thus, we have three possible next states:

<S/2, that man, >
<VP/3, man, S/2 : >
<NP/0, that man, VP/2 : S/2 : >

We now have to choose between these, removing one from the set and leaving the other two behind, to be reconsidered later if other possibilities do not work out. Let us say that we choose the first of them. Since there are no arcs leaving S/2, only the POP rule could be appropriate. This does not apply, however, as the stack is empty. So we cannot progress further from this state. Since the state is not a final state, we simply remove it from the list, leaving:

<VP/3, man, S/2 : >
<NP/0, that man, VP/2 : S/2 : >

Again, we have to choose which state to investigate next. Let us again choose the first one. From VP/3, we have no option but to PUSH for an S:

<S/0, man, VP/2 : S/2 : >
<NP/0, that man, VP/2 : S/2 : >

Again, selecting the first state in the list, we are forced to PUSH and get:

<NP/0, man, S/1 : VP/2 : S/2 : >
<NP/0, that man, VP/2 : S/2 : >

If we this time select the second state to investigate, we can proceed to:

<NP/0, man, S/1 : VP/2 : S/2 : >
<NP/1, man, VP/2 : S/2 : >

(because 'that' is a DET). Similarly, we can progress from this state to a similar state at NP/2:

<NP/0, man, S/1 : VP/2 : S/2 : >
<NP/2, , VP/2 : S/2 : >

If we continue selecting the second state in the set, we can POP to:

<NP/0, man, S/1 : VP/2 : S/2 : >
<VP/2, , S/2 : >

and then POP again to:

<NP/0, man, S/1 : VP/2 : S/2 : >
<S/2, , >

The second state in our list is now a successful final state, and so we can halt, having successfully recognized the string.

Here is an example of random generation from the networks, giving the intermediate states and the rule used at each stage. As in the FSTN case, for generation, we keep the list of words output so far, rather than the list of words to be processed in a state. The rules for generating next states have to be altered slightly to cater for this change. Since the generation is random, we only need to consider one alternative at each point and can discard the others.

<S/0, , >
  PUSH
<NP/0, , S/1 : >
  ABB' (NP)
<NP/2, John, S/1 : >
  POP
<S/1, John, >
  PUSH

<VP/0, John, S/2 : >
  ABB′ (V)

<VP/1, John saw, S/2 : >
  PUSH

<NP/0, John saw, VP/2 : S/2 : >
  ABB′ (DET)

<NP/1, John saw the, VP/2 : S/2 : >
  ABB′ (N)

<NP/2, John saw the mouse, VP/2 : S/2 : >
  POP

<VP/2, John saw the mouse, S/2 : >
  POP

<S/2, John saw the mouse, >
  SUCCESS!

Exercise 3.4 Why does it not matter for the final outcome which choices we make at which points in the recognition example that we walked through in the text? Does this apply in general? [*intermediate*]

Exercise 3.5 Write down a revised set of next state rules for RTNs, oriented towards generation, rather than recognition. [*easy*]

Exercise 3.6 In Chapter 2, we showed how a deterministic FSTN could be easily translated into a LISP function. Write down an example deterministic RTN and translate it directly into a program in such a way that each network gives rise to a single function. In this translation, the analogue of invoking a subnetwork is calling a function while the analogue of returning to a higher network is exiting from a function. [*intermediate*]

3.4   RTNs in LISP

We can represent recursive transition networks as list structures in the same way as finite-state networks. In general, we now need to present more than one network simultaneously, however. We also need to allow networks to be named and arcs to have network names as labels, as well as symbols, abbreviations and #s. The way that we will achieve this is to have a global variable networks, which will contain an association list associating names with networks. So here are the networks in LISP form:

```
(setq networks
'((S
      ((Initial (0))
       (Final (2))
       (From 0 to 1 by NP)
       (From 1 to 2 by VP)))
  (NP
      ((Initial (0))
       (Final (2))
       (From 0 to 1 by DET)
       (From 1 to 2 by N)
       (From 2 to 3 by WH)
       (From 3 to 2 by VP)))
  (VP
      ((Initial (0))
       (Final (1 2))
       (From 0 to 1 by V)
       (From 1 to 2 by NP)
       (From 1 to 3 by that)
       (From 3 to 2 by S)))))
```

Here, of course, NP is the name of a network, whereas V is only an abbreviation. Our network traverser can tell what the possibilities are, because the network names are the atoms that appear as keys in networks. When our network traversers come across a label that is not #, we will assume that if the label is not a key in networks, then it must be either an abbreviation or a simple symbol.

To make our network traversal programs of Chapter 2 work with RTNs, we need to revise our concept of state and incorporate this revision into the arguments for the relevant next functions. A state now has an extra component – a stack of locations to return to. Our previous next functions, for various recognition and generation tasks, took arguments as follows:

```
(defun next (node tape network)
    ...
```

where node was the name of the node in the network and tape was the list of symbols remaining to be processed. For RTNs, we will revise this to be:

```
(defun next (networkname node tape stack)
    ...
```

where networkname and node together say where the kangaroo is (in which network and at what node of that network), tape gives the list of symbols and stack represents the line of waiting kangaroos.

We need to have ways to manipulate the stack of locations; in particular, to push an item on to the top of a stack, yielding a new stack; to pop the top item off a stack, to discover what the item is and what is left of the stack; finally, it is useful to be able to test whether a stack is empty. In fact, it is very straightforward to implement stacks as lists, where the car of the list is the top element of the stack and the cdr of the list is the remaining stack. If we use this representation, pushing an item on to a stack amounts to using cons to create a new list with that item on the front, popping an item from a stack amounts to using car and cdr to access the first element and remaining elements of the list, and, finally, the empty stack is represented by the empty list, nil.

We now need some ways of manipulating locations themselves. Previously, when we were restricted to a single network, a location could be simply the name of a node. Now, we will represent a location by a pair of values:

```
(<networkname> <node>)
```

where <networkname> is the name of a network and <node> is the name of a node in that network. Having the network name explicitly available inside the location data structure means that we can quickly tell which network we are in and can switch networks quickly. It is also essential if we have used the same node names in different networks.

The top-level function for RTN recognition is very similar to the finite-state case. However, note that we pass in the *name* of the network (that is, an atom) through the first argument networkname, rather than the network itself (that is, a complex list structure). In RTN traversal, we are constantly passing around references to different networks; hence, it will make things like trace output much more comprehensible if we pass around the names rather than the list structures.

```
(defun rtn_recognize (networkname tape)
  (catch
    'rtn
    (dolist (initialnode (initial_nodes (get_network networkname)))
      (rtn_recognize_next networkname initialnode tape ()))
    nil))
```

Notice that each initial state considered has an empty stack (the last argument to rtn_recognize_next). We will frequently need to get the network list structure from the name of a network and the function get_network will do this job for us:

```
(defun get_network (name)
  (cadr (assoc name networks)))
```

Here is the next function (called rtn_recognize_next) for recognition with RTNs. As in the finite-state case, it exits as soon as it has made a successful traversal.

```
(defun rtn_recognize_next (networkname node tape stack)
  (if (member node (final_nodes (get_network networkname)))
      (rtn_recognize_pop tape stack))
  (dolist (transition (transitions (get_network networkname)))
    (if (equal (trans_node transition) node)
        (let ((label (trans_label transition))
              (newnode (trans_newnode transition)))
          (if (get_network label)
              ;; interpret label as network name
              (rtn_recognize_push label networkname newnode tape stack))
          ;; interpret label as symbol/abbreviation
          (rtn_recognize_traverse label networkname newnode tape stack)))))
```

For this definition, the main work is parcelled up in three subfunctions.
The function rtn_recognize_traverse contains a kernel (dealing with the SYM',
ABB' and JMP' rules), like the non-recursive recognize_next. Its job is to deal
with the consequences of traversing a single arc:

```
(defun rtn_recognize_traverse (label networkname newnode tape stack)
  (dolist (newtape (rtn_recognize_move label tape))
    (rtn_recognize_next networkname newnode newtape stack)))
```

This subfunction calls rtn_recognize_move to move the tape in all possible ways,
parcelling up each new tape into a new state which will be examined by
another rtn_recognize_next. As well as rtn_recognize_traverse, rtn_recognize_next also calls
the subfunctions rtn_recognize_push and rtn_recognize_pop, corresponding to the
push and pop rules. The pop rule can be tried if node is a final node in its
network. If the stack is empty and the tape is also exhausted, then we have
successfully finished the original traversal. If, on the other hand, the stack
is not empty, we call rtn_recognize_next with the stored elements on the top of
the stack:

```
(defun rtn_recognize_pop (tape stack)
  (if (and (null stack) (null tape))
      (throw 'rtn t)
      (if (not (null stack))   ; not finished
          (rtn_recognize_next
            (caar stack)    ; stacked networkname
            (cadar stack)   ; stacked node name
            tape
            (cdr stack)))))
```

With the push rule, which applies if an arc label is a key in networks, we
construct a new state for each initial node of the subnetwork. This state has
the same tape as the original state and a stack that has the destination of
the arc pushed on to it. So, when we emerge from that network, we will

continue from wherever this arc leads:

```
(defun rtn_recognize_push (label networkname newnode tape stack)
  (dolist (initialnode (initial_nodes (get_network label)))
    (rtn_recognize_next label initialnode tape
      (cons (list networkname newnode) stack))))
```

Note that even if the push rule does apply for a given arc, in rtn_recognize_next we still check for the label being an abbreviation, a symbol, and so on in the usual way (using rtn_recognize_traverse).

We still have not defined rtn_recognize_move, which finds all legal ways of moving the tape during the traversal of an arc. This function is exactly the same as the one used in the finite-state network recognizer:

```
(defun rtn_recognize_move (label tape)
  (recognize_move label tape))
```

Exercise 3.7   Assemble the various pieces of code and construct the relevant network data structures to implement the example RTNs given in the text.   [*easy*]

Exercise 3.8   Add extra code to the RTN recognizer so that it prints out messages to show what it is doing. Your program might print out messages like the following:

```
(Arriving at node 3 in network S)
(Looking for a NOUN)
(PUSHING for a S)
(POPPING)
(FAILING)
(FAILING back to node 3 in network S)
```

[*easy*]

Exercise 3.9   Reimplement RTN traversal using record structures instead of all the lists used in our implementation.   [*easy, for programmers*]

3.5   Pushdown transducers

We saw in the last chapter how an FST is simply an FSA that deals with two tapes. Similarly, we can construct a *pushdown transducer (PT)* as a pushdown automaton that deals with two tapes. To specify a PT, it suffices to augment the RTN notation so that labels on arcs can denote pairs of symbols, just as in the finite-state case. In general, a label in a PT (or, to be precise, an RTN that is interpreted as a PT) may specify any of the following:

- a symbol to be found on each tape – for example, fish_poisson – where either or both symbols may be #.
- an abbreviation for a set of such symbol pairs.
- the name of another PT to be traversed.

With the extra power of RTNs, we can write interesting transducers quite easily. For instance, an ELIZA PT can be constructed from the previous RTN translated into a transducer.

EXAMPLE: Eliza PT

```
        Name ELIZA:
         Initial 1
         Final 2
         From 1 to 2 by EVERYONE-ME
         From 1 to 2 by ...
         ... many more arcs ... .

        Name EVERYONE-ME:
         Initial 1
         Final 4
         From 1 to 2 by everyone_'who do you think'
         From 2 to 3 by VERB-GROUP
         From 3 to 4 by me_you
         From 4 to 4 by EQUAL.

        Name VERB-GROUP:
         Initial 1
         Final 2
         From 1 to 11 by has_has
         From 11 to 2 by V-PERF.
          ... .

      EQUAL abbreviates:
        a_a, about_about, acorn_acorn, ... .
      V-PERF abbreviates:
        forgotten_forgotten, punished_punished, hated_hated, loved_loved, ... .
```

It is similarly easy to produce a simple PT for limited English–French translation. Apart from the alterations to deal with gender in noun phrases, this PT is a direct translation of our previous RTN for English sentences.

EXAMPLE: PT for limited English–French translation

```
Name S:
  Initial 0
  Final 2
  From 0 to 1 by NP
  From 1 to 2 by VP.
Name NP:
  Initial 0
  Final 2
  From 0 to 1 by DET-FEMN
  From 1 to 2 by N-FEMN
  From 0 to 4 by DET-MASC
  From 4 to 2 by N-MASC
  From 2 to 3 by WH
  From 3 to 2 by VP.
Name VP:
  Initial 0
  Final 1, 2
  From 0 to 1 by V
  From 1 to 2 by NP
  From 1 to 3 by that_que
  From 3 to 2 by S.
N-MASC abbreviates:
  man_homme, horse_cheval, ... .
N-FEMN abbreviates:
  house_maison, table_table, ... .
NP abbreviates:
  John_Jean, Mary_Marie, Jean_Jeanne, ... .
DET-MASC abbreviates:
  a_un, the_le, this_ce, ... .
DET-FEMN abbreviates:
  a_une, the_la, this_cette, ... .
V abbreviates:
  sees_voit, hits_frappe, sings_chante, lacks_manque, ... .
WH abbreviates:
  who_qui, which_qui, that_qui.
```

Note that, when used to produce French output from English input, this system is doing little more than word-by-word translation, and it is easy to find examples where this will not work for French or other languages. On the other hand, the fact that the transducer incorporates a notion of what is a grammatical sentence in each language means that it could be used for other purposes – for instance, generating random pairs of legal and equivalent sentences.

Given that an RTN has successfully recognized a sentence as grammatical in some language, we might be interested to see which route the RTN interpreter took through the network for this sentence. That is, we might be interested to see a *trace* of which networks have been entered and exited, which word categories have been found when, and so on. One possibility would be to augment our RTN interpreter to keep track of this information and display it at the end of recognition. Alternatively, we could construct a transducer that produces this information as its output.

EXAMPLE: Using a PT to record a path through an RTN

```
Name S:
  Initial 100
  Final 200
  From 100 to    0 by #_(S
  From    0 to    1 by NP
  From    1 to    2 by VP
  From    2 to 200 by #_).
Name NP:
  Initial 100
  Final 200
  From 100 to    0 by #_(NP
  From    0 to    1 by DET
  From    1 to    2 by N
  From    2 to    3 by WH
  From    3 to    2 by VP
  From    2 to 200 by #_).
Name VP:
  Initial 300
  Final 100, 200
  From 300 to    0 by #_(VP
  From    0 to    1 by V
  From    1 to    2 by NP
  From    1 to    3 by that_that.
  From    3 to    2 by S
  From    1 to 100 by #_)
  From    2 to 200 by #_).
```

N abbreviates:
  man_N, house_N, table_N, ...
NP abbreviates:
  Mayumi_NP, Maria_NP, Gilbert_NP, ...
DET abbreviates:
  a_DET, the_DET, that_DET, ...
V abbreviates:
  sees_V, hits_V, sings_V, lacks_V, ...
WH abbreviates:
  who_WH, which_WH, that_WH.

This transducer, which is again derived straightforwardly from our English sentence RTN, can be used to transduce a sentence into a trace showing the networks that the RTN would traverse in accepting it. Each network has been augmented with extra arcs at the beginning and end (one for each initial and final state), which produce output on the second tape recording entry to and exit from that network. A symbol like '(S' on the output indicates entry to the S network; the symbol ')' on the output indicates exit from the network last entered. In addition, we have each instance of an abbreviation or particular word encountered leave behind a trace of its occurrence. Thus, for instance, the input sentence 'Mayumi sees that the man sings' would produce essentially the following output on the second tape:

(S (NP NP) (VP V that (S (NP DET N) (VP V))))

At present, our networks are so simple that it is not possible for a sentence to be recognized in more than one way. Hence, this transducer will always generate exactly one trace for each legal sentence. We can change this by allowing prepositional phrases in our sentences. At its simplest, a prepositional phrase consists of a preposition followed by a noun phrase – for instance, 'with the funny hat' and 'behind Washington'. A noun phrase can have any number of prepositional phrases at its end, as in:

The man with the funny hat behind Washington

In this case, the prepositional phrases are telling us more about whoever it is being described by the noun phrase. Prepositional phrases can also occur at the end of verb phrases to indicate where, when or how the action takes place, as in:

Maria sang with the choir in the large room.

Sometimes it is not clear whether a given prepositional phrase belongs to a noun phrase or to a verb phrase, as in:

Maria saw the woman with the telescope.

This ambiguity corresponds to different ways in which this could be recognized as a sentence.

___

Exercise 3.10   Add rules to the transducer just given to allow both a noun phrase and a verb phrase to include any number of prepositional phrases at its end. What outputs will the transducer produce for the sentences 'Maria sees the woman with the telescope' and 'Maria sees the woman in the park with the telescope'?   [*easy*]

Exercise 3.11   Modify the example English–French network and lexicon so as to be able to translate the following sentences into French:

John gives a horse to the man.
The man knows John lacks a house.

Ensure that 'to the' will translate into 'au' rather than 'a le'. *Hint*: You may need to use a pair like word_# or #_word in your transduction lexicon.   [*intermediate*]

Exercise 3.12 [*intermediate*]: Implement the functions rtn_transduce, rtn_transduce_next and rtn_transduce_move analogous to the finite state functions transduce, transduce_next and transduce_move. The resulting program should be able to handle pushdown transducers like the simple French translation system. The example French translation network appears in LISP form in lib eng_fre2. Here is how one of the networks looks as a list structure (remember that this is one component of the global list networks):

```
(VP
    ((Initial (0))
     (Final (1 2))
     (From 0 to 1 by V)
     (From 1 to 2 by NP)
     (From 1 to 3 by (that que))
     (From 3 to 2 by S)))
```

You will need to pay attention to the same factors that changed in converting a finite state recognizer to a finite state transducer – the requirements for initial and final states and the use of a pair of tapes. In fact, you can use the previous transduce_move as the value of rtn_transduce_move.   [*intermediate*]

3.6   Advantages and limitations of RTNs

We have demonstrated that RTNs have certain clear notational advantages over FSTNs. They allow commonly occurring subpatterns to be expressed as named subnetworks, and large networks to be built up in a modular way. In addition, they allow us to deal naturally with some of the recursive structures in natural languages. The result is a conceptual and notational system that is clean, clear and efficient. As we have seen, however, there is a price to be paid in the complexity of the network traversal algorithms, and we might still prefer FSTNs for a given application for this reason, even though the resulting networks might be larger.

As regards mathematical adequacy, we have illustrated some recursive language structures that can be recognized by RTNs but cannot in principle be captured by FSTNs. The classical example showing the difference in power between the two notations is the language $a^n b^n$. Whereas it is impossible for an FSTN to recognize precisely the legal strings in $a^n b^n$, it is rather easy to construct an RTN that does. Here is another simple language for which the same is true. Assume that we have just two symbols, '(' and ')', and we want to recognize whether a string of such symbols has correctly matching brackets. Thus, the following strings will be legal:

$$( ) (( )) ((( )))$$
$$(( ) ( ))$$
$$(( )) ((( )) ( ))$$

but the following will not:

$$) (( ) ( )$$
$$((( ))$$
$$(( )))$$

Although it is possible to construct an RTN to recognize the set of legal strings in this language (it needs to use recursion in a non-trivial way), it is not possible to do the same with an FSTN. Syntactic constructions with this formal character are rather common in natural languages, although English fails to provide a really clearcut example. However, if you imagine a language just like English except that the 'then' in the 'if ... then ...' construction is obligatory, and this is the only usage of the word 'then', then you can get a sense of the phenomenon as it might occur naturally.

Are there sets of inputs that even RTNs cannot recognize? The answer is yes: while it is possible to write an RTN that will recognize precisely the strings of a^nb^n, it is not possible to write one for the language $a^nb^nc^n$ – that is, the language of strings consisting of n number of as, followed by n number of bs, followed by n number of cs, for any n. Similarly, the language $a^mb^nc^md^n$ is not amenable to recognition by an RTN.

Exercise 3.13   Write RTNs that recognize exactly the legal strings of (a) a^nb^n and (b) the language of matching brackets described in the text. [*easy*]

3.7   Augmented transition networks

The foregoing examples show that certain kinds of outputs, such as sentences in other languages, can be computed from natural language sentences using transducers (PTs) built from RTNs. All the examples do, however, have a kind of family resemblance, in that the order in which items appear in the output echoes the order in which corresponding items appear in the input. Now, it is possible to write PTs that produce outputs in a *different* order from the corresponding inputs, but for such a situation we have to essentially include a different set of arcs for each possible input–output pair. When the input and output languages have large vocabularies, this leads to large networks, which cannot be expressed concisely even using our abbreviation mechanism. One solution to this problem would be to have a way of specifying how a *sequence* of outputs relates to a *sequence* of inputs, rather than having to specify input–output relations at the level of single arcs. Grammars, as presented in Chapters 4 and 7, provide a basis for describing sequences of phrases, and in Chapter 8 we will see how we can compute outputs from such grammars. Alternatively, we can keep to the network metaphor and enhance our networks with extra facilities to overcome the PT limitations. This is the approach taken with *augmented transition networks (ATNs)*.

Consider, for instance, what is required to enhance our translator to deal with more interesting noun phrases. In French, adjectives standardly follow the noun they modify, whereas in English they precede it. For instance, we would want 'a short name' to be translated to 'un nom court' (literally, 'a name short'). In fact, there are good reasons why we left out adjectives in our previous translators. If we try to extend the PT to include adjectives on the English side, we find that we have to write networks like the following:

```
Name NP:
  Initial 0
  Final 2
  From 0  to 1   by DET-MASC
  From 1  to 1a by short_#
  From 1  to 1c by green_#
  ...
  From 1a to 2a by N-MASC
  From 1b to 2b by N-MASC
  From 1c to 2c by N-MASC
  ...
  From 2a to 2   by #_court
  From 2c to 2   by #_vert
  ... .
```

where there are three arcs for each possible English adjective (and yet this network only deals with single adjectives!). The problem is that the French adjectives, which are known before the English noun is encountered, have somehow to be remembered and then produced on the second tape after the noun is translated. ATNs allow values to be remembered in this way during a network traversal by providing *registers* (variables) for storing information. Registers are rather like (local) variables in a procedural programming language like LISP. Thus, in our notation for ATNs, we will include a line declaring the registers used at the beginning of each network. Each arc of the network may then be annotated with instructions for how to shuffle information between these registers when it is traversed. Instructions can also be associated with the initial and final nodes of a network, specifying things to do when the network is entered or exited. In the latter case, the instructions will concern the single value that the network is allowed to return to the network that calls it, summarizing the result of its computations.

To make things more concrete, here is how we might tackle our noun phrase translation problem in an ATN. We will use the register FNP to keep track of the value (French phrase) to be returned by the NP network. In the French translation of a proper noun, this is simply whatever single French name corresponds to that English name, if there is one. In the French translation of a simple noun phrase, we need to have a French determiner, a collection of French adjectives and a French noun. We can introduce registers called FDET, FADJS and FNOUN to keep track of this information used in the translation of a noun phrase, and annotate the NP network informally as follows (for now, read '*' as meaning the current word):

```
Name NP:
  Registers FADJS, FNOUN, FDET, FNP
  Initial 0              set FADJS to the empty string
  Final 2                return FNP
  From 0 to 1 by DET     set FDET to French(*)
  From 1 to 1 by ADJ     set FADJS to FADJS + French(*)
  From 1 to 2 by N       set FNOUN to French(*)
                         set FNP to FDET + FNOUN + FADJS.
```

where + is a form of string concatenation that inserts spaces between words and French is a function that takes English words to their French translations, which we naively assume to be unique. The register FADJS is used here to hold a string that will translate a whole sequence of adjectives. As more English adjectives are discovered, their French translations are added to the end of the current value of this register.

Registers allow us to separate the times when parts of the output are computed from the position they occupy in the output. The idea is to recognize one structure but to be able to build as output a structure that may be only indirectly related to it.

We have assumed here that the French translation of any English word – that is, French(*) – can be easily computed. In general, ATN systems allow us to call arbitrary procedures defined in a standard programming language (often LISP) from the arcs of a network, and in an actual system this would probably be how this would be implemented. Note that the network could actually specify the category of the word to be translated, which would help when a given English word was ambiguous; for example, 'slight' could be a noun or an adjective, and would translate into 'manque d'égards' or 'léger' accordingly. Nevertheless, it is still very simplistic to assume that a word can be translated without any regard to the context, and no sensible machine translation system would be designed this way.

Usually in ATNs there is one special register, called '*', which automatically holds the value we are currently considering. When '*' is mentioned on an arc that is looking for a single word (either a specific word or a word covered by an abbreviation), it will always refer to the current word that the arc is looking at (as in the preceding network). On the other hand, when '*' is mentioned on an arc that introduces a PUSH to a subnetwork, it will always refer to the result returned by that subnetwork. This enables higher networks to deal with the result of lower networks. For instance, in our translation example, the S network needs to put together the French translations of the noun phrase and the verb phrase to make the translation of the whole sentence. Here is one way it could be done, using registers FSUBJECT and FPREDICATE to hold these values:

```
Name S:
  Registers FSUBJECT, FPREDICATE
  Initial 0
  Final 2                    return FSUBJECT + FPREDICATE
  From 0 to 1 by NP          set FSUBJECT to *
  From 1 to 2 by VP          set FPREDICATE to *.
```

Our translation rules for English noun phrases are inadequate in a number of ways, but one of the limitations provides grounds for introducing another feature of ATNs – extra tests on the arcs. The precise form of a determiner or adjective in French depends on the gender of the noun it qualifies, this being either masculine or feminine. Thus, we have:

> a green tree → un arbre vert   (a tree green)
>
> a green table → une table verte   (a table green)

Unfortunately, in our ATN we will not find out the gender of the noun phrase until the English noun is encountered, and by then we will have already generated the translation of the adjectives. One solution would be to actually keep the English determiner and adjectives in registers, and then translate them at the end of the phrase. A simpler solution, however, makes use of the trick used for French determiners in the ENG_FRE-2 FST, which relies on the fact that network traversal is organized as a search process, so that all possible traversals of the network will be found. We can outline two routes through the NP network, one corresponding to a masculine NP and the other corresponding to a feminine one. Each of these routes will produce adjectives with endings appropriate to the gender chosen and will then require there to be a noun of the appropriate gender at the end of the phrase. In any actual traversal, only one of them will lead to a successful solution, because the noun in the input string will have only one gender. As long as our implementation correctly searches through all possibilities, however, it will not matter whether it finds the correct path first or whether it starts off trying the possibility that fails. Because we have an ATN, rather than an FSTN, we can introduce a further twist and avoid duplicating all the NP arcs for the two different routes. Instead, we can use a register FGENDER to record the gender that we have chosen. So, the two different routes start with different arcs, setting the register to the two different values, but share exactly the same arcs after that. The arcs that the two routes have in common will then translate the determiner and adjectives on the basis of whatever value FGENDER has. To force the analysis to succeed only when the choice of FGENDER is the same as the gender of the

French noun, we add a special test to the arc from 1 to 2:

```
Name NP:
    Registers FADJS, FDET, FNP, FNOUN, FGENDER
    Initial 0              set FADJS to the empty string
    Final 2                return FNP
    From 0 to 1 by DET     set FGENDER to "masculine"
                           set FDET to French(*, "masculine")
    From 0 to 1 by DET     set FGENDER to "feminine"
                           set FDET to French(*, "feminine")
    From 1 to 1 by ADJ     set FADJS to FADJS + French(*, FGENDER)
    From 1 to 2 by N       set FNOUN to French(*)
                           the gender of FNOUN must be
                             the same as FGENDER
                           set FNP to FDET + FNOUN + FADJS.
```

where we now assume that the function French is provided with a gender as well as an English word, where this is required. Notice that, although we needed two arcs corresponding to the original choice of the gender, we did not need to duplicate the arcs for the adjectives and noun in the same way. The use of the register FGENDER enabled us to use each arc for both of the two alternatives. For this sort of approach to work, we obviously need a search mechanism that allows a register to have different values in different possible paths through the network. This has direct implications for the way one implements ATNs.

In our simple English–French translation example, we have seen how ATN registers can be used locally to reorder material to be output. The same idea can be used globally to keep track of phrases that appear extraposed from their canonical position. For instance, each of the following questions is identical in form to the word 'who' followed by an ordinary statement, except that somewhere in the statement there is a gap (indicated by ?) where we would normally expect a noun phrase. This gap corresponds to the position of the item whose identity is being questioned:

> Which employer [? will see Maria tomorrow]
> Who [will Mayumi see ?]
> Who [does Mayumi have a contract with ?]

In an ATN, it is relatively straightforward to remember (left) extraposed material (here, the questioned noun phrases) by assigning a value to a global register HOLD and to retrieve the relevant information again when an apparent gap is found.

3.8 Developing ATNs

To give an example of the flavour of ATN programming, we will now look at the outline of part of a hypothetical question–answering program using an ATN. To start with, we will deal with simple English declarative sentences; later, we will deal with questions as well. For simplicity, we will ignore tense in this example. The output of the network will be a simple proposition, qualified with the word add or search, according to whether the information is to be added to the system's database (is new information) or is to be searched for in the system's database (has been asked about in a question). We will see later how such a system might actually be implemented.

For this example, we will assume that a proposition can be represented by a sequence consisting of a verb followed by a sequence of names of objects qualified by their syntactic relation to the verb. In a programming language like LISP, it would be natural to represent these by lists. In this context, we will say that an object can be related to a verb by acting as its subject (arg0) or object (arg1), or by appearing as the object of some preposition. Thus, for declarative sentences, we wish to produce results such as the following:

```
Mayumi will see Maria:
  <add,
    <see,
      <arg0, Mayumi>,
      <arg1, Maria>
    >
  >
Mayumi will see Maria with Hans:
  <add,
    <see,
      <arg0, Mayumi>,
      <arg1, Maria>,
      <with, Hans>
    >
  >
```

Here is a network that will do this.

EXAMPLE: Simple ATN for English sentences

```
Name S:
  Registers PPS, AUXS, MOOD, MAINVERB, ARG0, ARG1
  Initial 0            set PPS to the empty sequence
                       set AUXS to the empty sequence
  Final 3              return
                       <MOOD, <MAINVERB,
                              <"arg0", ARG0>,
                              <"arg1", ARG1>
                       > ++ PPS>
```

From 0 to 1 by NP	set ARG0 to *,
	set MOOD to "add"
From 1 to 2 by V	set MAINVERB to *
From 2 to 2 by V	add MAINVERB to AUXS
	set MAINVERB to *
From 2 to 3 by NP	set ARG1 to *
From 2 to 3 by #	set ARG1 to the empty sequence
From 3 to 3 by PP	add * to PPS.

Name NP:
  Registers RES
  Initial 0

Final 1	return RES
From 0 to 1 by PN	set RES to *.

Name PP:
  Registers PREP, ARG
  Initial 0

Final 2	return <PREP, ARG>
From 0 to 1 by P	set PREP to *
From 1 to 2 by NP	set ARG to *.

PN abbreviates:
  John, Mary, Susan, Peter, ...

P abbreviates:
  with, behind, ...

V abbreviates:
  will, see, ...

(The operation ++ is concatenation of sequences.)

There are a number of things to note about this network. First of all, to reuse bits of the network (with different register assignments), ATN programmers tend to have large networks, rather than lots of small ones. So, there is no VP network here. This has been turned to advantage in the present context, because the translation of the predicate does not come out as a simple constituent of the translation of its sentence. Instead, components of the predicate appear at different points in the analysis of the whole sentence.

Secondly, note how the recognition of verb sequences is done, by the following arcs:

From 1 to 2 by V	set MAINVERB to *
From 2 to 2 by V	add MAINVERB to AUXS
	set MAINVERB to *

In this application, only the main verb (the last word in the sequence) is used, all the (preceding) auxiliary verbs being ignored (stored in a register AUXS whose value is not subsequently used). Until the last verb is reached, however, it is not known which is the main verb. So, it is arranged that at each moment MAINVERB is the last verb that has been encountered so far. In general, the value of this register will change several times when an input like the following is analyzed:

> Mayumi will have seen the play.

and so at times the traversal will be on a correct analysis path but the register will have an incorrect value. One of the techniques used in ATN programming is to put into a register a value that is probably (but not necessarily) correct, and then to change it if it turns out to be wrong. This is effectively a way of postponing a decision on the value – a form of least commitment. An alternative strategy, that of making a blind choice and leaving the search mechanism to rule out all but the correct possibilities, would be encoded as the following non-deterministic fragment:

> From 1 to 1 by V   add * to AUXS
> From 1 to 2 by V   set MAINVERB to *

The least-commitment strategy is often more efficient than making a blind choice, as maintaining alternative hypotheses tends to be expensive in ATN implementations. It relies, however, on the network explicitly noticing when the initial register assignment is wrong (here, when a verb follows a previous sequence of verbs) and there always being enough information in the registers to reconstruct the correct values when this happens.

We can elaborate this network further to deal with simple yes–no questions and to generate outputs such as the following:

> Will Mayumi see Maria:
> <search, <see, <arg0, Mayumi>, <arg1, Maria>>>

In this context, the form of a yes–no question is the same as that of the corresponding statement, except that the first of the sequence of verbs appears at the start of the sentence. It is fairly straightforward to make the network incorporate this generalization, by adding extra arcs:

> From 0 to 4 by V   set MAINVERB to *
> From 4 to 2 by NP   set ARG0 to *,
>   set MOOD to "search"

Note how little of the network has had to change for this. The use of the MOOD register allows large parts of the networks to be *shared* between statements and yes-no questions, in the same kind of way that the FGENDER register was useful before.

Finally, it would be nice to deal with simple WH questions, like 'Who will Mayumi see?' We will translate them into the same basic form, but with a special symbol, '?', indicating an element that is being asked about, thus:

Who will see Maria:
    <search, <see, <arg0, ?>, <arg1, Maria>>>

Who will Mayumi see:
    <search, <see, <arg0, Mayumi>, <arg1, ?>>>

Who will Mayumi see Maria with:
    <search, <see, <arg0, Mayumi>, <arg1, Maria>, <with, ?>>>

Now these WH questions are identical in form to the word 'who' followed by an ordinary yes–no question, except that somewhere in the yes–no question there is a gap where we would normally expect a noun phrase. This gap corresponds to the position of the item whose identity is being questioned:

Who [? will see Maria]

Who [will Mayumi see ?]

Who [will Mayumi see Maria with ?]

The first thing we need to do is recognize words like 'who' as forming simple noun phrases. We shall say that 'who' belongs to a category WH of question pronouns. In the event that a noun phrase takes the form of a question pronoun, we shall produce the special value "?" from the NP network:

From 0 to 1 by WH   set RES to "?"

Now we need to deal with such a noun phrase appearing at the start of a sentence. We can indicate that such a noun phrase has appeared by assigning a value to a register HOLD. Apart from setting this register, we want to continue as if this was a normal yes–no question:

From 1 to 4 by V   ARG0 must be "?"
                        set MAINVERB to *,
                        set HOLD to TRUE

Now we need to cater for the fact that somewhere later in the sentence an expected noun phrase will not appear and that the value "?" is to be used instead of the value returned by the NP network. We could add alternative arcs to this effect wherever a noun phrase is expected, but this would result in many messy changes. It would be much better to add to the NP network,

S network:

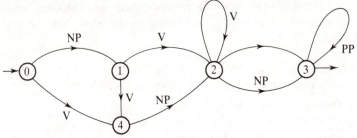

NP network:

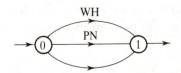

PP network:

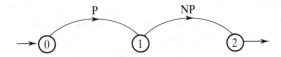

Figure 3.3   Final network for English ATN.

so that if HOLD is TRUE a "?" noun phrase can be appropriately hallucinated:

From 0 to 1 by #   HOLD must be TRUE
                          set RES to "?",
                          set HOLD to FALSE

The only thing that now needs to be done is to ensure that HOLD is given an appropriate value at the start of a sentence:

Initial 0   ...
                          set HOLD to FALSE

and finally to ensure that we do not allow ourselves to leave the sentence with any unused NPs:

Final 3
...
HOLD must be FALSE

The diagrammatic form of the complete network (with the annotations associated with registers removed) is shown in Figure 3.3.

Something like our HOLD register is a traditional device in ATN programming for dealing with what linguists call *unbounded dependencies*, *left extraposition*, *leftwards extraction* or *wh-movement* – where a phrase appears to have been moved leftwards out of its normal position. We should note that, whereas all other registers used so far (apart from '*') have only been used locally within individual networks, HOLD needs to be globally available to all networks. Hence, in ATN systems it is usually implemented by a special mechanism (as is '*').

Exercise 3.14   What does the linguistic description embodied in our example ATN for English sentences lose by not having an explicit verb phrase network?   [*easy*]

Exercise 3.15   How would we implement this 'grammar' (just the recognition part) using just RTN facilities? How many extra arcs need to be added to simulate the operation of HOLD? What if we wish to reject sentences like 'what green car does Mayumi believe [_ were responsible for the accident]?' where the left extraposed phrase does not have the right number features to be able to fill the 'hole'?   [*hard*]

Exercise 3.16   How might we use HOLD to deal with the unbounded dependencies in relative clauses? Consider examples like:

The strange man who$_i$ [I sold the tape to _$_i$] could well be a crook.

How does the use of HOLD have to change to cater for nested relative clauses, as in:

The man who$_i$ [I sold the tape that$_j$ [Hanni erased _$_j$] to _$_i$] may well be laughing.

[*hard*]

3.9   Implementation of ATNs

ATNs are just RTNS annotated with extra tests and actions, and so we can represent them as list structures simply by embellishing our existing notation. We will require that each network declare the registers that are to be used within it, just as many programming languages require a function to declare its local variables. In addition, a network will specify tests and actions to be performed:

- Initially, when the network is entered.
- Finally, when the network is exited.
- On all transitions, as each transition is made.

Here is our example ATN expressed in list notation (it also appears as lib atnarcs1). We use LISP lists to represent the sequences of symbols built by the program.

```
(setq networks
'((S
      ((Registers (pps auxs mood mainverb arg0 arg1))
       (Initial (0))              t ((setq pps ()) (setq auxs ()))))
       (Final (3))                t ((list mood
                                         (append
                                             (list mainverb
                                                  (list (quote arg0) arg0)
                                                  (list (quote arg1) arg1)
                                                  )
                                             pps))))
      (From 0 to 1 by NP)         t ((setq arg0 star) (setq mood (quote add))))
      (From 1 to 2 by V)          t ((setq mainverb star)))
      (From 2 to 2 by V)          t ((setq auxs (cons mainverb auxs))
                                         (setq mainverb star)))
      (From 2 to 3 by NP)         t ((setq arg1 star)))
      (From 2 to 3 by |#|)        t ((setq arg1 ())))
      (From 3 to 3 by PP)         t ((setq pps (cons star pps))))))
    (NP
      ((Registers (res))
       (Initial (0))              t (())
       (Final (1))                t (res))
       (From 0 to 1 by PN)        t ((setq res star)))))
    (PP
      ((Registers (p arg))
       (Initial (0))              t (())
       (Final (2))                t ((list p arg)))
       (From 0 to 1 by P)         t ((setq p star)))
       (From 1 to 2 by NP)        t ((setq arg star))))))))
(setq abbreviations
'((PN abbreviates john mary susan peter)
  (P abbreviates with behind)
  (V abbreviates will see)))
```

Each network now has an additional Registers statement, which specifies the (local) registers that are going to be used within that network. At the end of each Initial or Final statement, as well as at the end of each transition statement, there are two extra list components, specifying the tests and actions to be performed. Tests and actions are represented by lists containing normal LISP code, which may treat the local registers of the network and the global registers star (which represents *) and hold like normal LISP variables. The instructions in these lists will then be executed at appropriate times. Many ATN systems use a restricted language for actions and tests, which are then evaluated by an interpreter. We will not present such a language: firstly, because the common actions of assignment and building lists are so naturally expressed in a normal programming language and, secondly, because there seems to be no principled way of restricting the actions and tests that might be needed. We therefore allow actions and tests to be arbitrary LISP code, whose results may or may not be noticed, as appropriate. Tests are obviously expected to produce results, as are the actions associated with the final parts of networks (whose results will be used as the value of the * register in the calling network). On the other hand, any results returned by other action code will simply be ignored.

lib atnrecog implements a simple ATN traverser that works with ATNs represented as we have just discussed. Although the details of the implementation are unimportant and much of the following description can be skipped, it is important to have some conception of how the implementation of an ATN differs from that of an RTN. First of all, since the ATN list structures have more components that RTNs, we need to redefine our basic network accessing functions accordingly. Apart from redefining functions like initial_nodes to take account of the extra components, we need to introduce new functions to extract the tests and actions from various places in the networks:

```
(defun initial_tests (net)
  (nth 2 (assoc 'Initial net)))

(defun initial_actions (net)
  (nth 3 (assoc 'Initial net)))

(defun final_tests (net)
  (nth 2 (assoc 'Final net)))

(defun final_actions (net)
  (nth 3 (assoc 'Final net)))
```

(Remember that nth numbers the elements of a list starting with 0.) Here are two important functions to do with accessing registers:

```
(defun regs_used (net)
  (nth 1 (assoc 'Registers net)))
```

```
(defun initial_regs (net)
  (list
    (regs_used net)
    (mapcar #'not (regs_used net))))
```

regs_used just enables us to find out the local registers declared for a given network. initial_regs returns a list with two elements, the first being the list of register names and the second being a list with the same length, each element of which is nil:

```
(regs_used (get_network 's))

(PPS AUXS MOOD MAINVERB SUBJ OBJ)

(initial_regs (get_network 's))

((PPS AUXS MOOD MAINVERB SUBJ OBJ)
 (() ()   ()    ()         ()   ()))
```

When we store the values of the registers of a network, we will use precisely this representation, a list of the register names followed by a list of the register values, where each value is associated with the corresponding element of the register name list. Here, we use nil as the initial value of a register (as LISP does for local variables), and so the initial_regs of a network represent the registers together with their initial values.

ATNs are an extension of RTNs because of the use of registers. But registers produce added complication in the implementation, because we have to deal with alternative values of registers in different search paths. A state of an ATN recognition can now be represented by the following:

- R1. the current node (and network name).
- R2. the remaining symbols.
- R3. the stack of return points.
- R4. the values of the local registers.
- R5. the value of the HOLD register.

Of these, the first three are more or less the same as for the RTN case. The stack must, however, contain more complex objects in an ATN. When a POP occurs during recognition, the top element of the stack must hold enough information for the computation to resume in the higher network. This must include the values of the registers as they were when that network was pushed from and a record of any actions that have to be performed on the result of the subnetwork computation before the traversal in the higher network can be completed. It must also, as before, hold the network and node names specifying where the traversal in the higher network is to resume. The HOLD register needs special attention in the implementation as it is a global register, whereas all the other registers are local to particular subnetworks.

We can derive an ATN traverser from our RTN traverser in much the same way that we derived our RTN traverser from an FSTN traverser. That is, we can create an ATN traverser by appropriately enriching the notion of a state to include the values of the registers in all the networks being traversed. The appropriate next function header now looks like the following:

```
(defun atn_recognize_next (networkname node tape stack regs hold)
```

where regs is the set of registers and their values for the current network, and hold is the current value of the HOLD register. Where are the values of the registers in other active networks kept? They are kept in the stack, a stack element now being of the form:

```
(<networkname> <node> <regs> <tests> <actions>)
```

where <networkname> and <node> are as before – these specify in which network and to which node the system is to return. <regs>, <tests> and <actions> specify the current registers of that network and any tests and actions that have to be performed before the system can successfully return to that network. We will define the functions stacked_networkname, stacked_node, stacked_regs, stacked_tests and stacked_actions to retrieve these parts from the top element of a given stack. Notice that, although the HOLD register is global, its value is part of the search state; that is, it may have different values on different traversals of the network. This is why we do not actually implement it as a global variable in LISP. Here is the definition of atn_recognize_next. As with the RTN recognizer, the main work is dealt with by specialized functions to push, pop and traverse an arc:

```
(defun atn_recognize_next (networkname node tape stack regs hold)
  (if (member node (final_nodes (get_network networkname)))
      (atn_recognize_pop networkname tape stack regs hold))
  (dolist (transition (transitions (get_network networkname)))
    (if (equal (trans_node transition) node)
        (let ((label (trans_label transition))
              (newnode (trans_newnode transition)))
          (if (get_network label)
              ;; interpret label as network name
              (atn_recognize_push label networkname transition tape stack regs hold))
          ;; interpret label as symbol/abbreviation
          (atn_recognize_traverse label networkname transition tape stack regs hold)))))
```

As in the RTN case, the first thing for atn_recognize_next to do is to try to pop from the current network. If node is a final node in the current network, then atn_recognize_pop is called:

```
(defun atn_recognize_pop (networkname tape stack regs hold)
  (if (dotests regs (final_tests (get_network networkname)) hold nil)
    (let (
          (star_newhold
            (dopopactions regs (final_actions (get_network networkname)) hold nil)))
      (if (and (null stack) (null tape))
        ;; end of top-level network
        (throw 'atn (car star_newhold))
        (if (and stack
              ;; end of subsidiary network
              ;; do tests at end of original PUSH
              (dotests
                (stacked_regs stack)
                (stacked_tests stack)
                (cadr star_newhold)      ; hold
                (car star_newhold)))     ; star (result of POP)
          ;; execute actions at end of original PUSH
          (let ( (newregs_newhold
                  (doactions
                    (stacked_regs stack)
                    (stacked_actions stack)
                    (cadr star_newhold)   ; hold
                    (car star_newhold)))) ; star
            ;; proceed in original network, using stacked values
            (atn_recognize_next
              (stacked_networkname stack)
              (stacked_node stack)
              tape
              (cdr stack)
              (car newregs_newhold)
              (cadr newregs_newhold)))))))))
```

Before initiating a pop, this function checks that the final tests associated with the network are satisfied (calling function dotests). The final actions, executed by the function dopopactions, then produce two results, one of which becomes the new value of the star register, and the second of which will be the new value of the hold register. star is returned as the result of the whole analysis if both the stack and the tape are empty. If the stack is not empty, it is necessary to resume in a higher network, restoring the values that are saved in the stack. In this case, it is also necessary to apply the tests saved from the push arc before continuing.

After attempting to pop, the only other possibility is to find a network arc from node that can be traversed. Thus, atn_recognize_next iterates through the arcs that leave this node. If the label is the name of a network, it calls atn_recognize_push to attempt to enter that subnetwork. If the initial tests in that network succeed, we push to the new network, producing a new stack that has the networkname, trans_newnode of the arc, registers regs and the arc trans_tests and trans_actions pushed on the front:

```
(defun atn_recognize_push (label networkname transition tape stack regs hold)
  (let ((newnet (get_network label)))
    ;; try tests at start of proposed network
    (if (dotests (initial_regs newnet) (initial_tests netnet) hold nil)
      ;; execute actions at start of new network
      (let ((newregs_newhold
          (doactions
            (initial_regs newnet)
            (initial_actions newnet)
            hold
            nil)))
        ;; explore from all initial nodes
        (dolist (initialnode (initial_nodes newnet))
          (atn_recognize_next
            label
            initialnode
            tape
            (cons                              ; new value of stack
              (list
                networkname                    ; network
                (trans_newnode transition)     ; destination node
                regs                           ; registers
                (trans_tests transition)       ; post tests
                (trans_actions transition)     ; post actions
                )
              stack)
            (car newregs_newhold)
            (cadr newregs_newhold)))))))
```

Notice that the tests and actions associated with the push arc are saved up to be tried when the subnetwork is finally popped from. If the label is not the name of a network, we move the tape in the standard way according to what the label is, and we also check that the arc tests succeeds and compute the new registers and new value of hold that result from executing the arc trans_actions. This is done by atn_recognize_traverse:

```
(defun atn_recognize_traverse (label networkname transition tape stack regs hold)
  ;; try moving the tape
  (dolist (newtape (recognize_move label tape))
    ;; set the star register
    (let ((star (diff_tape newtape tape)))
```

```
;; try the arc tests
(if (dotests regs (trans_tests transition) hold star)
    (let (
        (newregs_newhold
            ;; execute the arc actions
            (doactions
                regs
                (trans_actions transition)
                hold
                star)))
        ;; continue from the destination node
        (atn_recognize_next
            networkname
            (trans_newnode transition)
            newtape
            stack
            (car newregs_newhold)
            (cadr newregs_newhold)))))))
```

This completes the definition of atn_recognize_next and its main subfunctions.

There are a few other main functions that remain to be defined. diff_tape is used to set the * register; it simply looks to see how much of the tape has been consumed by a transition. dotests is used to execute a set of tests, whereas doactions and dopopactions are used to execute a set of actions. dopopactions is for actions performed as a network is exited (which must return a value for *), whereas doactions is for other sets of actions (which do not produce results). doactions expects arguments as follows:

```
(defun doactions (regs actions hold star)
```

where regs is the current local registers and their values, actions is the list of actions to be performed, and hold and star are the current values of the appropriate global registers. The result will be a list of two values – the new local registers and the new value of the hold register after the actions have been performed. For instance, the call:

```
(doactions '((pps auxs mood mainverb arg0 arg1)
             (()  ()  ()    ()       ()  ()))
           '((setq arg0 star) (setq mood (quote add)))
           '()
           'np)
```

executes the actions:

```
(setq arg0 star) (setq mood (quote add))
```

in a network with registers pps, auxs, mood, mainverb, arg0 and arg1, all with values nil, in a context where hold is nil and star (the * register) is NP. This call will produce a list of two items – first of all the new values of the registers and secondly the new value of the hold register, here simply nil:

```
(((pps auxs mood mainverb arg0 arg1)
  (()  ()   add  ()        np  ())))
 ())
```

Notice how the register values returned reflect the changes to arg0 and mood. doactions works by creating a list of items representing a LISP function that contains the appropriate actions. In this example, the function that results would be essentially what would arise from the following definition:

```
(defun xxx (star hold pps auxs mood mainverb arg0 arg1)
  (setq arg0 star)
  (setq mood 'add)
  (list (list '(pps auxs mood mainverb arg0 arg1)
        (list pps auxs mood mainverb arg0 arg1))
      hold))
```

Finally, this function is called, by apply, with the appropriate arguments supplied, and the results are manipulated into the results of doactions. dotests and dopopactions are defined using very similar techniques.

Exercise 3.17   Using lib atnrecog and lib atnarcs1, run the example ATN on some test sentences. Extend the ATN as suggested in the text – to deal with yes–no and WH questions.   [*intermediate*]

Exercise 3.18   Add extra code to the ATN recognizer so that it prints out messages to show what it is doing. Your program might print out messages like the following:

```
(Arriving at node 3 in network S)
(Looking for a NOUN)
(Trying test (equal arg0 (quote =)))
(Test fails)
(PUSHING for a S)
(POPPING)
(FAILING)
(FAILING back to node 3 in network S)
```

[*intermediate*]

3.10   Some reflections on ATNs

The main contribution of ATNs is to introduce the notion of registers, assignment and tests into network notations. Registers can be used to keep track of pieces of text, pieces of output structure or features (like gender) of lexical items. Using registers, general tests can be made on acceptability (for example, gender agreement) and output can be built in a flexible order. The use of registers enables what would be different paths through an RTN to be merged into one, and search to be avoided by storing information before its exact significance is known. In addition, the use of global registers provides a technique for handling phenomena like the non-local dependencies found in some English relative clauses and questions.

A few words on the history of ATNs. We have noted that there are consistent structural relations between, for instance, a statement and the corresponding yes–no question, and a yes–no question and the corresponding WH question. In linguistics in the 1960s, the development of Chomsky's transformational grammar was largely motivated by observations like these. Chomsky and his co-workers described a set of transformations that could be used to derive more complex sentences (for example, WH questions) from simpler ones (for example, very simple declarative sentences). Unfortunately, it proved computationally infeasible to undo or reverse these transformations in a principled way, so as to build a language analyzer that would take arbitrary sentences and understand them in terms of their putative source representations. Woods and others developed ATNs essentially as a programming language for writing analyzers where the undoing of transformations could be carried out during processing. Unfortunately, it is not in general easy to translate any given transformation into ATN code. Nevertheless, ATNs, typically running in a left-to-right mode and using depth-first search, were probably the most prominent framework for natural language syntactic analysis in the 1970s.

Readers will hopefully have noticed how the flavour of ATNs is different from all the other formalisms we have discussed so far. Writing an ATN is much more like writing a computer program than writing either an FSTN or an RTN. When we write programs in conventional programming languages, a program will only do the task it is designed for. Similarly, our ATN for translating from English into French cannot be used (straightforwardly) for generating random English sentences or translating from French to English, say. With FSTNs and RTNs, we were writing specifications that could in principle be used for a number of tasks. To summarize, although they are based on the same network-traversing metaphor, ATNs are a *procedural* formalism, whereas FSTNs and RTNs are essentially *declarative*.

Although ATNs still get used, there are a number of trends in NLP that are now leading to their decline. The original theory of transformational grammar whose operations they sought to embody has changed out of all recognition. Furthermore, many linguists have begun to recognize the advantages of simpler formal frameworks. The importance of declarative formalisms is becoming increasingly realized in computer science, an issue we will examine further in Chapter 4. Finally, as we will see in

Chapter 6, the rise of charts as an efficient basis for parsing makes it clear that the depth-first search strategy adopted by most ATN implementations leaves something to be desired.

Our consideration of network-based language processors has led us to special-purpose programming languages for language analysis. Indeed, it can be shown that ATNs have the basic power to be used as a language for arbitrary programming tasks. Is there anything, then, that we can say theoretically about natural language analysis, apart from the fact that a general programming language is required for the job? Is there a future for declarative notations? In the next chapters we hope to show that both of these questions can be answered affirmatively.

SUMMARY

- RTNs use named subnetworks to generalize FSTNs.

- RTNs can represent recursive constructions in natural language.

- RTN traversal depends on a pushdown stack.

- PTs are to RTNs what FSTs are to FSTNs.

- PTs can be used to produce RTN parse trees.

- RTNs and PTs are descriptively more powerful than FSTNs and FSTs.

- ATNs augment RTNs with registers and register operations.

- ATNs are a procedural formalism.

Further reading

ELIZA is documented in Weizenbaum (1966). According to Woods (1970/1986), RTNs first appear in Conway (1963). For an elegant introduction to recursion in various forms, including RTNs, see Hofstadter (1979). Pushdown transducers appear to originate in Evey (1963). There is some relevant formal development in Choffrut and Culik (1983), and Wood (1987, pp. 352–5) provides a brief technical tutorial. Harel (1987) develops an elegant and sophisticated graphical formalism that can be used, inter alia, to define RTNs and PTs, as well FSTNs and FSTs.

The immediate precursors of Woods's own classic (1970/1986) paper on ATNs were Thorne et al. (1968), and Bobrow and Fraser (1969). Later work by Woods on ATNs includes his (1973), (1980) and (1987) papers, while Kaplan (1972) argues for their psycholinguistic plausibility.

Tutorial material on ATNs can be found in many sources, including Bates (1978), Charniak *et al.* (1980, pp. 257–74), Charniak and McDermott (1985, pp. 197–222), Johnson (1983), Tennant (1981, pp. 49–76) and Winograd (1983, pp. 195–271). Winston and Horn (1989, Chapter 28 and 29) show how an interpreter and a compiler for a restricted subclass of ATNs can be implemented in LISP. Pereira and Warren (1980/1986) provide an extended critique of ATNs, arguing for the use of declarative grammar formalisms instead.

CHAPTER 4

GRAMMARS

In ATNs, we have an immensely flexible medium for constructing natural language analyzers, but this flexibility is bought at the price of a procedural character that loses descriptive clarity and imposes a dependence on the type of application. In this chapter, we consider the advantages of basing a language processing system on a declarative description, a grammar, of the language concerned, which is neutral as regards the desired application. The concepts of context-free phrase structure grammars (CF-PSGs) are introduced, the notation of PATR being used to show how phenomena like subcategorization and unbounded dependencies can be elegantly described in a declarative formalism. Finally, the relation of CF-PSGs to other classes of grammars is considered.

4.1   Grammar as knowledge representation

A description of a recognizer or parser for a language is in some sense a description of that language, but it need not by any means be a perspicuous one. Moreover, it may well be an implementation-specific definition, but implementations – even implementations of a programming language that is thought to be well understood – can differ significantly and unexpectedly. It is for this reason that computer scientists have turned in recent years away from procedural definitions of the semantics for programming languages and towards the declarative descriptions of denotational semantics. Rather similar considerations hold when we consider writing programs that process natural language input: both syntactically and semantically, we need to have a secure definition of the natural language (or an approximation to a natural language) that we are processing if we are to have any idea how the system should behave under a wide range of conditions.

A language can be regarded as a set whose membership is precisely specifiable by rules. The set of compound linguistic expressions in a natural language is not finite, so we cannot list them all (cf., 'a slow machine', 'a very slow machine', 'a very very slow machine', ...). As far as is known, no natural language is a finite language. The range of constructions that make a language infinite is typically rather large. In English, a word like 'and' permits an unbounded number of phrases to be combined together and relative clauses can contain verb phrases which can contain noun phrases which can contain relative clauses which ... .

What we need are formal (that is, mathematical) systems that define the membership of the infinite sets of linguistic expressions and assign a structure to each member of these sets. Such formal systems are *grammars*. From this perspective, the various kinds of transition networks that we have looked at in the preceding chapters are grammars. However, the word 'grammar' is often used in a rather more restricted sense in current natural language work to refer to formal systems that meet not only the criterion just noted, but are in addition subject to two further criteria:

- Firstly, grammars, in the sense discussed in this chapter, are expressed in a declarative grammar formalism that only contains information about which objects combine together and what the properties of the resultant object are, a formalism that contains no extraneous procedural information about how to put the objects together, such as the control information implicitly encoded in transition networks.

- Secondly, grammars, as we shall present them, transparently provide each legal string with an implicit structural description, without the necessity of explicit structure-building annotations, as required in an ATN, for example.

Like FSTNs and RTNs, but unlike many ATNs, the grammars we shall present directly characterize the order of elements in the string, as opposed to attempting to reconstruct some hypothesized underlying order. And, like RTNs, our grammars will use simple recursion to manage the structural complexity. Grammars as we shall present them are declarative and, for the most part, based on a decomposition of syntactic categories (roughly 'parts of speech') into components known as features. One of the merits of such formalisms will only become apparent when we look at semantics in Chapter 8: grammars of this kind support a compositional approach to meaning, one in which every well-formed expression has a meaning of its own, a meaning that has been composed from the meaning of the subexpressions that make it up. In such a context, the syntactic structure imposed by the grammar on an expression is a key element in the determination of its meaning.

From the perspective of NLP, the study of grammar is a branch of knowledge representation: a grammar is simply a way of representing certain aspects of what we know about a language that is explicit and formal enough to be understood by a machine. Consider by analogy, a much simpler area of knowledge representation, the representation of mass: this involves mathematical questions (which is the appropriate number system to use – integers, reals, rationals, complex numbers, ...?), notational questions (do we use arabic numerals, roman numerals, points in a graph, ...?) and detailed descriptive questions (is **mass(ingot93) = 128kg** true, accurate, accurate enough, ...?). In this chapter, we will examine these three kinds of question as they apply to the grammars of natural languages.

One important mathematical question that has interested linguists, off and on, for the last 30 years is the question of just how powerful a formal system is needed to describe any natural language. We have already seen one example of this issue in Chapter 2 where we noted the inability of FSTNs to recognize exactly the strings in the language $a^n b^n$ – that is, the language consisting of strings containing some number of as followed by the same number of bs. And the RTNs considered in Chapter 3 can recognize exactly the strings of $a^n b^n$ but not those of $a^n b^n c^n$. There are a number of good reasons why a computational linguist should care about this question. If, for example, we are using an RTN for our language description and we encounter an $a^n b^n c^n$ construction in the language in question, then we will know that time spent trying to get our RTN to recognize the construction will be time wasted. Or suppose that we had access to hardware that would handle FSTNs ultrafast and observed that in actual occurrences of $a^n b^n$ constructions, the value of n never exceeded 3; then we might decide to compile our RTN descriptions down into FSTNs subject to an $n = 3$ upper bound (such a compilation is possible for any given finite upper bound on the value of n). Knowledge of the underlying mathematics can help to avoid wasting time and, sometimes, even suggest shortcuts. We will consider some of the general mathematical questions to do with power in a bit more detail in the final sections of this chapter.

The academic linguist's primary criterion in evaluating a type of grammar has always been its ability to capture significant generalizations within the grammar of a language and across the grammars of different languages. However, expressing significant generalizations is largely a matter of notation, and classes of grammars, taken as sets of mathematical objects, have properties that are theirs independently of the notations that might be used to define them. Thus, a class of grammars determines the set of languages that can be described by its members, the set of structural analyzes that can be assigned to sentences in these languages, and so on.

Like the academic linguist, the computational linguist needs to know what natural languages are really like, mathematically speaking. But, in addition, it is useful for the computational linguist to know what languages are roughly like, or mostly like, and whether particular languages (English, say, or Japanese) exhibit certain mathematical properties. These latter questions are of little interest to the academic linguist. Suppose, for example, that Swahili has certain features that show it to be a type Y language, mathematically. But suppose further that these features are statistically rather uncommon in every day Swahili usage, so that 99.5% of such usage can be parsed under the assumption that Swahili is of a mathematically more restrictive type and has a computationally more straightforward type X grammar. Suppose, finally, that we have a working parser based on a type X grammar for Swahili which handles 85% of the input it is offered and which, for numerous practical reasons (ill-formed input, dialectal variations, non-standard spellings, idiosyncratic stylistic forms, ...), cannot be further improved (85% is actually quite a good figure in a practical context). It is clear that under such conditions, a switch to a parser based on a type Y grammar would simply not be worth the effort since, ceteris paribus, it could effect at best an improvement from 85% to 85.5%.

Turning now to notational issues, the design and choice of grammar formalisms for NLP is a topic that has attracted considerable attention in the 1980s and much progress has been made. At least the following general criteria are relevant:

- linguistic naturalness,
- mathematical power, and
- computational effectiveness.

Firstly, those who use such formalisms need a notation that allows and encourages them to encode their linguistic descriptions in a manner that is easy to understand and modify, accords with the way they think about language, and expresses the relevant generalizations about the domain. For example, if all tensed verbs in a language appear in VP-initial position, then the formalism should allow us to say exactly that, and not force us into making 40 statements, one for each subclass of verbs, or into some cumbrous circumlocution making reference to all words showing some disjunction of particular endings, a circumlocution that just happens to pick out all the tensed verbs. Secondly, if we decide that natural languages are type Y, mathematically speaking, and we wish our grammars to take this fact into account, then the grammar description language will need to be able to express type Y grammars.

As will be seen in the final sections of this chapter, some notational restrictions on grammar formalisms can have the effect of seriously limiting the class of grammars that can be expressed. Conversely, apparently minor notational changes can radically increase the potential mathematical power of the systems characterized. We may not want this to happen, either because we wish to inhibit users of the formalism from devising unnatural analyzes, or for reasons of computational effectiveness, to which we now turn.

A grammar formalism used by an academic linguist is usually only read by other academic linguists. But a computational grammar formalism, like a programming language, has to be read and understood by both humans and machines. Furthermore, given the typical goals of NLP work, we want machines to be able to understand and employ the formalism in realistic amounts of time. Indeed, the issues that arise in the design of grammar formalisms are exactly those that arise in the design of any specialist declarative computer language for knowledge representation in some particular domain.

Some existing grammar formalisms were proposed to express linguistic theories. With such formalisms, the self-imposed limitations are often intended as empirical claims about the nature of natural languages. Others were designed for use as tools by the academic or computational linguist, and these are normally free of intended expressive limitations. The formalism we shall use in this chapter (and subsequently) to represent what are essentially context-free phrase structure grammars is called PATR, and this formalism belongs to the latter class. PATR has, in recent years, become a potential lingua franca for NLP work, and many other grammatical formalisms can be compiled into it.

All the kinds of grammar that have been used in computational linguistics have employed, in one form or another, the following:

- A representation for syntactic categories or 'parts of speech'.
- A data type for words (and hence a lexicon, dictionary or word list).
- A data type for syntactic rules.
- A data type for syntactic structures.

A grammar as a whole can be viewed as a use of a particular kind of data type composed of the first three items. A parser, then, is an algorithm that takes a grammar, together with a string, and attempts to return one or more instances of the syntactic structure data type. Thus, a complete grammar formalism provides, at least, a language for specifying syntactic categories, a language for representing lexical entries, a language in which to write rules (possibly rules of more than one type) and a language for exhibiting syntactic structures. These languages may be distinct, or two or more of them may collapse.

4.2 Words, rules and structures

A *lexicon* is minimally a list of words that associates each word with its syntactic properties. The most important of these properties is its (gross) syntactic category – for example, whether the word is a verb or a noun. In addition, depending on the sophistication of the overall grammar, the lexicon will contain information as to the subcategory of the word (such as whether a particular verb is transitive or intransitive), other syntactic properties (such as the gender of a noun in a language that makes gender distinctions), and perhaps also morphological and semantic information. In the very simplest grammars, then, a lexical entry might look like this (using PATR notation):

```
Word paid:
    <cat> = V.
```

which simply tells us that 'paid' is a word whose category (cat) is verb (V), whereas a slightly more sophisticated grammar might require a lexical entry like this:

```
Word paid:
    <cat> = V
    <tense> = past
    <arg1> = NP.
```

which tells, in addition, that the verb is in the past tense and that it is transitive – how <arg1> = NP comes to mean transitive will be explained later. Note that a feature description is always *partial* – when a feature is not mentioned, the description is consistent with it having *any* value.

The character of syntactic rules varies considerably depending on the precise character of the theory of grammar involved, and often such theories permit the use of more than one kind of rule. One very frequently employed type of syntactic rule is the *phrase structure rule*, and most current computational linguistic frameworks presuppose the existence of such rules. A phrase structure rule simply tells what a particular syntactic category (the 'left-hand side' – LHS) can be composed of (the 'right-hand side' – RHS). Thus, S → NP VP tells us that a sentence can consist of a noun phrase followed by a verb phrase, while VP → V NP tells us that a verb phrase can consist of a verb followed by a noun phrase. If you treat the arrow → as a convenient abbreviation for the expression 'can consist of' when looking at phrase structure rules, then you will not go far wrong. Phrase structure rules can also be used to introduce lexical items; thus, a rule like V → paid is just an alternative way of representing the information we encoded above as:

```
Word paid:
    <cat> = V.
```

In principle, then, we could at this stage, if we wished, collapse our rules and our lexicon into a single component, since both components use phrase structure rules in this example. In practice, however, we will sometimes treat lexical entries as grammatical rules and sometimes consider them as a separate component, depending on which seems clearest at a given moment.

So far, we have discussed grammar in the abstract without ever exhibiting an example of one. In this section and the next, we will look in some detail at what grammars look like and how they work. To start with, let us consider a very straightforward grammar (Grammar1) employing four syntactic categories; namely, noun phrase (NP), sentence (S), verb phrase (VP) and verb (V). We will supply the grammar with only three rules: one telling us that a sentence can consist of a noun phrase followed by a verb phrase, another which lets a verb phrase consist of a verb and a noun phrase, and a third which lets a verb phrase consist of a verb standing on its own. We also need a lexicon to supply us with some ready-made verbs and noun phrases. We will imagine that we are beginning to build a natural langauge front end to a hospital database, so all our lexical items will be drawn from this domain. The lexicon tells us that 'Dr Chan', 'nurses', 'MediCenter', and 'patients' are all noun phrases while 'died' and 'employed' are both verbs.

EXAMPLE: Grammar1

```
Rule {simple sentence formation}
    S → NP VP.
Rule {transitive verb}
    VP → V NP.
Rule {intransitive verb}
    VP → V.
```

Word Dr Chan:
    <cat> = NP.
Word nurses:
    <cat> = NP.
Word MediCenter:
    <cat> = NP.
Word patients:
    <cat> = NP.
Word died:
    <cat> = V.
Word employed:
    <cat> = V.

Grammars such as Grammar1 are called *context-free phrase struc-ture grammars (CF-PSGs)*. The key features of a CF-PSG are the employ-ment of a finite set of grammatical categories and a finite set of rules for specifying how LHS categories can be realized as sequences of RHS elements. An RHS element may then be either a category or a particular symbol of the language. When a CF-PSG rule specifies that an LHS category can be realized as a particular RHS, this realization is deemed to be possible regardless of the context in which the LHS category appears. The rule does not make any restriction on the context in which this can happen – hence, the term 'context free'. There are a variety of possible notations for CF-PSGs, the Backus–Naur Form used for programming language grammars being one, but we will use (a subset of) the PATR notation for Grammar1.

We have now completely defined Grammar1. But what is it good for? What can it do? Well, a grammar has two functions. The first is to define the sets of grammatical strings of words in the language under consideration (or, more realistically, part of that language). Such strings are said to be 'generated' by the grammar. This use of the word 'generate' does not imply the existence of any actual procedure that produces sentences; it indicates merely that certain strings are allowed as grammatical by the grammar. So, in the case of a natural language like English, a grammar should define the set of grammatical sentences, the set of grammatical verb phrases, and so on. In defining the sets of grammatical strings it will, by implication, also define the ungrammatical strings, since an ungrammatical string is simply a string that is not grammatical – that is, a string that is not 'generated' by the grammar. The second function the grammar has is to associate one or more structures with each grammatical string. The syntactic structure of a phrase can be thought of as a kind of justification that the phrase is grammatical. It displays the various parts of

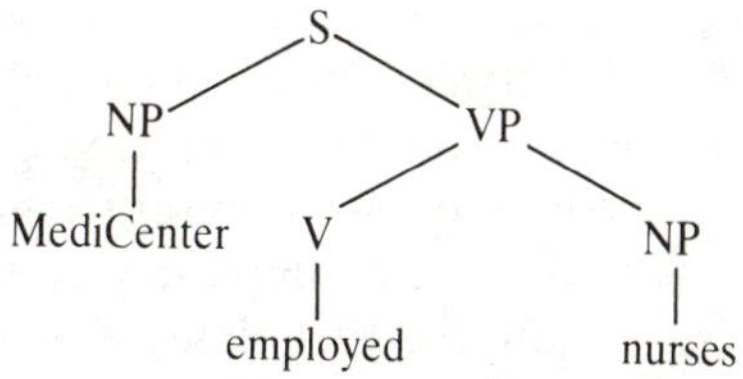

Figure 4.1 Phrase structure tree.

the phrase and the ways in which the combinations of parts are licenced by the rules of the grammar. As we will see, this breaking up of a phrase into parts is a key factor in the computation of the semantics of the phrase. Typically, if a given string has two different structures, then it will also have two different meanings, and hence be ambiguous. Part of the job of the grammar, then, is to make correct predictions about this kind of structural ambiguity.

What form do these structures take? The answer, in mathematical parlance, is *directed acyclic graphs (DAGs)*: all contemporary grammatical frameworks, without exception, employ some kind of directed acyclic graph to represent structure. We will not delve into graph theory here, however, and directed acyclic graphs will anyway receive more attention in Chapter 7. Conveniently, most, but by no means all, contemporary linguists have elected to use one particular kind of directed acyclic graph – namely, the tree – for their structural descriptions. And a tree is what it sounds like: it has a root, it has branches and it terminates in leaves. But computational linguists, like genealogists, conventionally exhibit their trees upside down, with the root poking into the sky and the leaves on the ground. Figure 4.1 shows such a tree.

How does Grammar1 define sets of strings and associate such strings with structures like the one shown in Figure 4.1? Consider the top of the tree: here we have an S which has as daughters an NP and a VP, and nothing else, appearing in that order. The first rule of Grammar1 says that an S can consist of an NP followed by a VP, and that is exactly what we have here. So, the grammar legitimates this part of the structure. If we turn our attention now to the VP, then again we find that the grammar contains a rule that corresponds to this part of the structure. Finally, we look in the lexicon and find that 'MediCenter' and 'nurses' are both NPs, as the tree claims, and that 'employed' is a V. So, every substructure in the tree corresponds to some rule in the grammar, and the tree is thus admitted by the grammar. Since the tree is a legitimate structure, it follows that the string of words made up of the leaves of the tree – namely, 'MediCenter employed nurses' – is, according to Grammar1, a grammatical expression of category S – that is, a sentence. This is not the only string of words that

Grammar1 will admit as a sentence – there are 39 more such strings, including 'Nurses died', 'Dr Chan employed patients', and so on.

We have represented our illustrative tree graphically, but such diagrams are not, given the limitations of present computers, a convenient data structure to use for NLP. The simplest way to handle trees is to manipulate them as lists, where the first element is the root category and subsequent elements are the daughter subtrees in order of occurrence. Thus, our tree would be represented as follows in LISP:

(S (NP MediCenter)(VP (V employed)(NP nurses)))

The general principle is that a tree is represented by a list whose first element is the top label and whose subsequent elements are the immediate subtrees in order. These elements are then themselves lists, representing the subtrees according to the same convention. In this scheme, a leaf node of a tree (here, an English word) is simply represented by itself. This kind of list would appear in a 'pretty-printed' format as follows:

```
(S
    (NP MediCenter)
    (VP
        (V employed)
        (NP nurses)))
```

We will conclude this section with some comments about the appropriate way to evaluate a particular grammar for a (fragment of a) language, given a grammar formalism and an underlying mathematical interpretation for that formalism. There are basically three empirical criteria:

(1)   Does it undergenerate?

(2)   Does it overgenerate?

(3)   Does it assign appropriate structures to the strings that it generates?

Once again, we are using the word 'generate' in a neutral sense here, simply discussing the adequacy of the grammar as a description of a set of strings and ignoring the procedural complications that would be involved if we wished to produce actual example sentences from the description.

A grammar for English undergenerates if there are some syntactically well-formed expressions of English to which the grammar assigns no structure. But the sets of rules that grammarians propose are rarely intended to generate the whole of a natural language and so questions of undergeneration are normally considered relative to the goals of the grammar. If the grammar is intended as a set of rules to handle all English relative clauses and yet it fails to assign a structure to 'that saw you' in 'the man that saw you', then the grammar is clearly empirically inadequate for reasons of undergeneration. In a computational context, undergeneration by the grammar is not necessarily a problem, if the goal is to *produce* appropriate language; on the other hand, it could prove fatal if the goal is to *recognize* or *understand*.

A grammar overgenerates if it legitimates strings that cannot be construed as grammatical expressions of the language in question, given the category assigned to them by the grammar. This appears simpler than the undergeneration criterion, since the grammarian's goals do not seem to be bound up with the criterion. However, two factors serve to make it less straightforward than it at first appears. Firstly, our intuitions about what is or is not grammatical are often hard to disentangle from our judgements about what is meaningful; for example, is 'stones bet stones stones stones' ungrammatical, or merely unlikely to have a useful meaning? And, secondly, the grammar may decide grammaticality on the basis of more than one component, so the fact that one component fails to forbid some string does not mean that the grammar as a whole will fail in this way. Of course, if all the components of the grammar are fully specified, then there should be no problem of evaluation. But often, in academic linguistic work, one or more syntactic components exist in name only (logical form, interpretative rules, and so on). This makes it difficult or impossible to evaluate the empirical adequacy of the rule components that are fully specified. In a computational context, overgeneration by the grammar is not necessarily a problem if the goal is to *recognize* or *understand* well-formed language. On the other hand, it could prove fatal if the goal is to *produce* well-formed language.

The question of whether a grammar assigns the correct structures is likewise a subtle one. Natural language expressions do not come to us with their structures ready marked: we have to infer the relevant structures indirectly by considering, for instance, what other phrases we could substitute for a given subphrase while maintaining grammaticality.

In addition to these empirical criteria, standard scientific considerations such as simplicity and generality apply to grammars in much the same way as they do to any other theories about natural phenomena. Other things being equal, a grammar with seven rules is to be preferred to one with 93 rules. And, other things being equal, a grammar for a fragment of English that can be converted into a grammar for the corresponding fragment of French with a few minor changes is to be preferred to a grammar for the English fragment that bears no relation whatsoever to its French counterpart. Likewise, a grammar for Swedish relative clauses that can be extended to handle a class of Swedish questions with the addition of a couple of rules and a feature is to be preferred to one that requires a complete new set of parallel rules and features to encompass the questions.

Exercise 4.1   Justify the claim that Grammar1 admits precisely 40 strings as sentences.   [*easy*]

Exercise 4.2   Every CF-PSG can be converted into an RTN that accepts exactly the same set of strings as the grammar defines. Write a compiler that will take an arbitrary grammar in the PATR format used by Grammar1, or a similar format of your devising, and convert it into an equivalent RTN represented in the way shown in Chapter 3.   [*intermediate*]

Exercise 4.3   The simplest way of doing the compilation of the last question will lead to RTNs with many redundant arcs. Write a program to optimize the resulting RTN by eliminating these redundant arcs.   [*hard*]

Exercise 4.4   Every RTN can be mapped into a CF-PSG that generates the same language. Write a compiler that will take an arbitrary RTN represented in the way shown in Chapter 3 and convert it into a CF-PSG that generates the same language. What aspect of RTNs makes this exercise somewhat less trivial than the reverse compilation?   [*hard*]

4.3   Grammars in LISP and random generation

In LISP programs, we will represent a grammar by a list of structures, one for each rule, and store the current grammar in a global variable called rules. Each rule is represented by a list of items. The first represents the LHS of the rule, and the rest represent the items on the RHS in sequence. In rules, English words are represented by the corresponding LISP atoms and grammatical categories are put inside lists to distinguish them from words. In grammars like Grammar1, where the only relevant feature for categories is cat, we need not explicitly mention the feature names in rules, and so, in writing rules for this kind of grammar, we will specify the category that has cat S simply by (S), for instance. Note that, although we will adopt this convention for rules, we will still build parse trees as described earlier – that is, with bare cat values like S, rather than lists like (S), as labels. Here is our representation of Grammar1 in LISP (also in lib cfpsgram):

```
(setq rules
'(((S) (NP) (VP))
  ((VP) (V))
  ((VP) (V) (NP))
  ((V) died)
```

```
((V) employed)
((NP) nurses)
((NP) patients)
((NP) MediCenter)
((NP) Dr Chan)))
```

Notice that we have included the lexicon in the set of rules without making any explicit distinction. Thus, for instance, we have interpreted the lexical entry:

```
Word employed:
    <cat> = V.
```

simply as another way to specify the rule

```
V → employed
```

One advantage of this approach is that it allows us to deal with 'Dr Chan' as a sequence of two words in a natural way. There are a number of reasons why, for efficiency, it might make sense to treat lexical entries differently from other rules, however. We will not make these optimizations here as they make the algorithms harder to follow.

One important way in which computers can be of use to formal linguists is by allowing them to experiment with different grammars and show them implications of the various choices they make, which might be hard to work out by hand. A useful tool in this context is a program that can randomly generate sentences that are judged legal by a grammar. Notice that it would not be so useful to have a random generator built to work only with a specific grammar, in the way that the ATN program developed in Chapter 3 was specific to a particular analysis of English, for linguists would then have to get involved with programming whenever they wanted to change a rule in the grammar. Instead, we want to have a program that can accept any grammar (in some formalism), written in a way not dissimilar to how a linguist would write one, and randomly produce legal sentences. In our LISP program (lib randgen), we will deal with CF-PSGs, represented by list structures as here.

Here is the top-level function of our random generator. The function generate takes a description of the kind of phrase to be generated (for example, (S)) and produces as its result a list of atoms (for example, (Dr Chan died)).

```
(defun generate (description)
    (if (atom description)
        (list description)
        (let ((rs (matching_rules description)))
            (if (null rs)
                (error "Cannot generate description")
                (generate_all (cdr (oneof rs)))))))
```

generate will be called recursively with descriptions of smaller and smaller phrases until it is called with a single atom as the description. In this case, the atom itself, packaged in a list, is returned as the result. If the description is not a single atom, it must be a list representing a syntactic category; so, to generate from it, the program must look for rules about what a phrase of this kind can consist of. matching_rules returns the list of all such rules, and one is then chosen at random using the function oneof. oneof simply takes a list and returns a random element, using the LISP function random to generate a number indicating the position of the element to be chosen:

```
(defun oneof (list)
  ;; randomly returns one of the given list
  (nth (random (length list)) list))
```

The RHS of the rule chosen is extracted (the LHS, which is the same as the original description, being ignored) and passed to generate_all. Since the RHS of a rule is just a list of the kind of items that generate can work from, generate_all simply calls generate on each element, concatenating the results together:

```
(defun generate_all (body)
  (if (null body)
      '()
      (append
        (generate (car body))
        (generate_all (cdr body)))))
```

matching_rules has to work through the grammar rules, collecting together in a list all the ones that start with the right category. It uses a function unify to compare the description it is generating from with the LHS of the rule. In a more general situation, where the description and LHS may specify values of several features, unify will have to be more complicated, as we will see. For our current purposes, however, it suffices for unify to test whether the two lists are equal:

```
(defun matching_rules (description)
  (let ((results ()))
    (dolist (rule rules results)
      (if (unify description (car rule))
          (setq results (cons rule results))))))

(defun unify (x y)
  (equal x y))
```

This simple program works well with small grammars but would have to be improved to work efficiently if we had hundreds of rules. One source of inefficiency is the search through the whole list of rules, which is carried out by matching_rules every time a category has to be generated from. If we grouped rules with the same category on the LHS together, perhaps as follows:

```
(setq rules
  '(((S)
      ((NP) (VP)))
    ((VP)
      ((V))
      ((V) (NP)))
    ((NP)
      (Dr Chan)
      (MediCenter)
      (nurses)
      (patients))
    ((V)
      (died)
      (employed))))
```

then matching_rules would only have to work through a list of groups, rather than a list of individual rules. Alternatively, rules could be stored in a LISP hash table or on the property lists of the LHS categories, for rapid retrieval, given the left-hand category.

If you have just written a large phrase structure grammar, this generation program might be useful to help you detect places where the grammar is not strict enough in its characterization of legality. Getting an example of an illegal sentence that can be generated is, however, not necessarily very useful. What we more often want to know is *how* the grammar managed to generate such an object. For this reason, it is interesting to see whether we can generate the *parse trees* of random sentences allowed by the grammar. In fact, our program can be altered straightforwardly to do this, the result being called lib randtree. In this modified program, generate returns a single parse tree, represented as a list in the way shown earlier, and generate_all returns a list of parse trees. Here are the new definitions (the other definitions do not need to be changed):

```
(defun generate (description)
  (if (atom description)
      description
      (let ((rs (matching_rules description)))
        (if (null rs)
            (error "Cannot generate from description ~S" description)
            (cons
              (category description)
              (generate_all (cdr (oneof rs))))))))
```

```
(defun generate_all (body)
  (if (null body)
      '()
      (cons
        (generate (car body))
        (generate_all (cdr body)))))


(defun category (description)
  (car description))
```

Notice how, now that generate returns a single item (parse tree), rather than a sequence of items (atoms), the call to append in generate_all is replaced by a call to cons.

Exercise 4.5   Write a program that automatically translates rule list structures in a more human-readable form into the format for rules such as those used in the text. Your program might take as input a list such as the following, for instance:

```
((Rule S → NP VP)
 (Rule VP → V)
 (Rule VP → V NP)
 (Word Dr Chan – (cat) = NP)
 (Word nurses – (cat) = NP)
 (Word died – (cat) = V))
```

You can assume that cat is the only feature used in the grammar.   [*easy*]

Exercise 4.6   Run the generation programs on Grammar1 and other grammars that you devise. Try tracing the function generate – the calling pattern mirrors the syntactic structure of the sentence precisely. This is not surprising given that, in Chapter 3, we were able to effectively get parse trees generated by a PT, simply by keeping a record of what the transducer had done in successfully getting through the sentence.   [*easy*]

Exercise 4.7   The first definition of generate_all is a source of inefficiency. Having built lists of atoms from the first item of a rule and the rest of the items, the program builds a new list consisting of the two joined together. Since this same process will be repeated as generate_all recurses down the RHS of a single rule, many lists will be built, only to be discarded almost immediately. Rewrite the program so that only one list is built – the final complete list of atoms.   [*intermediate*]

4.4   Subcategorization and the use of features

As the reader may already have noticed, the ungrammatical strings, '*Dr Chan died patients' and '*MediCenter employed' are among those that Grammar1 claims to be sentences (linguists use '*' to mark strings that are intuitively ungrammatical in the language under consideration, in this case English). The problem here involves what linguists call 'subcategorization'. Although 'died' and 'employed' are both verbs, as Grammar1 claims, they belong in different subcategories of the class of verbs. Specifically, 'employed' is transitive and requires a following NP, whereas 'died' is intransitive and cannot tolerate a following NP. We could patch up Grammar1 by replacing V with two categories, IV (intransitive verb) and TV (transitive verb), and revising the VP rules and lexicon accordingly, but such an approach rapidly proliferates a host of distinct parts of speech once a larger class of sentences is considered.

Instead of pursuing the *ad hoc* solution just mentioned, we will turn to a more principled approach: one that employs syntactic features. Most, if not all, contemporary theories of grammar employ features, and the extent and sophistication of their use has grown massively in the 1980s, although their use in computational linguistics goes back to the late 1950s. In a modern feature–theoretic syntax, atomic categories such as NP and V are replaced by sets of feature specifications. Each feature specification consists of a feature, say case, and a value for that feature, say accusative. The familiar names for categories such as NP and V can then be reintroduced as the value of a particular feature, which we shall call cat. In fact, we have already made this move in the lexical entries we have shown.

In the light of this, what we will do now is to rebuild Grammar1 using features, thus creating Grammar2, and solving the problem noted earlier with subcategorization. To make Grammar2 a little more interesting than it would otherwise be, we will also introduce a rule for coordination, which will allow us to illustrate the role of recursion in grammars. Having done that, we will then extend Grammar2 to Grammar3, and in so doing illustrate the descriptive power of feature–theoretic techniques on a range of syntactic phenomena.

We will employ just two features in Grammar2 – namely, cat(egory) and arg1(ument). cat will have as its values the labels that were used for categories themselves in Grammar1, but with one addition, C, which we will discuss later. arg1 will, for the moment, have just two values: 0 (that is, nothing) and NP. How are we to interpret these features and their values? Well, consider a category that has v as the value of its cat feature, which means that it is a verb, and NP as the value of its arg1 feature. We will interpret the latter to mean that it is the kind of verb that requires a following NP; that is, it is a transitive verb. A verb with 0 as its arg1 value will be a verb that requires nothing to follow; that is, it is an intransitive verb.

We now have the problem of how to write rules, given that we have moved away from unanalyzed (monadic) categories to bundles of featural information. To keep things clear, we will continue to write, for example:

Rule {simple sentence formation}
　　S → NP VP.

But this must now be construed as elliptical for something that would be more verbosely expressed as follows:

Rule {simple sentence formation}
　　X0 → X1 X2:
　　　　<X0 cat> = S
　　　　<X1 cat> = NP
　　　　<X2 cat> = VP.

So, in this verbose version of our rule notation, we have place holders X0, X1 and X2 in the rule itself, and then a collection of equations such as <X0 cat> = S, which is to be read as saying 'the value of X0's category feature is S'. In the abbreviated rule notation, we simply substitute the value of cat for the place holder in the rule and in accompanying equations. Given these remarks, we can now exhibit the rules employed by Grammar2.

EXAMPLE: Grammar2

Rule {simple sentence formation}
　　S → NP VP.
Rule {intransitive verb}
　　VP → V:
　　　　<V arg1> = 0.
Rule {single complement verbs}
　　VP → V X:
　　　　<V arg1> = <X cat>.
Rule {coordination of identical categories}
　　X0 → X1 C X2:
　　　　<X0 cat> = <X1 cat>
　　　　<X0 cat> = <X2 cat>
　　　　<X0 arg1> = <X1 arg1>
　　　　<X0 arg1> = <X2 arg1>.

Word died:
　　<cat> = V
　　<arg1> = 0.

Word recovered:
    <cat> = V
    <arg1> = 0.
Word slept:
    <cat> = V
    <arg1> = 0.
Word employed:
    <cat> = V
    <arg1> = NP.
Word paid:
    <cat> = V
    <arg1> = NP.
Word nursed:
    <cat> = V
    <arg1> = NP.
Word and:
    <cat> = C.
Word or:
    <cat> = C.

The first rule looks the same as its counterpart in Grammar1 and performs exactly the same function. The second and third rules in Grammar2 perform the desired functions of the second and third rules in Grammar1, but, together with the lexical entries shown, they ensure that a transitive verb will be followed by a noun phrase, whereas an intransitive verb will be followed by nothing. Grammar2 thus makes the correct claims about the grammaticality of the following examples:

    Nurses died.
    *Nurses died patients.
    *MediCenter employed.
    MediCenter employed nurses.

The grammar will assign structures to the first and last examples, but no structures are available for the second and third. The verbs 'die' and 'employ' belong to two featurally distinct categories in Grammar2: the former may not be followed by a noun phrase, the latter must be followed by a noun phrase. Hence, as far as Grammar2 is concerned, the second and third examples are ungrammatical.

The fourth and final rule is a schema, which takes us beyond the domain covered by Grammar1. This schema introduces the coordinate construction and says that a given category can consist of two further instances of the same category separated by an item of category C, which will turn out to be realized as 'and' or 'or'.

Turning now to the lexicon for Grammar2, while we can simply carry over the NP entries from Grammar1, we do need to revise the V entries, and add a couple of C entries. Notice that a few extra verbs have been added to enhance the plausibility of the examples given.

Apart from the introduction of features, which at this stage may appear to have been of much more trouble than it is worth, Grammar2 appears very little different from Grammar1. But there is one very fundamental difference between them. Grammar1 claimed that exactly 40 strings of words were grammatical instances of the category S, whereas Grammar2 admits infinitely many strings of words as grammatical instances of S. How can this be? The answer lies in the coordination schema we have introduced into Grammar2. This allows any category to split into two instances of the same category. These new instances may themselves split, and so on. This aspect of the grammar provides an example of recursion in syntactic rules (see the examples following Grammar3 for a rather different example of this phenomenon). Grammar2 permits recursion, whereas Grammar1 did not. This should become clearer from the example in Figure 4.2 which exhibits one of the infinitely many trees that Grammar2 admits as grammatical. As can be seen, we have two sentences coordinated, the second sentence itself containing a coordinate verb phrase. Thus, this example illustrates how the S category can reintroduce the S category, and how the VP category can reintroduce the VP category. The grammar imposes no limit on how many times categories can be reintroduced by the coordination rule, and so there is no limit on the number of expressions that Grammar2 can admit. Hence, Grammar2 admits all of the following examples:

Nurses died.

Nurses died and patients recovered.

Nurses died and patients recovered and Dr Chan slept.

Nurses died and patients recovered and Dr Chan slept and MediCenter employed nurses.

Nurses died and patients recovered and Dr Chan slept and MediCenter employed nurses and ... .

Although Grammar2 allows for the grammaticality of infinitely many sentences, we would rapidly grow bored with an enumeration of them. This is partly because the lexicon for Grammar2 is very small and so lengthy examples will force us into the repetition of lexical items. Let us therefore expand Grammar2 to Grammar3 and, in so doing, enlarge our lexicon by exploiting more fully the technique of using a feature (arg1) to

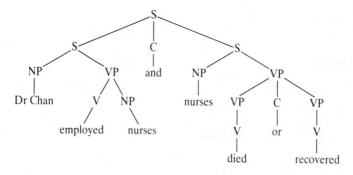

Figure 4.2 Phrase structure tree for sentence with coordination.

encode the category of complements that we employed for subcategorization in Grammar2. The rules for Grammar3 are those employed in Grammar2 with one addition, a rule for expanding prepositional phrases:

Rule {prepositional phrases}
 PP → P X:
  <P arg1> = <X cat>.

It is only when we come to the lexicon of Grammar3 that differences really become apparent. Grammar3 allows us to employ a much wider range of distinct subtypes of lexical item, including six different kinds of verb, by augmenting the lexicon of Grammar2.

EXAMPLE: Lexicon3

Word approved:
    <cat> = V
    <arg1> = PP.
Word disapproved:
    <cat> = V
    <arg1> = PP.
Word appeared:
    <cat> = V
    <arg1> = AP.
Word seemed:
    <cat> = V
    <arg1> = AP.

Word had:
    <cat> = V
    <arg1> = VP.
Word believed:
    <cat> = V
    <arg1> = S.
Word thought:
    <cat> = V
    <arg1> = S.
Word of:
    <cat> = P
    <arg1> = NP.
Word fit:
    <cat> = AP.
Word competent:
    <cat> = AP.
Word well-qualified:
    <cat> = AP.

Grammar3 provides us with structures for all the following examples, as well as an infinity of others:

> Nurses thought Dr Chan seemed competent.
> Dr Chan appeared well-qualified and disapproved of MediCenter.
> Patients had believed nurses thought Dr Chan had slept.

This last example illustrates recursion through the sentential (clausal) or verb phrase complements of a verb – we saw an RTN treatment of this phenomenon in Chapter 3. This is a very common form of recursion found in natural languages.

Our final example grammar will maintain the overall structure employed in Grammar2 and Grammar3. As Lexicon4 will be identical in every respect to Lexicon3, we shall not repeat it here. In fact, the only real change we will make in Grammar4 is the addition of a new feature, which we will call slash in virtue of a notational convention whereby we will use X/Y to represent a category X0 whose cat is X and whose slash is Y; that is, <X0 cat> = X and <X0 slash> = Y. The addition of this feature to the system requires certain consequential additions to the rules. Expressions like S/NP and VP/PP, then, stand for a particular kind of category, but what kind? What is the intuitive content of the notation? The answer is quite straightforward: an expression of category X/Y is an expression of category X from which an expression of category Y is missing. Thus, an S/NP (read S-slash-NP) is a sentence (or clause) that has got a noun phrase missing, whereas a VP/PP is a verb phrase that is missing a prepositional phrase. To make use of, or even to make sense of, these slash categories, we will need to make a number of additions to the rules that Grammar3 came equipped with.

EXAMPLE: Rules for Grammar4

Rule {simple sentence formation}
S → NP VP:
 <S slash> = <VP slash>
 <NP slash> = 0.

Rule {intransitive verb}
VP → V:
 <V arg1> = 0
 <V slash> = 0
 <VP slash> = 0.

Rule {single complement verbs}
VP → V X:
 <V arg1> = <X cat>
 <V slash> = 0
 <VP slash> = <X slash>.

Rule {prepositional phrases}
PP → P X:
 <P arg1> = <X cat>
 <P slash> = 0
 <PP slash> = <X slash>.

Rule {coordination}
X0 → X1 C X2:
 <X0 cat> = <X1 cat>
 <X0 cat> = <X2 cat>
 <C slash> = 0
 <X0 slash> = <X1 slash>
 <X0 slash> = <X2 slash>
 <X0 arg1> = <X1 arg1>
 <X0 arg1> = <X2 arg1>.

Rule {topicalization}
X0 → X1 X2:
 <X0 cat> = S
 <X1 empty> = no
 <X2 cat> = S
 <X2 slash> = <X1 cat>
 <X2 empty> = no
 <X0 slash> = <X1 slash>.

Rule {slash elimination}
 X0 → :
     <X0 cat> = <X0 slash>
     <X0 empty> = yes.

The first five rules of Grammar4 are simply revisions of those in Grammar3 to allow for our new feature: in each case, the value of slash (if any) on the mother is equated with the value of slash (if any) on the complement daughter, or all the daughters, in the case of the coordination rule. The sixth and seventh rules are wholly new. The essence of the topicalization rule can be more perspicuously expressed using our slash notation:

S → X S/X.

This rule says that a sentence can consist of some category followed by a sentence which is missing an expression of that category. And, these in turn, taken together with the rest of Grammar4, will permit such sentences as the following (without the commas):

> MediCenter, nurses disapproved of _.
> Of MediCenter, nurses disapproved _.
> Well-qualified, Dr Chan had seemed _.

As can be readily seen, the sentences that follow the comma in these examples all have something missing. The rule that is responsible for this missing item in Grammar4 is the last one, which can also be notated as follows:

X/X → .

This just says that an X missing an X can be realized as nothing. Thus, NP/NP, PP/PP and AP/AP are all allowed to appear as nothing in the structures defined by Grammar4.

Note that our modifications to the rules in Grammar3 mean, for example, that a sentence missing a Y can consist of a noun phrase followed by a verb phrase missing a Y (where Y might be NP, say). So, what the modified rules now permit is a transfer of information about a missing category from mother to daughter. The way this works should become clearer by looking at the relevant tree exhibited in Figure 4.3.

There is, in principle, no limit on the amount of intervening material that can occur between the *displaced* constituent at the front of the sentence and the *empty* constituent that corresponds to it and which occurs

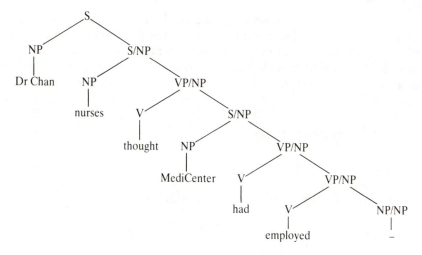

Figure 4.3   Phrase structure tree with slash categories.

within the sentence. Such constructions manifest what are known as *unbounded dependencies* and are surprisingly common in the world's languages. English, for example, makes extensive use of this type of construction, most notably in questions and relative clauses. In Chapter 3, we indicated how an ATN treatment might tackle such constructions using a global register HOLD to remember the displaced material. Such a procedural approach, which is specialized to parsing, differs substantially from the declarative description of the slash feature given in Grammar4. Although the analysis of topicalization given here is rudimentary, it does serve to illustrate the sort of feature-passing technique that is very common in current computational linguistic work on syntax.

The lexicon of Grammar3 is almost adequate for Grammar4, except for one problem. The grammar rules explicitly require that words like verbs and prepositions have 0 as the value of their slash feature. This is to prevent such words being extraposed from their normal position and untopicalized constructions having gaps. As a result, lexical entries need to state their value of slash explicitly, as in:

```
Word died:
    <cat> = V
    <slash> = 0
    <arg1> = 0.
```

It is straightforward, but laborious, to make the necessary alterations to all the lexical entries for Grammar3. The use of *macros* in lexical entries, an idea to be introduced in Chapter 7, is one possible way of making such global assignments of features to lexical items.

Notice that our use of features in Grammar2, Grammar3 and Grammar4 has been very restricted. We have simply replaced monadic category names like S and NP with small finite sets of attribute value pairs, where both attribute and value are drawn from small finite sets of atomic elements. Consequently, all these grammars could be converted into equivalent grammars with monadic categories quite unproblematically, although there are no obvious computational reasons for doing so. For instance, the rule:

Rule {simple sentence formation}
  S → NP VP:
    <S slash> = <VP slash>.

could be replaced by a finite number of rules like:

Rule
  S/S → NP VP/S.
Rule
  S/NP → NP VP/NP.
Rule
  S/VP → NP VP/VP.
Rule
  S/AP → NP VP/AP.

where S/S, VP/S, and so on, are to be read as single symbols, just like NP and S. Since the number of categories in these grammars is finite, and the rules are context free and finite in number, we have not left the domain of CF-PSGs, even though the descriptive apparatus used is much more sophisticated than that employed in Grammar1. We consider a mathematically more far-reaching use of the feature system offered by the PATR formalism at the end of this chapter.

The grammars we have been elaborating are what linguists would call 'toy grammars'. They serve to illustrate something of the way contemporary feature–theoretic grammars work, but they should not be taken too seriously as analyses of English. The fact that Grammar3 and Grammar4 work as well as they do owes a lot to the particular lexicon that they employ. The reader who has mastered the mechanics of at least Grammar3 might usefully consider the questions that follow.

Exercise 4.8 What is the purpose of the feature empty in Grammar4? What syntactic structure(s) would the grammar assign to the sentence 'MediCenter employed nurses' if the equations involving empty were removed? [*intermediate*]

Exercise 4.9 What happens if you try to add the past form(s) of the irregular verb 'go' to the lexicon? Can the analysis of 'had' be maintained in the light of such additions? What fact about the existing choice of verbs makes the treatment of 'had' seem superficially plausible? Does Grammar3, as it stands, permit any ungrammatical sentences containing 'had' to be generated?   [*intermediate*]

Exercise 4.10 All the verb forms given are in the past tense. What happens if you try to add the corresponding present tense forms?   [*intermediate*]

Exercise 4.11 The NP section of the lexicon does not contain any pronouns. What happens if you try to add 'I', 'him', and so on, to the NP lexicon? Which English pronoun can be added without leading to ungrammatical sentences?   [*easy*]

Exercise 4.12 The particular featural treatment of subcategorization adopted in Grammar2 suffers from a fundamental restriction. What is it? What English verbs lie outside its scope?   [*easy*]

Exercise 4.13 In Grammar4, there is a generalization to be made about the form of the rules that will transfer slash information from mother to daughter. This generalization is not, however, expressed in the form of Grammar4. What is the generalization?   [*easy*]

Being able to find fault in a grammar is one thing, but being able to repair or improve a descriptively inadequate grammar is a whole lot harder. The reader should pursue the following projects in order to get a feel for the latter enterprise.

Exercise 4.14 Grammar2 generates the ungrammatical string '*Dr Chan employed nurses and or and patients'. Work out the structure that it assigns to this string and consider how the grammar might be modified to eliminate it (and other similar examples).   [*intermediate*]

Exercise 4.15 Modify Grammar3 so that it can distinguish between a past participle and the past tense form. Add the relevant forms of the verbs 'go', 'eat' and 'know' to the lexicon. Check to see that 'had' now works properly.   [*intermediate*]

Exercise 4.16 Augment Grammar3 with a rule that will allow the generation of questions such as 'Had Dr Chan employed nurses?' Estimate how much work would be involved in getting the grammar to allow 'Was Dr Chan employed?' in a principled manner and make a list of the problems such an example gives rise to.   [*intermediate*]

Exercise 4.17 Add a feature (or features) to Grammar3 so that it can distinguish plural and singular. Encode this in the NP part of the lexicon in an appropriate manner. Augment the verbal part of the lexicon to include the present tense forms of the verbs. Now modify the rules so as to ensure subject–verb agreement. What problems would you encounter if you tried to add the verb 'be' to your modified grammar? [*intermediate*]

Exercise 4.18 Add a feature (or features) to Grammar3 so that it can distinguish between subject and non-subject noun phrases. Add 'she', 'him', 'they' and 'them' to the NP part of the lexicon. Make sure that the grammar does not legitimate such ungrammatical strings as '*them approved of she'. [*easy*]

Exercise 4.19 Add exactly one rule (and make no other changes) to Grammar4 to enable it to handle examples like 'Dr Chan, nurses thought seemed competent'. [*hard*]

Exercise 4.20 Add a rule (or rules) to Grammar4 so that it can handle two-word noun phrases like 'a doctor', 'the hospital', and so on. Augment the lexicon accordingly. Now add one further rule to permit noun phrases containing simple relative clauses such as 'a nurse doctors had employed' and 'the hospital Dr Chan approved of'. To do this, you will have to employ the slash feature. [*intermediate*]

Exercise 4.21 Augment Grammar4 with the rules necessary to permit questions such as 'Who had MediCenter employed?' and 'Who had Dr Chan thought MediCenter approved of?' [*hard*]

Exercise 4.22 If you have some mastery of a language other than English, try to work out a version of Grammar4 for that language using a lexicon that employs the relevant translations of the words appearing in Grammar4's English lexicon. [*intermediate project*]

4.5   Encoding feature specifications in LISP

Collections of feature names and associated values are easily represented in LISP. We will represent them using association lists, with feature names acting as keys. For instance, the following list:

```
((person 3) (number sing))
```

represents something with person and number features. The values for these are, respectively, 3 and sing. As before, we can represent a grammar rule by a list consisting of the LHS category followed by the RHS categories, these categories now being more complex than the single-element lists used previously. The main complication now is that a PATR rule can state that two features must have the same value, without specifying in advance what that value is to be. In our representation, where two features are required to share a value (by a PATR '=' statement), the two values will be denoted by occurrences of the same *variable symbol*. Variable symbols need to be distinguished from normal atomic values in some way, but apart from this only one aspect of their form is of importance. Where the same variable symbol occurs several times, the appropriate values have to be the same; where two different variable tokens appear, the values do not have to be the same. We have chosen to represent a variable symbol by an atom beginning with a '_', because this is easy to type, yet easily distinguished from the feature names and values that we are likely to use. A PATR rule can then be translated into the LISP notation by collecting up all the information provided about each given category into a single list, using multiple occurrences of the same variable to indicate where a value must be shared. For instance, the Grammar4 rule:

```
Rule {single complement verbs}
    VP → V X:
        <V arg1> = <X cat>
        <VP slash> = <X slash>.
```

could be translated into the following in LISP:

```
(((cat VP) (slash _y))
 ((cat V) (arg1 _x))
 ((cat _x) (slash _y)))
```

where the variable symbol _y is used to indicate that the slash of the VP must be the same as the slash of the second subphrase and the symbol _x is used to indicate that the cat of the second subphrase must be the same as the arg1 of the verb.

The LISP notation makes it relatively easy to see how a single rule using features corresponds to a number of context-free phrase structure rules. With the above rule, a possible CF-PSG rule can be derived first of all by filling out the representation to mention explicitly all possible features for all phrases. Thus, if cat, slash and arg1 are the only possible features, then the foregoing rule is 'filled out' to:

```
(((cat VP) (slash _y) (arg1 _v1))
 ((cat V) (arg1 _x) (slash _v2))
 ((cat _x) (slash _y) (arg1 _v3)))
```

where the extra variables _v1, _v2 and _v3 appear once each. It is now possible to consider a completely specified instance of this rule by choosing a possible concrete value for each variable, for instance:

```
_y  – NP
_x  – NP
_v1 – 0
_v2 – 0
_v3 – 0
```

This assignment of values to variables gives the following rule:

```
(((cat VP) (slash NP) (arg1 0))
 ((cat V) (arg1 NP) (slash 0))
 ((cat NP) (slash NP) (arg1 0)))
```

All we need now is a convention for translating each completely specified feature bundle into an atomic symbol. For instance, we could take the cat, slash and arg1 feature values in order, separated by underlines. We would then have the following context-free rule:

```
((VP_NP_0)
 (V_0_NP)
 (NP_NP_0))
```

Corresponding to different variable assignments, we will, of course, get different context-free phrase structure rules out at the end. But, as long as we are consistent about our conventions (for instance in translating at the end from feature bundles to symbols), the resulting grammar will be exactly equivalent to the original one.

The top level of a LISP program that carries out this translation might look like the following function, which prints out all the CF-PSG rules that correspond to a give rule:

```
(defun expand_rule (rule)
  (let ((newrule (fillout_rule rule)))
    (subst_values varlist newrule)))
```

fillout_rule produces a new rule where each category consists of a list of bare values for each feature in turn, obtained by adding new variables, like _v1 in the foregoing, for unmentioned features. It also creates, in the global variable varlist, a list with an entry for each variable symbol and the list of possible values it can have, for instance:

```
((_x NP S PP 0)
 (_v1 NP 0 N V PP))
```

How is it to know what possible features there are and what possible values they can have? The possible features, together with their possible values, will have to be declared in a global variable:

```
(defvar features
  '((cat S NP VP PP AP P N V O)
    (slash S NP VP PP AP P N V O)
    (subcat S NP VP PP AP P N V O)
    (empty yes no)))
```

subst_values is in charge of enumerating every possible concrete instance of the rule by substituting one of the possible values for each of the variables in the varlist:

```
(defun subst_values (varlist rule)
  (if (null varlist)
      (print rule)
      (dolist (val (cdar varlist))
        (subst_values (cdr varlist)
          (subst_value (caar varlist) val rule)))))
```

The function uses recursion to carry out the enumeration of all the possibilities. Each call of subst_values is in charge of trying out all possible values for the variable whose entry occurs first in the list. For each value in the car of varlist, it calls subst_value to actually substitute that value for the variable and then subst_values again to deal with the rest of the variables. When the recursion bottoms out, the actual value of the rule (with values for all the variables) is printed out. subst_value is easily defined:

```
(defun subst_value (name val thing)
  (if (equal name thing)
      val
      (if (consp thing)
          (cons
            (subst_value name val (car thing))
            (subst_value name val (cdr thing)))
          thing)))
```

In Chapter 7, we will look in more detail at the semantics of feature structures and develop LISP programs for more interesting applications.

Exercise 4.23 Complete the program to translate a grammar using features into a CF-PSG. In fillout_rule you will need to use the LISP function gensym to generate names for new variables. Translate the rules of Grammar4 into the LISP representation and run the program on it. How many context-free rules are generated? How might some of the sillier rules be excluded? [*intermediate*]

4.6   Classes of grammars and languages

In this section, we are concerned, not with the formalisms that have been employed in grammatical work, but rather with the underlying formal grammars that have been assumed, and with the classes of languages that they induce. The Chomsky hierarchy of languages, illustrated in Figure 4.4, is a crude dimension of grammar power whose lowest rung is the type 3 class of languages, also known as the regular languages or finite-state languages, and whose highest rung is the type 0 class of languages, also known as the recursively enumerable sets. In between come a number of other classes of languages including the indexed languages and the type 2 or context-free languages.

4.6.1   Context-free grammars and languages

The languages that can be described by CF-PSGs, which are the same as the languages that can be described by RTNs, are known as the *context-free languages (CFLs)*. CF-PSGs are relatively simple to write and to modify. They are associated with a successful tradition of work in computation, which has provided us with a thorough understanding of how to parse, translate and compile them. One of the motivations for taking an interest in CF-PSGs is the existence of relatively high-efficiency algorithms for recognizing and parsing CFLs. Context-free parsing is a basic tool of computer science, including NLP, and there have even been proposals for implementing CF-PSG parsers in special-purpose hardware.

Although equivalent in power, CF-PSGs are, in general, to be preferred to RTNs for the description of natural and formal languages. RTNs involve an ontology of states, along with properties of states (initial, final), neither of which are needed in CF-PSGs. And the standard way of thinking about RTNs is strongly conducive to a particular kind of processing ('top-down left-to-right depth-first' in the jargon of Chapter 5), whereas CF-PSG leaves all processing issues completely open. RTNs do have one minor advantage over CF-PSGs in that they can handle iteration directly (by an arc that loops back to the state it started from), whereas CF-PSGs are forced to use recursion to capture iteration.

Introductory linguistics and even AI textbooks and other pedagogically oriented works often claim that such phenomena as the dependencies between non-adjacent words exemplified in subject–verb agreement show English to be non-context free. This is not so. Even finite-state languages can exhibit dependencies between symbols arbitrarily far apart. To take an artificial example, suppose the last word in every sentence had to bear some special marking that was determined by what the first morpheme in the sentence was; a finite automaton to accept the language could simply encode in its state the information about what the

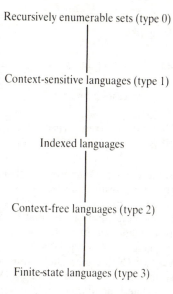

Recursively enumerable sets (type 0)

Context-sensitive languages (type 1)

Indexed languages

Context-free languages (type 2)

Finite-state languages (type 3)

Figure 4.4   The Chomsky hierarchy of languages.

sentence-initial morpheme was, and check the last word's marking against the state before accepting.

However, recently, at least one apparently valid instance of a natural language that is not a CFL has been found – Swiss German. What attitude should NLP research and development work take towards the few pieces of evidence that indicate that natural languages are not all CFLs? The fundamental thing that should be kept in mind is that the overwhelming majority of the structures of any natural languages can be elegantly and efficiently parsed using context-free parsing techniques. Nearly all constructions in nearly all languages can be parsed using techniques that limit the system to the analysis of CFLs.

EXAMPLE: Swiss German

The dialects of German spoken around Zürich, Switzerland, show evidence of a mathematically relevant pattern of word order in certain subordinate infinitival clauses: an arbitrary number of noun phrases (NPs) may be followed by a finite verb and a specific number of non-finite verbs, the number of NPs being a function of the lexical properties of the verbs. In addition, the semantic relations between verbs and NPs exhibit a crossed serial pattern: verbs further to the right in the string of verbs take as their objects NPs further to the right in the string of NPs. The crucial substrings have the form $NP^m V^n$. In a simple case, where $m = n = 5$, such a substring might have a meaning like:

Claudia watched Helmut let Eva help Hans make Ulrike work.

but with a word order corresponding to:

Claudia Helmut Eva Hans Ulrike watched let help make work
NP_1 NP_2 NP_3 NP_4 NP_5 V_1 V_2 V_3 V_4 V_5

In Swiss German, there is a specific property that makes this phenomenon relevant to the grammar power issue: certain verbs demand dative rather than accusative case marking on their objects, as a matter of pure syntax. This pattern will, in general, not be one that a CF-PSG can describe. For example, if we restrict the situation (technically, by intersecting with an appropriate regular language) to clauses in which all accusative NPs (NP_a) precede all dative NPs (NP_d), then the grammatical clauses will be just those where the accusative-demanding verbs (V_a) precede the dative-demanding verbs (V_d) and the numbers match up; schematically:

$$NP_a{}^m \quad NP_d{}^n \quad V_a{}^m \quad V_d{}^n$$

But this schema has the form of the language of strings of the form $a^m b^n c^m d^n$, where n is greater than 0, which can be shown not to be a CFL.

4.6.2 Finite-state grammars and regular languages

What is the smallest known natural class of formal languages that can reasonably be taken to include all the natural languages? The most restricted candidate that has ever been taken seriously is the class of finite-state, regular or type 3 languages. These are exactly the languages that can be recognized by FSTNs as presented in Chapter 2. They can also be characterized by grammars like Grammar1, but subject to the condition that every rule introduces at most one category (non-terminal) in the final position – alternatively, all rules introducing categories must place them in the initial position. Here is a finite-state grammar for the language generated by Grammar1, which happens to be a regular language:

Rule
    NP → Dr Chan.
Rule
    S → Dr Chan VP.
Rule
    NP → nurses.

Rule
  S → nurses VP.
Rule
  NP → MediCenter.
Rule
  S → MediCenter VP.
Rule
  NP → patients.
Rule
  S → patients VP.
Rule
  VP → died.
Rule
  VP → died NP.
Rule
  VP → employed.
Rule
  VP → employed NP.

However, there is a valid argument that not all natural languages are regular languages, which is based on the fact that a string of the following form:

A doctor (whom a doctor)^m (hired)^n hired another nurse.

only constitutes a legal sentence of English if m and n are the same. In ordinary grammatical terms, this is because each occurrence of the phrase 'a doctor' is a noun phrase that needs a verb such as 'hired' to complete the clause of which it is the subject.

The fact that natural languages are not regular does not necessarily mean that techniques for parsing regular languages are irrelevant to NLP. A number of scholars over the years have proposed that hearers process sentences as if they were finite automata (or as if they were pushdown automata with a finite stack depth limit), rather than showing the behaviour that would be characteristic of a more powerful device. To the extent that progress along these lines casts light on natural language parsing, the theory of regular grammars and finite automata will continue to be important in the study of natural languages, even though they are not regular languages. Indeed, we have already seen the utility of FSTs in the area of morphology in Chapter 2.

4.6.3   Indexed grammars and languages

If, in addition to a finite set of attribute value pairs, categories can also employ a single recursive feature called stack, say, and if rules are able to assign to, test and augment this feature, then the resulting expressive power is that of a class of grammars known as the indexed grammars. For example, suppose we allow categories X that can be described in the following way:

```
<X cat> = S,
<X stack top> = a,
<X stack stack top> = a,
<X stack stack stack top> = z.
```

and had a grammar with rules such as:

```
Rule {push endmarker on to stack}
  S → a A:
    <A stack top> = z
    <A stack stack> = <S stack>.
Rule {push 'a' on to stack}
  A0 → a A1:
    <A1 cat> = A
    <A2 cat> = A
    <A1 stack top> = a
    <A1 stack stack> = <A0 stack>.
Rule {copy stack from A to B}
  A → B:
    <A stack> = <B stack>.
Rule {pop 'a' off stack}
  B0 → b B1 c:
    <B0 cat> = B
    <B1 cat> = B
    <B0 stack top> = a
    <B0 stack stack> = <B1 stack>.
Rule {pop endmarker off stack}
  B → b c:
    <B stack top> = z.
```

Then we have a grammar for the language $a^n b^n c^n$, a language that is not a CFL. How have we managed to describe a non-context-free language in the same PATR notation that produced CF-PSGs like Grammar1 and Grammar4? By introducing the recursive feature stack, we have moved to a situation where there are *infinitely many* categories – a situation not permitted in CF-PSGs. Thus, for instance, for every n there is a category X that we can describe by:

$$<X \text{ stack}^n \text{ top}> = a$$

and no two such categories are the same.

The languages describable by indexed grammars – namely, the indexed languages – are a natural class of formal languages which form a proper superset of the CFLs and a proper subset of the context-sensitive or type 1 languages. They are of interest to NLP researchers because no phenomena are yet known which would lead them to believe that the natural languages do not form a subset of the indexed languages. In particular, it is clear that indexed grammars are available for the Swiss German facts and for most other sets of facts that have been even conjectured to hold problems for context-free description.

The indexed languages thus provide us, at least for the moment, with a kind of upper bound for natural language syntax. We can no longer be surprised by non-CFL patterns, although their rarity is a matter of some interest, but we should be very surprised at, and duly suspicious of, putatively non-indexed language phenomena.

SUMMARY

- Grammar design is a branch of knowledge representation.

- NLP grammars must satisfy both linguistic and computational criteria.

- Grammars define sets of strings and associate structures with them.

- Tree diagrams are used to represent syntactic structure.

- A lexicon associates words with their properties.

- Syntactic categories are bundles of grammatical information.

- Syntactic features can be used to define subcategories.

- PATR combines CF-PSG rules with a powerful feature system.

- Most constructions in most languages can be described by CF-PSGs.

Further reading

The methodological issues involved in the design of NLP grammar formalisms are usefully discussed in Shieber (1985a, 1987). The use of feature–theoretic grammar formalisms for NLP appears to have its origins in the work of Yngve in the 1950s (1958). The best introduction to the PATR grammar formalism is Shieber (1986a), while compilation of other grammar formalisms into PATR is discussed in Shieber (1986b).

Aho and Ullmann (1972) detail many of the properties of CFLs and CF-PSGs, Joshi (1987) gives a useful summary introduction to CF-PSG and some of its derivatives, and surveys of recent mathematical work on natural languages are to be found in Perrault (1984), and Gazdar and Pullum (1985). Fallacious or empirically ill-founded arguments mounted against the context freeness of natural languages are critically discussed in Pullum and Gazdar (1982), and Pullum (1984a), while a recent exemplar can be found in Rich (1983, p. 314). The non-fallacious argument based on Swiss German is due to Huybregts (1985) and Shieber (1985b), independently. The claim that natural languages are not in general finite state is thoroughly evaluated by Daly (1974). Useful discussion of the implications of the various claims and results for work in NLP can be found in Pullum (1983, 1984b).

Indexed languages and grammars were first discussed by Aho (1968) and a less technical presentation is available in Hopcroft and Ullman (1979). Their relevance to linguistic issues is the subject of Gazdar (1988).

CHAPTER 5

PARSING, SEARCH AND AMBIGUITY

A key feature of a grammar is the assignment of syntactic structures to a phrase that is judged a legal sentence of the language described. In Chapter 8, we will see how these structures are a vital element in the compositional computation of meaning. At this point, however, we consider the problem of parsing, which involves actually computing the structures assigned to a given phrase by a given grammar. As a declarative description of a language, a grammar does not specify how syntactic analyses are to be computed, and there is a vast space of possible parsing algorithms, even for the CF-PSGs. In this chapter, we survey the main dimensions of variation within this space – namely, bottom up/top down – depth first/breadth first – and the issue of storing intermediate results. Parsing sentences of natural languages is plagued by problems of global and local ambiguity. We consider some of the characteristics of this ambiguity problem.

5.1   A simple parsing problem

We will begin this chapter by considering a very simple problem; namely, how we might set about parsing the English sentence 'MediCenter employed nurses' given only Grammar1 from Chapter 4. The problem is simple for two reasons:

(1)   The example sentence contains none of the phenomena that make parsing written English less than straightforward.

(2)   By choosing an example from written English, we get a head start, as the datum comes to us partially preparsed.

Let us briefly consider this second point. Written English employs a convention whereby words are set off from each other by spaces. But spoken English is not like that – words are not, in general, separated by silences, the obvious temporal analogue of white space on paper. Nor are their boundaries otherwise marked. So, for spoken English, indeed the spoken form of any natural language, the problem is significantly harder: the written analogue would be parsing 'M e d i C e n t e r e m p l o y e d n u r s e s'. Now the parser not only has to do what our parser will have to do, but it also has to determine the appropriate word boundaries in the string. If that does not seem intuitively very difficult, then consider 'T h e n e a r l y i n g o n e s e r r e d'. Actually, the problem with speech is even worse, since one effect of running spoken words together is to change or even omit the sounds that appear word-peripherally. The parsing of speech is, thankfully, a topic that falls outside the remit of this book. But the problem of a parser having to determine the position of syntactically relevant boundaries in the absence of 'white spaces' does not simply go away when we turn our attention from speech back to the written form. Consider the following correctly written Turkish sentence:

çöplüklerimizdekilerdenmiydi

which translates into English as 'Was it from those that were in our garbage cans?' Clearly, a parser for written Turkish is going to have to determine the boundaries of those syntactic and semantic elements whose counterparts in written English would be words set off with white space.

With these matters in mind, let us now turn back to parsing our three-word example. For convenience, we repeat Grammar1 in its entirety here.

Rule {simple sentence formation}
    S → NP VP.
Rule {transitive verb}
    VP → V NP.

Rule {intransitive verb}
 VP → V.
Word Dr Chan:
  \<cat> = NP.
Word nurses:
  \<cat> = NP.
Word MediCenter:
  \<cat> = NP.
Word patients:
  \<cat> = NP.
Word died:
  \<cat> = V.
Word employed:
  \<cat> = V.

Exercise 5.1 Write a transducer that will find word boundaries in 'scrunched' (that is, white space removed) strings of English words drawn from some small set such as the names of the digits. Your program should map (f i v e s e v e n t w o), say, into (five seven two). *[easy]*

5.2 Bottom-up parsing

Given our three-word sentence:

 MediCenter employed nurses.

we can see where the word boundaries are, but what else do we already know about this string? Well, thanks to the lexicon of Grammar1, we know what syntactic category the first word belongs to. So, we can label that word NP and proceed from there. What we have done is find the first place in the string that matches the RHS of a rule or lexical entry. We can then label the sequence of words or categories that matched the RHS of the rule with the LHS of the rule:

 NP_____
 MediCenter employed nurses.

One way of parsing involves repeating this operation, at each stage, using the sequence of highest-level labels as the new string to operate on. So, we now continue, trying to further rewrite the string 'NP employed nurses'. Given only that, we can ask if there is any rule in the grammar whose RHS is simply NP – for example, K → NP. If there is, then we could explore the possibility of allowing this NP to be dominated by K in the structure we are trying to build up. But there is no such rule, so we are forced to consider the next word in the string, which we find to be of category V:

NP_____ V_____

MediCenter employed nurses.

Our task would now appear to be that of attempting to group these categories together in a manner permitted by the grammar. First, we check (again!) if any rule simply has NP and nothing else on the RHS, but there are no such rules in Grammar1. Now we need to know if there is a rule that allows us to group the sequence NP V together. To determine this, we look at the RHS of each rule in Grammar1 to see if it has the form NP V. None of them do. Turning our attention to the second item, we can then ask if any RHS is identical to V and, in fact there is, in the shape of the rule that allows a VP to consist simply of a V. So, we can add this information to the parse tree that we are trying to build up:

VP_____

NP_____ V_____

MediCenter employed nurses.

Now that we have found a VP following the initial NP, we can go back to the beginning of the string and ask if we have an initial sequence that can be subsumed under some category. Since we are acting out a rather stupid algorithm here, we will once again check to see if the single initial NP can be found as an RHS. Since the rule set provided by Grammar1 is a constant and not something that varies over the course of the parse, the answer will again be no. With that out of the way, we check to see if NP VP can be found as an RHS, and the answer is, of course, that it can. The only rule having NP VP as its RHS has S as its LHS, so we augment our parse tree with an S spanning the initial NP and the immediately following VP that we found. We are now looking for rules whose RHS matches parts of the string 'S nurses'. There is no rule whose RHS is 'S' or 'S nurses'. When we look 'nurses' up in our lexicon, we find it to be an NP, and so we progress to the following situation:

S_____

VP_____

NP_____ V_____ NP___

MediCenter employed nurses.

At this point, however, we cannot proceed. S itself does not occur as an RHS, nor does S NP, and nor does NP. So, there is nothing we can do with the sequence. Our goal is to find an S spanning the entire string, but this route has led us to an S spanning the first two words in the string and a dangling unattached NP at the end. Clearly, we have gone wrong somewhere.

Faced with this impasse, we will backtrack to the last point at which we were faced with a choice and explore one or more other possibilities. In doing so, we will unload the parts of the parse tree that we built subsequent to the choice point. Let's go back to the following situation:

```
              VP_____
NP_____  V_____
MediCenter employed nurses.
```

We have just seen that putting the NP and VP together here as an S led nowhere. A VP by itself does not exhaust the RHS of any of the rules in our grammar, so the only thing left to do is to look up the final word in the dictionary (again!), annotate the structure accordingly, and see where we can go from there:

```
              VP_____
NP_____  V_____  NP___
MediCenter employed nurses.
```

At this point, a dim parsing algorithm will once again combine the initial NP and V into a sentence. However, when this fails to work out, it will eventually try something else and check if the sequence NP VP NP occurs as an RHS (it does not), then if VP NP does (it does not) and, finally, whether the last NP can be subsumed under some other category (we have already checked this NP-as-RHS issue several times – the answer remains no). Again, we face an impasse: assuming that the parse tree contains this VP leads nowhere, as we have seen by exhaustively checking all the possibilities. So, we must backtrack still further, ridding ourselves of this VP hypothesis as we do so. After some further thrashing around, we arrive at the following configuration:

```
NP_____  V_____  NP___
MediCenter employed nurses.
```

Given our implicit order of proceeding, the next thing to check is whether V NP occurs as an RHS. It does, in the shape of the other VP rule in our

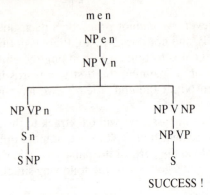

Figure 5.1   Search tree for bottom-up recognition.

grammar; that is, that which allows VP to dominate V followed by NP:

```
          _____VP_____
NP_____ V_____ NP___
MediCenter employed nurses.
```

Returning to the start of the sentence, we check (for the nth time) whether NP can exhaust an RHS, and then check if NP VP can. As previously, the answer to the latter question is yes, and so we can proceed to add S to our parse tree:

```
          _____S_____
          _____VP_____
NP_____ V_____ NP___
MediCenter employed nurses.
```

This S, unlike the one we found previously, spans the entire string, and so we have a success on our hands. The parsing strategy that we have been walking through has, at last, found a parse. If all we want is the first parse tree found and no others, then we can halt. If, however, we want our parser to find all the possible parsings of this string, then we will have to let it run a while longer. It will not find any more in this case, since this string is unambiguous with respect to Grammar1, but our parser only knows that it has found an S. It cannot know at this stage that this is the only spanning S to be found. To establish that, it must continue in just the manner we have already seen, chasing right to the end of every dead end until it has exhausted them all. But it would try our patience to follow it on this fruitless journey!

What has been illustrated is a kind of *bottom-up parsing*, as the parse tree is built from the bottom upwards. As we saw, bottom-up parsing involves searching through a space of alternatives, not all of which lead to a

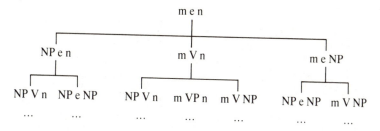

Figure 5.2 Redundancy through rewriting of lexical items.

successful solution. In Chapter 2, we discussed the notion of a search problem that involved exploring possible states, given a way of determining which possible states might arise from any state. As we saw there, it is convenient to display the possible states in a search problem as a *search tree*, with each state appearing above the states that could come next. Figure 5.1 shows part of the search tree for our bottom-up parser looking at the three-word sentence, where *m* represents MediCenter, *e* represents employed and *n* represents nurses.

A state of a bottom-up parsing process can be summarized by the sequence of highest-level labels of phrases that have been found. In fact, this is a characterization of a state of a bottom-up *recognizer*. For brevity, we only deal with recognizers in our search trees.

In our example, there is one main place where a choice has to be made. The choice is whether to rewrite the V into a VP or whether to continue and rewrite 'nurses' into an NP. In our example trace, the parser initially took the wrong decision here, and so had to back up and change its mind. Having made this decision, it eventually reached a dead end in the search tree, where a spanning sentence had not been found but no further rewritings were possible.

Note that we have not yet specified a precise algorithm for bottom-up parsing. Indeed, it is possible to imagine algorithms that involve much worse search spaces. For instance, in our example we have assumed in advance that there is no rule in the grammar like NP → MediCenter V which, although it does not initially apply, could later incorporate 'MediCenter' into a larger phrase, if that word is not immediately converted to an NP. So, we do not even consider failing to rewrite 'MediCenter' and moving on to 'employed' instead. The assumption that lexical items are only introduced in the grammar by rules whose RHSs are wholly lexical can obviously be enforced quite easily by the grammar writer. If this is done, then we can avoid search trees like that shown in Figure 5.2, where many states, like NP V n and m V NP, occur redundantly in different parts of the search space.

Another characteristic of our informal parser is that, having decided to rewrite NP V n into NP V NP, rather than NP VP n, it did not then

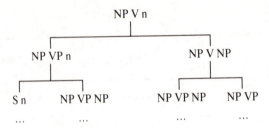

Figure 5.3 Redundancy through combining independent rewrites.

consider again rewriting the V into a VP, as this would again introduce redundancy, as shown in Figure 5.3.

We can write a very naive bottom-up parser quite easily in LISP (lib burecog). First of all, let us assume that we are provided with the rules of Grammar1, represented in LISP and stored in the global variable rules, as in Chapter 4. As in the previous discussion, we will present a *recognizer* rather than a parser, because this is simpler and the changes that make this into a parser are not great. We can think of determining whether a given string is grammatical as being the task of finding a sequence of rewrites that starts with the string and ends up with the symbol S, for instance:

```
(MediCenter employed nurses)
(MediCenter (V) nurses)
(MediCenter (V) (NP))
(MediCenter (VP))
((NP) (VP))
((S))
```

Each of these rewriting steps must be allowed by some rule of the grammar. For instance, the very last step is justified by the first rule saying that a sentence can be a noun phrase followed by a verb phrase. Notice that we have put grammatical categories inside lists to distinguish them from words. This is not necessary for this program, but it paves the way for programs that use more complex category descriptions. The function next, defined later, takes a list (representing a string of words and/or categories) as its argument and works out all possible ways of performing a single rewrite, using the rules of the grammar. Having obtained one of these rewrites, it calls next recursively on the new list. This next next finds out all possible rewrites of this, calling next on them, and so on. The original call of next, the calls of next generated by that, the calls of next generated by them, and so on, thus cause the whole search space of possible sequences of rewrites to be explored. Figure 5.4 shows part of the tree of next calls for the analysis of 'MediCenter employed nurses', where the words have been abbreviated as before. Notice that the tree of calls mirrors exactly the search tree.

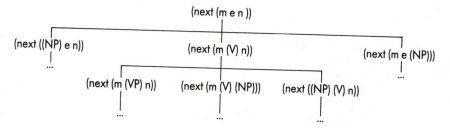

Figure 5.4   Call tree for bottom-up recognizer.

Here now is a possible definition for next:

```
(defun next (string)
  (if (equal string '((S)))
    (print '(yes))
    (do
      ((left nil (append left (list (car tape))))
       (tape string (cdr tape)))
      ((null tape))   ; do until end of tape
      (dolist (rule rules)
        (let ((newstring (rewrite tape (car rule) (cdr rule))))
          (if (null newstring)
            nil      ; rewrite failed
            (next (append left newstring))))))))
```

next finds all possible rewrites of its argument by working its way through the list from left to right. At any time, it keeps the list of items it has already worked through in the variable left and the list it still has to consider in tape. If it can find a rule in the grammar such that an initial portion of tape matches the body of the rule (using rewrite), then it can successfully produce a rewritten list and call next with it. The recursive next call is given a list consisting of all the elements to the left of the matched part, followed by the head of the grammar rule, followed by all the elements to the right of the matched part. The function rewrite is given the portion of the string after left and the LHS and RHS of a rule. It sees whether the elements of the RHS match the elements at the start of the string, and if so returns a new version of the string with the LHS substituted for the elements that the RHS matched:

```
(rewrite '((NP)(VP)(PP)) '(S) '((NP)(VP)))
((S) (PP))
```

Here is its definition:

```
(defun rewrite (string LHS RHS)
    (if (null RHS)              ; successful rewrite
      (cons LHS string)
      (if (null string)          ; end of string
        nil
        (if (equal (car string) (car RHS))
          (rewrite (cdr string) LHS (cdr RHS))
          nil))))              ; rule does not match
```

If we call next on a given list of atoms, when does the program terminate? The program only terminates when it has explored the whole search space; that is, when it has explored all possible ways in which the string could be a sentence. If there is at least one possible way, then, somewhere deep in the tree, a call of next will be generated with ((S)) as its argument. This call will print out the message (yes) and will then terminate without any more calls on next. Of course, other calls on next will, in general, have to run before the search is complete and the program as a whole terminates.

To make our recognizer into a parser, all we need to do is to enhance our representation of the sequence of words and categories to include parse trees instead of categories. Thus, our successful rewriting sequence will now look as follows:

```
(MediCenter employed nurses)
(MediCenter (V employed) nurses)
(MediCenter (V employed) (NP nurses))
(MediCenter (VP (V employed) (NP nurses)))
((NP MediCenter) (VP (V employed) (NP nurses)))
((S (NP MediCenter) (VP (V employed) (NP nurses))))
```

To implement this, we need to introduce a couple of changes in the next function. First of all, the termination condition needs to be changed, so that any tree labelled by an S is displayed when it appears as the only element in the list. In fact, we can generalize this to allow for any single tree to be accepted as a solution:

```
(if (equal (length string) 1)
    ...
```

Secondly, when next is called recursively, the new list should not contain just the LHS of the rule, but should contain the category label of the head, followed by the subtrees that have been found in the old list. Moreover, if the elements stored in the old list are parse trees, rather than simple categories, matching the sequence of elements with the body of a rule (where the elements are simple categories) is not so straightforward. We thus require the actions done for each rule in the grammar to be replaced by:

```
(let ((needed_others (initial_segment (cdr rule) tape)))
   (if (null needed_others)
      nil   ; rewrite failed
      (next (append left (list (cons (caar rule) (car needed_others)))) (cadr needed_others))))
```

where initial_segment is a function to be defined. initial_segment takes as its first argument the RHS of a rule; that is, an arbitrary list of individual atoms and category labels in lists, such as ((NP) and (NP)). As its second argument, it takes a sequence of items that could appear in the input list for next; that is, an arbitrary list of individual words and parse trees (represented as lists), such as ((NP Dr Chan) and (NP nurses) (V died)). It decomposes its second argument into two sublists and returns a list containing these as its result. The first sublist is the initial portion of the list that 'matched' against the rule body, while the second sublist is the rest of the list. For instance:

```
(initial_segment '((NP) and (NP))
   '((NP Dr Chan) and (NP nurses) (V died)))

(((NP DR CHAN) AND (NP NURSES)) ((V DIED)))
```

There is a very large space of possible parsing strategies and the strategy that we have walked through is merely one among many. But it serves to illustrate the kind of way that a parser works, the kinds of questions it needs to ask, and the kinds of blind alleys and wasteful repetitions that make the simplest algorithms inefficient. The basic observation to make about our parser is that it works from left to right: it does everything it can with the first item before exploring what it can do with the first two items, and so on. Clearly, there is no logical necessity about this. We could just as well have described a parser that worked from right to left. These two possibilities by no means exhaust the candidates: we could, to choose examples at random, have scanned the string looking for a verb and then worked outwards from the verb, or we could have worked zigzag fashion across the structure we were building. Notice, however, that parsers that attempt to parse a natural language as it is being produced, either as it is spoken or as it is typed, are forced to adopt a strategy that is basically left to right.

Our parser was bottom up, driven entirely by the data presented to it and building successive layers of syntactic abstraction on the base provided by that data. Parsers that work bottom up and from left to right, when they also index the rules of the grammar on the leftmost RHS category, are common enough to have been given a usefully mnemonic name 'left-corner parsers'. One major problem with bottom-up parsing is rules that have empty RHSs – that is ε-productions. If we had replaced our

VP rules with the following rules (where VCOMP is a category of verb complements):

> Rule {verb phrase}
> VP → V VCOMP.
>
> Rule {verb complement is NP}
> VCOMP → NP.
>
> Rule {verb complement is empty}
> VCOMP → .

which generate the same strings, we would have had difficulties. For if there is a rule with an empty RHS, that rule applies *anywhere* in the input string. Going bottom up, our parser is thus able to 'find' a phrase of the relevant category wherever it looks. With these rules, our parser would have been able to put VCOMPs all over the place and would have had to deal with intermediate structures like:

> VCOMP   NP   VCOMP   V   VCOMP   NP   VCOMP   VCOMP   VCOMP
>   MediCenter   employed   nurses

Fortunately, there is a simple algorithm to convert any CF-PSG to a grammar with no ε-productions that generates the same set of strings. The algorithm will not, in general, produce a grammar that induces the same parse trees as the original, however, and this may be a problem if we care about the syntactic structures that are built.

Exercise 5.2   Write a program that takes a grammar represented as a list of rules and carries out ε-production removal.   [*hard*]

Exercise 5.3   Run the recognition program with next traced to see what the search space looks like for the sentence in the text and grammar. How big is the search space? Where does the search space branch to the greatest extent?   [*easy*]

Exercise 5.4   Change the recognition program to terminate (almost) immediately it has shown that a string is grammatical. *Hint*: Make next return a result to indicate whether a solution has been found. Alternatively, define a top-level function that calls next and make use of throw and catch as in the finite-state recognizer fsrecog.   [*easy*]

Exercise 5.5 Define initial_segment and hence complete the parser. [*intermediate*]

Exercise 5.6   Write an improved version of the parser which avoids some of the redundancies in the search space (of the kinds mentioned) and which incorporates the heuristic that all lexical items appear only in lexical rules. *Hint*: When next spawns a recursive call for a possible rule R at a possible position P in the string, it will already have spawned recursive calls for all possible rules applying starting to the left of that position. To avoid duplicate analyses being tried by these other calls, the call that applies R at P should ideally prevent any of its descendants from applying one of these rules starting to the left of P. It can do this by requiring that any rule applied by a descendant use at least one of the items in the string which is at position P or to the right of it. next can be given an extra numerical argument pos which specifies that any rule used should use at least one item from the last pos items in the string.   [*hard*]

5.3   Top-down parsing

The naive bottom-up parser of Section 5.2 never formed hypotheses about what it was looking for or used such hypotheses to decide its next move. It only ever checked rules to see if there was a legitimate way of putting together the pieces already to hand. That is why it encountered problems with rules that involved putting together 'empty space'. By contrast, a pure (left-to-right) *top-down* (depth-first) *parser* would have proceeded roughly as follows:

> I am looking for an S.
>> What can an S consist of?
>> An S can consist of an NP followed by a VP.
>> So I need to look for an NP first.
>>> What can an NP consist of?
>>> There are no grammar rules expanding NP.
>>> There is a lexical entry listing 'nurses'
>>>> as a member of the category NP.
>>> Is the first word in the string 'nurses'?
>>> No.
>>> There is a lexical entry listing 'MediCenter'
>>>> as a member of the category NP.
>>> Is the first word in the string 'MediCenter'?
>>> Yes.
>> I have found an NP consisting of the word 'MediCenter'.
>> I now need to look for a VP.
>>> What can a VP consist of?
>> A VP can consist of a V.
>> I now need to look for a V.
>>> What can a V consist of?

***

There are no grammar rules expanding V.
There is a lexical entry listing 'died'
  as a member of the category V.
Is the next word in the string 'died'?
No.
There is a lexical entry listing 'employed'
  as a member of the category V.
Is the next word in the string 'employed'?
Yes.
  I have found a V consisting of the word 'employed'.
I have found a VP consisting of a V
  consisting of the word 'employed'.
I have found an S consisting of:
  an NP consisting of the word 'MediCenter'
  and a VP consisting of
  a V consisting of the word 'employed'.
Have I reached the end of the string?
No.
Oh dear, I must have done something wrong.
Try going back to *** and doing something different.
  I still need to look for a VP.
    What can a VP consist of?
    A VP can also consist of a V followed by an NP.
    I now need to look for a V.
      What can a V consist of?
    There are no grammar rules expanding V.
    There is a lexical entry listing 'died'
      as a member of the category V.
    Is the next word in the string 'died'?
    No.
    There is a lexical entry listing 'employed'
      as a member of the category V.
    Is the next word in the string 'employed'?
    Yes.
  I have found a V consisting of the word 'employed'.
Now I need to look for an NP.
  What can an NP consist of?
  There are no grammar rules expanding NP.
  There is a lexical entry listing 'nurses'
    as a member of the category NP.
  Is the first word in the string 'nurses'?
  Yes.
I have found an NP consisting of the word 'nurses'.
I have found a VP consisting of:
  a V consisting of the word 'employed'
  followed by an NP consisting of the word 'nurses'.
I have found an S consisting of:
  an NP consisting of the word 'MediCenter'
  and a VP consisting of

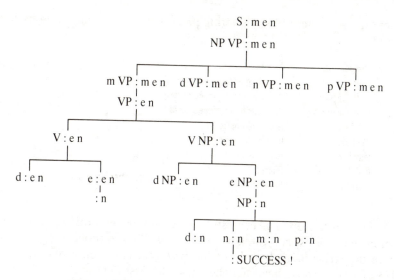

Figure 5.5   Search tree for top-down recognition.

a V consisting of the word 'employed'
  followed by an NP consisting of the word 'nurses'.
Have I reached the end of the string?
Yes.
I have succeeded.

Figure 5.5 shows the search tree for top-down parsing of the example sentence 'MediCenter employed nurses'. In top-down recognition, a state can be characterized by a sequence of goals and a sequence of remaining words. In our tree, we separate the goals from the remaining words with a colon (:). Thus, d NP : e n describes the state of the recognizer when it is trying to find the word 'died' followed by an NP and when the remaining words are 'employed nurses'.

We can write a top down recognizer similar to our bottom-up recognizer. Whereas a bottom-up recognizer needs to know only about what it has successfully found at any point, a top-down recognizer also needs to keep track of what it is trying to find – that is, its *goals*. So, our top-down version of next will take a first argument which is the list of categories (represented by names inside lists) and words (represented by LISP atoms) that it is trying to find, in the order it is to find them. When we call next originally, this list will simply be ((S)), indicating that the recognizer just needs to find an (S). The second argument to next will be the input string (list of atoms) which is to provide the words to satisfy these goals. Whereas in the bottom-up case we could think of a recognition as a sequence of rewrites of the original string resulting in ((S)), we must now think of generating sequences of goals–string pairs, with success indicated by both becoming empty:

Goals	String
((S))	(MediCenter employed nurses)
((NP) (VP))	(MediCenter employed nurses)
(MediCenter (VP))	(MediCenter employed nurses)
((VP))	(employed nurses)
((V) (NP))	(employed nurses)
(employed (NP))	(employed nurses)
((NP))	(nurses)
(nurses)	(nurses)
()	()

As before, each step in a successful sequence must be justified. If the first item in the goal list is a category, we are justified in proceeding to a pair where the string is unaltered but the first goal has been replaced by the RHS of a rule whose head matches it. If the first item in the goal list is a word which is the same as the first word in the string, we are justified in proceeding to a pair where the two identical words have been deleted.

So much for the legal moves. Our approach to searching through all possibilities (in lib tdrecog) will be as in the previous program: given a goals–string pair, next works out all the pairs that could immediately follow and calls next recursively on them. Thus, once again the tree of next calls will mirror the search space exactly. Here is our top-down version of next:

```
(defun next (goals string)
    (if (and (null goals) (null string))
        (print '(yes))
    (if (listp (car goals))
        (dolist (rule rules)
            (if (equal (car goals) (car rule))
                (next (append (cdr rule) (cdr goals)) string)))
        (if (equal (car goals) (car string))
            (next (cdr goals) (cdr string))))))
```

If you watch this program at work, a certain lack of intelligence manifests itself. For instance, from the state:

Goals	String
((V) (NP))	(believed nurses)

it generates all of the following:

(died (NP))	(believed nurses)
(employed (NP))	(believed nurses)
(approved (NP))	(believed nurses)
(appeared (NP))	(believed nurses)
(believed (NP))	(believed nurses)

that is, one state for every possible verb. If there were 500 known verbs, this would lead to 500 states to explore, even though only one of them could be equal to the next word in the string. This is indeed what a pure top-down analyzer would do. A more sensible move would be to use lexical rules bottom up but other grammar rules top down.

Top-down parsing does not have any problem with ε-productions, but (when performed left to right) encounters trouble with rules that exhibit *left recursion*. Here is another way we could have rewritten our VP rules:

Rule {simple verb phrase}
  VP → V.

Rule {complex verb phrase}
  VP → VP NP.

but now the rules will in fact generate more strings. Of these rules, the second is left recursive in that the first symbol on the RHS is the same as the LHS. With left-recursive rules in a grammar, a left-to-right, top-down parser will get into an infinite loop if it makes the wrong choices, and if we are asking for all parses it will, of course, in the end have to try all possible choices:

I now need to look for a VP.
What can a VP consist of?
A VP can consist of a VP followed by an NP.
  I now need to look for a VP.
  What can a VP consist of?
  A VP can consist of a VP followed by an NP.
    I now need to look for a VP.
    What can a VP consist of?
    A VP can consist of a VP followed by an NP.
    ...

When we are using complex feature-based categories, left recursion also arises when the first category on the RHS of a rule is more general than the one on the LHS (see Chapter 7 for a fuller discussion of the issues that features give rise to in parsing). Again, it is possible to transform a left-recursive grammar into an equivalent one with no left-recursive rules, and one that generates exactly the same set of strings (although it will not assign the same structures).

Exercise 5.7 Write a program that takes a grammar represented as a list of rules and converts it into another list of rules that generates the same language but from which all left recursion has been eliminated. [*hard*]

Exercise 5.8 Run the top-down recognition program with test grammars and sentences. Use tracing to look at the search tree. Under what circumstances will this program produce a search tree the same size as the bottom-up program? [*easy*]

Exercise 5.9 What would be involved in making this program into a parser? Why would it be more difficult than for the bottom-up program? The library program tdparse implements a top-down parser in a slightly different way. Its function find_trees is provided with a single goal and a string and returns a list of lists of the form:

    (<tree> <remainder>)

where <tree> is a parse tree for a phrase of type goal appearing at the start of the string and <remainder> is the list of words that remain after that phrase. For instance:

    (find_trees '(VP) '(employed nurses))

    (((VP (V EMPLOYED))
     (NURSES))
    ((VP (V EMPLOYED) (NP NURSES))
     ()))

find_trees makes use of another function find_subtrees, which takes a list of goals and produces a similar result, except that there are lists of parse trees:

    (find_subtrees '((NP)(VP)) '(MediCenter employed nurses))

    ((((NP MEDICENTER) (VP (V EMPLOYED) (NP NURSES)))
     ())
    (((NP MEDICENTER) (VP (V EMPLOYED)))
     (NURSES)))

Run this program to parse the sentence 'MediCenter employed nurses' and describe in English the sequence of actions that takes place, including what the parser looks for in the string and what parse trees it builds. [*intermediate*]

5.4 Comparing strategies

As with the case of the left-to-right, right-to-left dichotomy, the limiting cases of pure top-down and pure bottom-up by no means exhaust the strategies possible on this dimension. We could, for example, have a parsing strategy that begins by operating bottom up, until it has identified the categories of all the lexical items, and then operates top down in its search for the higher-level syntactic structures. With a more sophisticated grammar than Grammar1, we might employ a mixed parsing strategy that depended on the feature system: constituents carrying one class of feature would be hypothesized top down, whereas words identified as carrying features from another class would trigger attempts to build up the relevant constituents from the bottom.

How are we to decide which of top-down or bottom-up parsing would be better for a given application, or whether a mixed strategy is called for? It helps to consider the shape of the parsing search spaces for example sentences. Looking at the foregoing top-down and bottom-up search spaces, we see that a great deal of the branching in the top-down space occurs at the level of lexical items. If we altered our top-down algorithm to look ahead at the next remaining word, before spawning a state that required a specific lexical item, this would make the two trees for our example have exactly the same amount of branching. To see real differences between top-down and bottom-up search trees, we have to consider more complex grammars and sentences. Bottom-up parsing can try to build a phrase that top-down parsing would never consider, because such a phrase could never occur in the context of the surrounding phrases. Conversely, top-down parsing may hypothesize many kinds of phrase that bottom-up parsing will not consider, because relevant lexical items are not present.

The shape of the search trees does not, however, tell us everything about parsing efficiency. In the last paragraph, it was suggested changing the way the top-down parser deals with the prediction of lexical items, but in so doing we are just moving the equality test slightly forwards in time, and not affecting the number of such tests that would have to be made. In general, an important factor is the *number* of rules tried at each point of the analysis, because even rules that cannot actually be used in the analysis can cost the parser if they have to be tried. The number of rules tried depends crucially on the extent to which we can avoid repeating previous unsuccessful tries on material that has not changed, and also on the way in which the rules are stored. We will consider the problem of remembering previous rule failures in Section 5.6 as well as in the next chapter, but let us concentrate, for now, on the rule storage issue.

For top-down parsing, it is common practice to index rules by their LHS categories, so that it is easy to go from a category to all the rules that could expand it. For bottom-up parsing, a rule can be indexed by its leftmost RHS category (for left–right parsing) or by some other category, such as a category that appears in very few rules. Treating a lexical rule top down thus involves considering all the lexical rules for the relevant category. On the other hand, treating it bottom up only involves looking at the rules with a particular word on the RHS, and we would not expect there to be many of these. In general, we would like to parse instances of a category bottom up if there are many rules for that category but the indexing categories on the RHS of the rules index very few rules. Conversely, we would like to parse instances of a category top down if there are few rules for that category and the RHSs of those rules contain indexing categories that index many rules. These competing requirements may not, of course, be reconcilable.

5.5   Breadth-first and depth-first search

All the parsers presented so far have been depth-first parsers. A *depth-first* strategy is one in which each hypothesis is pushed as far as it can be before entering upon the exploration of another hypothesis. Thus, our bottom-up parser went as far as it could with the hypothesis that the verb 'employed' was the sole content of a dominating verb phrase before being forced to abandon this idea and explore instead the hypothesis of putting the verb together with the following noun phrase. A depth-first strategy then is a quintessentially sequential one. By contrast, a *breadth-first* strategy maintains a number of hypotheses at the same time, advancing each in turn by a single step. Ideally, as time goes by, hypotheses fail and the breadth-first device is left with a smaller space of hypotheses to consider.

Such a strategy is ideally suited to implementation on parallel machinery, but can be readily implemented by a sequential machine that distributes turns, rather like the way in which a card dealer distributes cards prior to a game like bridge. Here is how a particular bottom-up, breadth-first parser might have gone about parsing our three-word example sentence. Notice that 'a' and 'b' have been used in the following simply to make it clear which constituent is being referred to – they do not form part of the category name:

Assign categories to each lexical item:

MediCenter:	NPa.
employed:	V.
nurses:	NPb.

Check each category to see if it exhausts an RHS:

NPa:	no.
V:	can be dominated by VPa.
NPb:	no.

Check each adjacent pair of categories to see if they exhaust an RHS:

NPa V:	no.
NPa VPa:	can be dominated by Sa.
V NPb:	can be dominated by VPb.
VPa NPb:	no.

Check each triple of categories to see if they exhaust an RHS:

NPa V NPb:	no.
NPa VPa NPb:	no.

Check each new category to see if it exhausts an RHS:

VPa:	no.
VPb:	no.
Sa:	no.

Check each new adjacent pair of categories to see if they exhaust an RHS:

Sa NPb:	no.
NPa VPb:	can be dominated by Sb. [SUCCESS]

Notice that the left-to-right/right-to-left distinction is of much less potential significance in the context of a breadth-first parser than it is in the case of a depth-first one. Once again, the breadth- versus depth-first distinction is a dimension rather than a simple binary choice for the parser as a whole. It is quite common, for example, for parsers to begin by assigning all the words in the string to their (multiple possible) lexical categories (thus working in a breadth-first manner), but to proceed from then on in a largely depth-first manner.

Since the digital computers that we commonly use cannot do more than one thing at a time, when we implement a breadth-first search algorithm we need to introduce a device to enable the machine to spend its time evenly in different parts of the search space. We can do this in a simple breadth-first recognizer by collecting all the alternative possible states into a list. As this is a bottom-up recognizer, we can summarize all we need to know about a state by the list of words and categories that we have found so far (as in lib burecog). The breadth-first program proceeds in a sequence of cycles. Each cycle involves going through all the alternatives in the list, working out for each one what new states could follow from it. These new states are all collected into a list, which forms the list to be processed in the next cycle. Here is the breadth-first bottom-up recognizer:

```
(defun recognize (string)
  (do ((alternatives (list string))) ((null alternatives))
    (setq alternatives (next_states_list alternatives))))

(defun next_states_list (list)
  (if (null list)
      '()
      (append
        (next_states (car list))
        (next_states_list (cdr list)))))

(defun next_states (string)
  (if (equal (length string) 1)
      (print (car string)))
  (do (
      (left () (append left (list (car remaining))))
      (remaining string (cdr remaining))
      (results ())
```

```
   ((null remaining) results)   ; do until end of string
   (dolist (rule rules)
      (let ((newstring (rewrite remaining (car rule) (cdr rule))))
         (if newstring
            (setq results (cons (append left newstring) results))))))))
```

The function recognize is to be called with a list of words as its argument. The list of alternative states to explore from is kept in the variable alternatives. Each cycle involves going through the alternatives, computing next states. These are all collected up, using next_states_list, to form the new alternatives. The core of the function, matching parts of the string with the RHSs of rules (function rewrite), is as in our depth-first, bottom-up recognizer. next_states_list is given a list of search states and returns the result of appending together the next states from all the states in that list. The crucial function is, however, next_states, which returns the list of next states that follow from a given state. This function works its way down the string, keeping the remaining elements in the list remaining and the elements already encountered in left. It tries applying each possible rule at each position in the string (remaining holding the part of the string whose beginning will be matched against rule RHSs).

Exercise 5.10 Convert this recognizer (the code is in lib bubrecog) into a parser in the same way as was done with the depth-first, bottom-up recognizer. [*hard*]

5.6 Storing intermediate results

We noted earlier that a feature of our first parser was that it failed to store any intermediate results. That is a key reason for its obsessively time-wasting activity in rechecking things that it has already checked and which cannot have changed. You can think of it as an amnesiac if you like. But there has been a subtle shift in the breadth-first parser that we have just presented semi-formally: this device checks each *new* category to see if it exhausts an RHS and checks each *new* adjacent pair of categories to see if they exhaust an RHS. This makes it slightly harder to program, since the implementation now has to make it possible to keep a record of which categories and pairs have already been considered. Indeed, the program we have shown does not have this feature. But the pay-off is a more efficient parser that does not spend its time thrashing about exploring dead ends that it has already been down half a dozen times. This issue of storage of intermediate results is independent of the three distinctions already discussed, even though any parser needs to store *some* states, simply to remember what it is currently doing; in particular, a breadth-first parser, of necessity, has to remember the multiple hypothesis states that are currently being entertained. Storage of intermediate results also turns out to be the key to efficient parsing in a way that the other distinctions are not – at least, not in general. In Chapter 6, we will look in some detail at chart parsers, which are parsers that use a data structure called a chart to encode all intermediate results obtained in the course of a parse. The cost of this increase in efficiency is not simply one of implementation complexity: there is also a cost in terms of the space requirements of the parsing program.

Such a time versus space trade-off is a familiar one in computer science. Consequently, we would expect simple-minded amnesiac phrase structure parsers, like the one we have sketched out, to be linear in space, but exponential in time, in the worst case. This means that, at worst, they will make space (that is, memory) demands that vary in direct proportion (hence linear) to the length of the input string measured, in number of words, which is a very parsimonious use of space, but make time demands proportional to a constant k raised to the power of the string length measure – thus, $t = k^3$ for a three-word string, $t = k^{11}$ for an 11-word string, and so on. Such a worst-case demand for time is typically quite unacceptable for anything but the shortest strings. By contrast, the kind of phrase structure parser that stores intermediate results, such as those discussed in Chapter 6, can be expected to make space demands that are at worst quadratic in the length of the string; that is, they are proportional to n^2 where n is the length of the string. This is worse than linear but acceptable for strings of the length that are typically used in natural language communication. The time demands, on the other hand, are at worst cubic in the length of the string; that is, they are proportional to n^3 where n is the length of the string. This latter figure is really not good enough, but is vastly better than the exponential worst case just considered, and, in practice, this theoretical worst case of n^3 will be rarely, almost certainly never, encountered with the kinds of grammars appropriate to natural languages and the kind of strings such parsers are standardly faced with. The cubic worst-case time efficiency problem for natural language parsers, to the extent that it is a problem at all, is completely dwarfed in practice by a much more serious problem, that of pervasive natural language ambiguity. It is to this that we turn in the following section. The efficiency figures we have just been considering all relate to the time (or space) taken to recognize a string; that is, to the time to decide whether it is grammatical. The time taken to enumerate all parses of a string is affected by the degree of ambiguity and in the worst case is exponential.

5.7 Ambiguity

Let us add a single entry to the lexicon of Grammar1:

```
Word nurses:
    <cat> = V.
```

This now allows Grammar1 to admit sentences such as 'Dr Chan nurses patients'. What we have done is infect the lexicon of Grammar1 with a lexical ambiguity caused by the presence of this new entry alongside the existing entry for 'nurses':

```
Word nurses:
    <cat> = NP.
```

The introduction of this lexical ambiguity into Grammar1 does not mean that Grammar1 can now generate any ambiguous sentences – it cannot. If 'nurses' occurs as the first word or the third word of a Grammar1 sentence, then it must be of category NP, whereas if it occurs as the second word, then it must be of category V. However, this lexical ambiguity is going to cause extra work for at least one of the parsers already considered: a bottom-up parser finding 'nurses' will assign it to both the V category and the NP category, and explore where each trail leads.

Lexical ambiguity of this kind is omnipresent in languages like English. Most English words are nouns and many English nouns can be used as verbs. Moreover the ending '-s' is used both by almost all English nouns as their orthographic plural form and by almost all English verbs as their orthographic third-person singular form. The result is a large number of possibilities for ambiguity. To take another example from the many available, consider words of the form 'Xer'. Many of these, such as 'smoother' and 'cleaner', can either mean 'one that Xes' or mean 'more X'. Or consider words ending in '-ing' and compare the adjectival sense found in 'driving rain' with the verbal sense found in 'driving Chevrolets'. Open any English dictionary at a randomly selected page and look at the words listed on it: most of them will be given as belonging to more than one part of speech, or more than one syntactic category in our terminology, and most of them will be given as having more than one meaning. If a parser is part of a system intended to map English sentences into meanings, then it has to cope with both these aspects of lexical ambiguity. In contrast, an experimental or toy system engaged simply in assigning syntactic structures to strings can, if it chooses, simply ignore lexical meaning ambiguities that are not paralleled by a categorial ambiguity. Thus, for example, the semantic ambiguity of the noun 'bank' has no syntactic correlate in American English. (In British English, 'the bank are pressing me for repayment' is grammatical on the financial institution reading, but Americans find it ungrammatical on either reading.)

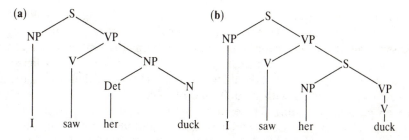

Figure 5.6   An example showing combined lexical and structural ambiguity.

There is a distinction to be made in principle between lexical ambiguity and structural ambiguity although, in practice, the former often gives rise to the latter, and is thus bound up with it. An American English sentence like 'I walked to the bank' contains a purely lexical ambiguity due to the two different senses of the noun 'bank': no structural ambiguity is involved. By contrast, a sentence like 'I observed the boy with a telescope' contains a purely structural ambiguity, corresponding to whether the speaker or the boy is in possession of the telescope, and no relevant lexical ambiguities. Often, we find the two together, as in the classic 'I saw her duck', where the structural ambiguity between sentential and NP complements to the verb 'saw' is triggered by the lexical ambiguity of 'her' (accusative pronominal NP versus possessive pronominal determiner) and 'duck' (verb of motion versus noun naming species of aquatic fowl), as illustrated in Figure 5.6.

Notice that ambiguity is potentially multiplicative rather than simply additive: a string containing one 2-way ambiguous item and one 3-way ambiguous item could, although it need not, have as many as six different structures (or meanings) as a result, not merely five as addition would suggest. Sometimes, other syntactic considerations ensure that the actual number of readings is less than the arithmetical potential maximum. Thus, 'I saw her duck' only has two readings, not four, despite the presence of two 2-way lexically ambiguous items in the string. Often, however, especially where purely structural ambiguity is concerned, the actual number of available readings coincides with or approaches the arithmetic maximum. What is disturbing for parser and grammar designers is that this figure can get very large, even for strings of a length typically encountered in practice. We will take a look at the primary sources of such multiplicative ambiguity shortly, but before we do so there are one or two matters in need of clarification.

In talking about ambiguity in this book, we are always concerned with what might be called grammatically available ambiguity, as opposed to some more intuitive notion. Thus, intuitively, 'flying planes made her duck' is unambiguous and has only the reading in which planes that were flying caused an animate female entity to move the upper part of her body to avoid them. But our intuitions make only this reading available to us (unreflectingly, at least) because, presumably, they are informed by a knowledge of planes, flying, and so on. As far as the syntax of English is concerned, and thus as far as a syntactically based parser for English is concerned, this sentence is ambiguous and has no less than four distinct structures associated with it, only one of which corresponds to the intuitively perceived reading. The expression 'flying planes' has two structures, which can be paraphrased as 'planes that fly' and 'the act of flying planes', as does 'made her duck', and these two 2-way ambiguities multiply out. This may seem perverse, but it is virtually inescapable: only a parser that could bring the meanings of the subexpressions together with sophisticated, wide-ranging, real-world knowledge (about ducks, planes, and so forth) could hope to escape constructing the three intuitively bizarre but grammatically available readings in a principled manner. In Chapters 8 and 10, we will consider limited ways in which semantic and pragmatic information can be used to filter out inappropriate parses, but there is no known general solution to the problem.

Returning to the main thread of this section, we will now consider the three major sources of pure structural ambiguity in English (and many other languages):

- PP attachment,

- coordination, and

- noun–noun compounding.

In English, prepositional phrases (PPs) can attach themselves, normally in a constituent-final position, to constituents of almost any syntactic category – sentences, verb phrases, noun phrases and adjectival phrases to name but four. This means that if we have a nest of constituents, all of them nested to the right, and a single final PP, then we have a degree of ambiguity that varies with the depth of the nest. This is best illustrated diagrammatically, as shown in Figure 5.7. Often, the differences in interpretation between these attachment positions can be quite subtle. Consider, for example, the various readings of 'I can leave for 10 minutes'.

If you look back to Grammar2 in Chapter 4, you will see a rule for coordination which, in a slightly simplified form, looks like this:

Rule {coordination}
$X \rightarrow X C X$.

where X can be any category and C can be realized as 'and' or 'or'. There is a small but crucial difference between this rule and the rule that you will find given, implicitly or explicitly, in logic textbooks for the logical

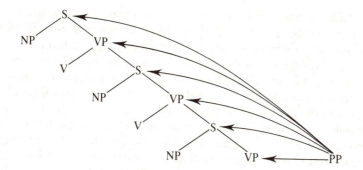

Figure 5.7 Possibilities for PP attachment.

counterparts of English 'and' and 'or'. The rule logicians use, in our notation, is:

Rule {unambiguous coordination}
X → (X C X).

The parentheses, which are expressions of the language being defined although not expressions having a meaning of their own, make all the difference in that they ensure that the sentences of logic are never ambiguous: you have to say either '(P and (Q or R))' or '((P and Q) or R)' and you are not allowed to say 'P and Q or R'. English and many other languages are just the opposite: they more or less force an ambiguous form on the user. Since coordination, like modification by PP, is one of the most frequently used constructions, the ambiguity of sentences like 'Mayumi and Hans or Beryl left early' is a real problem for natural language parsers. Programming languages sometimes *look* as if they are as ambiguous as English in respect of such constructions, but appearances are misleading: normally, the language defines an explicit precedence hierarchy among the operators and this eliminates the potential for ambiguity.

There is a sense in which the phrase 'widget hammer' is ambiguous: it could mean the same as 'widget used as hammer', 'hammer for hitting widgets', 'hammer used by widgets' and numerous other things beside. But this ambiguity is not structural. There is only one way in which two nouns can be put together in a fixed order. But now consider 'town widget hammer'. This is at least 2-way structurally ambiguous and can be parsed as ((town widget) hammer) or (town (widget hammer)), and thus gives rise to just the same issue as coordination. Like the latter, noun–noun compounding is extremely common in English, especially official, technical and bureaucratic English. You do not have to look hard to find things like 'Judiciary plea bargain settlement account audit'. Assuming that only binary noun combination is permitted, this innocent-looking bit of jargon has no less than 42 distinct structural descriptions.

Now consider a sentence from a press release with a couple of noun–noun compounds, a couple of PP modifiers at the end, as well as a few 'ands' and 'ors' for good measure. Since ambiguities multiply out, such a sentence may have literally tens of thousands of different structural descriptions, only one of which is associated with the intended meaning of the sentence used. This kind of ambiguity is not a theoretical problem (at least, not in the present context), but it is a very real practical problem for those who have to write parsers that are actually expected to form a component of a useful natural language system. In fact, there are two problems, one of which is how to determine what the intended structure is, which is not really the parser's problem at all. The other problem is how to cope with the sheer size of the set of partial structures that will be created during the parse of a fairly ambiguous string. A partial solution to the latter problem is provided by the chart data structure, introduced in Chapter 6, but more radical moves are probably called for.

Exercise 5.11   Write a small grammar for a fragment of English with, say, a dozen or more words in its lexicon, each of which belongs to at least two syntactic categories used by the syntactic rules. Study the behaviour, when using this grammar, of the various parsers developed in response to earlier exercises.   [*easy*]

Exercise 5.12   Devise a grammar and lexicon that will allow for the ambiguity of 'I saw her duck' and 'flying planes made her duck', and examine the behaviour of the various parsers already developed on these sentences.   [*easy*]

Exercise 5.13   Devise a grammar that will allow PP modifiers, coordination and noun–noun compounding. Using one of the parsers already written, explore how many distinct parses you get for a range of examples admitted by this grammar.   [*intermediate*]

5.8   Determinism and lookahead

Our discussion in the previous section concerned itself almost wholly with what we shall call global ambiguity; that is, cases where an expression is correctly assigned two or more structures and where those structures persist, or carry over, into the larger structures of which the expression forms a part. But of equal concern to the designer of parsers is the phenomenon of local ambiguity; that is, cases where an expression is correctly assigned two or more structures and where those structures may or may not persist, or carry over, into the larger structures of which the expression forms a part. The parsing of a wholly unambiguous sentence may nonetheless involve the exploration of a great deal of local ambiguity en route to the ultimate, single, structural description of the whole. Consider, for example, a right-to-left, bottom-up, depth-first parser working on the sentence:

The surgeon whose most famous pupil was Dr Chan founded MediCenter.

Such a parser may well try to build an analysis in which 'Dr Chan founded MediCenter' is a constituent, even though, ultimately, no such constituent is involved in the structure of the sentence. This sort of activity, as opposed to activity spent on global ambiguities, is time wasting, and much effort and ingenuity in computational linguistics has gone into trying to find ways to minimize or eliminate it.

One project aimed at its elimination can usefully be called the 'determinism' project, inspired originally by the work of Marcus. The aim of this project is to construct parsers that will parse (unambiguous) sentences deterministically; that is, construct parsers that (almost) never get fooled by local ambiguities, never have to backtrack, never change their mind, but which march inexorably to the single, correct, structural description. Why '(almost) never'? Well, 'never' may well be too ambitious. The human parser gags on certain unambiguous strings – those that have come to be known as garden path sentences, as in:

The horse raced past the barn fell.

The prime number few.

The granite rocks during the earthquake.

Since humans have difficulty with such examples, it is not unreasonable to permit a computer parser to also. In fact, many of those engaged in the determinism project have had cognitive science goals in mind, rather than engineering ones, since they have been attempting to model what they take the human parser to be like, not attempting to build fast parsers that never fail on well-formed strings.

Lookahead involves looking a bounded distance ahead in the string before deciding how to interpret a word or sequence of words. It can be regarded as a very constrained form of backtracking. Information about the frequency of different syntactic constructions may well have played a part in the evolution of the human parser and can be used in making plausible decisions, when lookahead does not suggest a single possibility. Deterministic parsers generally achieve adequate performance using a combination of lookahead and heuristics about the relative frequencies of different constructions.

Although Marcus-type parsers will only parse CFLs, they employ a more procedural notion of syntactic rule than that considered in Chapter 4. More recent work in this tradition has, however, employed the CF-PSG format for grammars and attempted to show how existing deterministic parsing techniques from computer science, such as shift–reduce parsing, can be used directly or else extended to handle natural language input. This work has begun to exploit, and explicate, two interesting observations made by psycholinguists about the way in which the human parser appears to work – namely, by 'right association' and 'minimal attachment'. The former says that, ceteris paribus, phrases get attached as far to the right as they can be, whereas latter says that, ceteris paribus, phrases are attached in a way that minimizes the amount of structure that has to be built.

SUMMARY

- A parser maps strings into their structures.

- Bottom-up parsers work up from the words in the string.

- Top-down parsers work down from syntactic category goals.

- Parsing involves search.

- Depth-first search pursues one hypothesis at a time.

- Breadth-first search pursues hypotheses in parallel.

- Simple parsers do not store intermediate results.

- Storage of intermediate results is the key to efficient parsing.

- Global and local ambiguity are key problems in parsing.

- Deterministic parsers seek to eliminate local ambiguity.

Further reading

Good introductions to the technical side of context-free parsing algorithms can be found in Aho and Ullman (1972, Sections 3.4, 4.1 and 4.2 and 1977, Chapters 4 and 5). Petrick (1987) presents an NLP perspective on parsing issues. Linguistic and cognitive science perspectives on some of these issues are developed in Johnson-Laird (1983, Chapters 12 and 13), Dowty *et al.* (1985), Pulman (1983) and Sampson (1983a). The application of context-free parsing algorithms in the NLP context is discussed by Gazdar and Pullum (1985), Martin *et al.* (1987), Tomita (1986) and

Winograd (1983, Sections 3.1–3.5, 6.7), among many others. CF-PSG-based NLP parsers have even been implemented in hardware – see Sanamrad *et al.*(1987).

Discussion of ambiguity is pervasive in the NLP literature. See Alshawi (1987), Heidorn (1982), Hirst (1986), Sparck Jones (1983) and Tait (1983), for a representative sample, while the sheer size of the problem posed by multiple structural ambiguities is established in Church and Patil (1982).

Marcus's approach to deterministic parsing is most fully developed in Marcus (1980), but Charniak (1983), Ritchie (1983a), Sampson (1983b), Winston (1984, pp. 307–14) and Winograd (1983, pp. 402–10) provide tutorial material on the topic, while Milne (1982) makes proposals to extend the coverage of Marcus-type parsers. A proof that Marcus-type parsers will only parse CFLs is to be found in Nozohoor-Farshi (1987). Thompson and Ritchie (1984, pp. 263–300) develop a rational reconstruction of a Marcus-style parser in LISP and provide all the relevant code in an appendix.

The notion of right association was introduced by Kimball (1973) and that of minimal attachment by Frazier and Fodor (1978). There is extensive subsequent literature on the claims these authors make, some of which call into question its empirical basis – see Schubert (1986) and the references therein. Work by Shieber (1983), Tomita (1984) and Pereira (1985) advocate the use of shift–reduce parsers in NLP to account for attachment preferences. Aho and Ullman (1972, Chapter 5) provide a thorough introduction to a variety of shift–reduce parsing algorithms.

CHAPTER 6

WELL-FORMED SUBSTRING TABLES AND CHARTS

This chapter considers how a parser can efficiently store intermediate results to cope with certain kinds of redundancy in the parsing search space. First of all, the notion of well-formed substring table (WFST) is introduced. A WFST is a mechanism enabling a parser to keep a record of structures it has already found, so that it can avoid looking for them again. The further extension represented in charts enables a parser, in addition, to record information about goals it has adopted. Recorded goals may have been unsuccessful or may still be under exploration, but in either case it would be inefficient for the parser to start pursuing them again from scratch. The organization of a chart parser is described, as is the way in which the components of the system can be manipulated to produce different search and rule invocation strategies.

6.1   Well-formed substring tables

For the purposes of this chapter, we will equip ourselves with Grammar5 as a fragment of a simple phrase structure grammar for English.

EXAMPLE: Grammar5

Rule {simple sentence formation}
S → NP VP.

Rule {intransitive verb}
VP → IV.

Rule {intransitive verb plus PP complement}
VP → IV PP.

Rule {transitive verb}
VP → TV NP.

Rule {transitive verb plus PP complement}
VP → TV NP PP.

Rule {transitive verb plus VP complement}
VP → TV NP VP.

Rule {simple noun phrase}
NP → Det N.

Rule {noun phrase with PP complement}
NP → Det N PP.

Rule {simple prepositional phrase}
PP → P NP.

Word the:
    <cat> = Det.

Word her:
    <cat> = Det.

Word her:
    <cat> = NP.

Word they:
    <cat> = NP.

Word nurses:
    <cat> = NP.

Word nurses:
    <cat> = N.

Word book:
    <cat> = N.

Word travel:
    <cat> = N.
Word report:
    <cat> = N.
Word report:
    <cat> = IV.
Word hear:
    <cat> = TV.
Word see:
    <cat> = TV.
Word on:
    <cat> = P.

Grammar5 will assign structures to such sentences as:

Nurses hear her.
The nurses report.
They see the book on the nurses.
They hear her report on the nurses.

Since the grammar has no number agreement mechanism and no case distinctions, it will also assign structures to a range of ungrammatical strings, such as '*The book hear they', as well as a typical collection of grammatical but silly sentences, such as 'They hear the book'. These apparent shortcomings are not our focus of interest here, however. Our concern initially is with the nature of the encoding of information about strings that a parser can glean from this grammar.

Consider the problem confronted by a top-down parser faced with the string 'They saw the nurses report'. Ignoring the parsing of the subject noun phrase, the top of the search tree looks as shown in Figure 6.1(a). (For brevity, we have assumed that the parser is intelligent with lexical categories and does not waste time looking for lexical items that are not present.) The main part of the tree (circled) shows the parser's efforts in looking for just a noun phrase after the transitive verb 'saw'. All the paths in this part of the tree lead to failure, because there is an intransitive verb after the noun phrase, but nevertheless along the way a noun phrase is successfully parsed. The worrying thing is that an almost identical tree is to be found when we look more closely at the next subtree (Figure 6.1(b)). Apart from the bottom left node, this tree is exactly like the previous one, except that there is an extra PP in front of each ':'. So, the parser is having to do exactly the same work looking for a noun phrase in this part of the tree. Moreover, the same thing happens yet again in the third subtree,

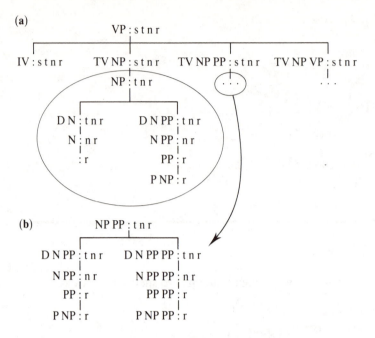

Figure 6.1   Parts of parsing search tree.

although this time there will be an extra VP in front of each ':', but the work done looking for the noun phrase will be the same. Here, perhaps the extra work may not matter much, but parsing a noun phrase can sometimes be a lengthy process, and it would be wasteful to carry out the same work three times.

In this example, we have discovered that there is *redundancy* in the parsing search space; that is, there are repetitions of essentially the same situation coming up again and again. How can we alleviate this problem? The trouble is that the parsers we have described have no *memory* of what they have done before. If our parser is exploring the search tree depth first from left to right, it will successfully parse the noun phrase 'the nurses' in the first subtree. But since this subtree leads to failure, everything in it will be discarded and the work will have to begin again in the second subtree. If the parser had kept some record of what it had found, it would not have had to repeat the work of finding it again.

The key idea, then, is for the parser to have some way of recording the constituents (and their structure) that it has found. We have already discussed the most familiar way of encoding structural information – namely, by means of trees such as that shown in Figure 6.2. Trees provide an excellent way of representing the completed structure of an unambiguous string that is admitted by the grammar, but our problem here is in representing partial structures that may or may not be part of a final

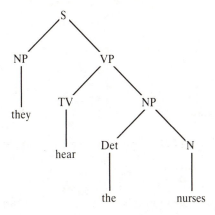

Figure 6.2 Representing a single, complete structure.

complete parse. Just because we find a possible noun phrase such as 'nurses' in one part of the search tree does not mean in general that this will have to be a noun phrase in a complete parse, since 'nurses' may be a verb or part of a larger noun phrase like 'the nurses'. So, we want to be able to store information about alternative partial analyses of the string, without committing ourselves to a premature decision as to which are correct.

There are a number of other occasions where such an ability might also come in useful. For instance, suppose we want to see the information that Grammar5 can provide about a string that it does not admit, such as:

The nurses book her travel.

Our grammar has some things it can say about this string, but it cannot assign a single tree to it. How then can we represent what it does have to say? One obvious answer is as a sequence of trees, as shown in Figure 6.3. We might well want to represent such a string in a natural language front end which is confronted with ill-formed input, a grammatical construction that falls outside its own set of rules, a misspelling or a word that is not in its lexicon. In such cases, a robust system will want the syntactic component to tell the semantic and pragmatic components as much as it has been able to find out about the syntactic structure, rather than simply breaking, reporting 'No parse available', and leaving other components to try and sort out the mess on their own on the basis of an unanalyzed string of words. This is really just like the situation in our original example, where we wanted a similar kind of communication between the computations in different parts of the parsing search tree. In the case of ungrammatical input, the grammar can only say less than a single complete tree would say.

Figure 6.3   Representing partial structures.

We also find strings where there is more to say than can be said by a single complete tree:

> They hear the report on the travel.

The grammar assigns two complete trees to this string. How then can we represent this fact? One obvious answer is as a set of (complete) trees, as illustrated in Figure 6.4. Again, a practical natural language understanding system needs to be able to represent syntactic ambiguities: they are ubiquitous but can often be resolved by the semantics or pragmatics, at least in principle. But suppose we encounter a string where the grammar can assign no complete tree, but can assign multiple, mutually inconsistent, partial analyses, as, for example, in the following example:

> They see his report on her.

Putting together our two previous answers, we seem to be led in the direction of a data structure consisting of a set of sequences of trees. But if we were to construct such a set for the example just given, or similar examples, then a problem will become apparent: even if the number of possible partial analyses is quite small, enumerating all possible sequences that cover the whole input string could result in a very large set. This is connected with the problem of ambiguities being multiplicative, which was discussed in Chapter 5.

The solution to these problems of structural representation lies in representing everything that would be required to enumerate the possible tree sequences; that is, the possible partial trees and what portions of the string they might account for, without actually doing the enumeration. The resulting representation is called a *well-formed substring table (WFST)*. Consider the beginning and end of the string to be numbered 0 and n, respectively, and the gaps between words to be numbered from 1 to $n - 1$ from left to right. Now, a WFST simply tells us, for each pair of points i, j

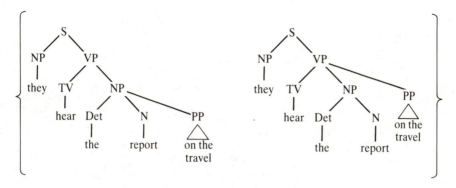

Figure 6.4   Representing alternative structures.

$(0 \leqslant i < j \leqslant n)$, what categories can span the substring of words found between i and j.

One way to think of a WFST, and the one that we shall adopt, is as a directed (each arc has a particular direction), acyclic (containing no cycles) graph with unique first and last nodes, a graph whose nodes are (conveniently and conventionally) labelled from 0 (the first node) to n (the last), where n is, as before, the number of words in the string, and whose arcs are labelled with syntactic categories and words. For illustration, Figure 6.5 shows the cases we have just considered represented in this fashion. It can be readily seen that a WFST can represent all three cases with equal facility and with no redundancy.

We can represent a WFST as a set of arcs, where an arc is a structure with the following attributes:

```
<START>  = ... some integer   ...

<FINISH> = ... some integer   ...

<LABEL>  = ... some category ...
```

A phrase structure tree of the conventional kind is also a directed acyclic graph, of course, but one in which the nodes are labelled with categories and the arcs are unlabelled. In our WFST, the arcs carry the category labels and the nodes have essentially arbitrary names, although we have used integers and exploited the '<' relation on integers to implicitly encode the head and tail of the (directed) arcs. Notice that a WFST encodes the order of phrases directly: a constituent with an arc going from i to j in the table precedes a constituent with an arc from m to n just in case $j < m$. This is in contrast to trees, which encode ordering directly for sister constituents

(a)

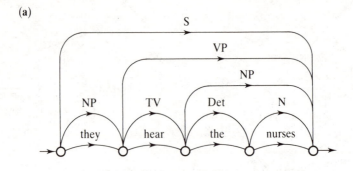

(b)

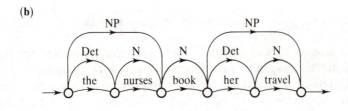

(c)

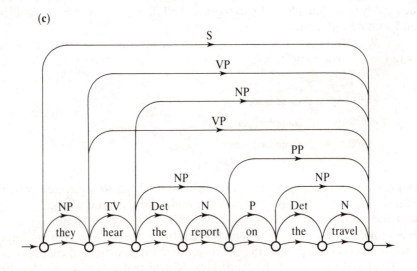

Figure 6.5 Representing (a) a single structure, (b) partial structures and (c) alternative structures in a WFST.

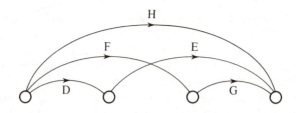

Figure 6.6   Recovering structural information from a WFST.

only. Trees do, however, encode immediate dominance relations, indicating which phrases are parts of which other phrases, directly whereas simple WFSTs, such as those considered here, do not. In fact, strictly speaking, our WFSTs as presented so far do not, by themselves, suffice to recover all the information encoded in our more verbose tree-based data structures. Simply by looking at the WFST, you cannot be sure of the rule (or rules) that legitimates a particular arc. Consider the WFST shown in Figure 6.6. Is the covering H warranted in virtue of H dominating D and E or in virtue of H dominating F and G? Without knowing what rules are in the grammar, we cannot tell. However, we can keep this information available if we make the label of an arc a parse tree – or a category, together with the sequence of arcs that correspond to the immediate subphrases – instead of a simple category.

How can a WFST be used by a top-down parser? We require that successfully found phrases be recorded in the table at some point. When a phrase of a particular category is then sought at a particular position in the string, the table is consulted. If there is an entry for the right kind of phrase starting at the right place, then the entries in the table are used as the possible analyses, rather than the work having to be done again. This strategy relies, however, on a particular convention about entering partial analyses into the table; namely, that an entry for a given category, starting at a given position, is not entered until *all* such entries can be entered. Otherwise, the second piece of computation, relying on the fruits of the first, will not incorporate all possible analyses into its investigations. A convention of this kind will be necessary even for a recognizer, because different possible analyses for a category, starting at a given position, may have different end positions.

WFSTs can be used by any kind of parser: they do not commit us to parsing bottom up, left to right or breadth first, although they permit us to do any of these things (or their familiar antitheses), and in any combination and any degree. The data structure itself is completely neutral, just as the more familiar phrase structure tree is. The use of a WFST simply allows a parser to refrain from rediscovering things that it has already found out.

We have motivated the WFST representation on a variety of intuitive grounds, but it turns out that the use of a WFST is also suggested by the complexity results on parsing of non-deterministic CF-PSGs. What the various n^3 CF-PSG parsing algorithms have in common is the implicit or explicit use of a WFST, and this single factor suffices to account for their cubic worst-case efficiency. Simpler algorithms that do not use a WFST typically have an exponential worst case. The intuition is a straightforward one: by storing intermediate results and by always testing for the presence of a category in the store before trying to build it, a WFST-based parser can avoid ever having to do the same thing more than once. The price to be paid is in the space consumed, but a WFST does not contain any redundancy, so this space demand is never worse than a multiple of n^2 (for a single parse). And since memory is cheap and natural language sentences are short, the price is an easily affordable one. Although they are very suggestive, these complexity results must be treated with care, unfortunately, as they reflect the complexity of finding the *first* parse only of a string. In practice, we will often be interested in finding *all* parses of a string, and the complexity of this, when the language itself is allowed to contain arbitrary ambiguity, is always exponential. Nevertheless, the complexity results do give an indication of the computational savings resulting from the use of a WFST and, as a result, many non-deterministic natural language parsers since the early 1970s have used a WFST of some sort or another.

Exercise 6.1 Adapt one of the top-down parsers previously presented to use a WFST. For this exercise, don't worry about the precise representation of the WFST – concentrate on the idea of the parser storing useful results and using this store to avoid duplicating work. [*intermediate*]

Exercise 6.2 In our main parsing example so far, the duplication of effort in looking for noun phrases could in fact have been avoided if the grammar had been restructured to factor out common parts of rule bodies. Although such a restructuring of the grammar can sometimes be effective, it can lead to a proliferation of new categories, with a corresponding loss of clarity, and it will not in any case cure all cases of duplication of work. Think of an example English grammar fragment and sentence where a WFST saves work but where the grammar *cannot* obviously be restructured in this way. *Hint*: Consider cases where a phrase of a particular kind needs to be found after another phrase, but where the phrase coming first may have several different analyses. [*intermediate*]

Exercise 6.3 Our discussion of WFSTs presupposed that our grammars contained no ε-productions. Which of our assumptions need to be changed to allow for such rules directly? [*easy*]

Exercise 6.4 Our WFSTs encode information about the categories of constituents that the parser has succeeded in finding, but no information about categories that the parser has *not* found to cover certain substrings. Explore the possibility of an elaborated WFST that could encode such negative information. What sorts of parser could benefit from such information? Design one. Are there types of parser to which the possibility of such an encoding would simply be irrelevant?   [*hard*]

Exercise 6.5 There are several ways we can implement a WFST; for example, we could use a binary three-dimensional array of size $n \times n \times c$ where c is the number of categories employed by the grammar and n is the length of the string in words. On this implementation, **wfst(0, 2, NP)** = 1 would mean that the first two words of the string could be taken to comprise an NP, while **wfst(3, 5, VP)** = 0 would mean that it was not yet known whether it was possible to treat the fourth and fifth words as a verb phrase. Modify one of the parsers given in the previous chapter so that it can access and update such an implementation of a WFST.   [*intermediate*]

6.2   The active chart

If we return to our original example, we can see that the use of a simple WFST will save work because it means that a successfully found noun phrase only needs to be found once. But it will not save the parser any time reinvestigating hypotheses that have previously failed. Moreover, if computations in different parts of the search space are both simultaneously in the middle of looking for noun phrases, there will be nothing to stop the work being done twice, even if it is successful in the end. The only way we can coordinate such work and avoid duplicating previous *attempts* at parsing is to have an explicit representation about the different goals and hypotheses that the parser has at any one time. The WFST as we have presented it is a good way of representing facts about structure, but what about structural hypotheses, conjectures or goals? By way of illustration,

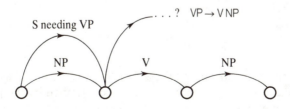

Figure 6.7   Representing goals and hypotheses.

(a)   **(b)**

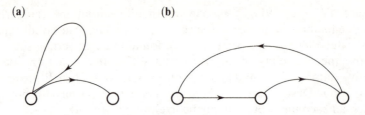

Figure 6.8   (a) Allowed cycle and (b) disallowed cycle in a chart.

consider Figure 6.7. This wholly informal object is intended to represent the state of analysis of a parser that:

- has established that the string may consist of an NP V NP sequence,
- is exploring the hypothesis that it can be analyzed as an S consisting of an NP VP sequence,
- has got to the point where it has decided to treat the NP it has already established as identical with the NP of the NP VP sequence, and
- needs to establish that the subsequent V NP sequence can be covered by VP.

We have already seen that WFSTs can readily represent partial analyses, but what we have here is a partial analysis together with a hypothesis. We plainly cannot represent such hypotheses in our WFST data structure as characterized earlier. However, two small changes to the data structure will give us what we need. Instead of requiring our directed graph to be strictly acyclic, we will relax things to permit single arcs ('empty arcs') that cycle back to the node they start out from, as in Figure 6.8(a), but we will continue to prohibit graphs that have cycles like that shown in Figure 6.8(b). The motivation for this minor relaxation of the acyclicity requirement will become apparent as we go on. The second change we need to make is to elaborate the label on arcs from a simple category to a decorated rule of the grammar. If S→ NP VP is a rule of the grammar, then the following objects ('dotted rules') are all well-formed arc labels:

S → .NP VP

S → NP.VP

S → NP VP.

Informally, the 'dot' in one of these labels indicates to what extent the hypothesis that this rule is applicable has been verified by the parser. The first kind of label, which will only ever occur on the kind of arc that cycles back to the node from which it emerged, denotes the hypothesis that an S

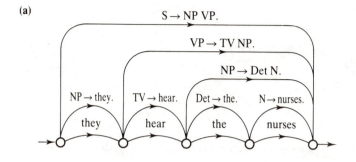

(a)

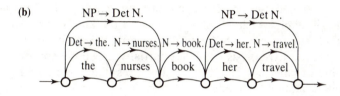

(b)

(c)

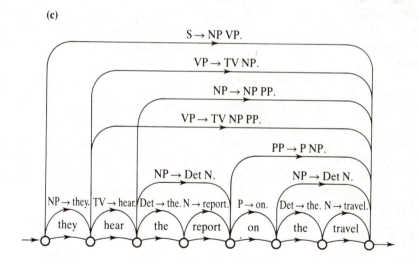

Figure 6.9 Representing (a) a single structure, (b) partial structures and (c) alternative structures in a chart.

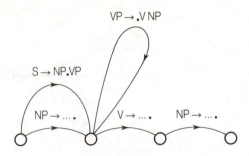

Figure 6.10   Representing goals and hypotheses in a chart.

can be found covering a substring that starts from the node in question and which covers that substring in virtue of the latter also being covered by an NP VP sequence. It indicates that such a hypothesis has been made, but that it has not necessarily been even partially verified. The second and third kind of label, which will never occur on the kind of arc that cycles back to the node from which it emerged, denote the same hypothesis, but indicate that the hypothesis has been partially or wholly confirmed. The second kind of label will only be found on arcs that cover an NP; that is, between nodes that are already spanned by an arc labelled NP→ <categories>., and thus indicates that the first part of the hypothesis, the presence of an initial NP, has been confirmed. The third kind of label indicates a fully confirmed hypothesis and will only be found on arcs that cover a string made up of an NP substring followed by a VP substring. This third kind of label is thus the closest equivalent to the earlier simple category labels that we used in WFSTs, only it provides a little extra information, since it indicates the sequence that warrants the presence of the category ascription.

A WFST that has been modified to include hypotheses in the manner described is known as an *active chart*, which we shall simply abbreviate to *chart* hereafter in accordance with common usage, following the work of Kay, and the family of parsers that exploit the chart as a data structure are known as *chart parsers*. A node in a chart is often referred to as a *vertex* and the arcs as *edges*. Arcs that represent unconfirmed hypotheses are known as *active edges* and those that represent confirmed hypotheses – that is, those with a label of the form C→ <categories>. are known as *inactive edges*.

Obviously, charts can represent everything that a WFST can. Figure 6.9 shows how our earlier example WFSTs would appear in chart notation. As we would expect, these charts only exhibit inactive edges. Figure 6.10 is the chart that corresponds to our informal hypothesis diagram in Figure 6.7. Notice that this contains two active edges.

We pointed out earlier that the WFST is completely neutral with respect to parsing strategy and this is true also of the chart.

We can represent a chart as a set of structures, each of which has the following attributes:

<START>   = ... some integer ...
<FINISH> = ... some integer ...
<LABEL>   = ... some category ...
<FOUND>   = ... some category sequence ...
<TOFIND> = ... some category sequence ...

where <LABEL> is the LHS of the appropriate dotted rule, <FOUND> is the sequence of RHS categories to the left of the dot and <TOFIND> is the sequence of RHS categories to the right of the dot. In this representation, an edge whose value for TOFIND is the empty sequence will be an inactive edge, and all other edges will be active. We will occasionally use an n-tuple notation in the text to abbreviate such records. Thus, the two tuples:

<0, 2, S → NP.VP>
<3, 5, NP → Det N.>

represent the following active and inactive edges, respectively:

<START> = 0
<FINISH> = 2
<LABEL> = S
<FOUND> = <NP>
<TOFIND> = <VP>

<START> = 3
<FINISH> = 5
<LABEL> = NP
<FOUND> = <Det, N>
<TOFIND> = <>

6.3   The fundamental rule of chart parsing

Now consider the problem of parsing in the light of the data structure we have just described, but remember that a chart is simply a set of edges. As in our previous presentations of parsing, we will initially ignore the problem of actually building phrase structure trees, since this will require some

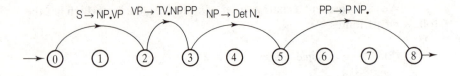

Figure 6.11   Example partial chart.

additions to the edge data structure. Suppose that we are in the middle of the parsing process and we look at the chart to find that it contains the following edges, among others:

$$\{<0, 2, S \rightarrow NP.VP>,$$
$$<2, 3, VP \rightarrow TV.NP\ PP>,$$
$$<3, 5, NP \rightarrow Det\ N.>,$$
$$<5, 8, PP \rightarrow P\ NP.>,$$
$$\dots \qquad\qquad \}$$

We can represent these edges diagrammatically, as shown in Figure 6.11. For clarity, we have omitted all the other edges that would need to be in the chart for the chart to have developed thus far. What we have here is two active edges and two inactive ones. The latter constitute a noun phrase and a prepositional phrase that we have already found. The first active edge represents a hypothesis about a sentence that has found a noun phrase, although not the one represented, and is looking for a verb phrase. The second active edge represents a hypothesis about a verb phrase that has found a transitive verb and is looking for a noun phrase followed by a prepositional phrase. Consider the first active edge. To satisfy the hypothesis, we need to find an inactive verb phrase edge in the chart that starts at vertex 2. But, let us suppose there is no such edge. We do, of course, have a hypothesis about the (eventual) presence of such an edge, but, until that hypothesis is confirmed, we are not in a position to do anything about the first active edge. Turning our attention now to the second active edge, we have a verb phrase hypothesis that is looking to find a noun phrase that starts at vertex 3. And we do indeed have such an edge. This means that our verb phrase hypothesis has been further, although not yet fully, confirmed. We can represent this further confirmation by adding another active edge to the chart – namely, $<2, 5, VP \rightarrow TV\ NP.PP>$. This is a hypothesis that is looking to find a prepositional phrase starting at vertex 5; but we have one of those in our chart, so this verb phrase hypothesis is (fully) confirmed and we can, accordingly, add an inactive edge to the chart to represent the verb phrase we have found – namely, $<2, 8, VP \rightarrow TV\ NP\ PP.>$. This

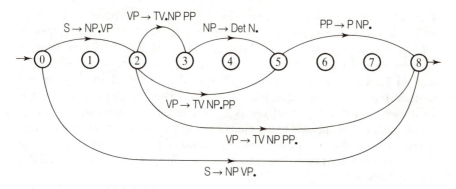

Figure 6.12   Application of the fundamental rule.

is where we have got to:

{<0, 2, S → NP.VP>,
<2, 3, VP → TV.NP PP>,
<2, 5, VP → TV NP.PP>,
<2, 8, VP → TV NP PP.>,
<3, 5, NP → Det N.>,
<5, 8, PP → P NP.>,
...   }

If we now return to our first inactive edge, we can see that its hypothesis is now also (fully) confirmed, since there is, indeed, a verb phrase that begins at vertex 2. So, we can add the inactive edge <0, 8, S → NP VP.> to our chart which now looks as shown in Figure 6.12. The fact that we have an S edge spanning the entire width of the graph means that we have succeeded in parsing the string as a sentence. There may well be further parses to find, but we have at least found one of them.

The process we have just described represents the essence of chart parsing. There is more to the latter than our informal walkthrough might lead you to think, but everything else is technical niceties. What we have done is to apply exactly the same rule three times: if an active edge meets an inactive edge of the desired category, then put a new edge into the chart that spans both the active and inactive edges. Kay calls this rule the *fundamental rule* of chart parsing. We have expressed it very imprecisely. What do 'meets' and 'desired' mean? What kind of edge do we add? But this imprecision can be readily remedied:

Fundamental rule

If the chart contains edges <i, j, A → W1.B W2> and <j, k, B → W3.>, where A and B are categories and W1, W2 and W3 are (possibly empty) sequences of categories or words, then add edge <i, k, A → W1 B.W2> to the chart.

This rule does not say whether the new edge is active or inactive, but then it does not need to since this is fully determined by whether W2 is empty or not. In a real implementation, however, it might well be convenient or efficient to add a simple flag to the edge data structure to signal activity or inactivity. Notice also that this rule only adds to the chart; it does not remove the active edge that has succeeded from the chart. This is as it should be since that active edge may be able to succeed in virtue of another inactive edge that appears in the chart at a later stage. If we remove it, then we run the risk that our parser will fail to find all possible parses, or, to put it in logician's parlance, we run the risk that our parser will exhibit *incompleteness*.

We can easily implement a chart parser in LISP by using a global variable chart to store the active and inactive edges of the chart (the complete code is in lib chart). We will represent each edge by a list of the following form:

(<start> <finish> <label> <found> <tofind>)

where:

- <start> (an integer) is the position in the chart where the edge starts,
- <finish> (an integer) is the position where the edge ends,
- <label> (a category) is the type of phrase that the edge is involved with,
- <found> (a list) is the list of constituents that have already been found,
- <tofind> (a list) is the list of constituents that remain to be found.

For a chart recognizer, the found and tofind lists need only be lists of categories. Thus, the following example represents an edge that is trying to find an NP starting at position 0 (the beginning of the string). So far, a Det has already been found between the start and finish points. However, before a complete NP can be found, an Adj and an N must be found (starting at the current finish point):

```
start finish label found tofind
(0    3    (NP) ((Det)) ((Adj) (N)))
```

We will make use of the following functions to access the components of an edge:

```
(defun start (edge)
  (nth 0 edge))

(defun finish (edge)
  (nth 1 edge))
```

```
(defun label (edge)
  (nth 2 edge))

(defun found (edge)
  (nth 3 edge))

(defun tofind (edge)
  (nth 4 edge))
```

For a chart parser, we will require that the edges remember more about what they have already found. So, we will require the found list to be a list of parse trees. We will come back to this case shortly, and let us initially consider the recognizer case. In this case, a first attempt to formulate the fundamental rule of chart parsing looks like the following:

```
(dolist (active_edge chart)
  (if (not (null (tofind active_edge)))
    (dolist (inactive_edge chart)
      (if (and
            (null (tofind inactive_edge))
            (equal (start inactive_edge) (finish active_edge))
            (equal (label inactive_edge) (car (tofind active_edge))))
        (setq chart
          (cons
            (list
              (start active_edge)
              (finish inactive_edge)
              (label active_edge)
              (append (found active_edge)
                (list (label inactive_edge)))
              (cdr (tofind active_edge)))
            chart))))))
```

That is, we need to look for pairs of entries in the chart, such that the first (the active edge) ends where the second (the inactive edge) starts, the second has no tofind categories and the label of the second is the same as the first tofind category of the first.

This piece of code for applying the fundamental rule in all possible ways, although suggestive, is unfortunately not quite what we need. First of all, the additions to the chart are taking place during two nested dolist iterations. In each of these loops, the LISP system is keeping track of how far through the chart it has searched so far. When we add new items, the chart changes and LISP will almost certainly get confused, so that we will either check pairs of edges several times or fail to check some combinations. A second problem is that we have no control over which new edges are added when – it just depends on the order in which dolist happens to find things. Finally, we can make the checking of the fundamental rule more efficient by doing it only when we add a new edge. So, instead of having to check for all combinations of edges in the database, we simply check, whenever an edge is added to the chart, whether there is something that combines with that edge. Here now is the core of our chart parser program, the function which adds a new edge to the chart, checking for applications of the fundamental rule:

```
(defun add_edge (edge)
  (setq chart (cons edge chart))
  (if (null (tofind edge))   ; added edge is inactive
      (progn
        (dolist (chartedge chart)
          (if (not (null (tofind chartedge)))   ; look for active edge
              (check_and_combine chartedge edge)))
        (inactive_edge_function edge))
      (progn   ; otherwise added edge is active
        (dolist (chartedge chart)
          (if (null (tofind chartedge))   ; look for inactive edge
              (check_and_combine edge chartedge)))
        (active_edge_function edge))))
```

The actual testing for the application of the fundamental rule is now done by the function check_and_combine. check_and_combine tries to combine an active and inactive edge using the fundamental rule. When it wishes to add a new edge to the chart, instead of changing the chart directly, it calls agenda_add to put the new edge on the agenda of additions to be made:

```
(defun check_and_combine (active_edge inactive_edge)
  (if
    (and
      (equal (start inactive_edge) (finish active_edge))
      (equal (label inactive_edge) (car (tofind active_edge))))
    (agenda_add
      (list                         ; new edge
        (start active_edge)
        (finish inactive_edge)
        (label active_edge)
        (append (found active_edge)
          (list
            (tree (label inactive_edge) (found inactive_edge))))
        (cdr (tofind active_edge))))))
```

As well as calling check_and_combine, add_edge also calls the functions inactive_edge_function and active_edge_function according to whether the edge added is inactive or active. We will appropriately define these functions later to obtain bottom-up or top-down parsing as required. Finally, we have now produced the core of a parser by having lists of parse trees for the found elements of edges. The function tree constructs a parse tree for a phrase,

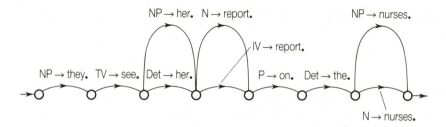

Figure 6.13 Initialized chart.

given the category of the phrase and the list of the parse trees of the constituents.

Now that we have the fundamental rule, there are three further matters that we need to address before we have all the ingredients to make a fully functioning chart parser. These are:

- initialization,
- rule invocation strategy, and
- search strategy,

We shall deal with all of these in turn.

6.4 Initialization

We cannot apply the fundamental rule to a chart that contains no edges. There needs to be at least one active edge and one inactive edge for anything to happen. The task of ensuring that there are some inactive edges to be found is the job of initialization. Ignoring morphology for the moment, it is quick and easy to look up words in the lexicon and find what categories they belong to. The results of such a dictionary look-up can be placed in the chart directly as inactive edges, right at the start without the need for any phrase-level parsing. So, for example, given the string 'they see her report on the nurses', we can use the lexicon included in Grammar5 to immediately build the chart shown in Figure 6.13. In doing so, we have *initialized* the chart. Notice that some pairs of adjacent vertices are connected by more than one edge, which is due to the category ambiguity exhibited by several of the words in the example string.

We have now covered most of the content of the top-level function chart_parse for the parser. chart_parse expects a goal (a category) and a string (list of words). It returns all the possible parse trees in a list. Before going into its main loop, chart_parse must perform initialization, and for this, it calls the function initialize_chart. This, when the chart is run using a bottom-up strategy, simply produces inactive edges for all the words in the string:

```
(defun initialize_chart (goal string)
  (do*
    ((vertex 0 (+ vertex 1))
     (remaining string (cdr remaining))
     (word (car string) (car remaining)))
    ((null word))
    (agenda_add
      (list
        ;; (start finish label found tofind)
        vertex (+ 1 vertex) word nil nil))))
```

Note that for simplicity we have entered the words rather than their categories. Given that we are representing lexical entries as normal grammar rules, we will see normal bottom-up parsing will fill in the categories for us. When all applications of the edge-adding rules have been made in the main loop, chart_parse then looks for complete parses by looking for edges of the form:

(0<L><goal><trees>())

where L is the number of words in the string and goal is the name of the category that we are interested in – for example, (S). In any edge of this form, trees will be the sequence of parse trees for the immediate constituents of the goal category – for example, ((NP Dr Chan) (VP (V employed)(NP nurses))). These can be easily combined with the goal category – for example, (S) – to produce a parse tree of the string:

```
(defun chart_parse (goal string)
  (setq agenda nil)
  (setq chart nil)
  (initialize_chart goal string)
  ...main loop...
  (let ((parses ()))
    (dolist (edge chart parses)
      (if (and
            (equal (start edge) 0)
            (equal (finish edge) (length string))    ; end of string
            (equal (label edge) goal)                 ; recognizes goal
            (null (tofind edge)))                     ; edge complete
        (setq parses
          (cons
            (tree goal (found edge))                  ; parse tree
          parses)))))))
```

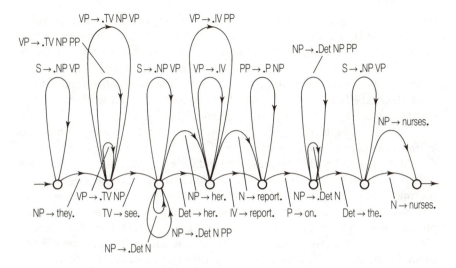

Figure 6.14   Application of the bottom-up rule to the initialized chart.

6.5   Rule invocation

The edges that the initialization step provides are not sufficient for parsing to begin: we still need a way of creating new active edges if anything is to result from the application of the fundamental rule. One simple principle to ensure that such an edge gets added is the following: every time you add an inactive edge with label C to the chart, add a new empty active edge, starting from the same vertex, for every rule in the grammar that requires a constituent C as its leftmost daughter. An empty active edge is an active edge that has yet to find any of its components and which thus starts from, and finishes at, the same vertex. This rule invocation strategy will give us a kind of bottom-up parsing – we shall consider alternative rule invocation strategies later. The exact way in which this strategy works may become clearer from the following formulation:

> ***Bottom-up rule***
> If you are adding edge <i, j, C → W1.> to the chart,
> then for every rule in the grammar of the form
> B → C W2, add an edge <i, i, B → .C W2> to the chart.

The bottom-up rule will apply when most inactive edges are added to the chart, and the result is a set of active edges to be added. If we imagine that we had applied this rule while initializing the chart depicted in Figure 6.13, then we would have obtained a chart of the form shown in Figure 6.14.

Here, active edges have been added to the chart corresponding to rules whose leftmost daughters have been found. Clearly, there is plenty in this chart for the fundamental rule to work on, and, every time that the latter succeeds in adding an inactive edge to the chart, our bottom-up rule will probably also apply, providing yet more work for the fundamental rule to do. Indeed, the bottom-up rule and the fundamental rule are all we need to ensure that all possible analyzes are found.

Notice that in this parsing strategy a rule is retrieved as soon as the leftmost element on its RHS has been found. This indexing on the leftmost daughter means that the strategy is a kind of left-corner parsing. Another interesting feature is the use of active edges. The use of active edges in this parsing strategy means that, unlike the bottom-up parsers presented in Chapter 5, the parser is in a sense maintaining hypotheses about other phrases that might be present. The fact is, however, that nothing more will happen to these active edges until further required phrases have been found (bottom up). So, if an active edge with label S→ .NP VP is added to the chart on the discovery of an NP, there is nothing that this hypothesis can do apart from, using the fundamental rule, absorb any following NPs (including the one found) into a new active edge and then absorb all VPs that are found after them to make inactive S edges. The active edges are thus simply providing an efficient way of storing rules that might possibly apply (bottom up) at a later stage. When we consider the top-down rule, we will see that there are much more positive ways of using active edges than this.

Top-down and bottom-up styles of parsing are implemented in our program by the functions active_edge_function and inactive_edge_function, which are called whenever an active, or inactive, edge is added to the chart. In our implementation, the looking up of lexical items will then take place when inactive_edge_function is called for the original word-labelled edges. Any parsing strategy will need to refer to the rules of the grammar – we will assume that these are available in the global variable rules, as in Chapter 4. We will not, for the present, deal with general feature specifications, but will confine ourselves to monadic categories like (S). Here are the functions for bottom-up parsing:

```
(defun inactive_edge_function (edge)
  (dolist (rule rules)
    (if (equal (label edge) (cadr rule))   ; the first daughter in the rhs
      (agenda_add
        (list
          (start edge) (start edge) (car rule) nil (cdr rule))))))

(defun active_edge_function (edge) t)
```

Quite how the operation of the bottom-up rule will interact with that of the fundamental rule depends on the order in which the various edges are added to the chart. This question brings us to our third ingredient – search strategy.

Exercise 6.6 Explain how the following edges can be added to the chart in Figure 6.14 by the operation of the two rules:

(1)   An inactive NP edge covering 'the nurses'.

(2)   An inactive PP edge covering 'on the nurses'.

(3)   An inactive NP edge covering 'her report on the nurses'.

(4)   An inactive VP edge covering 'saw her report on the nurses'.

(5)   An inactive S edge covering the whole string.

(6)   An inactive NP edge covering 'her report'.

(7)   An active S edge S → .NP VP starting and finishing before 'her'.

(8)   An active S edge S → NP.VP covering 'her report'.

(9)   An active S edge S → .NP VP starting and finishing before 'the nurses'.

(10)   An active S edge S → NP.VP covering 'the nurses'.

(11)   An active S edge S → NP.VP covering 'her report on the nurses'.
[*easy*]

6.6   Search strategy

Every active edge represents a hypothesis that needs to be explored. If it succeeds, even partially, then it is likely to generate further hypotheses (active and inactive edges), due to the operation of the fundamental rule and the rule invocation strategy that we adopt. With a serial machine, we have to make choices about the order in which to pursue these hypotheses. The basis on which we make these choices is our search strategy. In chart parsing, it is convenient to have a data structure, an *agenda*, for storing hypotheses to be explored or edges to be added to the chart, so that we can avoid investigating identical hypotheses and make a reasoned decision about what to investigate when.

One possibility is to regard the agenda as a stack: as new edges are produced, we push them on to the stack. Then, when we have to select an edge to work on, we take the one on the top of the stack. This will produce behaviour rather like depth-first search, as the following example indicates.

Imagine, for instance, that we have the following stack of edges to add to the chart, where e1 is at the top:

e1: e2: e3

Popping e1 off the stack, we might find that the addition of this edge leads to three more edges – e11, e12 and e13 – being proposed. If we push these on to the stack, the result is:

e11: e12: e13: e2: e3

Popping e11 off the stack, we might find that this results in three new edges – e111, e112 and e113. So, the next state of the stack is:

e111: e112: e113: e12: e13: e2: e3

Now, if the multiple edges produced at each stage represent alternatives, such as alternative categories for a word or alternative ways that a particular phrase type might be realized, then what we are doing at each point is taking one of the possibilities and pursuing it as far as possible before trying an alternative. For instance, because new edges are pushed on to the top of the stack, the edge e2 will never be considered until all the edges e111, e112, e113, e12 and e13, and all edges arising from them, have been added. Similarly, e3 will never be considered until all these edges, and also all edges arising from e2, have been added.

Another strategy is to regard the agenda as a queue, which is like a stack except that new items are added to the opposite end from which items are removed. In such a scheme, as new edges are produced, we push them on the end of the queue. When we have to select an edge to work on, we take the one at the front of the queue, whatever it is. This will produce something more like breadth-first search. For instance, in the foregoing example, the sequence would be:

e1: e2: e3	select e1
e2: e3: e11: e12: e13	select e2
e3: e11: e12: e13: e21: e22: e23	select e3
e11: e12: e13: e21: e22: e23: e31: e32: e33	select e11

and so on, where e21, e22 and e23 are the new edges arising from the addition of e2, and similarly for e3. This time, if the different edges at each point represent alternatives, the system spends only a small amount of time on each possibility before switching its attention to the next.

Lots of other strategies are imaginable, of course, by manipulating the agenda in various ways. For example, we could position active edges according to how near completion they are – for example, empty edges to the end, those with only one category to find to the front, or conversely; or according to their categories – noun phrases to the front, other categories to the end, or whatever; or according to information gleaned from another component – the semantics, say. We can favour edges that result from particular grammar rules over edges that result from others, attempting to exploit statistical results about language use or human parsing preferences.

If we want our parser to produce all possible parses, then the chart will eventually go through exactly the same work and produce exactly the same results whatever search strategy we impose. So, if we do not care what order the parses are produced in, then the choice of search strategy is essentially arbitrary. But, if we only want one parse, or we only want parses that meet certain additional constraints which may not be inherent in the rules alone, or if we have some other process running in parallel like semantic interpretation of constituents, then the choice of search strategy becomes a matter of concern and has efficiency implications (see below).

The main loop of the parser is entirely concerned with manipulating the agenda:

```
(do
   ((edge (car agenda) (car agenda)))
   ((null agenda))
   (setq agenda (cdr agenda))
   (add_edge edge))
```

agenda, a global variable, holds the list of edges waiting to be added to the chart. This list holds the edges in priority order, because the loop deals with the edges in the order they appear in the list. In general, of course, add_edge will cause new edges to be added to the agenda, so that agenda may grow between iterations.

So far, however, our parser remains fairly neutral about the search strategy to be adopted. However, by providing appropriate definitions for the remaining functions, we can force it to work in a number of different ways. As we have seen, the search strategy is determined by how new edges are to be added to the agenda. The following definition of agenda_add causes new edges to be added at the beginning (given highest priority), which gives rise to a kind of depth-first search strategy:

```
(defun agenda_add (edge)
   (setq agenda (cons edge agenda)))
```

6.7   Housekeeping

In addition to the matters already discussed, a real implementation of a chart parser needs to take care of certain vital housekeeping matters. When one of our rules proposes a new edge, we only want to add it to the chart if it is not already there. So, edge addition needs to be preceded by a check to see if the edge exists. Without this check, the chart would not be removing any duplication from the search space, of course.

An equally important piece of housekeeping for a parser, rather than a recognizer, is the organization of the building of the phrase structure tree for the string under consideration. As with a WFST, the idea is to have elements of the edge data structure be trees, rather than simple categories. The elements to which this applies is the sequence of FOUND categories for an edge. Thus, the FOUND of an edge will be the sequence of parsè trees of the FOUND phrases, rather than simply the categories.

The fundamental rule must be altered to take tree building into account. The fundamental rule creates a new edge with one more FOUND phrase than the active arc that helped to spawn it. We must ensure that the new item in the sequence is a tree, not a bare category. Fortunately, we can easily construct the parse tree from the participating inactive edge by using the existing label of the edge, together with the sequence of trees for its subphrases, given in the existing FOUND structure.

We can readily deal with the necessary housekeeping by minor additions to the code already shown. The following will ensure that agenda_add checks for duplicate edges:

```
(defun agenda_add (edge)
  (if (or
        (already_in edge agenda)         ; left recursion check
        (already_in edge chart))
      nil                                ; do not add to agenda
      (setq agenda (cons edge agenda))))) ; add to front of agenda

(defun already_in (edge edgelist)
  (member edge edgelist :test #'equal))
```

For the already_in check we use member, but using equal (rather than eql) as the relevant equality test, because eql will not succeed if it is provided with two different lists with the same elements.

The function add_edge already calls tree so as to put trees rather than categories in the found list. This function to build a tree from a category and a list of subtrees is as follows:

```
(defun tree (cat subtrees)
  (if (consp cat)
      (cons (car cat) subtrees)
      cat))
```

Exercise 6.7   How does the chart parser described in the text behave if the grammar contains a rule $A \to A$, for some category A? Is this correct? Does the same behaviour occur if it is only a recognizer? If some phrase can be recognized as being of category A by the other rules of the grammar, what effect does the addition of this rule have on the number of structural analyses of that phrase? Are there other kinds of rules where similar problems can arise? Suggest some possible solutions.   [*hard*]

6.8 Alternative rule invocation strategies

As we have seen, the chart data structure itself is neutral with respect to the search strategy employed, since we can go depth first, breadth first or whatever way we want. The same neutrality extends to the rule invocation strategy. Our illustration was of a bottom-up rule, but we could just have well have substituted a top-down strategy:

Top-down strategy

(1)   At initialization, for each rule A → W,
where A is a category that can span a chart (typically S),
add <0, 0, A → .W> to the chart.

(2)   If you are adding edge <i, j, C → W1.B W2>
to the chart, then for each rule B → W,
add <j, j, B → .W> to the chart.

Here, the first clause ensures that the parsing process gets started by a bunch of empty active S edges added to the first vertex. The second clause entails that every active edge spawns further empty active edges that are looking to find the first (non-preterminal) category in the to-be-found list. Note that once again, for clarity, we have omitted discussion of building the parse tree. Applying the first clause to our initialized chart example gives us the chart shown in Figure 6.15(a) and applying the second clause gives that in Figure 6.15(b)

In addition to the straightforward top-down and bottom-up rule invocations, lots of other strategies can be constructed by, for example, making the rules sensitive to particular classes of categories or rules. Thus, we might, say, combine a basically top-down strategy with bottom-up rule invocation triggered by closed class 'function words', or by verbs. Or we might combine a basically bottom-up strategy with top-down invocation of just the rules responsible for unbounded dependency and ellipsis constructions. In devising such strategies, we must always address the question of the *completeness* of the parser; that is, whether or not it is guaranteed to find all possible parses. It is straightforward to construct hybrid strategies that are guaranteed to miss possible parses, and this is unacceptable in most contexts. For instance if, given Grammar5 (see page 182), we decided to parse bottom up, left to right, except that prepositions would be sought top down, we would never recognize a single prepositional phrase because a top-down prediction of a preposition will never arise.

The functions initialize_chart, active_edge_function and inactive_edge_function are easily redefined for top-down parsing. Top-down parsing has to be started by the addition of initial active edges for all rules which can expand the goal category. The function add_rules_to_expand adds active edges at a given vertex corresponding to all possible rules with a given category on the

(a)

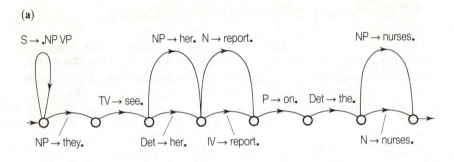

(b)

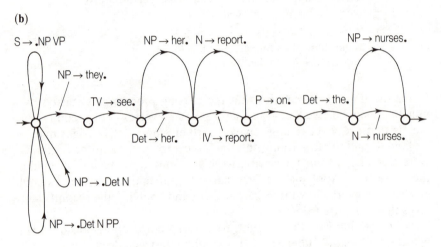

Figure 6.15 Applying the top-down rule to the initialized chart.

LHS. Note that in bottom-up parsing, no special actions are performed when active edges are added. For top-down parsing, this situation is reversed:

```
(defun inactive_edge_function (edge) t)

(defun active_edge_function (edge)
    (add_rules_to_expand (car (tofind edge)) (finish edge)))

(defun add_rules_to_expand (goal vertex)
    (dolist (rule rules)
       (if (equal goal (car rule)) ; the lhs of the rule
          (agenda_add
             (list vertex vertex (car rule) nil (cdr rule))))))
```

```
(defun initialize_chart (goal string)
  (do*
    ((vertex 0 (+ vertex 1))
     (remaining string (cdr remaining))
     (word (car string) (car remaining)))
    ((null word))
    (agenda_add
      (list
        ;; (start   finish      label found tofind)
           vertex (+ 1 vertex) word nil    nil   )))
  (add_rules_to_expand goal 0))
```

Exercise 6.8   Consider the classical problems of top-down and bottom-up parsing discussed in the last chapter: left recursion and ε-productions, respectively. Do the chart-based algorithms given here solve these problems? Or can they be simply converted to algorithms that do solve them?   *[hard]*

6.9   Efficiency

The efficiency of a given chart parser on a given input is inversely related to the amount of excess structure present in the chart at the end of the (attempted) parse. If the input string is ungrammatical and yet the chart is full of edges, then clearly the parser has been doing lots of work to no good effect. Ideally, we would like the parser to build very few edges for such an input, and for it then to be able to report that the string had no parses. Likewise, if the string is grammatical and the chart is full of edges, then the parser will have been maximally efficient if every inactive edge present is employed in some structure assigned to the string, and if every active edge present represents a hypothesis that ultimately proves successful, such as results in the addition of an inactive edge. Unused inactive edges, and active edges that lead nowhere, represent wasted activity and thus directly reflect the inefficiency of the parser. The goal of experimenting with the rule invocation strategy is to reduce this wastage to a minimum.

The efficiency of a chart parser is also greatly dependent on how well the data structures used are tuned to support the basic parsing operations that are performed again and again. A chart parser spends a lot of its time retrieving information from the chart and the grammar; for instance:

- When an inactive edge has been added to the chart, it looks for active edges that require the relevant category at the point where the inactive edge begins, in order to apply the fundamental rule.

- When an active edge has been added to the chart, it looks for inactive edges for the first category that the active edge requires, which start where the active edge ends, in order to apply the fundamental rule.

- When an inactive edge has been added to the chart, it looks for all grammar rules where the first category on the RHS is the same as the category of the edge, in order to apply the bottom-up rule.

- When an active edge has been added to the chart, it looks for all grammar rules whose LHS is the first category that the edge requires, in order to apply the top-down rule.

If each time the parser went looking for an edge of a particular type it had to look through every edge in the chart, performance would slow down dramatically as soon as the chart achieved any size. This is the sort of performance that we would expect if the chart was represented as a simple list of edge data structures, as ours is. A better implementation would keep the edges of the chart in a data structure that was indexed by the starting and/or finishing points of the edges, and possibly also by certain relevant categories in the edges – for instance, by the label of an inactive edge and the first tofind category of an active edge. In this way, the search could proceed rapidly to a small set of potentially relevant edges, without having to consider the whole chart.

Exercise 6.9   Run this parser with the rules given in Grammar5. Try both parsing strategies. What kinds of redundant edges are added given each strategy?   [*intermediate*]

Exercise 6.10   The use of a list to represent the chart is wasteful in a number of ways. When a new edge is added, checking the fundamental rule involves searching through the whole list for edges that may combine with it. However, edges that may combine with an inactive edge must finish where the edge starts, and edges that may combine with an active edge must start where the edge finishes. Devise an alternative representation that facilitates the finding of edges that start or finish at a given point. For instance, you could have two arrays or vectors edges_starting and edges_finishing that associate with positions in the chart (numbers) lists of edges that start or finish there. Inactive edges could then be entered in edges_starting and active edges in edges_finishing. Alter the program to make use of this new representation of the chart.   [*intermediate*]

SUMMARY

- WFSTs provide storage of intermediate results.

- Charts are WFSTs that store results and hypotheses.

- A chart is a set of annotated arcs called 'edges'.

- An inactive edge is a result.

- An active edge is a hypothesis about structure.

- Initialization sets a chart up with inactive edges for each word.

- Chart parsers are driven by the fundamental rule.

- Charts are neutral with respect to parsing and search strategy.

Further reading

The first CF-PSG parsing algorithms to systematically exploit the efficiency improvements to be gained by storage of intermediate results in WFSTs are those of Earley (1970) and Younger (1967), while the complexity issues are usefully explored in Sheil (1976).

Contemporary chart parsing has its origins in the General Syntactic Processor of Kaplan (1973) and the MIND parser of Kay (1973). Kay himself provides a comprehensive technical discussion in his (1980/1986) paper.

Tutorial introductions to the technique are provided by Winograd (1983, pp. 116–27) and Allen (1987, pp. 60–73). Thompson and Ritchie (1984) develop a chart parser in LISP and provide all the relevant code in an appendix.

Among many recent research papers on chart parsing are Thompson (1981, 1983), Kilbury (1985), Ramsay (1985), Slack (1986), Wittenburg (1986), Pareschi and Steedman (1987), Sågvall Hein (1987), Steel and De Roeck (1987), and Wiren (1987). Chart parsers have also found uses in speech understanding (Görz 1981, 1982; Thompson 1985).

FEATURES AND THE LEXICON

This chapter deals in some detail with two related topics that have an important bearing on morphological, syntactic and semantic aspects of NLP. The first topic concerns the nature and use of the feature structures now widely used to represent morphological, syntactic and semantic information. Issues here include the combination of feature structures (unification), inclusion relations between them and the consequences that their use has for the nature of the parsing process.

The second topic is the lexicon, a topic that has become increasingly important during the 1980s, partly because of the ubiquity of feature-based NLP systems. The latter have permitted computational linguists to adopt very simple and compact grammatical rule systems at the cost of pushing almost all of the syntactic facts about the language into the lexicon. The organization of the latter thus becomes a matter of crucial concern.

7.1   Feature-theoretic syntax

Consider the following grammar for a fragment of French.

EXAMPLE: Initial grammar of French

Rule
  S → NPa VPa.
Rule
  S → NPb VPb.
Rule
  S → NPc VPc.
Rule
  S → NPd VPd.
Rule
  S → NPe VPe.
Word je:
    <cat> = NPa.
Word tu:
    <cat> = NPb.
Word elle:
    <cat> = NPa.
Word nous:
    <cat> = NPc.
Word vous:
    <cat> = NPd.
Word ils:
    <cat> = NPe.
Word tombe:
    <cat> = VPa.
Word tombes:
    <cat> = VPb.
Word tombons:
    <cat> = VPc.
Word tombez:
    <cat> = VPd.
Word tombent:
    <cat> = VPe.

This grammar generates exactly six French sentences, of which 'elle tombe' ('she falls') is typical. All six sentences intuitively have exactly the same structure, yet our grammar employs five distinct rules, nearly one for each. This is wasteful and obscures an evident generalization about simple French sentences. Furthermore, if we try and extend this grammar to encompass the imperfect 'elle tombait' ('she was falling' – compare 'je tombais') or three-word sentences such as 'elle est tombée' ('she has fallen' – note the feminine form of the past participle), then we need still more S expansion rules, even if we decide to treat the auxiliary 'être' form as an element of the verb phrase in the latter case.

We already have a solution to this descriptive problem to hand – namely, the syntactic feature apparatus that we introduced, although hardly discussed, in Chapter 4. Accordingly, let us revise our grammar.

EXAMPLE: Revised French grammar

Rule
  S → NP VP:
    <NP per> = <VP per>
    <NP num> = <VP num>.

Word je:
    <cat> = NP
    <per> = 1
    <num> = sing.
Word tu:
    <cat> = NP
    <per> = 2
    <num> = sing.
Word elle:
    <cat> = NP
    <per> = 3
    <num> = sing.
Word nous:
    <cat> = NP
    <per> = 1
    <num> = plur.
Word vous:
    <cat> = NP
    <per> = 2
    <num> = plur.

Word ils:
        `<cat>` = NP
        `<per>` = 3
        `<num>` = plur.

Word tombe:
        `<cat>` = VP
        `<per>` = 1
        `<num>` = sing.

Word tombe:
        `<cat>` = VP
        `<per>` = 3
        `<num>` = sing.

Word tombes:
        `<cat>` = VP
        `<per>` = 2
        `<num>` = sing.

Word tombons:
        `<cat>` = VP
        `<per>` = 1
        `<num>` = plur.

Word tombez:
        `<cat>` = VP
        `<per>` = 2
        `<num>` = plur.

Word tombent:
        `<cat>` = VP
        `<per>` = 3
        `<num>` = plur.

    This grammar generates exactly the same six French sentences as our original grammar, but it does so with only a single rule. The apparent cost, of course, is in the lexicon, each of whose entries now seems more verbose, and where one form 'tombe' now has two entries while previously one sufficed. In fact this cost is more apparent than real, as any attempt to extend our original grammar will soon demonstrate. Furthermore, the verbal entries shown are wholly predictable, given only the stem and the conjugation class, so there is no real need to list them all in this way (see the later sections of this chapter for some discussion of how to organize the lexicon so as to avoid the listing of predictable forms).

7.2   Feature structures as graphs

Our use of features so far largely corresponds to the traditional view of features in linguistics, especially in phonology, but also in their limited syntactic use in the 1960s and 1970s. Under this view, categories (known in phonology as segments or, crudely, phonemes) are made up of sets of attribute value pairs, where both attributes and values are atomic. A conventional notation for such objects – for example, for the category associated with the French pronoun 'nous' – is the following feature matrix:

$$
\begin{bmatrix}
\text{cat} & \text{NP} \\
\text{per} & 1 \\
\text{num} & \text{plur}
\end{bmatrix}
$$

Crucially, such objects never assign more than one value to any attribute and (typically) are not required to assign a value to every attribute; thus, this feature matrix contains no value for the attribute case. Mathematically, this means that feature matrices are partial functions from the set of attributes into the set of values.

An alternative way of thinking about features mathematically, and one that has proved productive in recent years, is as simple graphs, as illustrated in Figure 7.1. A graph of this kind is known as a *directed acyclic graph (DAG)*. The graph is directed because the arcs have directions, indicated by arrows, and it is acyclic because there are no cycles in it – it is not possible to get from a node to itself just by following the arrows. In this example, the arcs are labelled with attributes and the terminating nodes are labelled with atomic values. In the toy grammars for natural language fragments that we have presented in the book so far, values have all been atomic, which is to say that they have had no internal structure. This keeps things simple for pedagogic purposes, but does not do justice to the sophistication of contemporary feature theory, in which the value of a

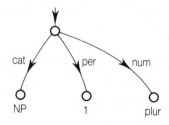

Figure 7.1   Directed acyclic graph.

feature in a category may itself be a syntactic category; that is, features are allowed to take categories as their values. This allows features such as slash and arg1, introduced in Chapter 4, to encode not just gross categorical distinctions, as flagged by NP, PP, and so on, in our example grammars, but also linguistically important information having to do with, for example, case, person, number and gender. Category-valued features allow many significant grammatical generalizations to be captured rather straight-forwardly. For example, a category-valued version of our slash feature is able to capture the regularities underlying the class of unbounded depen-dency constructions, which includes relative clauses, WH questions, topicalization, and so on. This is because, for instance, a category-valued slash can bundle together in one place all the relevant features (person, number, gender) that must be shared between an extraposed NP and the context of the 'hole' it is to be paired with.

We can, if we wish, recode our little grammar of French to use a category-valued feature arg0 to handle the agreement – the reason for our choice of the name arg0 will become apparent below. Our S expansion rule can simply require the subject to be identical to the value of the arg0 feature in the VP. We can thus put into the arg0 feature for a verb all the require-ments it places on its subject – category, person, number, and so on – and in a single equation express the fact that all these requirements must be satisfied. This rule is shown, along with the revised lexical entries necessary for the verb forms. The lexical entries for the pronouns remain as in the previous example and so are not repeated here.

EXAMPLE: Capturing agreement with a category-valued feature

Rule
    S → X VP:
        <VP arg0> = <X>.

Word tombe:
        <cat> = VP
        <arg0 cat> = NP
        <arg0 per> = 1
        <arg0 num> = sing.
Word tombes:
        <cat> = VP
        <arg0 cat> = NP
        <arg0 per> = 2
        <arg0 num> = sing.

Word tombe:
    <cat> = VP
    <arg0 cat> = NP
    <arg0 per> = 3
    <arg0 num> = sing.
Word tombons:
    <cat> = VP
    <arg0 cat> = NP
    <arg0 per> = 1
    <arg0 num> = plur.
Word tombez:
    <cat> = VP
    <arg0 cat> = NP
    <arg0 per> = 2
    <arg0 num> = plur.
Word tombent:
    <cat> = VP
    <arg0 cat> = NP
    <arg0 per> = 3
    <arg0 num> = plur.

We can use our graph-theoretic notation to good effect in displaying the structure of the verbal categories assumed in our revised version of the French grammar fragment. Figure 7.2 shows the category to which the word 'tombons' belongs. We will refer to a feature as being *category valued* if and only if it is not atom valued. Thus, arg0 is category valued, whereas cat, per and num are all atom valued. Notice that our use of notation such as <arg0 num> = plur can be seen to specify a path in the DAG (<arg0 num>) and tells us the label on the node at the end of that path (plur).

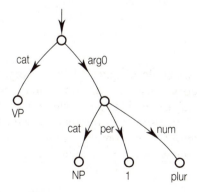

Figure 7.2   DAG for 'tombons'.

Grammars standardly invoke principles of feature matching to ensure the identity of certain features on adjacent nodes. Such principles are equations that say that certain features appearing on one node must be identical to the features appearing on another. Most current work assumes a principle that is responsible for equating one class of feature specifications as they appear on the mother category and the daughter which manifests the morphology associated with those features. This daughter is known as the *head* of the phrase. Most phrases only have a single head. Thus, for example, a verb phrase inherits the tense of its verb since the latter is the head of the verb phrase. There is no straightforward way of specifying this principle on a grammar-wide basis with the notational resources that we have used so far, but we can stipulate the effects of the principle on a rule-by-rule basis quite simply if we assume that the relevant features are all to be found on a single branch of the DAG. Let us call the label on this branch head. Then we can write a typical VP rule as follows:

```
Rule
  VP → V NP PP:
    <V head> = <VP head>.
```

This requires that the value of the head feature on the V and that on the mother VP be identical. If the head of the V contains an attribute value pair that is inconsistent with a pair in the head of the VP, then the rule is inapplicable. The values of head here will, typically, not be atomic but will themselves be DAGs.

So far, the feature graphs that we have presented have always been trees. However, when we have category-valued features it is convenient to take advantage of the flexibility offered by general DAGs. Consider the following extended VP rule:

```
Rule
  VP → V NP PP:
    <V head> = <VP head>
    <VP verb> = <V>.
```

There are two ways we could imagine a VP category described by such a rule being represented as a graph, as illustrated in Figure 7.3. Note that the repeated values of the head features have been omitted. The first involves having two *copies* of the substructure that appears twice, whereas the second involves a *sharing* of the common substructure. Which of these we choose depends on what we want '=' to mean and what we expect to follow from what. From:

<VP head> = <VP verb head>   and   <VP verb head num> = sing

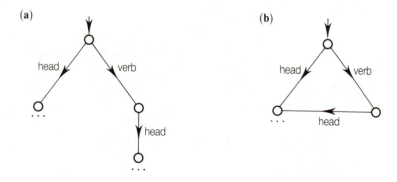

Figure 7.3   Alternative representations for VP category.

we would like it to follow that:

<VP head num> = sing

which is to say (among other things) that the VP inherits all the head features of its verb. If we interpreted the first statement in terms of there being two copies of the head substructure, there would be nothing to prevent us adding to the verb head part of the DAG to include number information, but leaving the head part untouched. As a result, the inheritance would not necessarily arise. On the other hand, in a sharing interpretation, '=' means that two structures are the *same* structure, rather than that they just happen to have the same values for all features. It is therefore impossible to add to one without making the same addition to the other. The sharing approach is also more attractive from a computational perspective, as the data structures are smaller if only one copy needs to be maintained. In conclusion, then, we will interpret '=' as specifying that two categories or parts of categories must share, rather than simply have the same value. The vital point computationally is that we can represent two substructures sharing even before everything is known about them. Then the problem of updating one, when an addition is made to the other, is trivial.

To deal with DAGs that display sharing, we must allow terminating nodes to remain unlabelled. For instance, the minimal DAG that satisfies:

<feature1> = <feature2>

does not have any labelled nodes, as shown in Figure 7.4. Unfortunately, once we allow unlabelled terminating nodes, it becomes possible for there to be several different graphs that convey exactly the same information. This arises because it is always possible to add spurious unlabelled nodes to a DAG without adding any extra information. Although a DAG can

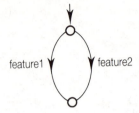

Figure 7.4 DAG with unlabelled nodes.

express the fact that a category contains no information about a given feature, it is not possible for a DAG to express the fact that a category *cannot* have a value for a given feature. Therefore, a DAG that specifies the presence of a feature without any extra information about its value cannot ever conflict with any other DAG, as regards that feature, and, as a consequence, makes no real statement about that feature. Saying that a DAG has a value for a given feature without either giving some information about that value or saying that the value shares with some other value, conveys no real information. As a result, we must consider the two DAGs depicted in Figure 7.5, for example, to be fully equivalent.

Exercise 7.1 Find an informant who knows French well and find out the facts about the following construction:

> Elle est tombée.
>
> *Elle est tombé
>
> *Elle a tombée
>
> *Elle a tombé
>
> *Elle a parlée
>
> Elle a parlé.

Add a version of a VP → V VP rule to the French grammar that uses the arg0 feature and then modify the grammar so that it can handle the facts about French past participle agreement that you have uncovered.   [*intermediate*]

Exercise 7.2 Rework Grammar4 from Chapter 4 so that both arg1 and slash are category-valued features. Add pronominal noun phrases to the lexicon

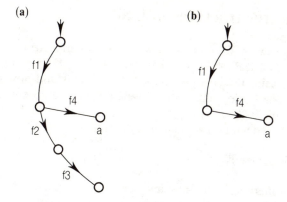

Figure 7.5 Two fully equivalent DAGs.

and demonstrate that your revised grammar takes care of the following facts:

She disapproved of him.

*Her disapproved of she

Her, he disapproved of.

Him, she paid.

*He, she paid

[*intermediate*]

Exercise 7.3 Draw DAGs that satisfy the following equations:

(a) <f1 f2> = a
     <f1 f3> = b
     <f1 f4> = <f1 f5>

(b) <f1 f2> = <f1 f3 f4>
     <f2 f3> = a

(c) <f1 f2> = <f1 f3>
     <f1 f2 f4> = a

Restrict yourself to DAGs that contain no unnecessary sharing or feature values. [*easy*]

7.3   Feature structures in LISP

We already saw in Chapter 4 how simple feature structures could be represented by LISP lists. Now that the notion of DAGs has been introduced, it is easier to see what the notation means and how easy it is to extend it to handle more interesting cases. We have represented collections of features and values using association lists, each sublist providing a feature name and value. For instance, the following list:

((person 3) (number sing))

represents something with person and number features. The values for these are, respectively, 3 and sing. Where a value is itself a complex collection of features, an embedded list can be used for the appropriate element. For instance, in the following:

((cat V) (arg0 ((cat np) (case nom) (number sing))))

the value of the arg0 feature is a complex object. This has values for at least the features cat, case and number. Both of these two example descriptions are tree-shaped, and in order to represent general DAGs we need to have a way of representing sharing between different parts of a category. As we have seen, a variable symbol can be used to indicate that two features must be given the same value – that is, that the features share. Thus:

((cat VP) (head _x) (verb ((head _x))))

represents a DAG in which the head and the head of the verb share a value, whereas:

((cat VP) (head _x) (verb ((head _y))))

represents a DAG in which they may not. In fact, since _x and _y only appear once each in the data structure, unless _x and _y are given some other significance, the information conveyed by this structure is exactly the same as that conveyed by:

((cat VP))

Our implementation of DAGs needs to be able to describe the situation when two DAGs share a value, but where some information is already known about that value. In such a case, we want to show all the known information about the value in both places and, in addition, indicate that the *remainder* of the description of the value is also shared. We use a special notation for talking about the remainder of the information about a given item. Where & appears in the position normally occupied by a feature name in the last element of a list, the item following it is taken to denote the rest of the appropriate description. When this remainder value is itself a list, it is as if that list was simply spliced on the end of the original list. For instance:

((cat V) (& ((number sing) (person 3) (& ((tense pres) (& _x))))))

means exactly the same as:

((cat V) (number sing) (person 3) (tense pres) (& _x))

and we would not normally use such a long-winded form. Normally, we put a variable symbol after the & and use multiple occurrences of the same symbol to indicate sharing of the remainder. For instance:

((cat VP)
(head ((number sing) (& _x)))
(verb ((head ((number sing) (& _x))))))

denotes a structure where the head shares with the head of the verb, but where in addition we know that the number of the head is sing. As a description, a DAG is always *sideways open*, which means that it can always be consistently extended by adding information about new features that are not mentioned in it. So, where we have previously used a list without an explicit remainder entry:

((person 3) (number sing))

for a description, we do not mean 'the person is 3, the number is sing and no other features have values'. What we actually mean by this is 'the person is 3, the number is sing and any other features could have any values'. Therefore, we should really use an explicitly open-ended form with a remainder:

((person 3) (number sing) (& _x))

The programs that we will develop for operating on DAGs will assume that DAGs are represented by lists with explicit remainders, and so we will adopt this more verbose representation from now on.

Notice that it is quite possible to construct a LISP list using the & notation that does not correspond to any legal DAG. Here are two examples of such illegal structures:

((cat V)   (& _x) (number sing) (& _y))
((cat VP)   (head ((number sing) (& _x)))
            (verb ((head ((number plur) (& _x))))))

The first does not correspond straightforwardly to a DAG because we are given two different descriptions of the remainder; in fact, we would not allow it anyway because we require the only & to be in the final element). The second involves two subDAGs that share their remainders but which do not share their number features. This cannot happen in a DAG (try drawing a picture of it). On the other hand, some possibly unexpected structures do indeed correspond to legal DAGs, such as the following:

```
((cat V)    (& ((number sing) (& ((person 3) (& _x))))))
((cat VP)   (head ((number sing) (person 3)  (& _x)))
            (verb ((head ((person 3) (number sing) (& _x)))) (& _y))
 _x
```

The first of these is the same as:

```
((cat V) (number sing) (person 3) (& _x))
```

whereas the last one illustrates the fact that we can use a simple variable symbol to denote a degenerate case of a DAG (one which provides no information whatsoever).

Exercise 7.4   Draw diagrams of all the legal DAGs represented by LISP lists in Section 7.3. What LISP lists would represent the DAGs given in the figures appearing so far in this chapter?   [*easy*]

7.4   Subsumption and unification

Computational implementations of principles of feature matching, such as those already mentioned, crucially depend upon notions of *subsumption* and *unification*. Of these, the idea of unification has proved to be profoundly influential, finding its way into most current work on NLP and generative grammar. Assuming, for the sake of illustration, the theory of categories elaborated earlier, we can define subsumption as follows:

Subsumption

A category A subsumes a category B if and only if:

- every atom-valued feature specification in A is in B,
- for every two feature values that share anywhere in A, the corresponding values share in B, and

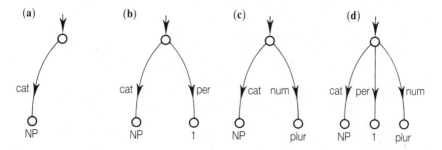

Figure 7.6 Example categories. Note that (d) is the unification of (b) and (c).

- for every category-valued feature specification in A, there is a value for that feature in B, and the value of the feature in A subsumes the value in B.

If A subsumes B, then we may refer to B as an *extension* of A or say that 'B *extends* A'. Intuitively, a category provides information by specifying feature values and specifying sharing between values. Category A properly subsumes category B if A contains less information than B; that is, it is a less informative description. Thus, every piece of information in A must be present in B, but not vice versa. In detail, our recursive definition says first of all that any specification for an atom-valued (non-category-valued) feature in a category is also in all extensions of that category. It also guarantees that if a category specifies a value *v* for some category-valued feature, then any extension of that category specifies a value for that same feature that is an extension of *v*. Finally, it specifies that information about sharing must be preserved in any extension, although, of course, an extension is allowed to contain extra sharing information as well. In the example of Figure 7.6, category (a) subsumes both category (b) and category (c), but neither (b) nor (c) subsumes the other. Categories (b) and (c) each subsume category (d), however.

Note that an extension of a category may contain a specification for any feature that is unspecified in that category. The extension relation is thus a generalization of the relation 'is a superset of', and is one that takes proper account of category-valued features and sharing. It also provides a way of ordering categories, as illustrated in Figure 7.7; namely, the set of categories can be displayed in a *lattice diagram* with less informative categories shown above their extensions or the more informative categories.

An important operation on categories is that of unification. This notion is closely analogous to the operation of union on sets. Unification is undefined for categories containing feature specifications that contradict each other.

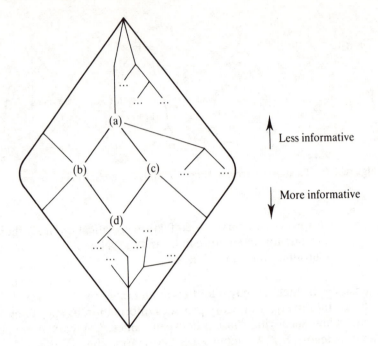

Figure 7.7 Lattice of possible categories.

Unification
The unification of two categories is the smallest category that extends both of them, if such a category exists, otherwise the unification is undefined.

In terms of the lattice diagram, the unification of two categories is the highest category that is below both of them. It contains the pooled information from the two categories, but no more. In the example given earlier (see Figure 7.6), category (d) can be seen to be the unification of the set containing categories (b) and (c). Category (d) is also the unification of the set containing categories (a), (b) and (c). However, if we look for the unification of (b) with the category in Figure 7.8, we find it to be undefined.

The counterpart of intersection in this domain is generalization, defined as follows:

Generalization
The generalization of two categories is the largest category that subsumes both of them.

In the lattice diagram, the generalization of two categories is the lowest category that comes above both. In the foregoing examples, category (a) is

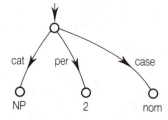

Figure 7.8 Further example category.

the generalization of the set containing categories (b) and (c). Category (a) is likewise the generalization of the set containing categories (a), (b) and (c), and of the set containing (d) and the category of Figure 7.8.

It is going to be vital to be able to compute the unification of two categories, represented as DAGs, in order to build the structures specified by the grammar during parsing. Our definition of unification does not help us very much in this respect, but there is, fortunately, a simple algorithm for computing the unification of two DAGs. The unification is built by putting together the information in the two original categories to build a new one. Basically, we walk through the graphs simultaneously, starting at the two initial nodes, copying information into a new graph as we go. Most of the time, we will have a finger on a node in the first graph, a finger on a node in the second graph and a thumb on a node in the new graph that corresponds to the two of them. To start with, our fingers will be on the initial nodes of the two original graphs, while our thumb will be on a new initial node of the new graph, which is all that there is of that graph so far. As we point at each node in the first graph, and simultaneously at a node of the second graph, we look to see what labels there are on arcs leaving these nodes. When a label appears on arcs in both graphs, we build an arc with that label in the new graph, and we move our fingers and thumb across these arcs, as shown in Figure 7.9.

What we have done here is to copy across information common to both original DAGs. We then continue from where we moved to, carrying on the copying operation for all the rest of the original graphs that can be reached along that route. Having done that, we return to the nodes that the identically labelled arcs came from and consider all the rest of the emanating arcs similarly. Where we come to a labelled arc in one graph that has no corresponding arc in the other graph, we copy across the information to the new graph anyway, effectively ignoring the second graph. In this way, we also obtain, in the new graph, information that is only present in one of the originals. To preserve information about sharing values, one further complication is required. If we ever reach a node in one of the original graphs that we have already visited, the last arc traversed in the new graph should be routed to the node in the new graph that corresponded to that node before, and any transcribing should continue from that point. If our fingers

(a)

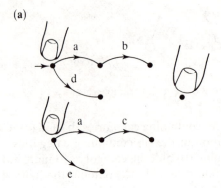

(b)

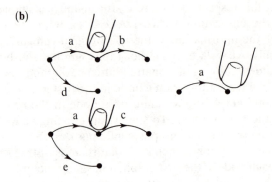

(c)

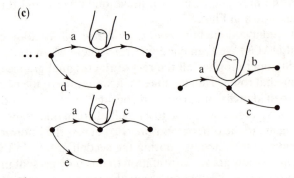

Figure 7.9   Unification in progress.

simultaneously reach nodes that have been visited before, the corresponding nodes in the new graph and all paths reachable from them should be merged together.

This informal algorithm, and many unification algorithms used in practice, suffer from the problem that structures with cycles can be built. To prevent this, the algorithm should contain what is known as an *occur check*; that is, a test to make sure that a structure is not unified with a structure that properly contains that structure. Such a test normally exacts a high cost in running time, which is why it is often omitted from implementations of unification.

This roughly sketched unification algorithm is, unfortunately, rather expensive, even without the occur check, as the graph resulting from the unification has to be constructed from scratch, even though it may be hardly any different from either of the two original graphs. So, in practice, a *destructive* algorithm for unification is often used. This involves making changes to the data structure representing one of the original DAGs so that the graph with the changes made to it will be the result. Of course, making changes inside an existing data structure is potentially dangerous, as it means that the original data structure can no longer be used to represent whatever it used to be. But, in many cases, when the original data structure is no longer needed, the destructive approach is safe and efficient. In destructive unification, information that is in one graph and not in the other is copied directly into the second graph (and sometimes vice versa). Sharing is dealt with in the same way as previously.

Implementing a destructive form of unification unfortunately forces us to worry about low-level issues such as when data structures can be safely reused. Because of this, we will use an implementation where (successful) unification results instead in an *extension recipe* for how to extend either of the two DAGs to produce the new DAG. This contrasts with a destructive version of unification, which would actually change one of the lists to become the result of the unification. If we actually want to construct the resulting DAG, we can then apply the recipe obtained from unification as a separate stage.

How might we specify a recipe for extending a DAG into a new one? Such a recipe will have to indicate places in the original DAG where extra information has to be added, together with what that information is. The obvious way to indicate places where information can be added in a DAG is to put variable symbols in those places. An extension recipe, then, only needs to provide an association between (some of) the variables occurring in the original DAG and the information that is to be added in these places. Such a recipe is called a *substitution*. There are two consequences that follow from choosing this kind of extension recipe. First of all, where two values share, the use of the same variable in both places will ensure that any substitution will put exactly the same information in both places. Secondly, if we do not provide an explicit variable for some open-ended part of a DAG – for example, for some remainder – we cannot expect the recipe to tell us what extra information needs to be added there.

The library file lib subst provides a number of useful functions for manipulating variable symbols and substitutions. These functions are used by a large number of our example programs. A substitution is represented by an association list (in fact, the functions we define may create substitutions with extra nil elements at the end as well). Each two-element sublist contains a variable symbol and a (possibly atomic) DAG that is to be associated with it. For instance, the result of unifying the two structures:

```
((cat _x) (number 3) (& _z))
((number _y) (cat np) (& _w))
```

is a substitution equivalent to:

```
((_y 3) (_x np) (_z _w))
```

In fact, it is not necessary to know about the representation used to be able to use the functions in lib subst; it suffices to know what results they compute and what kinds of arguments they must be provided with. Here is a brief description of the most useful functions in the library:

(isvar item) returns t/nil
: Tests whether a data structure is a variable symbol or not.

(newvar) returns a variable
: Creates a new variable with a name different from any existing one. This function uses the LISP function gensym to generate a new symbol that consists of a '_' followed by a number.

empty_subst
: A LISP variable holding the data structure representing the empty substitution (which records no values as being associated with variables).

(lookup_subst item substitution) returns an item
: A function that, if the input item is a variable symbol, retrieves whatever value is associated with it in the substitution. If the input item is not a variable symbol, or if there is no associated value, that item is returned unchanged.

(add_subst variable item substitution) returns a substitution
: A function that produces a new substitution from an old one. The new substitution is just like the old one except that, in addition, it associates the given item with the given variable symbol.

(apply_subst substitution structure) returns a new structure
: A function that carries out the recipe provided by a substitution, producing a new (extended) structure from an old one.

(compose_substs substitution substitution) returns a substitution
: A function that takes two substitutions and produces a new one which, when applied, will carry out the operations specified in the first recipe, followed by those specified in the second recipe.

lib dagunify provides, among other things, a function unify that produces a substitution from two given DAGs (or nil, if the DAGs do not unify). Although it is not important to understand the details of the code, we will briefly consider the flavour of the approach. The objective of unification is to build up a substitution that, if applied, will be able to transform both of the DAGs into the same extended DAG. This substitution starts off as empty_subst, and each of the functions invoked in unification takes the current value of the substitution as one of its arguments and returns a new extended substitution as its result (or nil, if an inconsistency is detected). The current substitution has to be constantly consulted during unification, as a variable could be encountered that has already been assigned a value by it.

```
(defun unify (dag1 dag2)
   (combine_values dag1 dag2 empty_subst))
```

The key function in unification is obviously combine_values, which takes two DAGs and the current substitution as arguments and returns a (possibly extended) substitution as its result:

```
(defun combine_values (dag1 dag2 substitution)
   (let* (
         (realdag1 (lookup_subst dag1 substitution))
         (realdag2 (lookup_subst dag2 substitution)))
      (if (equal realdag1 realdag2)
         substitution
         (if (isvar realdag1)
            (add_subst realdag1 realdag2 substitution)
            (if (isvar realdag2)
               (add_subst realdag2 realdag1 substitution)
               (if (and (listp realdag1) (listp realdag2))
                  ;; make sure that everything in dag1 is in dag2
                  (do
                     ((subst substitution))
                     ((isvar realdag1)
                     ;; finally put the rest of dag2 at the end of dag1
                     ;; (as long as subst is not nil)
                     (and subst (add_subst realdag1 realdag2 subst)))
                     (let* (
                           (feature (caar realdag1))
                           (value (lookup_subst (cadar realdag1) subst)))
                        (if (equal feature '&)
                           (setq realdag1 value)
                           (let (
                                 (subst_dag2 (put_value_in (list feature value) realdag2 subst)))
                              (setq realdag2 (cadr subst_dag2))
                              (setq subst (car subst_dag2))
                              (setq realdag1 (cdr realdag1))
                              (if (null subst) (return nil))))))
                  nil))))))
```

If the two DAGs are already equal, then the existing substitution can be returned unchanged and all is well. Alternatively, if one is a variable symbol – the function isvar from lib subst tests this – then it suffices to add an element to the substitution that associates this with the other DAG. In any other case, both DAGs must be complex objects (lists) for unification to succeed. What we need to do is to go through the explicit feature–value pairs mentioned in the first DAG, for each one adding to the substitution as necessary, so that the second DAG contains the same pair. Finally, we add to the substitution to associate whatever information there is in the second DAG and which we have not already encountered with the remainder variable at the end of the first DAG. For instance, with the two DAGs:

((cat VP) (& _x))   and   ((number sing) (& _y)))

we start by putting into the substitution entries for extending the second DAG to contain the information explicitly encoded in the first. At this point, the substitution will be something like:

((_y ((cat VP) (& _z))))

If we applied this substitution to the second DAG at this point, the result (after some cosmetic flattening) would be:

((number sing) (cat VP) (& _z))

We now associate with the remainder variable _x the parts of the second DAG that we have not already seen in the first DAG, adding to the substitution to make:

((_x ((number sing) (& _z)))
(_y ((cat VP) (& _z))))

This substitution now has the property that it yields the same DAG, whichever of the two original DAGs it is applied to. combine_values iterates through the feature specifications (feature and value) found in the first DAG. For each one, it attempts to add to the substitution in such a way that the second DAG will have the same value for this feature. Procedure put_value_in is used for this. As well as adding to the substitution as necessary, put_value_in also returns what remains of the second DAG if the entry for the given feature is removed. As we cycle through the features of the first DAG in turn, each time we use (in the variable realdag2) the result returned from the previous put_value_in, rather than the original DAG. This means that realdag2 gets smaller and smaller so that, when we reach the end of realdag1, it then holds all the featural information of the original realdag2, which did not have any analogue in the original realdag1. It is this final value that we then associate with the remainder variable (now in realdag1) of the original first DAG.

Exercise 7.5   Using only the functions in lib subst to construct the relevant lists, construct a substitution that associates: a with _x, b with _y and _y with _z. Finally, use the same functions to do the following with this substitution:

> Find out the values associated with _x, _y and _z and
> apply it to the DAG ((f1 _x) (f2 ((f21 c) (f22 _z) (& _q))) (& _r)).

[*easy*]

Exercise 7.6   Read and understand the definition of apply_subst that is given in lib subst. Write an alternative definition that, instead of producing a new structure, destructively alters the old structure, adding in the new information.   [*intermediate, for programmers*]

7.5   The status of rules

Having now discussed the structure of complex categories at some length, it is appropriate to review the status of rules in this scheme. A PATR rule says that, in the language described, certain LHS categories can be realized as certain sequences of RHS categories, but it does not provide the possible LHS and RHS categories by enumeration. Instead, it provides us with a description of the categories that can appear in this relationship. For instance, the rule:

```
Rule
   S → NP VP:
      <NP head> = <VP head>
      <S subj> = <NP>.
```

which, expanded into its full form, is:

```
Rule
   X0 → X1 X2:
      <X0 cat> = S
      <X1 cat> = NP
      <X2 cat> = VP
      <X1 head> = <X2 head>
      <X0 subj> = <X1>.
```

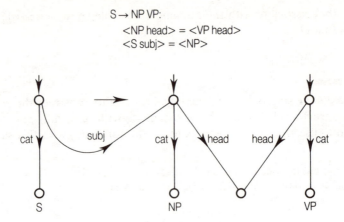

$S \rightarrow NP\ VP$:
$<NP\ head> = <VP\ head>$
$<S\ subj> = <NP>$

Figure 7.10   Minimal DAGs satisfying a rule.

says that:

> Every category X0 can be realized as a category X1 followed by a category X2 as long as the cat of X0 is S, the cat of X1 is NP, the cat of X2 is VP, the head of X1 is the same as the head of X2 and the subj of X0 is X1.

As far as the rule is concerned, as long as these stipulations are obeyed, then X1 followed by X2 is indeed a legal way of realizing X0. It does not matter if any of the categories have other features not mentioned in the rule, or if there are extra sharing relationships in addition to those specified – the minimal conditions provided are enough to ensure legality.

One way to interpret such a rule computationally is as a test for grammaticality. Given three categories X0, X1 and X2, we could proceed through the conditions of the rule and verify whether they are satisfied by the categories. Another way to interpret the rule, one that could be used by a parser, is as a way of generating possible categories X0, X1 and X2, perhaps given some initial information about one or more of them. For instance, a top-down parser might want to know what X1 and X2 could be, given some information about X0. In this case, the problem amounts to the following:

> Given some categories C0, C1 and C2, are there extensions of these categories, X0, X1 and X2, which satisfy the rule? If so, what is the least information that has to be added to C0, C1 and C2 to produce a legal sequence of categories?

Such least extensions can be computed by successively extending the initial categories to additionally reflect each '=' constraint in turn. For instance, we could start off by extending X0 so that it had S for its cat value. This would obviously fail if X0 already had a cat value that conflicted with S, but would succeed if X0 had no cat value or had one that was already S. After dealing with the cat constraints, we would come to the others. As we have already noted, the interpretation of feature constraints like <X1 head> = <X2 head> is that the values at the end of the two paths are to be identical. So, to satisfy this constraint, we would extend X1 and X2 so that in the extensions the two head values were identical. In the extended DAGs, what value would we expect to find at the end of each of the paths? Clearly this value would be a DAG containing at least all the information that was previously known about the two paths individually. And the information provided does not legitimate any structure apart from that previously available from the two paths. We would, therefore, expect the value at the end of the two paths to be the *unification* of the two previous values. If the unification is not defined, then an adequate extension cannot be computed, and so the rule is inapplicable in this case. So, we can generate the minimal extension categories X0, X1 and X2 by starting with the initial categories, C0, C1 and C2, and performing a series of unifications. In this, we treat each '=' constraint in turn, as an instruction to generate a new set of categories, where some values are replaced by the unification of two previous values.

7.6   Representing PATR grammars in LISP

A PATR grammar rule consists of two parts – a framework phrase-structure rule and a set of extra conditions. We can easily represent PATR conditions by LISP list structures. For instance, the VP rule of Grammar4 can be represented as follows:

```
(Rule (VP -> V X)
    (VP cat) = VP
    (V cat) = V
    (V arg1) = (X cat)
    (V slash) = 0
    (VP slash) = (X slash))
```

Notice that we spell out the cat values explicitly in the LISP notation. Here is another rule – the 'slash elimination rule':

```
(Rule (X0 -> )
    (X0 cat) = (X0 slash)
    (X0 empty) = yes)
```

We will now represent a grammar as two lists, rules and lexical_rules. The above list structure would be suitable as an element of rules whereas the following would be a possible value for lexical_rules:

```
(setq lexical_rules
 '((Word (approved)
         (cat) = V
         (slash) = 0
         (arg1) = PP)
   (Word (disapproved)
         (cat) = V
         (slash) = 0
         (arg1) = PP)
   (Word (of)
         (cat) = P
         (slash) = 0
         (arg1) = NP)
   (Word (Dr Chan)
         (slash) = 0
         (cat) = NP)
   (Word (nurses)
         (slash) = 0
         (cat) = NP)
         (cat) = NP)))
```

The lexicon and rules of Grammar4, apart from the conjunction rule, can be found in this LISP format in lib patrgram. In fact, the moment we start wanting to do something with grammars, it becomes clear that extra information is needed for our programs to be able to present information to us in a concise and relevant way. Our categories may now have entries for a number of different features, but usually we are only interested in seeing certain features in parse trees and other structures built by programs. We will thus assume that every LISP PATR grammar comes equipped with two functions, as follows:

(category dag substitution) returns a printable value
> Given a basic DAG and a substitution, possibly specifying extra extensions to that DAG, extracts the main useful category information.

(tree cat subtrees) returns a tree
> Given a value returned by category and a list of subtrees, returns the parse tree with the value as its label and the given subtrees.

The appropriate functions in lib patrgram are as follows:

```
(defun category (d subst)
 (let (
       (cat (find_feature_value 'cat d subst))
       (slash (find_feature_value 'slash d subst)))
   (if (equal slash 0)
       cat
       (list cat '/ slash))))
```

```
(defun tree (cat subtrees)
  (cons cat subtrees))
```

where find_feature_value (defined in lib dagunify) is used to extract the value of a given feature from a DAG. So, we have decided that, for this grammar, we usually wish to see the values of the cat and slash features, the '/' notation being used when the slash is not 0. In this case, we have decided to build parse trees conventionally, but with other grammars we may make other decisions – for instance, we may decide to suppress the subtrees when they are complex.

To make use of PATR rules, we need to have a way of constructing DAGs that satisfy the sorts of conditions specified in rules, testing whether given DAGs satisfy the conditions and so on. The file lib lisppatr contains a number of useful functions, which will now be outlined (although a detailed understanding of the code is not important). The key function that we will use is the function apply_condition which, given such a list of conditions, a DAG and a current substitution, produces an extended substitution which, when applied to the DAG, produces an extended DAG in which the conditions are satisfied. For instance:

```
(setq dag '((VP _x) (V _y) (X _z) (& _r)))
(setq subst
  (apply_condition '((VP slash) = (X slash)
                     (V subcat) = (X cat)
                     (V slash) = 0) dag empty_subst))
  (apply_subst subst dag)
```

produces a DAG like the following:

```
((VP ((SLASH #:_814)  (& #:_811)))
 (V  ((SUBCAT #:_818) (& ((SLASH 0) (& #:_819)))))
 (X  ((SLASH #:_814)  (& ((cat #:_818) (& #:_817)))))
 (& _R))
```

where the variables like #:_814 arise because of the use of newvar to create new variables as the necessary extensions of the DAG are recorded. (Note that these symbols, created by gensym, are not 'interned', which means that if you try to read in two occurrences of #:_814 you will get two *different* symbols; if you want to read in structures like this and be able to name multiple occurrences of the same symbol, you should first remove the #: prefixes.) Here is the definition of apply_condition. There is actually one other clause in the definition, which we will come back to later.

```
(defun apply_condition (entry dag subst)
  (if (null entry)
      subst
      (if (consp (car entry))
          ;; path1 = path2
```

```
    (let*
      ((end1_subst1 (apply_path (car entry) dag subst))
       (end1 (car end1_subst1))
       (subst1 (cadr end1_subst1)))
      (if subst1
        (let*
          ((end2_subst2 (apply_path (nth 2 entry) dag subst1))
           (end2 (car end2_subst2))
           (subst2 (cadr end2_subst2)))
          (if subst2
            (let ((newsubst (combine_values end1 end2 subst2)))
              (if newsubst
                (apply_condition (cdddr entry) dag newsubst)
                nil))
            nil))
        nil))
    (error 'Illegal PATR entry ~S' entry)))))
```

The most interesting part deals with a condition of the form first = rest. Each of first and rest may be a list of feature names, like (verb head number), specifying a value in a DAG by the path used to reach it, and rest may alternatively be a simple value, like S or no. The function apply_path is used to get hold of the values that first and rest indicate, these being put into the variables end1 and end2. Finally, the substitution is extended, by combine_values, to make these values unify.

```
    (defun apply_path (path dag subst)
      (if (null path)
        (list dag subst)
        (if (atom path)
          (list path subst)
          (if (consp path)
            (let ((subst_val (get_value (car path) dag subst)))
              (if (car subst_val)
                (apply_path (cdr path) (car subst_val) (cadr subst_val))
                subst_val))
            (error 'Ill-formed path ~S' path)))))
```

The function apply_path actually needs to return two values. Sometimes, if the DAG does not explicitly mention all the features necessary to follow the path, it may need to add to the current substitution in order to force the values to exist in the desired extension. Therefore, it needs to return a list containing both the value found and the (possibly enlarged) substitution.

With apply_condition, we have the raw material for making use of PATR rules. lib lisppatr contains definitions of two functions, corresponding to the two main ways in which we need to use rules:

```
    (lhs_match dag rule) returns (substitution daglist)
    (rhs_match daglist rule) returns (substitution newdaglist)
```

The function lhs_match is used when we have a category (DAG) and wish to know whether a given rule might provide a way of rewriting this. This would obviously be relevant to a top-down parser. If successful, the function returns a list of DAGs corresponding to the RHS of the rule, together with a substitution that indicates necessary extensions to the original DAG. For instance:

```
(let* (
  (goal '((cat S) (& _r)))
  (subst_rhs
    (lhs_match
      '((cat S) (& _r))
      '(Rule (S -> NP VP)
          (S slash) = (VP slash)
          (NP slash) = 0
          (S cat) = S
          (NP cat) = NP
          (VP cat) = VP))))
  (print (simplify_features (car subst_rhs) goal))
  (print (cadr subst_rhs))
  t)
((CAT S) (SLASH #:_34) (& #:_31))
(((SLASH 0) (CAT NP) (& #:_37)) ((SLASH #:_34) (CAT VP) (& #:_39))) T
```

where simplify_features, defined in lib dagunify, is a version of apply_subst that flattens out extra remainders in DAGs. Given a DAG and a PATR rule, for instance:

```
((VP -> V X)
  (VP cat) = VP
  (V cat) = V
  (V arg1) = (X cat)
  (V slash) = 0
  (VP slash) = (X slash))
```

lhs_match operates by:

- Producing a skeleton DAG with top-level features named according to the phrase names in the rule (here, VP, V, X).

- In the skeleton, giving the LHS phrase name (here, VP) the DAG provided and giving each other feature a distinct variable as its value.

- Using apply_condition to produce a substitution enforcing the conditions of the rule.

- Applying this substitution to the skeleton DAG and extracting the components to form the output list.

The function rhs_match works in a very similar way, but is the kind of thing that would be used by a bottom-up parser. Given a list of DAGs and a PATR rule, it looks to see whether an initial sublist of the list could be extended to satisfy the conditions on the categories in the RHS of the rule. In this case, it constructs a list consisting of a DAG for the LHS of the rule, followed by the remaining DAGs of the original list. It bundles this, together with the substitution needed to appropriately extend the used DAGs, into a single list which serves as its result.

lib lisppatr does provide one other very useful function, make_dag, which allows us to construct a minimal DAG satisfying a given set of conditions. Using make_dag takes much of the pain out of specifying DAGs for programs:

```
(make_dag '((cat) = S (slash person) = 3 (slash) = (pred slash)))

((CAT S)
 (SLASH ((PERSON 3) (& #:_2123)))
 (PRED ((SLASH ((PERSON 3) (& #:_2123))) (& #:_2127)))
 (& #:_2125))
```

7.7   Random generation revisited

How can we adapt our random generator to deal with the more interesting sorts of grammars exemplified by Grammar2, Grammar3 and Grammar4? The basic generation algorithm can be used again, but we must be more sophisticated about representing and comparing complex categories. When we are using a grammar rule for generation, we have to pay special attention to structures that share, which is denoted by multiple occurrences of the same variable. Imagine we are trying to generate a phrase covered by the category:

```
((cat S) (& _r))
```

and decide to use the following rule:

```
Rule {topicalization}
  X0 → X1 X2:
    <X0 slash> = <X1 slash>
    <X0 cat> = S
    <X1 empty> = no
    <X2 cat> = S
    <X2 slash> = <X1 cat>
    <X2 empty> = no.
```

Using lhs_match on the LISP version of this rule, we obtain the following list of categories to generate from:

```
(((SLASH 0) (EMPTY NO) (CAT _x) (& _r1))
 ((CAT S) (SLASH _x) (EMPTY NO) (& _r2)))
```

As we work through this list in order, we find that first of all something of the form:

```
((SLASH 0) (EMPTY NO) (CAT _x) (& _r1))
```

must be generated. We have a completely free choice as to what _x must be, so it would be quite acceptable for us to generate something with cat NP, say. When we come to the next part of the rule, we have to generate:

```
((CAT S) (SLASH _x) (EMPTY NO) (& _r2))
```

but we no longer have a free choice for _x. Whatever _x is chosen here must be the same as the _x that was chosen for the first subphrase – that is, NP. We need to have a way of remembering what choice was made for the cat feature of the first subphrase so that we can ensure that the slash feature of the second subphrase is the same. Fortunately, we have already marked this restriction in the DAGs by using the same variable symbol _x in both places. All we need to do is keep track of what value is associated with _x where it first arises and ensure that in subsequent occurrences of _x the same value is used. We can keep track of the values associated with the variables in a rule by keeping a current substitution, which notionally has to be applied to each DAG we deal with.

In our previous version of generate, we defined a function unify that tested whether the LHS of a rule was appropriate for generating from a given description, using equal. Now that we allow arbitrary features, we could use our DAG version of unify, taking account of the fact that the LHS of a rule may specify any number of features in any order. In practice, however, the function lhs_match is just what we need, and we can use that to obtain, from an initial category, the RHS sequence of categories that a given rule specifies, if the category is matched with its LHS. Here are the main functions of the new generation program; the whole program is to be found in lib randfgen. They are very similar to the main functions in lib randgen:

```
(defvar current_substitution)
```

```
(defun generate (dag)
  (if (atom dag)
    (list dag)
    (let ((rs (matching_rules dag)))
      (if (null rs)
        (throw 'generate nil)
        (let ((subst_rhs (lhs_match dag (oneof rs))))
          (setq current_substitution
            (compose_substs current_substitution (car subst_rhs)))
          (generate_all (cadr subst_rhs)))))))

(defun generate_all (body)
  (if (null body)
    '()
    (append
      (generate (apply_subst current_substitution (car body)))
      (generate_all (cdr body)))))
```

The main difference from the previous program is in the maintenance of the global variable current_substitution, which must hold any values already associated with variables that will be encountered later on in the generation process. In generate, any assignments to variables obtained by unifying the DAG with the LHS of a rule must be added to the current substitution. This is done by compose_substs, defined in lib subst. In addition, before attempting to generate from a given DAG, in generate_all, we always apply the current substitution to it, to get the latest values associated with any variables. The function matching_rules is much as before, although it uses lhs_match:

```
(defun matching_rules (dag)
  (let ((results ()))
    (dolist (rule rules)
      (let ((subst_rhs (lhs_match dag rule)))
        (if (car subst_rhs)
          (setq results (cons rule results)))))
    (dolist (rule lexical_rules)
      (let ((subst_rhs (lhs_match dag rule)))
        (if (car subst_rhs)
          (setq results (cons rule results)))))
    results))
```

The global variable current_substitution needs to be given an initial value before we can start generating. It makes sense to put this initialization in a top-level function and always to invoke the generator through this function:

```
(defun g (description)
  (setq current_substitution empty_subst)
  (catch 'generate
    (generate description)))
```

Our new version of generate contains provision for the program immediately to exit from g if it ever comes to a DAG for which there are no matching rules. This enables us to have loops like:

(loop (print (g (make_dag '((cat) = S (slash) = 0)))))

and not to have the program crash if it gets into a dead end. But why do we get dead ends with this program? This never used to happen in our earlier generation programs. With Grammar4, dead ends occur through the inter-action of several rules. It is easier to demonstrate why dead ends occur by inventing a single rule that causes problems and might plausibly be in a grammar.

Consider a language where verbs appear at the ends of verb phrases (there are many such Subject–Object–Verb (SOV) languages – Eskimo, Japanese, Persian and Turkish to name just four). For such a language, a grammar might include a rule like the following:

```
Rule {SOV VP expansion}
   X0 → X1 X2:
      <X0 cat> = VP
      <X2 cat> = V
      <X2 subcat> = <X1 cat>.
```

Imagine our program is generating a random VP and uses this rule. It will end up with a list of two DAGs like the following to generate from:

((cat _x) (& _r1))
((cat V) (subcat _x) (& _r2))

First of all, it has to generate a phrase of any category (_x). Having done this (and necessarily obtained a value for _x in the current substitution), the program has to generate a verb whose subcat feature has this same value. Unfortunately, there are unlikely to be verbs with all possible subcat values, and so for some _xs that we choose (for instance, C, N) it may be impossible to find an appropriate verb. We might be tempted to criticize the grammar for this problem: the grammar says that _x can have any value, and the rule is thus incorrect. But such a criticism is based on a misunderstanding. The rule should be read as saying '... is a legal phrase if ... and the cat feature of the first subphrase is the same as the subcat feature of the second.' It is our interpretation of this rule in procedural terms – namely, 'generate any phrase and then generate a phrase whose subcat feature has the same value as the first phrase's cat feature' – that is wrong. This interpretation will never generate incorrect sentences, but sometimes it will get into hopeless dead ends. A better implementation of random generation would have to build in some kind of search mechanism for trying different possible values of _x.

You may well get frustrated running lib randfgen, since, through randomness, it frequently gets into dead ends and often seems to avoid the most interesting sentence constructions. One way out of this is to make the program less random. For instance, you could define your own version of oneof which asks you which rule to choose, as follows:

```
(defun oneof (list)
  (if (equal (length list) 1)
      (car list)
      (let ((n 1))
        (dolist (x list)
          (print (list n x))
          (setq n (+ 1 n)))
        (print '(which one ?))
        (let ((input (read)))
          (if (and (integerp input) (< 0 input) (<= input (length list)))
              (nth (- input 1) list)
              (oneof list))))))
```

Using this version of oneof, you can steer the program to generate any legal sentence, or you can reply with random numbers if you wish the machine to try making the decisions. (If you get tired with this way of running the program and wish to reinstate the original oneof, just load lib randfgen again.)

————

Exercise 7.7 Load the example grammar in lib patrgram and generate some random phrases from it, using lib randfgen. Here is the sort of thing to type in:

    (print (g (make_dag '((cat) = S (slash) = 0))))

Use tracing (of generate and generate_all) to follow what the generator is doing. Of course, the important information in current_substitution will not be shown by this. Modify the program to print out the result of applying current_substitution to the DAG when generate is called.   [*easy*]

Exercise 7.8 Use the random generator with the directive version of oneof. With the grammar rules in lib patrgram, what sequence of numbers do you have to provide to make the program generate the following sentences:

Nurses seemed well-qualified.

Dr Chan disapproved of MediCenter.

Competent Dr Chan seemed.

Patients thought patients had approved of Dr Chan.

Dr Chan appeared well-qualified patients thought.

[*intermediate*]

Exercise 7.9   Add the conjunction rule to the list of rules. If you are using the library version of oneof, what problems does this introduce for random generation? What bugs in the grammar does the generator reveal? [*intermediate*]

Exercise 7.10   Alter generate to produce parse trees, generating labels using the slash and cat features.   [*intermediate*]

Exercise 7.11   Update the library program tdrecog, encountered in Chapter 5, to work with PATR-style grammars. It would make sense to make use of the function lhs_match roughly as in the generate function in the text.   [*hard*]

Exercise 7.12   In matching_rules, we compute the substitutions obtained by the various unifications and then throw this information away. When control returns to generate and a particular rule is chosen, the unification for that rule then has to be done again. This is wasteful. Alter the program to avoid this.   [*intermediate, for programmers*]

7.8   Chart parsing with feature-based grammars

We have presented chart-parsing algorithms using phrase structure grammars like Grammar1 with monadic categories, but of course we have made use of grammars with more structure than this to cover interesting natural language constructions. What exactly are the issues to be faced when implementing a parser (a chart parser, say) for a grammar that allows complex categories? There are really three basic options for how to parse when a grammar allows complex categories:

(1)   Expand the grammar into a monadic CF-PSG.

The simplest use of features can be viewed as a way of specifying sets of rules in an abbreviated way. For instance, the rule:

```
Rule
  S → NP VP:
    <NP num> = <VP num>.
```

can be seen as a shorthand for the two rules:

```
Rule
  S → NP_sing VP_sing.
Rule
  S → NP_plur VP_plur.
```

In this case, all we need to do is to expand out the rule set and parse using the standard techniques. But this strategy is really only feasible for small toy grammars, since otherwise the set of rules will be quite vast. The size of the set of rules that deal only with coordination is likely to be at least as great as the size of the set of categories. The size of a set of categories based on n binary features is 3^n (it would only be 2^n if all features had to be fully specified), so even with a modest set of, say, 24 binary features, we have 3^{24} (282 429 536 481) categories. The size of the grammar impacts directly on both the space (memory) and time requirements of parsing. In practice, therefore, even if the induced category set is finite, we have little choice but to employ the feature system directly while parsing, one way or another.

(2)   Parse using a monadic CF-PSG backbone.

If there is a feature (or set of features) such that every DAG in every grammar rule specifies a definite value for that feature, an initial parsing can take place using the monadic CF-PSG derived by just considering this feature and forgetting the others. For instance, some grammars specify a specific value for the cat feature of each category and in such cases we could parse only using this feature. Of course, if other features are neglected in the parsing, the parser can be expected to waste time exploring hypotheses and formulating potential analyses that would be excluded by the full grammar. A filtering process would then be required to determine which complete analyses found by the initial parsing were actually valid, and what the values of the other features were. For instance, if the S-expansion rule just given was part of a grammar and sentences were parsed using only the cat feature, sentences analyzed using this rule would have to be checked to ensure that the num values of the noun phrase and verb phrase were compatible. Parsing with a context-free backbone suffers from the fact that a filtering process is needed after the main parsing process and also that the parsing search space is widened by ignoring other features (how much depends on the extent to which constraints on these features can actually reject parses, rather than enable structures based on the backbone features to be built). In addition, this approach will not be feasible when there is no single feature that is given a value in every DAG in the grammar. For instance, the conjunction rule of Grammar2 does not specify a value for the cat feature of each daughter, and so the cat feature cannot be used to make a monadic backbone for Grammar2.

(3)   Incorporate special mechanisms into the parser.

The basic parsing problem is the same, whether categories are atoms or arbitrary feature structures. All that is required is that the basic operations of the parser (testing for equality, looking for rules, and so on) be redefined to accept a different data structure for categories. This simple fact, unfortunately, masks a number of special problems that arise in parsing directly with complex categories. Nevertheless, in the end, this is probably the most effective approach, and we will survey here some of the special problems that arise and some standard ideas for their solution.

Let us start by surveying the main differences between parsing with monadic categories and with grammars involving complex categories. First of all, the raw material of the grammar, the rules and lexical entries, are different. Secondly, we must start using DAGs in appropriate places in the chart. As we saw in Chapter 6, an edge in a chart recognizer is a structure with the following components:

<START>	= ... some integer ...	(where the edge starts)
<FINISH>	= ... some integer ...	(where the edge finishes)
<LABEL>	= ... some category ...	(the main goal of the edge)
<FOUND>	= ... some category sequence ...	(the subphrases already found)
<TOFIND>	= ... some category sequence ...	(the subphrases left to find)

Previously, we thought of the LABEL, FOUND and TOFIND components as representing a dotted rule, where <LABEL> is the LHS of the rule, <FOUND> is the sequence of RHS categories before the dot and <TOFIND> is the sequence of RHS categories after the dot. Any edge in the chart will now have as its LABEL a DAG representing the phrase that is found or being sought as well as DAGs for its FOUND and TOFIND categories. Although there may not be a rule in the grammar that specifies exactly this sequence of DAGs, the entries in the LABEL, FOUND and TOFIND components taken together form a sequence of DAGs that must be legitimated by a single grammar rule or lexical entry.

The DAGs in an edge will not in general be completely specified for all features, and, as with rules, we must take each edge to be a statement about all possible categories that extend the categories specified. For instance, an active edge with the dotted rule depicted in Figure 7.11(a) indicates that we have found an NP with person 3 and that, if we can find a VP with person 3, then we will have found an S with mood the same as the mood of the VP. It does not matter if the VP found has extra features to those specified. On the other hand, an inactive edge with the dotted rule shown in Figure 7.11(b) indicates that we have found a VP with particular values for num and mood. Since no other features are mentioned, the assumption is that the words we have found simply bear no information about these other features, and so any extra information about the features would be completely compatible with what we know. In particular, if we ever wanted to find a VP with 3 as the value for person or one with FOO as the value of BAZ, then this VP would serve adequately each time.

How does the operation of the fundamental rule look when we have DAGs as categories? Imagine that we wish to combine the two edges of

(a)

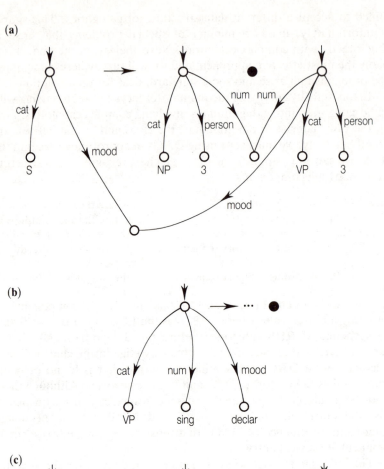

(b)

(c)

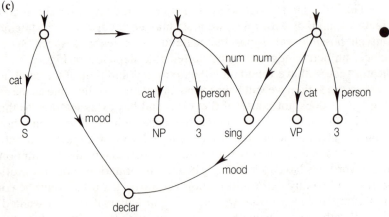

Figure 7.11   (a) Dotted rule for active edge. (b) Dotted rule for inactive edge. (c) Result of applying the fundamental rule.

Figure 7.11 by the fundamental rule and that they start and finish at appropriate places. Clearly, the rule applies here, as the active edge only requires a VP with person 3, and this is compatible with the information in the inactive edge. What do we know about the S that we have found and its immediate constituents? From Figure 7.11(c), we can see that the mood of the S is the same as the mood of its VP; from Figure 7.11(b), we can see that this is declar. From Figure 7.11(a), we can see that the num of the NP is the same as the num of the VP; from Figure 7.11(b), we can see that this is sing. Hence, the dotted rule for the combination should look as shown in Figure 7.11(c). What we have done here is to extend the whole sequence of DAGs just enough so that the DAG for the required VP and the DAG for the found VP are unified. As a consequence, in the resulting dotted rule, all the pieces of information from the various parts of the complete sentence are combined in the right ways. In general, then, the result of an application of the fundamental rule is a new edge similar to the contributing active edge, except that it:

- extends it by having in the place of the first required category the result of unifying that category with the category found, and
- has the dot moved on one place to the right.

The other chart-parsing rules involve retrieving rules from the grammar whose parts correspond to categories appearing in the chart. Once again, unification is the appropriate operation that corresponds to the equality test used in the monadic case. For instance, in an application of the top-down rule a grammar rule must be found whose LHS DAG can be unified with the DAG for the first TOFIND phrase.

7.8.1   Copying

Our sketch of how the fundamental rule can work with complex categories has glossed over important issues about the multiple use of edges. In a chart parser, every active and inactive edge must be preserved until parsing has finished, because it may need to combine together with an edge that has not yet entered the chart. Consider, for instance, the processing of the sentence

An employee with two supervisors can apply to the area head.

and imagine that we are keeping track of the number (sing or plur) of phrases like NPs and VPs. Now, our chart parser might well find the VP 'can apply to the area head' fairly early; the num feature for this phrase will be unspecified, as the phrase could serve as either a singular or a plural VP. A bottom-up parser might well combine this phrase with the plural NP 'two supervisors' to yield a complete sentence. This application of the fundamental rule will result in an edge where the NP and the VP will both be plural, as the subject and predicate of a sentence must share their num values. It would be wrong to keep any of the new information obtained about the VP in any place but the new edge, however, because the original VP edge will eventually have to combine with the incomplete singular NP 'an employee with two supervisors' and hence be seen (in this context) as a singular phrase. In this example, the original VP edge must remain unscathed by its combination with the first NP if it is to correctly combine with the second.

A further twist to the story about multiple uses of edges is introduced by the fact that in a chart parser a given edge can contribute several times towards a single analysis. For instance, active edges corresponding to the rule:

```
Rule
  X0 → X1 X2:
    <X0 cat> = VP
    <X1 cat> = VP
    <X2 cat> = PP.
```

would contribute several times to the analysis of a VP that contained more than one final PP. The actual categories involved each time would, however, be different, and so the representation adopted needs to be able to keep the different values separate.

What implications do these issues have for chart parser implementation? First of all, they mean that *destructive* unification cannot be used in the generation of new edges, as this is only safe if the graphs that are changed will never be needed again. Thus, in applying the fundamental rule, we cannot safely overwrite the active edge and reuse the data structures to build the new edge – the partial solution that it represents must be preserved for possible later use. Secondly, the fact that a given edge can contribute twice to an analysis means that we have to be careful about using variables to stand for parts of DAGs that can be extended. If the same DAG is to be used twice in the same analysis, we cannot use the same variables to represent both extensions at the same time.

The obvious solution to these problems is to always use copies for unification. In the new copies, we can always ensure that fresh variables are used so as not to conflict with variables used elsewhere. Copying is, however, expensive, and a number of schemes for structure sharing have been devised in an attempt to reduce the amount of copying required. The new edge created by the fundamental rule will in general be quite similar, although not identical, to the active edge that participated. So, we can devise implementations of these data structures where the new structure is represented, not as a completely new object, but as the original active edge together with a record of the changes (additions) necessary to convert that structure into the new one. In a LISP implementation, this might be done by using substitutions to represent changes, and by representing an edge by a pair consisting of a skeleton edge and a substitution. Such a representation will make it harder to see exactly what the contents of a given edge are. On the other hand, it will make the job of building new edges much easier.

7.8.2 Duplication checking

The crucial advantages of chart parsing come from the way in which duplication of effort is avoided. When categories are monadic, it is trivial to check whether an edge is already present in the chart, because either there is an edge mentioning the same categories or there is not. When categories have complex internal structure, however, there are more possible relations between a new edge and an edge already in the chart than simply being the same or different, and so our duplication tests must be more sophisticated. If we already have an active edge looking for a noun phrase of any num at some position in the string, for instance, we do not want to add a new edge that is looking for a plural noun phrase at that point, even though the edges are different. On the other hand, if we already have an edge looking for a plural noun phrase, it is quite reasonable to add a new one that will accept any noun phrase, because otherwise possible solutions will be lost. In fact, the test that a new edge must pass before being added to the chart is that it is not subsumed by any existing edge.

Exercise 7.13 If there is already an active edge looking for a plural noun phrase at some point in the chart and a new edge is generated that will accept any noun phrase at that place, the new edge will pass the subsumption check and be added to the chart. This means, however, that if there is a sequence of words that can be recognized as a plural noun phrase, this phrase will be recognized twice, once as a plural noun phrase and once as an 'any' noun phrase. What possible techniques might be introduced to avoid this duplication? [*hard*]

Exercise 7.14 If category-valued features are allowed, even the subsumption check will not necessarily prevent the parser getting into infinite loops. This is because we can keep on generating edges, spanning the same part of the input string, none of which is subsumed by any previous one. Write down some grammar rules where this could happen in a top-down parser. How might we solve this problem? [*hard*]

7.8.3   Indexing

In Chapter 6, we discussed the utility of indexing in a chart parser, both for the chart itself and for the grammar. In general, a top-down parser needs to index the grammar rules on the LHS categories and a (left-to-right) bottom-up parser needs to index them on the first categories on their RHS. The existence of complex categories gives us a greater choice on indexing strategies. Where there is a conventional cat component to each category (as we have assumed), a simple strategy is to index on the cat values – this reduces to something essentially the same as the monadic category case. This strategy will not work straightforwardly, however, if rules do not always specify cat values for all constituents. For instance, in our treatment of topicalization:

> Rule {topicalization}
>   X0 → X1 X2:
>   <X0 cat> = S
>   <X2 cat> = S
>   <X2 slash> = X1.

there is no obvious way to index this rule for a bottom-up parser, because the first category on the RHS could have any value for its cat feature (at least, this is true of the rule as we have presented it, which is something of an oversimplification). If indexing is on the basis of the cat feature, the only solution seems to be to lump together all rules of this kind in a bundle to be tried bottom up, whatever the category of a FOUND phrase happens to be. If there are many such rules, or indeed many rules indexed by any given category, some form of secondary indexing (using other features) will be needed to cut down further the rules considered in any instance. In general, then, the designer of an efficient chart-parsing system needs to allow for indexing on a tunable set of features (such as cat, arg1, slash) that may well need to be changed as the grammar develops.

7.8.4   Conflating similar edges

As it is set up, a chart parser will eventually enumerate all possible analyses of a given string by the time it halts. Each of these will yield a, possibly complex, DAG for the category describing the string, as well as a tree expressing its constituent structure, if we decide to build it. Now, if we are only interested in the category itself, and this will be the case where our task is only recognition or where the (possibly extensive) information in the topmost category is all we need for some task, we will be uninterested in alternative analyses that give rise to DAGs containing exactly the same information. Since the information in a category is obtained entirely from the grammar rule used to recognize it and the categories of the immediate subphrases, we will likewise be uninterested in alternative analyses of a smaller phrase that all yield essentially the same category. We are thus led to consider a strategy of conflating inactive edges for similar categories, even if the internal structure of the edges (the FOUND lists) is not identical in every respect.

Consider, for example, a recognition task involving a grammar that describes categories entirely in terms of the values of cat and num features. A given noun phrase, occupying a given portion of the string, may well have three possible analyses, say, but if these are all singular in num, it is only necessary to consider one such analysis. Similarly, if there are three possible ways of finding a verb phrase after that noun phrase, all occupying the same portion of the string and being likewise singular, we only need to consider one of them. If we can avoid adding the extra edges to the chart in both cases, it will only be necessary to apply the fundamental rule once, rather than nine times, to recognize a sentence consisting of a noun phrase followed by a verb phrase. This is obviously a considerable saving.

This idea of conflating similar edges can be extended to a technique of *packing*, which is useful even when we *are* interested in the complete internal structure of phrases. When there are two different analyses covering the same portion of the string and yielding equivalent categories, the technique is to conflate these into a single edge which indicates that there are several possible internal analyses (FOUND lists) for the phrase. When the resulting 'packed' edge is combined with another edge, it is left in its packed form – the two analyses are not expanded out. Only when a complete inactive edge covering the whole string has been found are all the possible analyses worked out (if this is required) by unpacking all the packed subphrases and combining together all the alternative analyses in all possible ways. If all possible analyses are eventually required, the packing and unpacking of the edges contributing to these analyses will not make much difference to the amount of work done. On the other hand, if there is a possible phrase with several analyses but which does not contribute to any complete analysis of the string, packing the relevant edges together can save an appreciable amount of work, because the (in the end futile) work done in combining this phrase with other phrases only has to be done once, rather than once for each possible internal analysis.

7.8.5   A modified LISP chart parser

lib fchart presents a version of the chart parser of lib chart, modified to deal will full PATR-style grammars. The modifications are actually quite minor. For instance, here is the revised function check_and_combine, which deals with applying the fundamental rule:

```
(defun check_and_combine (active_edge inactive_edge)
  (if (equal (start inactive_edge) (finish active_edge))
    (let ((subst (unify (label inactive_edge) (car (tofind active_edge)))))
      (if subst
        (let (
          (subtrees
            (append (found active_edge)
              (list
                (tree
                  (category (label inactive_edge) subst)
                  (found inactive_edge))))))
          (agenda_add
            (rename
              (apply_subst subst
                (list                    ;; new edge
                  (start active_edge)
                  (finish inactive_edge)
                  (label active_edge)
                  subtrees
                  (cdr (tofind active_edge)))))))))))
```

The only real difference from the previous code is the use of unify to compare the label of the inactive edge with the first tofind category of the active edge. If the unification succeeds, the resulting substitution subst needs to be applied to the whole of the new edge added to the agenda. In addition, the whole edge is copied by the use of the function rename, defined in lib subst, so that no two edges in the chart ever have two variables in common. As in the previous chart parser, in add_edge, when an edge is added, every edge of the chart has to be considered in the search for a relevant edge that could combine with it – this chart parser employs no indexing mechanisms whatsoever.

Although a top-down definition of the active_edge_procedure can be taken across directly from our simple chart parser, we now introduce into add_rules_to_expand a test to check that edges being added to the chart are not subsumed by existing edges. For this, it is sufficient to make sure that the label on a new arc (the LHS of the rule) is not subsumed by a category that has already been sought at that particular vertex. As with the random generator, the function uses lhs_match to attempt to match the goal with the LHS of a rule. This yields the pair subst_rhs, consisting of a substitution and a list of RHS DAGs. At this point, we look to see whether we have already looked for a category subsuming this LHS at this position in the chart (function subsumed_goal). If so, we do not add the new edge. Having worked our way through all the rules, we then record the fact that we have tried all rules for this category at this point (function record_goal):

```
(defun add_rules_to_expand (goal vertex)
  (dolist (rule rules)
    (let
      ((subst_rhs (lhs_match goal rule)))
      (if (car subst_rhs)
        (let* (
          (LHS (apply_subst (car subst_rhs) goal))
          (RHS (cadr subst_rhs)))
          (if (not (subsumed_goal LHS vertex))
            (agenda_add
              (rename
                (list
                  vertex
                  vertex
                  LHS
                  nil
                  RHS)))))))))
  (record_goal goal vertex))
```

The parser maintains in the global variable existing_goals a list of DAGs representing the categories that have previously been sought and the relevant positions in the chart. Each of these has entries for just two features, goal (a DAG representing the category sought) and vertex (the position where it has been looked for). The functions subsumed_goal and record_goal simply access this global variable:

```
(defun subsumed_goal (goal vertex)
  (let ((goaldag
    (list
      (list 'goal goal)
      (list 'vertex vertex)
      (list '& (newvar)))))
    (dolist (g existing_goals nil)
      (if (subsumes g goaldag)
        (return t)))))

(defun record_goal (goal vertex)
  (setq existing_goals
    (cons
      (list
        (list 'goal goal)
        (list 'vertex vertex)
        (list '& (newvar)))
      existing_goals)))
```

The function subsumes (defined in lib subsumes) is used to test whether the DAG for the current goal is subsumed by one of the previous ones. Only if it is not is the new edge added to the agenda.

Exercise 7.15 Run the modified chart parser on example sentences allowed by patrgram and any extensions to it that you have derived. Produce a list of proposed modifications that would improve the efficiency of the parser. [*easy*]

Exercise 7.16 lib fchart only has the relevant functions for top-down parsing (but with lexical look-up done bottom-up). Define the appropriate functions for full bottom-up parsing. Comment on the appropriateness of Grammar4 for top-down versus bottom-up parsing. [*hard*]

Exercise 7.17 lib fburecog provides a bottom-up recognizer akin to lib burecog, but modified to deal with PATR grammars and to avoid some redundancies in the manner of lib buparse2. Use it to recognize some sentences allowed by patrgram and any extensions to it that you have derived. [*easy*]

7.9   Representation of lexical knowledge

The lexicon of an NLP system has to provide a systematic and accessible encoding of a variety of information about words. Minimally there has to be some syntactic information. In a toy system, this may amount to no more than an atomic syntactic category label. In an NLP system that is intended to parse a significant fragment of a language, however, the lexicon will need to provide information on a range of syntactic matters including at least some of the following, although exactly what is provided depends on both the language and the type of word involved: part of speech, subcategorization possibilities, case, finiteness, number, person, gender or noun class, aspect, mood, reflexiveness and WH-ness. If that is all that the lexicon provides, then two consequences follow. Firstly, and rather obviously, the parser will be no use for anything but parsing, since such a lexicon is not providing any information that will enable us to distinguish the meaning of 'the man loves the woman' from that of 'the woman hates the man'. As far as the information in our lexicon is concerned, these two strings of words might as well be identical. Secondly, and perhaps less obviously, such a lexicon will have to exhaustively list every inflectional form of every word, regardless of whether the form is regular or not. Since our hypothesized lexicon only contains syntactic information, it has no way of representing the fact that 'loves' is an entirely predictable variant of the word 'love'. If we know what there is to know about the word 'love', including the fact that it is morphologically regular, then there should be no need for a lexicon to say anything explicit about 'loves'.

These considerations must lead us to conclude the following:

- If a lexicon is to be useful for something other than mere parsing, then it must include semantic information about the words that it contains (or defines).

- If a lexicon for a language that has any kind of regular inflectional morphology (and the vast majority of languages do have) is to avoid large-scale redundancy, then it must list word roots or stems, together with sufficient morphological and syntactic information for the regular forms of words to be deduced. This in turn means that the lexicon must make explicit provision for irregular forms.

In practice, many NLP systems treat the lexicon as a necessary evil that is of little theoretical interest and which is implemented by a collection of relatively unprincipled programs. Modern grammatical frameworks are, however, increasingly emphasizing the centrality of the lexicon, and so we will attempt to look a bit more carefully at what information needs to be represented and how. We will begin by trying to consider just the syntactic information that the lexicon needs to encode and how it may best be encoded. There are really only three types of purely syntactic information associated with words:

(1)   The basic part of speech – for example, that the word is a verb.

(2)   What, if anything, the word combines with – that is, its complements and possibly its subject.

(3)   Certain syntactically relevant inherent properties – for example, gender in the case of nouns.

All three types of information are generally encoded within the syntactic category of a word in a feature-based syntax. Here are a couple of examples:

```
Lexeme Mädchen:
    <cat> = N
    <gender> = neut.
```

This lexical entry tells us that the German word 'Mädchen' is a neuter noun.

```
Lexeme love:
    <cat> = V
    <arg0 cat> = NP
    <arg0 case> = nom
    <arg1 cat> = NP
    <arg1 case> = acc.
```

This lexical entry says that the English word 'love' is a verb that subcategorizes for an accusative object NP (that is, that 'love' is a transitive verb) and combines with a nominative subject NP (like all other English verbs). It is clear from this that we are using the arg0 feature to code up information about the subject of the verb and arg1 to code up information about the direct object. What should we do with verbs that require (or allow) more than one complement? An obvious strategy would simply be to grant ourselves as many features like arg0 and arg1 as the language in question requires. Then, when we come to a word like the verb form 'give', we can make our lexicon provide the relevant information like this:

```
Lexeme give:
    <cat> = V
    <arg0 cat> = NP
    <arg0 case> = nom
    <arg1 cat> = NP
    <arg1 case> = acc
    <arg2 cat> = PP
    <arg2 pform> = to.
```

The verb 'bet' would force us to have an arg3 feature as well, but four such argument features would be sufficient for a grammar of English. These verb features will be used by rules such as the following:

```
Rule
VP → V X1 X2:
    <V arg1> = X1
    <V arg2> = X2
    <V arg3> = 0.
Rule
VP → V X1 X2 X3:
    <V arg1> = X1
    <V arg2> = X2
    <V arg3> = X3.
```

English contains thousands of simple transitive verbs like 'love'. If each one is given a separate fully specified entry like the one given here, then our English lexicon is going to be very large indeed. One simple way to avoid this is through the use of abbreviations expressed as *macros*:

```
Macro syn_iV: {intransitive verbs – "die"}
    <cat> = V
    <arg0 cat> = NP
    <arg0 case> = nom.
Macro syn_tV: {transitive verbs – "eat"}
    syn_iV
    <arg1 cat> = NP
    <arg1 case> = acc.
```

Macro syn_dtV: {ditransitive verbs – "give"}
    syn_tV
    <arg2 cat> = PP
    <arg2 pform> = to.
Macro syn_datV: {dative verbs – "hand"}
    syn_tV
    <arg2 cat> = NP
    <arg2 case> = acc.

The idea of a macro is to have a single symbol, for instance syn_iV, which abbreviates a whole set of feature specifications – for instance <cat> = V, <arg0 cat> = NP, <arg0 case> = nom. In a lexical entry, whenever we include the name of a macro, it is as if we included the whole set of specifications that that name abbreviates. We can even have macro definitions that invoke other macros, as syn_tV does with syn_iV. The advantage of macros is that we can have much shorter lexical entries that look like this:

Lexeme die:
    syn_iV.
Lexeme elapse:
    syn_iV.
Lexeme eat:
    syn_iV.
Lexeme eat:
    syn_tV.
Lexeme give:
    syn_tV.
Lexeme give:
    syn_dtV.
Lexeme give:
    syn_datV.
Lexeme hand:
    syn_dtV.
Lexeme hand:
    syn_datV.
Lexeme love:
    syn_tV.

Notice that many words will have several lexical entries in virtue of the various syntactic classes to which they belong.

Macros seem to be a useful abbreviatory device for the writer of the lexicon, but how are we to interpret them computationally? There are several possible points at which macro names appearing in a definition might be expanded out into their full form. First of all, they might be expanded out when the lexicon is created. That is, the lexicon might be a

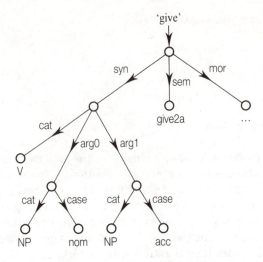

Figure 7.12   Lexical entry for 'give'.

data structure that directly associates lexemes with DAGs, each DAG being fully specified in the structure. The disadvantage with this would be that the lexicon would be a very large structure. It would be better to store the descriptions in roughly textual form and then expand out the macro definitions for a lexical entry when that entry was actually required for some purpose. Then the amount of information stored about any given lexeme could be relatively modest. In practice, this seems to be the preferred option. Yet another alternative would be to postpone the expansion of macros even longer. That is, retrieving the entry for a lexeme might actually return some kind of DAG that contained unexpanded macro names. The macros would then only be expanded when that DAG, or a relevant portion of it, needed to be unified with another DAG.

Multiple entries for what is morphologically the same verb are not required merely to indicate syntactic variants, as they also correspond to semantic differences. This brings us to the semantic information needed in lexical entries. The sense of 'eat' in 'we eat' is a function with one argument – that is, something that needs to combine with one object to produce a proposition – whereas that in 'we eat fish' is a function with two arguments – that is, it needs to combine with two objects. We will distinguish such senses as eat1a for the one-argument case, eat2a for the two-argument case, and so on. The final alphabetic character in these sense names is to provide for the case of words with semantic variants with the same number of arguments; thus, say, give3a in 'we gave fish to Felix', but give3b in 'we gave Felix fish'. For the purposes of this chapter, we will assume that eat1a, eat2a, give3a, give3b, and so on, are simply logical constants to be found in our language of semantic representation, and we will completely ignore the logical relationships that there might be between these constants. Given such a simplistic view of semantics, all the lexicon has to do, then, is to tell us what constants correspond to what words. This can be easily done with the featural apparatus that we already have, which we will now employ in the manner suggested by the example shown in Figure 7.12.

From now on, we assume that lexical entry DAGs split initially into syn (syntax), sem (semantics) and mor (morphology) branches, rather than simply consisting of the syn branch. Pedantically, this means we now have to recast our syntactic class abbreviations in the manner illustrated by this example:

```
Macro syn_iV:
    <syn cat> = V
    <syn arg0 cat> = NP
    <syn arg0 case> = nom.
```

This allows us to recast our lexical entries like this:

```
Lexeme die:
    syn_iV
    <sem> = die1a.

Lexeme elapse:
    syn_iV
    <sem> = elapse1a.

Lexeme eat:
    syn_iV
    <sem> = eat1a.

Lexeme eat:
    syn_tV
    <sem> = eat2a.

Lexeme give:
    syn_tV
    <sem> = give2a.

Lexeme give:
    syn_dtV
    <sem> = give3a.

Lexeme give:
    syn_datV
    <sem> = give3b.

Lexeme hand:
    syn_dtV
    <sem> = hand3a.
```

```
Lexeme hand:
     syn_datV
     <sem> = hand3b.
Lexeme love:
     syn_tV
     <sem> = love2a.
```

These entries still lack morphological information, and it is to this that we now turn. An English verb can appear in an absolute maximum of eight distinct forms, of which one is always idiosyncratic (the root) and one is always predictable (the present participle or gerund form in -ing) once you know the root. For instance, here are the various forms for the most irregular verb in English, 'be':

```
root  – be
form1 – am
form2 – are
form3 – is
form4 – was
form5 – were
form6 – been
form7 – being
```

We use the feature root to encode the root, and form1 to form7 as features for encoding the other seven potential verb forms. Here, form1 to form3 are the first, second and third-person present tense forms, respectively; form4 is the first-person singular past tense form; form5 is the second-person singular past tense form; form6 is the past participle form; and form7 is the present participle form. Fortunately, a wholly regular English verb is only mani-fested in four distinct forms, all of them predictable from the root:

```
root  – stamp
form1 – stamp
form2 – stamp
form3 – stamps
form4 – stamped
form5 – stamped
form6 – stamped
form7 – stamping
```

We will adopt an analysis (largely for reasons of perspicuity) in which each of the forms has a stem and a suffix, representing the basic word from which they are formed (always the root for regular verbs), together with the ending that is added for this form. Given this framework, we can provide an abbreviation for wholly regular verbs, as follows:

```
Macro mor_regV:
    <mor form1 stem> = <mor root>
    <mor form1 suffix> = ε
    <mor form2 stem> = <mor root>
    <mor form2 suffix> = ε
    <mor form3 stem> = <mor root>
    <mor form3 suffix> = ε
    <mor form4 stem> = <mor root>
    <mor form4 suffix> = ed
    <mor form5 stem> = <mor root>
    <mor form5 suffix> = ed
    <mor form6 stem> = <mor root>
    <mor form6 suffix> = ed
    <mor form7 stem> = <mor root>
    <mor form7 suffix> = ing.
```

where ε indicates the empty suffix. Now, where we specify the stem and suffix for a given form, we are assuming that the stem and the suffix will be combined in the word using the rules of English orthography, so that 'love' with 'ing' gives rise to 'loving' and not 'loveing'. We will discuss later how these rules might be implemented. Given this macro under its intended interpretation, we can exhibit the lexical entry for 'love':

```
Lexeme love:
    <mor root> = love
    mor_regV
    syn_tV
    <sem> = love2a.
```

The first line here is self-evidently redundant, since the name of the lexical entry is identical to the root form. We can by convention always name a lexical entry in this way. Accordingly, we will henceforth treat:

```
Lexeme xxx:
    yyy
    ...
    zzz.
```

as abbreviating:

```
Lexeme xxx:
    <mor root> = xxx
    yyy
    ...
    zzz.
```

This means that our entry for 'love' can be simplified to:

```
Lexeme love:
    mor_regV
    syn_tV
    <sem> = love2a.
```

Given our various macros and other conventions, this entry contains all the information contained in the verbose equivalent shown here:

```
Lexeme love:
    <mor root>        = love
    <mor form1 stem>  = love
    <mor form1 suffix> = ε
    <mor form2 stem>  = love
    <mor form2 suffix> = ε
    <mor form3 stem>  = love
    <mor form3 suffix> = ε
    <mor form4 stem>  = love
    <mor form4 suffix> = ed
    <mor form5 stem>  = love
    <mor form5 suffix> = ed
    <mor form6 stem>  = love
    <mor form6 suffix> = ed
    <mor form7 stem>  = love
    <mor form7 suffix> = ing
    <syn cat>         = V
    <syn arg0 cat>    = NP
    <syn arg0 case>   = nom
    <syn arg1 cat>    = NP
    <syn arg1 case>   = acc
    <sem>             = love2a.
```

Not all the verbs in our example lexicon fragment are regular, however. Both 'eat' and 'give' have wholly idiosyncratic past tense forms together with -en past participles. Their present tense and participle forms are regular, however, and we will use another macro definition to capture a class of verbs including both of these:

```
Macro mor_presV:
    <mor form1 stem>  = <mor root>
    <mor form1 suffix> = ε
    <mor form2 stem>  = <mor root>
    <mor form2 suffix> = ε
    <mor form3 stem>  = <mor root>
    <mor form3 suffix> = ε
```

```
<mor form4 stem> = <mor form5 stem>
<mor form4 suffix> = ε
<mor form5 suffix> = ε
<mor form6 stem> = <mor root>
<mor form6 suffix> = en
<mor form7 stem> = <mor root>
<mor form7 suffix> = ing.
```

Equipped with these abbreviations, our lexicon now looks like this:

```
Lexeme die:
    mor_regV
    syn_iV
    <sem> = die1a.
Lexeme elapse:
    mor_regV
    syn_iV
    <sem> = elapse1a.
Lexeme eat:
    mor_presV
    <mor form4 stem> = ate
    syn_iV
    <sem> = eat1a.
Lexeme eat:
    mor_presV
    <mor form4 stem> = ate
    syn_tV
    <sem> = eat2a.
Lexeme give:
    mor_presV
    <mor form4 stem> = gave
    syn_tV
    <sem> = give2a.
Lexeme give:
    mor_presV
    <mor form4 stem> = gave
    syn_dtV
    <sem> = give3a.
Lexeme give:
    mor_presV
    <mor form4 stem> = gave
    syn_datV
    <sem> = give3b.
Lexeme hand:
    mor_regV
    syn_dtV
    <sem> = hand3a.
```

```
Lexeme hand:
    mor_regV
    syn_datV
    <sem> = hand3b.
Lexeme love:
    mor_regV
    syn_tV
    <sem> = love2a.
```

Now that we have a way of expressing certain kinds of lexical knowledge, we can think about how this knowledge is to be used in an NLP system. For the moment, let us consider this from the point of view of a language analysis system. Such a system is presented with a sequence of unanalyzed words as its input and needs to determine the relevant features for each word – that is, syntactic features for parsing and semantic features for determining the meaning. But, as all the lexical knowledge is about word roots, to determine the relevant features, we need to determine how the word can be analyzed as being some form of a root which is in the lexicon. For this, we need to be able to analyze a word in terms of the possible stems and suffixes that make it up. This is a relatively straightforward task for English, and we leave further investigation of it as an exercise for the reader. Basically, the approach is to look at the end of the word for a regular English suffix and propose the part of the word before this as a possible root. This process will have to be modified to take account of the rules of English orthography, so that, for instance, 'loving' can be analyzed as stem 'love' with suffix 'ing'. In addition, especially if the process has no access to the lexicon, we must be prepared for several possible results to be obtained. For instance, without any knowledge of actual English words, we could not determine whether 'loaves' is to be analyzed as having the stem 'loaf' or the stem 'loave'.

Having determined possible stems and suffixes for a given word, our language analyzer can in principle extract the information from the relevant lexical entry and start parsing. But this is not quite the end of the story. Even if we have a language of semantic representation that can make sensible use of constants like die1a and hand3b, and a morphological interpreter that can analyze words to give possible stem and suffix values, we still have no link between the syntax and the morphology. This lexicon tells us that 'give' has 'given' as the (morphologically interpreted) value of its form6 feature, but it says nothing about the specific syntactic contexts (for example, after 'have') in which the form6 form of the verb might be expected to appear. All it provides is the syntactic features that all forms of 'give' have in common. What we clearly need is a way of deriving the particular syntactic features of specific inflected word forms from the lexical entries. We can achieve this by augmenting our lexicon with a definition of the possible ways an inflected word can be related to a lexeme as appearing in the lexicon.

One way of looking at the relations between a word and a lexeme is in terms of a *word form clause (WFC)*, which states the conditions under which the relations can hold. Then, when we have a word and a possible lexeme that it might be related to, we attempt to find a WFC that can be applied. As in the application of a grammar rule, we try to construct an extension of the DAG representing the word, which will only contain information about the stem and suffix, and the DAG representing the lexeme, which contains only general information that applies to all forms of the lexeme, in such a way that the WFC conditions are satisfied. The computation of these extensions then results in the word inheriting extra syntactic and semantic properties from the lexeme, as well as specific properties spelled out in the WFC. Here is a WFC for the third-person singular, present tense form class of English verbs:

```
WFC third_sing:
    <word mor form> = <lexeme mor form3>
    <word syn> = <lexeme syn>
    <word syn cat> = V
    <word syn arg0 per> = 3
    <word syn arg0 num> = sing
    <word syn tense> = pres
    <word sem> = <lexeme sem>.
```

This WFC says that a word is the third singular form of the lexeme if the following conditions can be satisfied. The form of the word must be the same as the form3 form of the lexeme; that is, the stem values must both unify, as must the suffix values. Moreover, the syn path of the word must unify with the syn specifications shown; it must unify with the syn of the lexeme and have the mentioned extra properties. Finally, the sem of the word must unify with the sem of the lexeme.

Here is how we would use WFCs in a language analysis program. From an output of the morphological analyzer, we can build a partial description of a word, consisting of its <mor form>, with a stem and a suffix. For instance, for the word 'loves', we could build the following:

```
Word loves:
    <mor form stem> = love
    <mor form suffix> = s.
```

We now need to determine a lexical entry and a way in which this word is related to that entry. Let us assume that we try the lexeme 'love' and the relation third_sing. So, we now attempt to find extensions for the 'loves' DAG, which plays the role of the word, and for the DAG for the lexeme 'love', which plays the role of the lexeme, in such a way that the conditions of the WFC are satisfied. That is, we attempt the unifications specified in the third_sing WFC, with word taken to indicate the word DAG and lexeme the

DAG provided by the lexical entry for 'love'. In this case, all the unifications succeed. If they did not, we would have to try another possible WFC or lexical entry. As a result of the unifications, we find an extension to the word DAG, describable as follows:

```
Word loves:
        <mor form stem> = love
        <mor form suffix> = s
        <syn cat> = V
        <syn tense> = pres
        <syn arg0 cat> = NP
        <syn arg0 case> = nom
        <syn arg0 per> = 3
        <syn arg0 num> = sing
        <syn arg1 cat> = NP
        <syn arg1 case> = acc
        <sem> = love2a.
```

This is then the kind of category structure that we can use for parsing.

To summarize, here is how lexical access works in our hypothesized language analyzer. Incoming words are processed by a morphological analyzer to yield possible stem and suffix values. For each such result, possible lexemes are retrieved from the lexicon. For each possible partial word description and possible lexeme that it may be related to, possible WFCs are invoked. Each such successful invocation results in a full word description (DAG) which can be used in later stages such as parsing. In a system where we have many lexical entries and WFCs, indexing of the lexical data structures will be vital for efficient processing. Relevant lexemes can be efficiently retrieved for combining with partial word descriptions if the lexical entries are indexed on the possible stem values in the various forms; for instance, the 'give' entry should be accessible rapidly from both of the stems 'give' and 'gave'. In addition (for English), a WFC can be indexed on the possible suffixes that may indicate the relations; for instance, third_sing may be applicable if the suffix is 's' or ε, but not if the suffix is 'ed'.

It is considerably less clear how lexical access should function in a language generation system. In such a system, we might expect the semantics of a desired word to be specified, as well as some of the syntactic features (determined by the syntactic context in which the word will appear). The approach might then be to retrieve possible lexical entries, indexed on their semantic components, followed by possible WFCs, indexed on certain syntactic features that they add. An attempt can then be made to apply each WFC to each retrieved lexeme together with a word about which only the specified syntactic features are known. Each such successful application will yield a fuller description of a possible word that could be generated, including a stem and a suffix. Composing the stem–suffix pair could then produce the final surface form of the word. These remarks presuppose that a choice between roughly synonymous words can be made arbitrarily, whereas in practice the choice of an appropriate word needs to take into account matters of style and context in important ways.

Exercise 7.18 Rather than introducing the features arg0 through arg3, a potentially more elegant way of dealing with the items with which a verb may be associated would be to have a feature called subcat, say, whose values are lists of categories built up using features first and rest. Write down some sample lexical entries using this idea, together with the rules needed to unpack them. [*intermediate*]

Exercise 7.19 The macros mor_regV and mor_presV have a lot of structure in common. Express elements of this common structure as further macro definitions, and use these in the definition of macros for classes of verbs including 'drink' and 'meet'. The path <mor form5 stem> is also a rather opaque specification to appear in many lexical entries. Add a more mnemonic form such as <mor past_stem> and use it in your definitions. [*easy*]

Exercise 7.20 Design an FST to carry out the process of morphological analysis. Such an FST should accept an input consisting of the sequence of letters in a word and produce as output the sequence of letters in a possible stem, followed by a special token indicating a possible suffix. Such an FST will, of course, be non-deterministic. You may well find it useful to have the FST actually process the tapes in reverse order. So, for instance, given the input sequence 'y l i p p a h', it would yield an output 'L y p p a h', where L is some special token indicating the suffix 'ly'. [*intermediate project*]

7.10   Implementing a lexicon in LISP

The basic components for implementing a lexical component in LISP have already been presented. lib lisppatr, through functions like apply_condition, allows us to construct list structures representing PATR conditions and then to construct DAGs that satisfy the conditions. In LISP, we can

associate PATR conditions with macro names by using a property
patr_macro:

```
(setf (get 'syn_iV 'patr_macro)
 '((syn cat) = V
   (syn arg0 cat) = np
   (syn arg0 case) = nom))

(setf (get 'syn_tV 'patr_macro)
 '( syn_iV
   (syn arg1 cat) = np
   (syn arg1 case) = acc))
```

Moreover, we can extend apply_condition, which, as we have seen, takes a list
of PATR conditions and a DAG and returns a substitution extending the
DAG so that it satisfies the conditions, to look up the definitions of macros
appearing in conditions. This just involves adding an extra clause:

```
(let
  ((newsubst
    (apply_condition (get (car entry) 'patr_macro) dag subst)))
  (if newsubst
    (apply_condition (cdr entry) dag newsubst)
    nil))
  ...
```

This is what we need for a straightforward implementation of the kinds of
lexical entries we have discussed. Given such macro definitions, we can
construct DAGs satisfying the macros, for instance:

```
(setq subst (apply_condition '(syn_tV) '_x empty_subst))
(simplify_features subst '_x)
((SYN ((CAT V)
       (ARG0 ((CAT NP) (CASE NOM) (& #:_14)))
       (ARG1 ((CAT NP) (CASE ACC) (& #:_20)))
       (& #:_16)))
 (& #:_6))
```

Here, simplify_features is just like apply_subst, except that it removes unnecessary
remainder entries in DAGs. For actual lexical entries, we need to have a
function, lookup_conditions, that associates lexemes (represented by LISP symbols) with conditions. One way of implementing this would be to use the
property list of lexemes (represented as LISP symbols):

```
(defun lookup_conditions (lex)
  (get lex 'lexicon))

(defun set_conditions (lex conds)
  (setf (get lex 'lexicon) conds))
```

We can then set up lexical entries as follows:

```
(set_conditions 'love
  '((mor root) = love
    (sem) = love2a
    mor_regV
    syn_tV))
```

A WFC can be thought of as a set of conditions that must be satisfied for a particular relationship to hold between a word and a lexeme. Alternatively, we can think of it as a set of conditions that can be satisfied by a particular kind of DAG that only has values for word and lexeme as its top-level features:

```
(setq example_wfc
  '((word mor form) = (lexeme mor form3)
    (word syn) = (lexeme syn)
    (word syn cat) = V
    (word syn arg0 per) = 3
    (word syn arg0 num) = sing
    (word syn tense) = pres
    (word sem) = (lexeme sem)))
```

Exercise 7.21   Set up some more of the macros and lexical entries discussed in the text. Write a function lookup_lex which, given a lexeme, accesses the PATR definition in lexicon and returns a DAG representing the category of that item.   [*easy*]

Exercise 7.22   Write a function apply_wfc which, given such a WFC, a DAG representing a word and a DAG representing a lexeme, either of which may be a variable or contain variables, returns the extension of the word required for it to be in the appropriate relation with the lexeme (or nil, if the word cannot possibly be in this relation). For instance, your function might produce output as in the following example:

```
(apply_wfc
  example_wfc
  (make_dag '((mor form stem) = love (mor form suffix) = s))
  (lookup_lex 'love))
((MOR ((FORM ((STEM LOVE) (SUFFIX S) (& #:_10997))) (& #:_11041)))
 (SYN ((CAT V)
       (ARG0 ((CAT NP) (CASE NOM) (PER 3) (NUM SING) (& #:_11047)))
       (ARG1 ((CAT NP) (CASE ACC) (& #:_11037)))
       (TENSE PRES)
       (& #:_11049)))
 (SEM LOVE2A)
 (& #:_11051))
```

Your function will have to create a DAG with appropriate word and lexeme features, use apply_condition to enforce the WFC and then extract the relevant part of the resulting structure. [*intermediate*]

Exercise 7.23 Implement a lexical retrieval system for a language analyzer along the lines suggested in the text. [*intermediate project*]

Exercise 7.24 Develop a set of WFCs for English inflection and test them against a small lexicon. [*easy*]

Exercise 7.25 The sense that eat1a represents is systematically related to that of eat2a, likewise give3a to give3b. The relation crucially depends on the nature of the argument structure expressed in the syntactic component of the lexical entry, but is completely ignored given the way we have chosen to define things. Explore the possibility of making do with fewer primitive word senses by exploiting the relevant syntactic–semantic relations. [*hard*]

Exercise 7.26 Add 'be', 'do' and 'have' entries to the lexicon. [*easy*]

Exercise 7.27 Provide a full lexical entry for the French verb 'tomber' and define any macro needed to keep the entry simple and perspicuous (you will need a French-speaking informant or a comprehensive French grammar book in order to do this exercise). [*intermediate*]

Exercise 7.28 Develop a set of lexical entries and associated macros and WFCs for a representative set of English nouns, including 'cat', 'child', 'datum', 'dog', 'ox', 'scissors', 'sheep', 'shoe' and 'trousers'. [*intermediate*]

7.11 DAGs versus terms

The decision to treat complex categories as DAGs is motivated by a number of considerations. Complex categories have parts and there needs to be a way of referring to a given part of a category; hence, the use of feature names. The parts may themselves have parts; hence, the meaningfulness of a sequence of feature names specifying a path and the directed graph notions that arise from this. We sometimes need to deal with two objects that have a part in common; hence, we need graphs rather than trees. On the other hand, there is no obvious need to allow structures to contain themselves as proper parts; hence, the graphs are acyclic. These reasons should not, however, lead us to neglect other possible kinds of objects that we might use as complex categories, and there is an obvious alternative candidate suggested by work in logic programming – the *logical term*.

A logical term has one of the following forms:

- A constant – for example, **sing**, **3**, **apple**.
- A variable – for example, **X, Y, Z** – distinguished from constants.
- A complex term – for example, **s(sing, X), f(f(f(2))), s(h(2, sing), apple)**.

A complex term is a *function symbol*; for instance, **f** or **s**, followed by a sequence of *arguments* (other logical terms), enclosed in parentheses and separated by commas. Logical constants are analogous to the atomic symbols that we have used in DAGs, whereas a complex term can be thought of (and is often implemented computationally) as a sequence of items, consisting of the function symbol followed by the arguments. A complex term can be used to represent an object that has parts (and parts of parts, ...) in the same way as a DAG. For instance, the term:

    s(h(2, sing), apple)

with the following interpretation in terms of sequences:

    <s, <h, 2, sing>, apple>

can be used to represent an object that has three attributes. One of these has the simple value s, another has the simple value apple, and the other has a complex value, which itself has three attributes, with values h, 2 and sing. Variables in complex terms can be used to represent values that are unspecified, with multiple occurrences of the same variable indicating a shared value. So, the term:

    s(h(2, X), X)   or   <s, <h, 2, X>, X>   .

denotes an object whose third attribute is the same as the third attribute of its second attribute (we are assuming a convention in which variables always appear in upper case). In PATR notation:

    <1> = s
    <2 1> = h
    <2 2> = 2
    <2 3> = <3>

Although there is an obvious underlying similarity between terms and DAGs, there is an immediate difference in how information is encoded. In a DAG, an attribute is identified by a feature name; in a term, it is identified by its numerical position. This makes DAGs easier to use than terms for humans – it is easier to remember the name of a feature than the numerical position that is assigned to it in a structure. On the other hand, it also makes terms easier to use than DAGs for computers. A term (sequence) can be represented as a sequence of items in memory, which permits the accessing of a given component in constant time. In the representation of a DAG, however, a certain amount of search is required to find the value of a given feature. This means that, whereas DAGs may be a good way for a grammar writer to think, it may make sense to have the operations on DAGs that they specify compiled into more efficient operations on terms.

Subsumption and unification of terms is defined component wise, with two complex terms failing to unify if they differ in a function symbol or in the number of arguments. So, here is the definition for complex term subsumption:

Complex term subsumption

A complex term A subsumes a complex term B if and only if:

- A and B have the same function symbol and number of arguments,
- each argument of A subsumes the corresponding argument of B, and
- for every two components that share anywhere in A, the corresponding components share in B.

This brings out another difference between terms and DAGs. Because DAGs are sideways open, a DAG can always be extended by adding a value for a new feature that is not currently mentioned in it. On the other hand, a term has a fixed number of arguments (attributes) and adding an extra argument changes it into a very different, and incompatible, object. This means that, in specifying a category as a term, we have to specify a value (if necessary, a variable) for every feature that might ever have a value in extensions of the category. So, using terms as categories can be problematic in grammar development if we are not initially sure exactly what features the extensions of a category might have. On the other hand, once our repertoire of features has stabilized, the sideways openness of DAGs is no longer strictly required.

In compiling DAGs and DAG operations into terms and term operations, it is necessary to decide what features in the DAGs will give rise to function symbols and which feature will correspond to each argument position. Since the function symbol of a complex term cannot be a variable, the function symbol can only be used for a feature that has an atomic value in every description that will ever be used. If there is no such feature, then it is necessary to pick a dummy function symbol that will be the same in every description and encode all the features in the arguments. In many grammars, there is a cat feature whose value is always known and atomic. In such a situation, it is natural to use its value as the function symbol. Thus, the grammar rule:

```
Rule
  s → np vp:
    <np per> = <vp per>
    <np num> = <vp num>.
```

could compile into something like:

s → np(X, Y), vp(X, Y).

Grammar rules of the latter form are the basis of grammar formalisms, such as DCGs (Definite Clause Grammars), which have been developed in logic programming.

LISP arrays would be a good data structure to implement complex terms, because they are more compact than lists and permit the accessing of particular elements in constant time. We will, however, use lists to represent complex terms, with the first element of a list being the function symbol and the subsequent elements the arguments, in order. Thus we will represent the term:

s(h(2, sing), x)

by the following LISP data structure:

```
(s (h 2 sing) _x)
```

We will make further use of complex terms in Chapters 9 and 10, and will make use there of lib tunify and lib tsubsume, which implement unification between and subsumption of terms. These library files define functions termunify and termsubsumes, which behave just like unify and subsumes, except that they expect lists representing terms, rather than lists representing DAGs, as their arguments. Finally, lib termify provides a function termify_dag which will translate a DAG into a term, according to a set of rules specified by the programmer.

Exercise 7.29 Take one of the programming exercises in this chapter involving a PATR grammar (for instance, using the chart parser). Write down rules to specify how the DAGs that arise from this grammar can be compiled by termify_dag into terms. Convert the whole grammar into an equivalent one where each rule is a list of terms (use lhs_match to produce a list of DAGs and then termify_dag to make them into terms). Define new versions of category and tree to use the term representation. Finally, rerun the exercise, using the term versions of unify and subsumes. Beware of the fact that termify_dag will not deal correctly with DAGs that have shared remainders; hence, you will not be able to use grammar rules that specify such DAGs. You will need to redefine the functions used for accessing rules, for instance, as follows:

```
(defun lhs_match (dag rule)
  (let* (
          (lhs (car rule))
          (rhs (cdr rule))
          (subst (termunify dag lhs)))
    (if subst
        (list subst (apply_subst subst rhs))
        '(() ()))))

(defun rhs_match (dags rule)
  (let* (
          (lhs (car rule))
          (rhs (cdr rule))
          (needed (length rhs)))
    (if (< (length dags) needed)
        '(() ())
        (let ((subst (rhs_match_list rhs dags empty_subst)))
          (if subst
              (list
                subst
                (cons
                  lhs
                  (nthcdr needed dags)))
              '(() ()))))))

(defun rhs_match_list (rhs dags subst)          ; subst already applied
  (if (null rhs)
      subst
      (let ((newsubst (termunify (car rhs) (car dags))))
        (if newsubst
            (rhs_match_list
              (apply_subst newsubst (cdr rhs))
              (apply_subst newsubst (cdr dags))
              (compose_substs newsubst subst))
            nil))))
```

[*hard*]

SUMMARY

- Contemporary NLP grammars make extensive use of features.

- Features can be encoded in DAGs.

- DAGs are a more convenient representation than terms.

- Features simplify the treatment of agreement.

- Featural information is combined through unification.

- Chart parsers can manipulate feature structures directly.

- Lexical entries encode featural information about words.

- Macros can help to simplify lexical entries.

- WFCs express relations between inflected words and lexical entries.

Further reading

The notion of unification has its roots in Robinson's (1965) work on theorem proving and has found its way into computational linguistics through the work of Kay (1979) and the logic programming tradition (Colmerauer 1978). Recent statements of Kay's own perspective can be found in Kay (1984, 1985b). Shieber (1986a) and Carlson and Linden (1987) provide introductions to unification-based linguistic formalisms in general, Shieber (1988) argues that their use permits a single parameterized theorem prover to serve for both parsing and generation, Karttunen (1986) reports on a development environment for such formalisms and Pereira *et al.* (1987) document a panel discussion on the state of the art in 1987. The classic reference for definite clause grammars is Pereira and Warren (1980).

Apart from PATR, the best-known linguistic formalisms based on DAG unification are FUG (Kay 1985a), GPSG (Gazdar *et al.* 1985), HPSG (Pollard and Sag 1988), JPSG (Gunji 1987) and LFG (Kaplan and Bresnan 1982). There is also now a rapidly growing literature on realizing categorial grammars within a unification formalism, a literature that includes Bouma (1988), Calder *et al.* (1988), Wittenburg (1986), Uszkoreit (1986), Moortgat (1988), Zeevat (1988), and much of the contents of Haddock *et al.* (1987), and Klein and van Benthem (1987). Hellwig (1986) shows how unification techniques can be applied in the context of a dependency grammar.

Shieber (1986b) discusses the possibility of reconstructing GPSG in PATR, while in Shieber (1987) he examines a number of reductions between various unification grammars, including FUG and LFG. Tutorial introductions to the linguistic analyses that have been provided within GPSG and LFG can be found in Sells (1985) and Horrocks (1987). In presenting DAG unification, we have restricted ourselves to feature theory for the purposes of illustration. However, some current linguistic theories allow unification to be performed on structural descriptions (as in LFG), and even on whole grammars (as in FUG).

Pereira and Shieber (1984), Kasper and Rounds (1986), Moshier and Rounds (1987), Beierle and Pletat (1988), Johnson (1988), Mellish (1988) and Gazdar et al. (1988) present work on the underlying logic, mathematics and semantics of unification-based linguistic formalisms. Barton et al. (1987) present results on the complexity of GPSG and LFG, and Ritchie (1984, 1985, 1986) performs a similar service for FUG.

Extensions to DAG unification to permit such operations as negation and disjunction are discussed in Kasper (1987), Nakazawa et al. (1988) and Karttunen (1984). The latter suggests that generalization, rather than unification, may be the appropriate operation to employ in composing the syntactic properties of coordinate constituents.

Karttunen and Kay (1985) and Pereira (1985) discuss structure-sharing techniques while Wroblewski (1987) presents an alternative route to efficient graph unification. Tomita (1986) develops the notion of a 'shared-packed forest' as a space-efficient WFST. Frisch (1986) shows how the use of restricted quantification over features can reduce the parsing search space, Shieber (1985c) argues for a generalization of the monadic CF-PSG backbone technique for parsing with unification-based formalisms, while Haas (1987) makes the case for parallel parsing in this connection. For a very different kind of angle on parallel parsing, see Waltz and Pollack (1984).

A good introduction to issues of current concern with respect to NLP lexicons is to be found in Ritchie (1987), and the recent upsurge of interest in such issues is well represented in the Proceedings of COLING-86, which contains around 20 papers that deal with them.

Among these issues are the nature of lexical representation (De Smedt 1984, Flickinger et al. 1985, Evans and Katz 1986, Evans and Scott 1986, Evans and Gazdar 1989a, 1989b); the organization of lexical databases (Barnett et al. 1986, Domenig and Shann 1986, Isoda et al. 1986, Evens 1988, Neff et al. 1988, Neuhaus 1986, Wehrli 1985); the use of existing computer-readable commercial dictionaries (Boguraev et al. 1987a, Briscoe and Boguraev 1988, Calzolari and Picchi 1988, Mitton 1986); automatic dictionary construction (Boguraev et al. 1987b, Trost and Buchberger 1986, Jacobs and Zernik 1988); tools for lexicon creation (Ahlswede 1985, Alshawi et al. 1985, Daelemans 1987); and efficient lexical access (Cercone et al. 1983).

CHAPTER 8

SEMANTICS

Issues of syntactic structure are relatively well understood within NLP, but standard techniques for dealing with the meanings of linguistic utterances are harder to come by. The last three chapters of this book will attempt to summarize current ideas and techniques from this still very open-ended research area.

In this chapter, we begin by looking at the semantics–pragmatics distinction, at the notion of compositionality and at how meaning can be identified with reference. Then we turn to the business of translating syntactic representations into semantic ones and provide an extended illustration involving translation into a simple database query language, implemented with our existing featural apparatus and capable of handling basic quantification. We conclude with some further consideration of the ambiguity problem and show how one rather limited kind of semantic disambiguation can be implemented.

8.1 Compositionality

Philosophers of language and linguists have attempted to classify the aspects of meaning that an utterance may have, and have distinguished between the semantics of the sentence uttered and the pragmatics of the utterance. Conventionally, the semantics are to do with the truth or satisfaction conditions of the sentence, ignoring those aspects of the utterance meaning that are influenced by the context of its use or its intended purpose. The pragmatics are everything to do with the context and the intentions of the speaker and addressee, and to a large extent this category is used to sweep up all the difficult aspects of meaning that researchers wish to postpone considering. This chapter deals mostly with those aspects of meaning that are regarded as semantics, whereas in Chapter 10 we will consider more pragmatic aspects of meaning.

Those people who argue for the semantics–pragmatics distinction tend to claim that the truth-conditional, context-independent component of the meaning of an utterance is an important component of the utterance's full meaning, even if it is not the whole story. Thus, if I am sitting in the same room as you and you are next to an open window, I might say:

It is cold in here.

as a kind of polite request for you to close the window. Of course, the truth conditions of the sentence are something quite different – they involve a claim about the world. On the other hand, it could be argued that, to respond appropriately to this utterance, one strategy would be to grasp the truth conditions and then subsequently work out for what purpose I might wish to call your attention to this particular fact about the world. This is the standard model of the semantics–pragmatics relation at the present time, and the one that we shall assume.

How can we sensibly organize the process of semantic interpretation; that is, the derivation of the meaning of a sentence? The answers that people have found to this question are various, but one principle attributed to the philosopher Frege stands out in just about every approach that has been made. It can be informally stated as:

The meaning of the whole is a function of the meanings of the parts.

According to this principle, known as the *principle of compositionality*, the meaning of a sentence can be expressed in terms of the meanings of the phrases within it. The meanings of these in turn depend on the meanings of the subphrases within them. And so on, until we are down to the meanings of individual words, or even the meanings of the morphemes that make up the words.

Adopting Frege's principle does not make the extraction of the meaning a trivial process. It merely gives us a framework for organizing our ideas and decomposing the problem. In particular, we must resolve the following questions:

- What are the appropriate subphrases to consider when we want to obtain the meaning of a phrase?

- Just how does the meaning of a particular phrase depend on that of its subphrases?

- What are the meanings of the minimal units (the phrases, words or morphemes that do not themselves subdivide into smaller meaningful units)?

- What kinds of things should meanings be anyway? Are they symbols in the machine? Are they things in the world? Are they some kind of relationship between the two?

As for what the appropriate subphrases of a phrase are, we might hope that these would be precisely those that are given by the syntactic structure. So, for instance, when we have a rule in the grammar that says:

```
Rule
  S → NP VP.
```

then, as well as saying something about what forms a sentence can take – a sentence can be a noun phrase followed by a verb phrase – it might say something about how the meaning is to be extracted – the meaning of the sentence is some function of the meaning of the noun phrase and the meaning of the verb phrase. Of course, it might turn out to be asking too much for the same breakdown of a phrase into subphrases to yield both syntactic and semantic generalizations. We can, nevertheless, hope that there is some consistent relation between syntax and semantics in natural languages, and that a semantically appropriate grammar also captures syntactic generalizations.

Assuming that a syntactic analysis divides up phrases into semantically appropriate subphrases, it remains for us to specify just how the meaning of a complex expression (for example, the truth conditions of a sentence) depends on the meanings of the parts (for example, the noun phrase meaning and the verb phrase meaning). It is desirable to be able to cope with every possible way that complex phrases can be made up of immediate subphrases. This leads to an approach where syntactic and semantic rules are paired: corresponding to each syntactic rule that says how a phrase can be constituted, there is a semantic rule that says how the meaning of such a phrase is composed out of the meanings of the parts. Many approaches to semantic interpretation adopt this strategy, which is known as the *rule-to-rule hypothesis*.

There are various ways we can implement semantic rules computationally. In one method, direct use is made of the phrase structure tree of

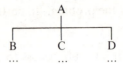

Figure 8.1 Excerpt from parse tree.

the natural language utterance in obtaining the meaning. Imagine we have the following rule in a phrase structure grammar:

Rule
A → B C D.

A semantic rule attached to this rule specifies how the meanings of phrases of types B, C and D, when these phrases appear in this order, can be combined to give the meaning of a phrase of type A. This is exactly equivalent to specifying how the meaning of a phrase of type A can be constructed, given that its parse tree is of the form shown in Figure 8.1. Thus, on this view, semantic rules can be seen as mappings from local phrase structure trees to meanings. We pursue this idea further in the sections that follow.

8.2 Meaning as reference

To introduce the idea of compositional semantic interpretation, we will imagine a hypothetical question–answering system that knows about airlines. For simplicity, we will only deal with the declarative form of English sentences, but each sentence will actually be treated as a yes–no question. In this context, we can choose to identify the meaning of a sentence with that sentence's truth value; that is, either true or false, depending on whether the implied question should be answered yes or no. Here are some example sentences and their meanings (their truth values):

Delta is a subsidiary – false

Virgin Airways is independent – true

Republic is independent – false

British Airways is a subsidiary and
British Caledonian is independent – false

Sentences similar to these can be generated by the following grammar:

```
Rule
    S → NP VP.
Rule
    S → S CONJ S.

Word Delta:
    <cat> = NP.
Word "Virgin Airways":
    <cat> = NP.
Word "is independent":
    <cat> = VP.
Word "is a subsidiary":
    <cat> = VP.
Word and:
    <cat> = CONJ.
```

In compositional semantic interpretation, we associate with each rule of the grammar, a rule for how the meaning of such a phrase is to be constructed from the meanings of its constituent phrases. First of all, consider the noun phrase entries. What meaning can we sensibly assign to the word 'Delta'? A natural response is that this phrase refers to the airline of that name. To avoid confusion about what this is, ideally, our rule for the meaning of this noun phrase would actually present this entity, by having it attached to the page somehow, for example. This is clearly out of the question, however, and so we will have to make do with some representation of the entity referred to – perhaps a photograph, a logo, a picture or any symbol that is conventionally associated with that entity and nothing else. In our rules, we will use a '#' prefix to denote such a representation of an entity. We can therefore write our meaning rule as follows:

```
Word Delta:
    <cat> = NP
    <meaning> = #Delta.
```

In other words, 'If a noun phrase takes the form 'Delta', then the meaning of the noun phrase is [Delta logo].' We can write similar rules for the other noun phrases naming entities, although it is not clear that we have really achieved anything so far.

Now, what kind of meaning are we to associate with a verb phrase? One clue comes from the fact that we have to construct the meaning of a sentence from the meanings of its noun phrase and its verb phrase. So somehow, for instance, for the sentence 'TWA is independent' we have to produce a truth value (true or false) from an object represented by #TWA, together with whatever meaning we get from the verb phrase 'is independent'. How would we determine in the real world whether TWA is independent? One way would be to look in a reference book to get a list of all the airlines who are independent and see whether TWA appears in that list. How can we be sure that the entity mentioned in the list is indeed the TWA we are interested in (it might even be referred to by other phrases, such as 'Carl Icahn's 1986 acquisition' rather than by 'TWA')? In an ideal reference book, we would expect to find a photograph, description or other symbol, #TWA, that uniquely identifies it. We can make our meaning for the verb phrase 'is independent' embody the essentials of an ideal reference book; that is, we can make it be a set of symbols like #TWA. When we wish to construct the meaning of a sentence containing this verb phrase, we simply look to see whether the meaning of the subject is in the set that is the meaning of the verb phrase. If so, the sentence is true, otherwise the sentence is false.

We write a set of elements by enclosing them in {brackets}. Thus, the following would be the meaning of 'is a subsidiary':

{#Manx_Airlines, #People_Express, #Eastern_Airlines, ...}

The following basic operations on sets are standard, and we will make use of them:

- Testing whether a given object X is an element of a given set S; that is, whether $X \in S$. This has the value TRUE or FALSE.
- Computing the intersection of two sets S1 and S2, represented as $S1 \cap S2$ – that is, the set of all elements that are in both S1 and S2.

Given this terminology and notation, we can express semantic interpretation rules for verb phrases and sentences:

```
Rule
  S → NP VP:
     <S meaning> = TRUE if <NP meaning> ε <VP meaning>
                 = FALSE otherwise.

Word "is independent":
     <cat> = VP
     <meaning> = {#Texas_Air, #Virgin_Airways, #US_Air, ...}.
Word "is a subsidiary":
     <cat> = VP
     <meaning> = {#Manx_Airlines, #People_Express, #Air_Cal, ...}.
Word "is US based":
     <cat> = VP
     <meaning> = {#Delta, #Pan_Am, #American_Airlines, ...}.
```

Finally, we can provide a rule for the conjunction of two sentences. The conjunction is true only if each individual sentence is true:

```
Rule
  S0 → S1 C S2:
    <S0 meaning> = TRUE if   <S1 meaning> = TRUE
                        and <S2 meaning> = TRUE
                   = FALSE otherwise
```

Notice that for these meanings we have started putting expressions that could require arbitrary kinds of computation on the right-hand side of the '=' signs (previously, we could only refer to constants and the values of other features). Although it is convenient to express the meaning relations in this way, in actual fact this kind of compositional meaning construction behaves in many ways differently from the way that other feature values are constructed. For instance, quite apart from the fact that computations other than unification are invoked here, information always flows from the meanings of the subphrases to the meaning of the whole phrase, whereas, because of the way unification works, information about other features can flow the other way. So, in computational terms, we might well think of meaning construction being performed by some special operation distinct from that which handles other features. We will see shortly that meaning expressions *can* sometimes be constructed by normal unification operations.

Let us now investigate how we might extend this scheme to handle more interesting noun phrases, so that we can consider sentences like:

An airline is independent.

Every airline is US based.

First of all, consider how we might represent the meaning of 'an airline'. Whereas 'Delta' refers to a specific entity, 'an airline' seems to leave it open which airline is actually referred to. Thus, a good idea might be to make the meaning of a noun phrase a set of objects. A word like 'Delta' gives rise to a set with exactly one element, {#Delta}, whereas a phrase like 'an airline' may give rise to a set with many elements, as in {#Aden_Airways, #Air_Cal, #Air_Mauritius, ...}.

Since we have changed the kind of thing that the meaning of a noun phrase is, we must make changes in the places where noun phrase meanings are used – that is, in working out the meanings of sentences. The new rule for sentences is now the following:

```
Rule
  S → NP VP:
    <S meaning> = FALSE if <NP meaning> ∩ <VP meaning> is { }
                = TRUE otherwise,
```

But now consider a phrase like 'every airline'. We might be tempted to give this the set of all airlines as its meaning, were it not for the fact that this is just what we would currently assign to 'an airline'. And there is clearly a big difference between 'an airline is independent' and 'every airline is independent', say. Unfortunately, there is no way to fix this problem without serious changes in our rules. One way to distinguish between 'an airline' and 'every airline' is in terms of the properties that they have. Thus, we can say correctly that 'an airline' is a subsidiary (because People Express is), that 'an airline' is independent (because Virgin Airways is), and so on. On the other hand, there is less we can say about 'every airline', although certainly 'every airline' is an airline. So, since 'an airline' and 'every airline' differ in the properties that they have, we can capture the distinction between them by identifying the meaning of a noun phrase with the set of properties that the object(s) referred to have. How are we to view these properties? Simply as sets, in the same way that we have interpreted verb phrase meanings. So the meaning of a proper name such as Delta is to be taken as the set of all sets having #Delta as a member. Thus:

```
Word Delta:
    <cat> = NP
    <meaning> = {{#Delta},
                 {#Delta, #Aden_Airways},
                 {#Delta, #Air_Cal},
                 ...
                 {#Delta, #Aden_Airways, #Manx_Airlines},
                 ...}.
Word "an airline":
    <cat> = NP
    <meaning> = [the set of all (sets of entities having at least one airline as a member)].
Word "every airline":
    <cat> = NP
    <meaning> = [the set of all (sets of entities that contain all the airlines as a subset)].
```

We can actually leave our meanings of verb phrases unchanged and simply change our sentence meaning rule to accommodate this new theory of noun phrase meaning. Whereas previously we allowed the verb phrase to specify a set of objects, and we were interested to see whether the noun phrase meaning belonged to that set, now we have the noun phrase meaning providing a set of sets, and we look for the verb phrase meaning in that set. Thus:

```
Rule
 S → NP VP:
    <S meaning> = TRUE if <VP meaning> ∈ <NP meaning>
                = FALSE otherwise.
```

However, there are a number of problems with this kind of approach to meaning in a computational context. One obvious difficulty is dealing with all those sets. We could represent a set implicitly by a procedure that will tell us whether a given object is an element. A more fundamental problem is that it is not clear that truth values are the appropriate meanings for sentences when we are putting meanings together in a compositional way. Consider sentences like:

Carl Icahn believes Delta owns Manx Airlines.

If we imagine sentences like this to be described by syntactic rules like the following:

Rule
  S → NP VP.
Rule
  VP → SV S.
Rule
  VP → TV NP

then the sentence 'Delta owns Manx Airlines' is a constituent of the original sentence. Now, according to compositionality, the only contribution that 'Delta owns Manx Airlines' can make to the meaning of a phrase containing it is its own meaning, which, in this case, is the truth value FALSE. Here we have construed the meaning of a sentence as its truth value, which means that the only thing about X that we are allowed to consult in determining whether 'Carl Icahn believes X' is true is its truth value. But, clearly, any normal person believes a number of sentences that are in fact true and a number of sentences that are in fact false. So, the truth value of 'Carl Icahn believes X' simply cannot be determined by reference to the truth value of X.

Of course, it is conceivable that we might be able to get round this specific problem by changing our syntactic rules. A better solution, however, would be to introduce a more sophisticated notion of meaning for a sentence than its truth value. This turns out to be easier said than done, and the issue of developing a notion of sentential meaning that will compose appropriately with the meanings of sentential complement-taking verbs like 'believe' and 'prove' remains an open research problem in philosophical logic.

Exercise 8.1 Write LISP functions to carry out semantic interpretation of sentences about airlines, or in a similar domain, as you wish, as outlined in this section. You should assume that you can obtain parse trees (perhaps use the chart parser chart to do this) from the sentences and should write functions to build semantic interpretations, given the information in these trees. The simplest way is to have one function for each category. Such a function will know about the different shapes of parse trees of that category, will work out what kind of tree it is given and will then compute the semantic interpretation, using other similar functions for the subphrases of other categories. For instance, here is a possible S function:

```
(defun interpret_s (tree)
  (if (equal (car tree) 'S)
    (member (interpret_np (cadr tree)) (interpret_vp (caddr tree))))
  nil)
```

where interpret_np and interpret_vp are similar interpretation functions (for NPs and VPs). [*intermediate*]

Exercise 8.2   Write a grammar for English number names, such as 'three hundred and forty two' and write interpretation functions, in the manner of the last exercise, to translate from parse trees to actual numbers. [*intermediate*]

8.3   Translation to a meaning representation language

Obtaining the truth value of a sentence may have its uses, but it is easy to imagine other ways we may wish to manipulate the meaning of a sentence. For instance, we might wish to determine whether we believe a given sentence, what conclusions follow from a sentence together with our existing beliefs or we might want to tell whether two different sentences mean the same thing. For these sorts of applications, we require a more informative notion of the meaning of a sentence than just a truth value. Thus, it has become traditional to approach the meaning of a sentence by translating it into an expression in another, artificial, language which is intended to represent the meaning. For such a process to have any point, we need to have a *meaning representation language (MRL)* that is better behaved in some way than the original natural language. For example:

- Whereas natural language statements may be ambiguous, we might require statements in an MRL to be unambiguous.

- Whereas it is hard to specify rules for how to determine when an arbitrary natural language statement is true, we might require that an MRL comes complete with rules that enable us to derive the conditions that the world would have to satisfy for an arbitrary statement to be true (the statement's truth conditions).

- Whereas it is difficult to determine what follows from a natural language statement, we might require that an MRL comes complete with rules of inference that enable us mechanically to derive new statements that follow from a given statement.

Semantic rules can be regarded as mappings from local phrase structure trees to meaning representations. If meaning representations are themselves structured objects, as expressions in formal languages are, then we can consider the mapping to be one that produces phrase structure trees for meaning representations. We then have mappings from trees to trees. In fact, things are not quite this simple, for the production of a meaning representation relies on the meaning representations of the subphrases. Thus, a semantic translation rule says that a local tree of a particular shape maps on to a local tree of another particular shape, provided that the subtrees of the original tree are mapped into subtrees of the new tree in a specified way. The mapping of the subtrees will in general require the use of other semantic translation rules in a recursive manner.

Viewing semantic translation to an MRL as local tree mapping does not necessarily commit us to a decision about when semantic translation rules are invoked. That is, the meaning of each phrase could be computed as soon as the parse tree for that phrase has been built, or the meaning could be worked out after a syntactic parse tree for the whole sentence has been constructed. Obviously, in the former case, however, the parse trees do not really have to be built, as their only purpose is immediately to determine which semantic translation rule is to be invoked. This recursive tree transformation can be regarded as a kind of transduction, where the input and output tapes are structured objects, rather than simple sequences of symbols. Given the kind of grammars we have been using in earlier chapters of this book, we have a natural place to attach information about what kind of output should correspond to a whole sequence of input phrases – the rule.

Assuming, for the moment, that both the natural language and the MRL can be described by the same sort of grammars, there is no difference between the kinds of objects that are the parse trees of natural language sentences and those that are the parse trees of semantic expressions. Thus, there is no reason why we have to consider the mapping as going from natural language sentences to meaning representations, rather than the reverse. Indeed, as we found with transducers, the same set of rules may support multiple purposes if we simply reconsider what the inputs and outputs are. A common technique in natural language generation systems, which might be called message-driven generation, is to make use of compositional rules that map from structures of the original semantics (the message) into structures representing linguistic objects.

Another method of semantic interpretation, which we will pursue further in the following sections, works as follows. As soon as the parser recognizes the presence of a phrase consisting of some sequence of subphrases (that is, the parser can apply a complete syntactic rule), the meaning of the whole phrase is immediately worked out from the meanings of the parts. In such a regime, the meaning of a single word would be constructed as soon as the parser encountered it. In addition, the parser would have to keep track of which syntactic rule it is currently using and what the meanings of the subconstituents found so far are. In this approach, there is a direct translation between the natural language and the semantic representation without any intermediate levels of representation. Such an approach enforces a local rule-to-rule interpretation regime, whereas in a tree-mapping approach, which carries out interpretation only on complete sentence parse trees, a compositional interpretation rule would be free to recognize and operate on local trees arising from the application of several grammar rules.

Exercise 8.3   One simple way of representing a whole number which makes some of its internal structure apparent is as a list of Arabic numerals. Thus, we can represent the number 345 in this simple MRL as:

(3 4 5)

Write a grammar for number names in some natural language, or use such a grammar that you have already written for a previous exercise, and write functions that translate from expressions of the Arabic numeral MRL into parse trees for your natural language grammar.   [*easy*]

Exercise 8.4   Add to the programs developed for the last exercise a grammar for number names in *another* natural language and functions for translating parse trees for strings of that language into elements of the Arabic numeral MRL. Combine the two stages of translation, so that parse trees for one natural language are mapped on to parse trees for the other natural language, via representations in the MRL.   [*intermediate*]

8.4   A database query language

To illustrate what translation into an MRL might look like, we will consider how to translate from simple sentences into formulae of a restricted logical language which we call DBQ. DBQ can be viewed as a restricted form of the predicate calculus with extensions that enable it to function as a simple database query language.

If we have an appropriately structured database of information about a given domain, in principle any DBQ query can be treated as a question addressed to the database and can be answered by a process of *evaluation*. The evaluation of a query amounts to attempting to verify that the complex proposition it represents is true. To verify the truth of the main proposition, a query evaluator may have to verify the truth of various subsidiary propositions. Some special propositions in DBQ are always true and cause things (answers) to be printed out when they are encountered during evaluation. We will consider the problems of query evaluation in Chapter 9, but for the present purposes we will concentrate on DBQ simply as the target language for semantic interpretation. An expression in DBQ represents a proposition, in the same way as an expression of the predicate calculus, and in Chapter 9 we will use a special syntax for DBQ queries, which is similar to that of the predicate calculus. As we shall see, however, for us to talk about a DBQ expression as it is being constructed, it is much more convenient to regard a DBQ expression as a DAG and to use our existing PATR notation to express constraints on its parts.

Let us return to our database of information about airlines. Corresponding to the primitive relations expressed in that database, DBQ allows us to express simple statements involving relations like 'is independent' and 'is an airline'. Such basic propositions are expressed using the features predicate, arg0 (and arg1, if the predicate relates two objects). For instance:

```
<predicate> = independent
<arg0> = TWA
```

denotes the proposition that TWA is independent (independent here representing the property of independence in much the same way that TWA represents Trans World Airlines) and:

```
<predicate> = took_over
<arg0> = Carl_Icahn
<arg1> = TWA
```

denotes the proposition that Carl Icahn took over TWA. DBQ also allows formulae to be combined by connectives such as and and or. In such a situation, the features connective, prop1 and prop2 are used. For instance:

```
<connective> = and
<prop1 predicate> = independent
<prop1 arg0> = US_Air
<prop2 predicate> = airline
<prop2 arg0> = Piedmont
```

says that US Air is independent and Piedmont is an airline. This is shown diagrammatically in Figure 8.2.

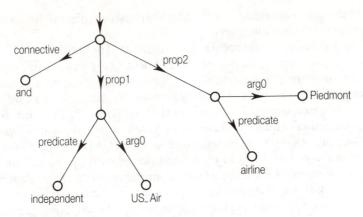

Figure 8.2 'US Air is independent and Piedmont is an airline'.

Finally, as in predicate calculus, DBQ allows for the construction of propositions that quantify over sets of individuals. In DBQ, however, quantifications are always *restricted*. That is, for instance, we cannot say that absolutely everything has some property, but instead we have to specify some class of objects and say that they all have the property. For a quantified proposition, we use the features quantifier, variable, restriction and body. Thus:

```
<quantifier> = all
<restriction predicate> = airline
<restriction arg0> = <variable>
<body predicate> = independent
<body arg0> = <variable>
```

The variable feature is a token that stands for an element of the set being quantified over. The restriction, which must mention the variable, delimits the set of individuals we are interested in; here, we say that it is the set of things that are airlines. The body, which must again mention the variable, tells us what predicate we are interested in testing for members of the restriction set; here, we are interested in seeing whether they are independent. Finally, the quantifier tells us how many elements of the set we want to satisfy the body predicate: all means that we require all the elements of the set to satisfy it, whereas exists means that we require at least one of the elements to satisfy it. So, the proposition represented here is that every airline is independent. We have just presented a notational variant of the predicate calculus formula:

$$(X)[airline(X) \rightarrow independent(X)]$$

Note that it does not really matter what value is associated with the variable feature, as long as the appropriate parts of the restriction and the body share that value. This corresponds to the fact that variables, in predicate calculus, can be viewed simply as pointers to places inside formulae and that, for instance, the above formula would mean exactly the same if X was replaced by Y throughout.

There are other kinds of DBQ formulae that, during query evaluation, involve the printing out of answers, apart from a final yes or no, but we will not consider these at present.

Exercise 8.5   Assuming the existence of primitive predicates for properties and relations like airline, independent, hotel_chain, took_over and out_sold, draw diagrams for the DBQ representations of 'TWA outsold Pan Am', 'every hotel chain took over an airline' and 'every independent airline outsold Manx Air'. [*easy*]

8.5 Computational semantics as feature instantiation

Features can serve a variety of purposes in a natural language analysis system. Certain features, such as case in English, are introduced to capture syntactic or morphological regularities that have no obvious simple semantic function. Others are obviously important for capturing allowable syntactic patterns but have direct semantic significance as well. For instance, number agreement can be thought of as an arbitrary syntactic phenomenon, and yet whether a noun phrase is singular or plural normally has an effect on its meaning. In a language processing system, we could take this a stage further and introduce features that are very important for the characterization of meaning, but which do not constrain the set of allowable sentence patterns in any straightforward way. Indeed, we could represent meaning entirely in terms of features and values, allowing the meaning to be built up in exactly the way that syntactic structure is built up during analysis.

In this section, we look at some example syntactic rules where the feature equations define meaning structures, rather than syntactic structures. The fact that we have chosen to represent DBQ expressions by DAGs means that we can talk about the internals of semantic structures by expressing constraints on the values of features. We could have included syntactic features, other than category information, in the rules, as well as semantic features, but we have missed them out for clarity.

What kinds of questions might we want to construct in asking questions about airlines, and how might we translate them into DBQ queries? AIRLINES-1 is a very small grammar for the airlines domain, with appropriate translation rules. As before, we will only deal with declarative sentences, although we treat them pragmatically as questions.

EXAMPLE: AIRLINES-1 grammar

```
    Rule
      S → NP VP:
        <S sem predicate> = <VP sem>
        <S sem arg0> = <NP sem>.
    Rule
      S0 → S1 CONJ S2:
        <S0 sem connective> = <CONJ sem>
        <S0 sem prop1> = <S1 sem>
        <S0 sem prop2> = <S2 sem>.

  Word Delta:
        <cat> = NP
        <sem> = Delta.
  Word "is independent":
        <cat> = VP
        <sem> = independent.
  Word "is a subsidiary":
        <cat> = VP
        <sem> = subsidiary.
  Word "is a hotel chain":
        <cat> = VP
        <sem> = hotel_chain.
  Word and:
        <cat> = CONJ
        <sem> = and.
  Word or:
        <cat> = CONJ
        <sem> = or.
```

Given these rules, the following description would be returned as the semantic analysis (that is, the DAG that stands as the value of the sem feature) of the sentence 'Delta is an airline and Delta is independent':

```
    <connective> = and
    <prop1 predicate> = airline
    <prop1 arg0> = Delta
    <prop2 predicate> = independent
    <prop2 arg0> = Delta
```

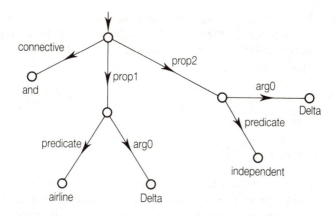

Figure 8.3   'Delta is an airline and Delta is independent'.

This is shown diagrammatically in Figure 8.3. Of course, in this example, our semantic interpretation is a fairly straightforward transliteration of the original sentence. With a more complex grammar, however, the semantic structures returned can be quite different in shape.

8.6   Transitive verbs and quantification

How does our simple grammar need to be extended to cover sentences like 'every airline took over a hotel chain'? In general, we need to have several semantic features associated with each phrase. Thus, with a sentence, we associate a single attribute, sem(antics), albeit an attribute with a structured value. A noun phrase is more complicated. One thing that a noun phrase may provide is a token, the referent, representing what is referred to. For instance, the noun phrase 'Delta' indicates that its referent is the airline of that name. In addition, we use two other semantic features for noun phrases. The sem feature has as its value some proposition that is conveyed about the referent. For instance, the noun phrase 'an airline' indicates that its referent is an airline. Finally, the hole feature indicates a place within the sem where extra information, derived from outside the noun phrase, can appear in the final meaning representation. In the case of a simple proper name, the noun phrase itself conveys no information about the referent, other than the DBQ name for it, and so any sem information about it comes from outside via the hole feature:

    Word Delta:
        <cat> = NP
        <referent> = Delta
        <sem> = <hole>.

In constructing the sem of a simple sentence, we take the sem of the subject noun phrase, where we fill the hole in that with the sem of the verb phrase. Finally, we indicate to the verb phrase what the referent of the subject was by using the subject feature arg0:

```
Rule
  S → NP VP:
    <S sem> = <NP sem>
    <NP hole> = <VP sem>
    <NP referent> = <VP arg0>.
```

Notice that here, in contrast to our previous practice, we are using the arg0 feature of a verb phrase to keep track of the pieces of semantic structure corresponding to the noun phrases that appear around it, rather than to keep track of the syntactic features of these noun phrases. A verb phrase has to produce an sem and can access the referent of its subject through the feature arg0. So, here is an example intransitive verb entry:

```
Word "is independent":
  <cat> = VP
  <sem predicate> = independent
  <sem arg0> = <arg0>.
```

Let us briefly take stock and see what these rules will do for us, given the example sentence 'Delta is independent'. Relevant portions of the feature structures can be described as follows:

The sentence
```
<cat> = S
<sem predicate> = independent
<sem arg0> = Delta
```

The subject noun phrase
```
<cat> = NP
<referent> = Delta
<sem predicate> = independent
<sem arg0> = Delta
<hole> = <sem>
```

The verb phrase
```
<cat> = VP
<sem predicate> = independent
<sem arg0> = Delta
```

We can make life more interesting by introducing a rule that allows a verb phrase to contain a transitive verb followed by a noun phrase. The sem of a transitive verb is constructed from two referents, the arg0 and the arg1, which are set up by the verb phrase rule:

```
Rule
  VP → TV NP:
    <VP sem> = <NP sem>
    <NP hole> = <TV sem>
    <TV arg0> = <VP arg0>
    <TV arg1> = <NP referent>.


Word "took over":
    <cat> = TV
    <sem predicate> = took_over
    <sem arg0> = <arg0>
    <sem arg1> = <arg1>.
```

So the structures built for 'Carl Icahn took over TWA' would be:

The sentence

```
<cat> = S
<sem predicate> = took_over
<sem arg0> = Carl_Icahn
<sem arg1> = TWA
```

The subject noun phrase

```
<cat> = NP
<referent> = Carl_Icahn
<sem predicate> = took_over
<sem arg0> = Carl_Icahn
<sem arg1> = TWA
<hole> = <sem>
```

The verb phrase

```
<cat> = VP
<sem predicate> = took_over
<sem arg0> = Carl_Icahn
<sem arg1> = TWA
```

The transitive verb

```
<cat> = TV
<arg0> = Carl_Icahn
<arg1> = TWA
<sem predicate> = took_over
<sem arg0> = Carl_Icahn
<sem arg1> = TWA
```

The object noun phrase
```
<cat> = NP
<referent> = TWA
<sem predicate> = took_over
<sem arg0> = Carl_Icahn
<sem arg1> = TWA
<hole> = <sem>
```

We can also allow simple quantification in the sentences; indeed, it is because of this that our analysis so far has been quite convoluted. We have already seen how DBQ can represent the statement that a given proposition is true for all possible (restricted) values of a referent, using the quantifier all. Similarly, the quantifier exists is used to indicate that there exists an object (satisfying a restriction) that makes a given proposition true. Here is the rule for introducing quantifiers of this kind:

```
Rule
  NP → Det N:
    <NP sem quantifier> = <Det sem quantifier>
    <NP sem variable> = <NP referent>
    <NP sem restriction> = <N sem>
    <NP sem body> = <NP hole>
    <NP referent> = <N referent>.
```

where nouns have lexical entries such as the following:

```
Word airline:
    <cat> = N
    <sem predicate> = airline
    <sem arg0> = <referent>.

Word "hotel chain":
    <cat> = N
    <sem predicate> = hotel_chain
    <sem arg0> = <referent>.
```

and where the category Det includes 'a' and 'every':

```
Word a:
    <cat> = Det
    <sem quantifier> = exists.

Word every:
    <cat> = Det
    <sem quantifier> = all.
```

Here, by way of example, is, in LISP form, the DBQ DAG that we get from the sentence 'an airline took over every hotel chain':

```
((sem ((quantifier exists)
       (variable _x)
       (restriction ((arg0 _x) (predicate airline) (& #:_211)))
       (body ((quantifier all)
              (variable _y)
              (restriction ((arg0 _y) (predicate hotel_chain) (& #:_237)))
              (body ((arg0 _x)
                     (arg1 _y)
                     (predicate took_over)
                     (& #:_262)))
              (& #:_242)))
       (& #:_215)))
 (& #:_192))
```

And here is what we get for 'every hotel chain took over an airline':

```
((sem ((quantifier all)
       (variable _x)
       (restriction ((arg0 _x) (predicate hotel_chain) (& #:_137)))
       (body ((quantifier exists)
              (variable _y)
              (restriction ((arg0 _y) (predicate airline) (& #:_163)))
              (body ((arg0 _x)
                     (arg1 _y)
                     (predicate took_over)
                     (& #:_188)))
              (& #:_168)))
       (& #:_141)))
 (& #:_118))
```

As these examples show, in the case of sentences containing more than one quantifier, our semantic interpretation rules only produce one reading, whereas there are frequently several. Are we talking about a single airline that was taken over by every hotel chain, or a possibly different airline for each hotel chain? The alternative readings of these examples can be obtained by switching around the occurrences of the quantifiers in the semantic representation. The problem of ascertaining the appropriate *scopes* of quantifiers is a serious one for a database front end program: a more sophisticated approach than ours might build a semantic representation that was neutral with respect to scoping decisions and subsequently enumerate all possible scopings for semantic (or user) screening of some kind.

Semantic interpretation carried out by feature instantiation is naturally done during parsing, rather than as a separate process operating on parse trees. It is similar in spirit to the idea embodied in ATNs; that is, that the structure built by a parser need not echo exactly the sequence of phrases as they were encountered. ATNs were likewise well suited to building semantic structures directly. The main advantage of ATNs was that the operations carried out (assignment, testing equality) were close to those operations that traditional computers could execute most efficiently. On the other hand, assuming that unification suffices as the only operation for building semantic structures, a grammar written in this manner can serve as a much more abstract characterization of a language than an ATN could provide, and one that can be turned to applications other than parsing. For instance, we could imagine a natural language generation program operating by exhaustively generating all the legal sentences of the language whose meaning unified with a given structure. We would expect that the constraint of unifiability with the given target would constrain the search considerably. This would be a kind of 'grammar-driven' generation, as distinct from the message-driven kind of generation discussed earlier.

Exercise 8.6 Draw diagrams for the DBQ expressions representing the meanings of the following phrases: 'airline' (an N), 'every airline' (an NP), 'took over an airline' (a VP), 'Delta took over an airline' (an S).   [*easy*]

Exercise 8.7 Provide appropriate entries for the new lexical items in the following sentences. What DBQ expressions do the rules assign to the sentences?

(a) Every transatlantic_carrier is_independent.

(b) Delta bought_out a travel_agent.

(c) Every UK_airline acquired a hotel_chain.

(d) A US_airline outsold every UK_airline.

[*easy*]

Exercise 8.8 In simple examples such as 'Carl Icahn took over TWA', the hole feature on NPs appears to be otiose. Can you eliminate it from the analysis and yet continue to handle the quantified examples correctly? If you cannot, explain why.   [*intermediate*]

Exercise 8.9 Add the following lexical entry to the grammar described in Section 8.6:

```
Word who:
    <cat> = NP
    <sem quantifier> = all
    <sem restriction> = <hole>
```

```
<sem body predicate> = printout
<sem body arg0> = <sem variable>
<sem variable> = referent.
```

What semantic representations are produced for the sentences 'who took over TWA?', 'TWA took over who?', 'who took over a hotel chain?' [*intermediate*]

Exercise 8.10   Extend the existing grammar to deal with adjectives, prepositional phrases and simple relative clauses. Your grammar should produce semantic translations for sentences like 'every large airline took over a small airline', 'every transatlantic carrier in Europe is independent', 'an airline that took over a hotel chain outsold Delta'.   [*hard*]

Exercise 8.11   lib airlines holds the grammar developed here for generating DBQ queries in LISP format. Use it, together with the library program lib fburecog (or lib fchart), to derive semantic representations from example sentences. You will see that lib airlines redefines the functions category and tree for this grammar. What is the purpose of this? How is it that lib fburecog, which implements a recognizer, is nevertheless able to yield complete semantic representations?   [*intermediate*]

Exercise 8.12   Experiment with the idea of generating airlines sentences from DBQ queries using lib randfgen to generate a random sentence, given only sem information about the top-level category. What problems do you encounter? How might the approach be improved to make a serious language generation system?   [*hard*]

8.7   Ambiguity, preferences and timing

As we have already noted, semantic translation in a language-understanding system can be postponed until a parse tree is available for the whole input sentence. Or, semantic translation can be interleaved with syntactic parsing, each syntactic fragment being translated as soon as it is complete. This might have seemed like an unnecessary distinction to make. Does it really make any difference when semantic translation takes place? Surely the same work has to be done regardless?

To see how it might make a difference when semantic translation takes place, we need to consider what happens when syntactic parsing yields multiple alternative analyses of an input. In general, we would hope that the result of semantic translation would give us some basis for comparing different analyses on grounds of semantic plausibility, maybe even allowing us to reject analyses that only yield obviously anomalous translations. For instance, we would expect the syntactic analysis of:

> Get a screwdriver with a narrow blade.

to yield results according to the following bracketings:

> Get (a screwdriver (with a narrow blade)).
> (Get a screwdriver) (with a narrow blade).

The first alternative seems to correspond to a sensible reading for the command, but the second forces us to see the blade as some kind of means for getting a screwdriver. This is clearly possible (in some situations it might be necessary to prise screwdrivers out of narrow cracks, and a blade would be useful for this!), but this interpretation is more of a strain somehow. We might expect an intelligent understander, everything else being equal, to prefer the first reading, because it does not violate any of our expectations, whereas the second reading forces us to rethink what might count as a way of getting a screwdriver. We might even reject the second reading out of hand in some applications – where tools were always easily available, for instance. In Chapters 9 and 10, we will see how these sorts of anomalies might be signalled by appropriate inferences, but for now it suffices to assume that they can be and that semantic considerations can give us some kind of preference ordering for syntactic analyses.

Now, semantic preferences can be expressed below the level of whole sentences, and this can be to our advantage if we use an interleaved style of semantic interpretation. For instance, we would normally expect the sequence:

> Defrauding airlines ...

to continue with something like:

> ... can make passengers ineligible for travel.

rather than with something like:

> ... can be indicted by a grand jury.

That is, we are relatively unhappy talking about airlines defrauding passengers, rather than passengers defrauding airlines. This semantic preference leads us in this instance to prefer a syntactic analysis of the initial fragment using rules like:

```
Rule
  NP → VP
    <VP head mor suffix> = ing.
```

rather than rules like:

```
Rule
   NP → Adj N.
Rule
   Adj → V
      <V mor suffix> = ing.
```

and this preference can be expressed in an interleaved semantic interpretation system before any more input words are processed.

If we are only interested in obtaining the most plausible semantic interpretation of the sentence, we can make use of this preference in ordering our parsing agenda and demote (or even remove) hypotheses that require the initial fragment to be analyzed in the second way. This means that we will not have to consider all the possible ways that the second analysis can combine with different analyses of the rest of the sentence, unless another preference is broken in a further development of the first. Thus, certain unlikely analyses can be killed off before they grow too far. If we had to wait until syntactic analysis of the whole input was complete before expressing any semantic preferences, we would have to follow through all possible syntactic analyses right to the end, before evaluating semantic plausibility and choosing an interpretation.

The efficiency arguments for interleaved semantic interpretation are not, unfortunately, conclusive. Whether using semantic checks to screen implausible syntactic analyses early is better than using them to screen completed parses later on depends on the relative efficiency of syntactic and semantic processing, as well as the extent to which local syntactic ambiguity can be resolved by syntax alone. For instance, in the sentence:

Defrauding airlines makes passengers ineligible for travel.

the ambiguity of the initial phrase can be fully resolved by number agreement considerations when this phrase is seen combined with the word 'makes'. This disambiguation is purely syntactic, and so any lengthy analysis carried out by an interleaved semantic interpreter to investigate the relative plausibility of the two readings of 'defrauding airlines' would be wasted.

8.8   Building semantic checking into the grammar

Imagine our NLP system encountering, say, the sentence:

The hole that had been drilled by the woman in the wrench turned out to be very useful.

Now consider the following possible noun phrase which might be suggested by our syntactic parser but which we might expect to be semantically dispreferred:

the woman in the wrench

There are at least two possible reasons for rejecting this phrase. We may use the fact that, in general, women cannot be in wrenches, and so this occurrence, as a special case, is anomalous. Or, we may reject the phrase because, normally used, it should refer to a particular person in the current context, and there is no woman in a wrench in the context of use. These two types of semantic reasoning could be called *context independent* and *context dependent*, because the first makes no appeal to the context of use, whereas the second does. Although the second type may require complex context-dependent inferencing, which will be discussed to some extent in Chapters 9 and 10, the first type of reasoning may be quite simple and, in restricted domains, it may be possible to almost completely formalize it. This leads to the possibility that context-independent semantic checking might be integrated with syntactic parsing in interesting ways.

The easiest way to incorporate reasoning about semantic appropriateness into our existing parsing framework is to use semantic features. Most of our grammars so far have made non-trivial use of syntactic features, but in addition we have already used some semantic features in grammars to build semantic representations. We can, in fact, enumerate a number of options as to what kinds of features we wish to include in a grammar:

(1)   Syntactic features only.
(2)   Syntactic features plus semantic features for building semantic structures only.
(3)   Syntactic features plus semantic features for checking only.
(4)   Arbitrary syntactic and semantic features.
(5)   Collapsed syntactic and semantic features.

Our very first grammars were of type 1. With such a grammar, there is no choice but to have semantic interpretation be a separate process (from parsing) that recognizes syntactic structures and constructs semantic analogues. Our airlines grammars were of type 2. We will see later a grammar of type 3, where the purpose of semantic features is only to filter out anomalous parses. There is no reason why we could not include semantic features of both kinds in the grammar and produce one of type 4. In such a grammar, it may not even be very clear which features are present primarily for syntactic reasons and which for semantic. We might thus take the final step (to type 5), forgetting about the syntax–semantics distinction and encoding directly the systematic regularities of the language in a restricted domain. This approach would yield a so-called 'semantic grammar'.

To see what a grammar of type 3 might look like, consider the following example sentences:

> Get a screwdriver with a narrow blade.
> Get a screwdriver with your left hand.

Imagine that we are interested in building a natural language-understanding system capable of dealing with the commands issued by a carpenter to a carpenter's apprentice. We might explain why, in this domain, in the first command the phrase 'with ...' must modify the screwdriver, whereas in the second the 'with ...' phrase must modify the 'get' action, as follows. In the carpentry domain, the word 'with' is 2-way ambiguous. In both cases it is of category P, but one sense expresses a relation between an object and one of its components, whereas the other sense relates an action with an instrument for carrying out that action. We can formalize this through the features arg0 type, the type of object that can be modified, and arg1 type, the type of object that can appear after the preposition:

```
Word with:
    <cat> = P
    <arg0 type> = action
    <arg1 type major> = physobj
    <arg1 type minor> = instrument.
Word with:
    <cat> = P
    <arg0 type major> = physobj
    <arg1 type major> = physobj
    <arg1 type minor> = component.
```

Notice that, through the features major and minor, we have allowed the amount of detail specified about a given object to vary. So, for instance, in the second 'with' entry the arg0 type can be any (physical) object, whereas the arg1 type must be a component, as well as being a physobj. For us to check that these requirements are met, we must record the features of the objects denoted by nouns and noun phrases, using the feature type:

```
Word hand:
    <cat> = N
    <type major> = physobj
    <type minor> = instrument.
Word blade:
    <cat> = N
    <type major> = physobj
    <type minor> = component.
```

and we must ensure that the conditions are satisfied in the grammar rules:

```
Rule
  PP → P NP:
    <PP arg0 type> = <P arg0 type>
    <P arg1 type> = <NP type>.
Rule
  VP1 → VP2 PP:
    <VP1 cat> = VP
    <VP2 cat> = VP
    <PP arg0 type> = action.
Rule
  NP1 → NP2 PP:
    <NP1 cat> = NP
    <NP2 cat> = NP
    <NP1 type> = <NP2 type>
    <PP arg0 type> = <NP2 type>.
```

Through these specifications of semantic constraints in the grammar rules, we hope to ensure that semantically anomalous analyses (for the carpentry domain) never arise. The technique we are using is the same as the one that we use in syntax to ensure that a singular noun phrase can never combine with a plural verb phrase.

Here are some more rules, completing a tiny fragment of what we might want for the carpentry domain. These rules allow adjectives and verbs to encode semantic expectations, just as prepositions do above.

```
Rule
  VP → TV NP:
    <TV arg1 type> = <NP type>.
Rule
  NP → Det NB:
    <NP type> = <NB type>.
Rule
  NB → N:
    <NB type> = <N type>.
Rule
  NB1 → Adj NB2:
    <NB1 cat> = NB
    <NB2 cat> = NB
    <NB1 type> = <Adj arg0 type>
    <NB1 type> = <NB2 type>.

Word get:
    <cat> = TV
    <arg1 type major> = physobj.
```

```
Word a:
    <cat> = Det.
Word your:
    <cat> = Det.
Word screwdriver:
    <cat> = N
    <type major> = physobj.
Word narrow:
    <cat> = Adj
    <arg0 type major> = physobj.
Word left:
    <cat> = Adj
    <arg0 type major> = physobj.
```

Now, if we use this grammar to parse 'get a screwdriver with a narrow blade', we get the following parse tree:

```
(VP (TV get)
    (NP (NP (Det a) (NB (N screwdriver)))
        (PP (P with) (NP (Det a) (NB (Adj narrow) (NB (N blade)))))))
```

whereas, if we use it to parse 'get a screwdriver with your left hand', we get a quite different structure:

```
(VP (VP (TV get) (NP (Det a) (NB (N screwdriver))))
    (PP (P with) (NP (Det your) (NB (Adj left) (NB (N hand)))))))
```

Of course, the successful disambiguation of sentences in this way all depends on our ability to codify the types of objects that occur in the application domain and the ways that individual word senses behave with respect to these types. Even in the carpentry domain, it is clear that this analysis would no longer work if we extended the grammar to deal with doll-making ('hand' behaving as a component of a doll) or carving ('blade' behaving as an instrument). Whether we can successfully enumerate all possible word senses and gain any mileage from a set of semantic features depends crucially on how self-contained the application domain is. The domain of weather forecasts is, for instance, much more likely to yield a successful use of semantic features than the domain of romantic novels.

It may well happen, if we go much further in formalizing a grammar of carpenter's commands, that certain combinations of features and values start to come up very frequently. For instance, the combination:

```
<cat> = NP
<type major> = physobj
```

will come up in any context where the grammar requires a noun phrase denoting a physical object. We could start introducing new primitive categories in such situations as a way of keeping our feature structures small. For instance, we could replace all occurrences of the above with:

```
<cat> = PHYSOBJ
```

We could then start encoding specialized forms that certain of these can have. For instance, a tool can be referred to using a manufacturer's name, as in 'the Stanley screwdriver':

```
Rule
  PHYSOBJ → TOOL.
Rule
  PHYSOBJ → MATERIAL.
Rule
  TOOL → Det MANUFACTURER BASICTOOL.
```

We could then include specific rules for classes of verbs that subcategorize for these specific categories:

```
Rule
  VP → FETCH_VERB TOOL.
Rule
  VP → USE_VERB TOOL TO VP.
```

covering strings like 'get the screwdriver' or 'use the screwdriver to open the tin'. This is the route towards creating a semantic grammar for the domain – that is, type 5. This may be worthwhile if the forms of phrases are very dependent on semantic characteristics, but will result in an unnecessary proliferation of cases if traditional general notions like NP capture the data fairly well. For instance, it might well be worthwhile introducing special categories for a grammar of times covering, for example, 'half past one' or 'three minutes to two', or addresses covering, for example, '1033 W. Mayfield Boulevard, Portland', because such phrases have unique and conventional forms. But the grammar of phrases referring to telephones might just be a minor variant on a standard NP grammar.

The use of features to encode semantic information in the grammar is a relatively unprincipled technique, but is one that has been frequently used by computational linguists and falls under a rubric known as *selectional restrictions*. In implementations of selectional restrictions, the values of the semantic features are often known as *semantic markers* and, as here, a failure of semantic features to match is generally taken to indicate a totally unacceptable interpretation. This kind of technique may be worth the effort in certain limited natural language domains and, thus, may be gainfully employed from an engineering perspective (if portability is not a consideration). However, it is unprincipled, since it is clear that it makes no sense to try and encode *all* potentially relevant real-world knowledge into the syntax as annotations on categories: the syntax is a small, bounded, finite object whereas the real-world knowledge is nothing of the kind. The principled way to approach the problem is to have a real semantic component and a genuine real-world knowledge and inference component, and to allow the parser access to these components, or, more pedantically, access to what these components have to say about the constituents that the parser is considering, throughout the process of parsing. To cope properly with problems of this kind, then, a parser needs to be able to ask not simply 'Can I put constituent of category A together with constituent of category B to form a category of constituent C?' but also 'Does constituent A have an interpretation that can be combined with an available B constituent interpretation to form a (sensible) interpretation for constituent C?' Attempts have been made along these lines but given the relatively underdeveloped state of computational NLP semantics and pragmatics, as compared to syntactic parsing, say, there is much room for further progress.

Exercise 8.13   A LISP version of our carpenter's grammar is in lib disambig. Using this grammar, together with a suitable parser or recognizer – for example, lib fchart – analyze the following sentences and note the results obtained:

(a)   Get a screwdriver with a narrow blade.

(b)   Get a screwdriver with your left hand.

Extend the treatment of adjectives, in such a way that 'heavy hole' and 'deep screwdriver' are not accepted, but 'heavy screwdriver' and 'deep hole' are.   [*intermediate*]

Exercise 8.14   Convert the feature-based chart parser fchart to use a semantic plausibility score to decide what to take off the agenda first. The new parser will need to keep an extra numerical field in each edge, specifying how plausible the edge is, and the plausibility scores will have to be combined at the various places edges are joined together. Each rule of the grammar will also need to include a plausibility score, and in general for any rule there will be two versions: one with the semantic preference enforced and one with the preference relaxed. For instance:

```
((VP -> TV NP) 100        ;;; 100% plausible
 (VP cat) = VP
 (TV cat) = TV
 (NP cat) = NP
 (TV arg1 type) = (NP type))
```

```
((VP -> TV NP) 90              ;;; 90% plausible
 (VP cat) = VP
 (TV cat) = TV
 (NP cat) = NP))
```

To avoid spending time on duplicate analyses, the parser should stop when it finds the first (maximally plausible) parse.   [*hard project*]

SUMMARY

- Semantics accounts for the truth conditions of sentences.

- Compositionality makes semantics dependent on syntax.

- It is tempting to identify NP meanings with referents.

- Such an identification is inadequate for quantified NPs.

- NLP semantics often proceeds by translating English to logic.

- DBQ is a logical language for database query.

- Simple English sentences can be translated into DBQ.

- Features can be used for semantics as well as syntax.

- Semantic features can be used to reduce syntactic ambiguity.

Further reading

Most of the topics addressed in this chapter are abundantly documented in the literature and so this section simply points at some representative recent work, rather than making any attempt at comprehensive citation. Although the literature on natural language semantics is large, the topic still lacks a satisfactory basic text. Dowty *et al.* (1981) comes closest, but readers without a thorough background in logic and set theory will find it hard going; reading McDermott (1978/1986) may persuade you to make the effort. However, a very useful background discussion can be found in Johnson-Laird (1983, especially Chapter 8). Lyons (1977) provides encyclopaedic coverage of most topics in semantics and pragmatics from a linguist's, as opposed to a logician's, perspective, while Hirst (1986) and Allen (1987, Part II) provide the most comprehensive overview, from an NLP perspective, of the topics covered in this chapter. An extensive discussion of compositionality and the issues it gives rise to is to be found in Partee (1984).

A variety of approaches to compositional semantics in NLP during the decade 1978–88 can be tracked through the following sources: Friedman *et al.*

(1978a, 1978b), Hobbs and Rosenschein (1978), Moran (1982), Rosenschein and Shieber (1982), Smith (1982), Warren and Friedman (1982), Schubert and Pelletier (1982/1986), Hirst (1983), Pelletier and Schubert (1984), Pinkal (1986), Hinrichs (1986, 1987), and Charniak and Goldman (1988). An influential recent paradigm that has emerged from this tradition is situation semantics originating in Barwise and Perry (1983) and receiving extensive formal development in Fenstad *et al.*(1987). The implications of this approach for NLP are explored by Barwise (1981), Evans (1981), Israel (1983), Mukai and Yasukawa (1985), Sugimura (1986), Lespérance (1986), Cooper (1987) and Nakashima *et al.* (1988). Although most contemporary work on semantics, both within NLP and without, is compositionally organized and owes a large debt to logic, this kind of perspective is not universally shared: see, for example, Riesbeck (1986), and Winograd and Flores (1986) for dissenting views.

The semantic properties of natural language quantifiers and the noun phrases that contain them form the subject matter for Cooper (1983), van Benthem and ter Meulen (1985), and Gärdenfors (1987). The question of how to assign, or avoid having to assign, the appropriate relative scopes to multiple quantifiers is addressed by Bunt (1984), Grosz *et al.* (1987), Hobbs (1983), Reyle (1985), Saint-Dizier (1985), Hurum and Schubert (1986), Hobbs and Shieber (1987), Hurum (1988), Keller (1988) and Moran (1988), among others.

The classic paper on quantification in the question–answering context is Woods (1978/1986). Groenendijk and Stokhof (1984) and Engdahl (1986) are both monographs dealing in detail with the semantics of questions and the interactions between questions and the quantifiers that they may contain. Webber (1987) gives an overview of question answering in AI. Main and Benson (1983) provide a denotational semantics for a question–answering system. A number of similar languages to DBQ have been used in natural language front ends to databases, starting from the work of Woods (1968) and Colmerauer (1978). Winston and Horn (1989, Chapter 30) give implementation details in LISP for a rather simple question–answering system based on an ATN.

Semantic checking, as described in this chapter, is discussed under the rubric of selectional restrictions in the linguistics literature. An enormously influential attack on the theoretical basis of selectional restrictions is to be found in McCawley (1968). Few linguists have expressed much interest in the topic in the two decades since this paper was published. However, Thomason (1972) provides one way of making formal sense of such restrictions. Within NLP, Wilks (1975, 1985) has remained a consistent champion of using semantic checking techniques to arrive at preferred readings (but not to exclude readings) in parsing. Ritchie (1983b) provides a useful critical discussion of semantic grammars and the role of semantic processing in parsing. Further discussion of these themes, from a variety of points of view, is to be found in Sparck Jones and Wilks (1983, Parts V and VI) and Dahlgren (1988). Mellish (1983, 1985) develops a theory of noun phrase interpretation in NLP which is both local and incremental, while Haddock (1987) shows how this kind of incremental interpretation can be integrated with categorial grammar parsing.

CHAPTER 9

QUESTION ANSWERING AND INFERENCE

Inference mechanisms can play a number of useful roles in language-processing systems. For instance, they can help a system to:

- Answer questions whose answers are distinct in form from any single piece of information that the system already possesses.

- Make predictions about possible future natural language inputs.

- Make decisions about assimilating new information into existing beliefs.

- Solve problems about how the world does or might behave.

- Detect that two statements are semantically equivalent or that a statement is anomalous.

In this chapter, we concentrate mainly on the kinds of inferences that a language-processing system might be required to make, generally illustrating the ideas by referring to question–answering systems. It is with such systems that our discussion begins. In Chapter 10, we will consider other uses of inference for the processing of natural language in context.

9.1   Question answering

Translating from a natural language sentence to an MRL expression can be useful in a number of ways, but how can we evaluate whether real understanding has occurred? Suppose somebody came up to you and claimed to have a natural language-understanding program that translated English sentences into an MRL. They might give you some examples of sentences and their translations:

Mayumi sings   ⇒   SING(M)
Beryl sees Hanni ⇒   SEE(B, H)

How would you evaluate their claim? You would certainly want to know what the denotations of the symbols SING, M, SEE, B and H are; that is, which objects and relations in the world they are supposed to indicate. You would also want to know the rules for constructing formulae in the MRL (the language's syntax). And you would want to know the rules for determining whether a given formula is true or not in any given context (the language's semantics). For although the truth or falsity of a formula in a given context might not always be of direct interest, the ability to determine (or know what would be involved in determining) the truth value in a given context is a fundamental part of knowing what the formula means. This is because knowing in what circumstances a formula would be true in some context (knowing the formula's truth conditions) amounts to knowing what the formula is claiming about the world. Armed with the appropriate syntax and semantics for the MRL, you could ascertain that the example sentences were indeed translated into expressions with the correct meaning.

But this would not be enough to demonstrate that the program had understood these sentences. To demonstrate understanding, it is not sufficient to show that the translation into an MRL, together with the semantics of the MRL, provides correct meanings for natural language sentences. If it were, we could simply use our natural language as an MRL and have the identity translation. It is not even sufficient to show that the semantics of the MRL is something that can be formally specified. For that offers no guarantee of any understanding, apart from that achievable by a human reader who is able to work out the semantics of meaning representations.

The kinds of tests for understanding that we need must examine the machine's ability to manipulate the symbols of the meaning representation language in a way that reflects their actual meaning. If a machine has sensory inputs of some kind, we might require that its manipulation of symbols like SING and SEE have some association or correlation with certain kinds of auditory or visual input or output. If the machine is able to accept or produce natural language utterances, we might require that its actions be in accordance with what we would expect from a language understander. But, above all, we might require that the way in which symbols are organized and used in the machine reflects somehow the organization and ways of the world. For instance, we would expect that there would be a connection between the way in which the symbol SING is used and the ways in which other symbols like SONG and MELODY are used, since there are obvious connections between the (real) concepts that these symbols presumably denote. Obviously, we cannot have a comprehensive model of the world in our machine, but whatever model the machine has should parallel the real world in all the respects relevant to the current application.

Question answering is one task that we can use to test the understanding of a natural language processing system. Other tasks include translation, the production of explanations and summaries, and various problem-solving tasks. We will concentrate here on question answering because it is relatively easy to build a simple question answerer from the materials we have already developed. In addition, natural language question–answering systems (QA systems) are providing an increasingly attractive way for humans to extract information from large computer databases. In its simplest form, which is dealing with yes–no questions, question answering includes being able to determine whether or not a given natural language statement, or, rather, its MRL equivalent, is true. That is, a QA system that can deal with any question (within some natural language fragment) in any context (one of a set of possible databases) will have to know the truth conditions of formulae in the MRL and hence, to act appropriately, will have to understand natural language queries in a non-trivial way.

Chapter 8 provided a syntax and informal semantics for the DBQ meaning representation language. Formulae of this language make use of general symbols like and and all, as well as special symbols for objects and relations that will depend on the particular database at hand. But are our semantic interpretation rules correct to translate the English word 'and' into a construction involving the connective and? What exactly does the symbol all mean to the machine? Can it really manipulate these symbols in a way that reflects the meanings of English sentences? What we will do next is specify informally an algorithm for evaluating a DBQ formula; that is, determining whether it is true or false in some given database. The operations for determining the truth of a given type of construction in the language will reflect the meaning that the construction has for the machine. The extent to which these operations reflect the original natural language meaning will remain unanswered, although there is certainly an intuitive reasonableness to the operations, at least when they are dealing with simple examples. If DBQ were to be taken seriously as an MRL, then it would be important to provide a formal semantics for it, and to determine to what extent the operations of the question–answering algorithm respected and embodied this semantics. This would enable us to factor out the question of the appropriateness of DBQ translations of natural language statements from the question of the extent to which the DBQ semantics is reflected in the machine.

For semantic translation, it was convenient to regard DBQ formulae as DAGs, as this allowed us to accumulate separately the different pieces of information that went into the construction of a given formula. For question–answering purposes, however, we can take a DBQ formula to be a fully constructed object, and it will be useful to exploit this and introduce a more concise LISP syntax similar to that of typed predicate calculus (predicate calculus where all variables are annotated with the type of object that they can range over). There are three kinds of DBQ formulae: their representations in PATR and their concise representations are as follows:

Old notation	*New notation*
<predicate> = p <arg0> = a0 <arg1> = a1	(p a0 a1)
<connective> = c <prop1> = p1 <prop2> = p2	(c p1 p2)
<quantifier> = q <variable> = v <restriction> = r <body> = b	(q v r b)

For example:

Old notation	*New notation*
<quantifier> = all <restriction predicate> = airline <restriction arg0> = variable> <body predicate> = employer <body arg0> = variable>	(all _x (airline _x) (employer x))
<connective> = and <prop1 predicate> = airline <prop1 arg0> = Delta <prop2 predicate> = hotel_chain <prop2 arg0> = Hilton	(and (airline Delta) (hotel_chain Hilton))

In translating from the old notation to the new, we replace all values for the variable feature by variable symbols in such a way that two such symbols are the same, exactly, when the two values share in the DAG. As before, we indicate variable symbols by using atoms beginning with '_'. Where a database predicate is involved, the number of objects in the list will, of course, depend on the predicate concerned. For instance:

(airline _x)

might represent the proposition that _x is an airline and:

(took_over _x _y)

might represent the proposition that _x took over _y. Here are some examples of queries in the LISP notation, together with natural language questions that they might correspond to:

```
(all _x
    (airline _x)
    (us_based _x))
'every airline is US based'
(all _x
    (airline _x)
    (printout _x))
'what airlines are there?'
(all _x
    (and (airline _x)
         (exists _y (hotel_chain _y)
                    (took_over _x _y)))
    (printout _x))
'what airlines took over a hotel chain?'
(all _x
    (and (hotel_chain _x)
         (exists _y (owns _x _y)))
    (printout _x))
'which hotel chains have subsidiaries?'
```

Exercise 9.1   Use lib termify to translate DBQ formulae as DAGs into the more concise LISP list structures used here.   [*intermediate*]

9.2   Evaluating DBQ formulae

Our algorithm for evaluating DBQ formulae will not actually provide truth values directly for a formula, but will produce a set of *substitutions* reflecting possible values for variables appearing in the formula that yield true propositions. It is simplest to see this for formulae of the first type (involving simple predicates). Imagine that we have a database about car parts which includes information about which firms supply which parts. We will assume that a relation supplies is represented in the database by a long list of entries specifying exhaustively who supplies what, as follows:

Who	*What*
smith_corp	radiators
jones_inc	spark_plugs
morgan_bros	radiators
jones_inc	batteries
smith_corp	tyres
morgan_bros	pumps

Questions about this relation can be phrased in DBQ by using the predicate supplies. We will use the first (arg0) argument position associated with supplies to indicate the supplying firm and the second (arg1) position to indicate the type of part. Then, the following are possible DBQ formulae involving this relation:

(supplies _x radiators)
(supplies _x _y)

The result of evaluating the first of these formulae will be the set of possible values for _x which would result in the formula matching something in the database. So what we get is:

(((_x smith_corp))
((_x morgan_bros)))

The result of evaluating the second of the formulae will be the set of pairs of values for _x and _y that result in the formula matching something in the database. In this case, the result corresponds to the whole relation represented by:

(((_x smith_corp) (_y radiators))
((_x morgan_bros) (_y spark_plugs)) ...)

In general, a DBQ formula involving a predicate and associated arguments will be assumed to correspond to a primitive relation, each true case of which is explicitly listed in the database. The evaluation of such formulae is dealt with by the database and returns the set of possible variable bindings that allow the formula to match a true fact recorded there.

Let us now consider the more complex kinds of DBQ formulae. In general, there needs to be a special way of evaluating each kind of conjunction and each kind of quantifier. Consider the and conjunction. We want the truth value of an and proposition to be true if and only if each of the two component propositions is true. A value of a variable will satisfy such a complex proposition only if it satisfies both of the subpropositions. So, here is a way of generating the possible substitutions for a conjunction:

> To evaluate (and P1 P2):
>> Let the set of answers computed so far be empty
>> Evaluate P1, to give the set of substitutions S1
>> For each element s1 of S1:
>>> Apply s1 to the proposition P2, yielding P2'
>>> Evaluate P2', giving the set of substitutions S2
>>> For each element s2 of S2:
>>>> Combine s1 with s2, and add the result to the
>>>> set of answers computed so far
>> Return the set of answers computed so far

We have made use here of the operations of *applying* and *combining* substitutions. We have already come across these operations via the LISP functions apply_subst and compose_subst. Consider the evaluation of the following DBQ formula:

   (and (supplies _x radiators) (supplies _x _y))

Evaluating the first part ((supplies _x radiators)) of the and proposition against our database results in the first of the set of substitutions given above:

   S1:
   (((_x smith_corp))
   ((_x morgan_bros)))

Each of these two substitutions is dealt with separately. First of all, the substitution ((_x smith_corp)) is considered. The second part of the and proposition is rewritten so that all occurrences of _x are replaced by smith_corp – this is *applying* the substitution to the formula. As a result, we now have the following formula:

   (supplies smith_corp _y)

Evaluating this gives rise to the second set of substitutions:

   S2:
   (((_y radiators))
   ((_y tyres))))

To get possible answers, we *combine* the elements of S2 one by one with the element chosen from S1. This just means getting the pairs of substitutions to pool their information. So, we get the following two answers:

   (((_x smith_corp) (_y radiators))
   ((_x smith_corp) (_y tyres)))

To complete the set of answers, we need to consider the second substitution in S1. Applying this to the second part of the and proposition gives:

(supplies morgan_bros _y)

and evaluating this gives:

S2:
(((_y radiators))
 ((_y pumps)))

Once more we combine these substitutions with the one selected from S1, this time generating the two answers:

(((_x morgan_bros) (_y radiators))
 ((_x morgan_bros) (_y pumps)))

Now that we have dealt with all the elements of S1, we can enumerate the set of substitutions that result from evaluating the whole formula:

(((_x smith_corp) (_y radiators))
 ((_x smith_corp) (_y tyres))
 ((_x morgan_bros) (_y radiators))
 ((_x morgan_bros) (_y pumps)))

Notice that the algorithm for evaluating an and proposition invokes the evaluation algorithm recursively on the parts of the formula. The algorithm will act similarly for other conjunctions and quantifiers. The recursion will bottom out every time because each recursive call is operating on a smaller piece of formula than the one that invoked it. So, eventually, the recursive calls will cause the evaluation of simple predicate formulae, which can be done by the database without any further recursive calls.

In evaluating a DBQ formula, we will only be interested in substitutions for variables that appear outside the formula. For instance, in the and example it was important to remember the possible values of _x satisfying the first subformula, in order to use them in evaluating the second. Now, the assumption will be made here that a quantified formula will never contain variables that are used outside (that is, *free* variables). So, this means that when a quantified formula is evaluated we need only ever produce one of two possible answers:

()
(list empty_subst)

The first of these answers says that there are *no* substitutions that will make this formula true, whereas the second says that there *is* a substitution that will make the formula true, but it is *empty* because the formula has *no* free variables. Here is the part of the evaluation algorithm dealing with the all and exists quantifiers:

> To evaluate (all V R B):
>> Evaluate R, to give the set of substitutions S1
>> If there are none, simply return (list empty_subst)
>> Otherwise, for each element s1 of S1:
>>> Apply s1 to the proposition B, yielding B′
>>> If B′ evaluates to give at least one substitution,
>>>> continue going through the elements of S1
>>> Otherwise immediately return ()
>> If you get successfully through all the elements of S1,
>>> return (list empty_subst),

> To evaluate (exists V R B):
>> Evaluate R, to give the set of substitutions S1
>> If there are none, simply return ()
>> Otherwise, for each element s1 of S1:
>>> Apply s1 to the proposition B, yielding B′
>>> If B′ evaluates to give at least one substitution,
>>>> immediately return (list empty_subst)
>>> Otherwise continue going through the elements of S1
>> If you get through all the elements of S1 without any success,
>>> return ()

Intuitively, the all algorithm goes through all the values of the variable satisfying the restriction and checks that they satisfy the body. Only if they all satisfy can it return (list empty_subst) – that is, true. On the other hand, the exists algorithm is content to return (list empty_subst) if there exists any value of the variable that makes both the restriction and the body true. Consider, for example, the evaluation of:

> (all _x (supplies _x radiators) (supplies _x tyres))

given our example database. The evaluation of the restriction part provides the following set of substitutions:

> S1:
> (((_x smith_corp))
> ((_x morgan_bros)))

Taking the first of these and applying it to the body, we get:

> (supplies smith_corp tyres)

which evaluates to (list empty_subst). So, we continue with the second substitution in S1. This time, the second formula to be evaluated is:

(supplies morgan_bros tyres)

which yields (). Because of this, the evaluation of the whole formula returns (). The evaluation has indicated that 'everyone who supplies radiators supplies tyres' is false, because Morgan Brothers supply radiators but not tyres.

Notice that this strategy of evaluating the restriction R in order to substitute values into the body B will only work if the evaluation of the restriction actually produces substitutions for the variable. Not every DBQ formula will, however, produce substitutions for all the variables in it when it is evaluated. For instance, evaluating an all formula, whether or not it is successful, never yields any interesting substitutions. So, in order for query evaluation as we have sketched it to work, we must require that a restriction formula be one of the following:

(1)   A simple proposition mentioning the variable – for example, (owns _x _y) mentions _x and _y).

(2)   A conjunction with such a proposition as its first conjunct.

If a DBQ formula is derived from the analysis of an English sentence, this restriction is rarely a problem, because most NPs provide, via the noun, a simple proposition about the referent which will appear in the restriction part of the relevant DBQ formula. For instance, 'every airline' gives rise to a DBQ formula where the restriction is the simple proposition (airline _x), where _x is the variable quantified over in the formula.

We have now sketched out the main components of an evaluation algorithm for DBQ formulae. Put together, these form a recursive algorithm for evaluating a formula by recursively evaluating its components in particular ways. The algorithm returns a set of substitutions, rather than a truth value, but for a formula with no free variables the possible results, (list empty_subst) and (), do indicate true and false, respectively. The algorithm as sketched can also be extended to handle other conjunctions, logical operators and quantifiers, such as or, not and most.

When a DBQ formula is treated as a database query, it is assumed that the person posing the query is interested in whether the proposition expressed is true or not. In general, they may be interested in knowing for what objects a given proposition is true, as well as knowing whether there are such objects. So, DBQ allows the specification of certain extra actions that are to be carried out during query evaluation. Such actions are treated as propositions that are always true, but which cause side effects to occur when their truth is verified. The only action we will actually use is that of printing out the value of a variable (that makes some proposition true). This will give rise to a DBQ form like:

```
(printout _x)
```

We really need to introduce a clause into the algorithm for such things, as follows:

```
To evaluate (printout X):
        Print out X
        Return (list empty_subst)
```

Of course, to introduce such actions sensibly into our DBQ formulae, we need to know when they will be encountered in the evaluation process. Thus, for instance, we want a printout action only to be encountered *after* a particular value has been put in the place of the relevant variable.

The algorithm for query evaluation is easily translated into LISP. lib dbq provides a function query which takes a query, represented as a LISP list structure, and returns the list of substitutions that make it true. We have already represented substitutions in LISP and lib dbq uses lib subst to manipulate these. The operations of applying and combining substitutions are thus provided by the functions apply_subst, or lookup_subst if the argument is a variable, and compose_substs, respectively. Sets of substitutions are represented by lists, with nil representing the empty set, which stands for false in this context. As we have seen, the empty list and the list consisting just of the empty substitution have a particular significance for DBQ, and so we will give them special names:

```
(defparameter NO nil)
(defparameter YES (list empty_subst))
```

The definition of query takes the form of a case statement which seeks to establish what kind of DBQ formula is involved. Once the type is established, query calls a special-purpose function for that kind of formula:

```
(defun query (formula)
  (if (listp formula)
    (case (car formula)
      (all
        (process_all
          (cadr formula)          ; x
          (caddr formula)         ; p1
          (caddr (cdr formula)))))  ; p2
```

```
(exists
  (process_exists
    (cadr formula)         ; x
    (caddr formula)        ; p1
    (caddr (cdr formula))))  ; p2

 ...

  (otherwise (retrieve-all formula)))
(retrieve-all formula)))
```

Notice that the various functions (process_all, process_exists, and so on) are called with the remaining top-level elements of the DBQ formula as their arguments. process_all is the function that deals with all constructions:

```
(defun process_all (x p1 p2)
  (dolist (subst (query p1) YES)
    (if (equal (lookup_subst x subst) x)
        (error "ALL condition doesnt bind variable ~S" (list x p1)))
    (if (null
          (query
            (apply_subst
              (add_subst x (lookup_subst x subst) empty_subst)
              p2)))
        (return NO))))
```

Notice how the code checks that the all condition finds a value for the variable. This should always happen with formulae arising from natural language queries. Here is how the and case looks in LISP:

```
(defun process_and (p1 p2)
  (let ((results ()))
    (dolist (subst1 (query p1))
      (dolist (subst2 (query (apply_subst subst1 p2)))
        (setq results
          (cons
            (compose_substs subst1 subst2)
            results))))
    results))
```

When the recursion reaches a simple proposition, the function retrieve_all is called. retrieve_all takes a simple proposition and returns a list of substitutions, corresponding to all ways the proposition can be found in the database. For the current purposes, it suffices to have the database represented as a list of facts kept in a global variable database:

```
(setq database
 '((supplies smith_corp radiators)
   (supplies jones_inc spark_plugs)
   (supplies morgan_bros radiators)
   (supplies jones_inc batteries)
   (supplies smith_corp tyres)
   (supplies morgan_bros pumps)))
```

although this would obviously be very inefficient if the database was large. retrieve_all works its way through the elements of database, comparing each one with the query and returning a substitution. The function performing this comparison is called termunify, and this of course implements term unification, as discussed in Chapter 7.

Exercise 9.2 Sketch out, by analogy to the clauses given in the text, extra clauses to enable the DBQ evaluation algorithm to handle the following kinds of formulae:

(a)   (or P1 P2) – P1 is true or P2 is true

(b)   (not P) – P is not true

(c)   (most V R B) – most values of V that satisfy R also satisfy B

[*intermediate*]

Exercise 9.3 The DBQ quantifiers all and exists correspond, at least approximately, to the English determiners 'all/each/every' and 'a/one/some', but there is no DBQ quantifier that corresponds to the English 'the'. In singular phrases, the use of 'the' tends to presuppose that an object satisfying the given description exists and is unique; if this is not true, there cannot be any simple yes or no answer to the question. Thus, if you are asked 'Is the railway network in Greenland efficient?' you could not answer simply yes or no, because there is no railway network in Greenland. Describe the extensions necessary to DBQ and the DBQ evaluation algorithm to have a quantifier the, analogous to the other quantifiers, which produces a special undefined result if there are no, or more than one, values of the variable that satisfy the condition.   [*intermediate*]

Exercise 9.4 A question–answering system using the algorithm described might produce correct answers but would definitely not produce cooperative ones. Consider, for instance, the question 'Does everyone who supplies jet engines accept VISA cards?' where jet engines, not being car parts, are not supplied by anyone in our database. This query should be translated into the following DBQ formula:

(all _x (supplies _x jet_engines) (accepts _x visa))

and the answer would be yes, because it is (vacuously) true that everyone in the empty set accepts VISA cards. But this would be a very unhelpful answer for a person who erroneously thought that jet engines were available from the dealers in the database and wanted to use their VISA card to buy one. How might the DBQ evaluation algorithm be altered to give a better response? How might a similar strategy handle uses of the word 'the', as in 'Does the firm that supplies pumps and tyres accept VISA cards?' [*hard*]

Exercise 9.5   lib europe contains a small LISP database of information about European countries. Produce, by hand or by program, DBQ formulae that correspond to the following English questions about these countries:

(a)   Sweden borders Norway?

(b)   Which countries border Sweden?

(c)   Each country borders a country?

(d)   Each country that borders Sweden borders Denmark?

Use lib dbq to answer them.   [*easy*]

Exercise 9.6   Using the library files dbq, fburecog (or fchart), airlines, airdb1 (which contains a database of information about airlines) and termify, develop an elementary natural language database front end that will answer a range of simple English questions about airlines. You will need to add to the lexicon and/or database to ensure that the same relations are covered in both.   [*intermediate*]

9.3   Standard logical inference

The DBQ evaluation algorithm presented in Section 9.2 bottoms out when it reaches a simple proposition involving a predicate and associated objects. At this point, it is assumed that the database will have an exhaustive listing of the true cases of the appropriate relation. This is highly reminiscent of our first approach to semantic interpretation, where we represented the meanings of words by sets. Given that DBQ formulae result from a fairly simple translation of natural language sentences, our assumption seems to be that the database must contain a listing for every English content word that might be appropriate in the domain. And yet this is clearly ridiculous, because there will be many ways of asking essentially the same question:

> Does Morgan Brothers accept VISA cards?
>
> Can I pay Morgan Brothers with a VISA card?
>
> Is Morgan Brothers registered with VISA?
>
> Does Morgan Brothers take part in the VISA scheme?

and also many questions whose answers are closely related to one another:

> Does Morgan Brothers accept credit cards?
>
> Will Morgan Brothers accept my VISA card?
>
> Does Morgan Brothers accept international credit cards?
>
> Do I have to pay Morgan Brothers by cash?

If we had to include a separate listing for each of the properties and relations, such as 'accept', 'pay', 'register', 'take part', 'VISA' and 'credit card', that might be mentioned, we would have to have a huge database with a great deal of information represented many times. Moreover, our machine would be showing very limited understanding of the subject matter, because it would have no explicit representation of the fact that certain concepts like 'pay' and 'accept' are fundamentally related to one another. The difficulty of constructing such a system would directly reflect the shallowness of such a model of the world.

One important respect in which a natural language understanding system should be able to model the world is in being able to determine what follows from what. If a language-processing system cannot determine, for instance, that if someone has influenza then they are unwell, then its model of the world (at least as far as medical matters are concerned) is surely lacking. We have already noted that one advantage of a formal MRL might be that it provides formal rules of *inference* for validly deriving new statements from information provided as statements in the language. We might hope to harness the potential thus offered to provide accurate and computationally feasible inference mechanisms as part of an understanding system. As we will indicate later, it is not clear that this can be done in a general way, but there are interesting models of some capabilities that such inference systems might have.

DBQ (without printout actions) is really just a restricted form of the predicate calculus, and so it is natural to look towards standard notions of logical inference to see whether they can be used to enhance our question answerers. Translating to a logical language like DBQ does not commit us to any particular account of how English words correspond to predicates. For instance, we are no more committed to translating 'Mayumi sings' to (sings mayumi) than to any of the following, say:

DBQ notation	*Standard logic notation*
(a b)	a(b)
(exists _x (mayumi _x) (sings _x))	$\exists X\ \text{mayumi}(X) \wedge \text{sings}(X)$
(m sing)	m(sing)
(fact world25 m sing)	fact(world25, m, sing)
(all _x (world25 sing _x) (contain _x m))	$\forall X\ \text{world25}(\text{sing}, X) \supset \text{contain}(X, m)$

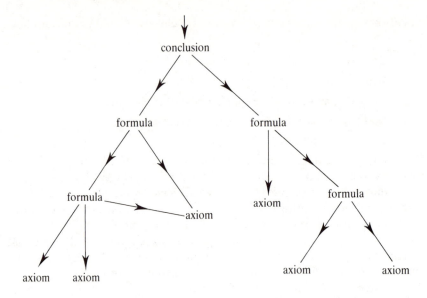

Figure 9.1 A proof as a DAG.

All that we need to do is to provide appropriate and consistent interpretations for the predicates and constants that we use in the translation. On the other hand, using predicate calculus does commit us to standard notions of validity and inference, but also provides computational techniques for making inferences (from the work on automatic theorem proving). In this section, we will briefly discuss some of the features of standard logical inference, to indicate why it is computationally unattractive and hence why some researchers in computational linguistics have felt a need either for restrictions of it or for other kinds of inference systems.

The standard notion of logical inference assumes that we start with a set of *axioms*, or facts that we are sure are true, together with a desired *conclusion* that we wish to establish. In a QA system, the axioms might be the background database and the conclusion the statement expressed by a question. Inference involves constructing a DAG, called a *proof*, where each node is labelled with a formula: the desired conclusion is at the initial node and all final nodes are labelled by axioms. For the inference to be valid, each formula in the graph must be licenced by an *inference rule* that shows that it follows from the set of formulae that immediately succeed it in the graph. This is illustrated in Figure 9.1.

For simplicity, we will use a restricted notation for inference rules based on a small subset of the programming language Prolog. In this language, a general rule about the world is expressed in the form **conclusion if condition**, and indicates that whenever the **condition** is true, so is the **conclusion** (many expert systems use rules with roughly this flavour). Thus, a rule says that if you have already established that the conditions of the

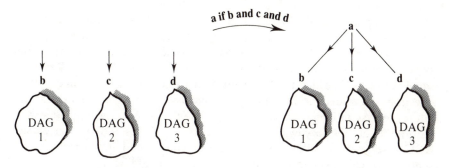

Figure 9.2 Operation of an inference rule.

rule are true – that is, you have complete DAGs starting at nodes labelled with these formulae – then you are entitled to combine the conclusion with these DAGs to make a new legal DAG, as shown in Figure 9.2.

The **condition** of a rule may be a collection of conditions, separated by the word **and**. Conditions and conclusions all take the form of a predicate, followed optionally by a number of associated objects, enclosed in brackets and separated by commas (a minor variant of the DBQ notation). Given suitable interpretations for the predicates **accepts**, **public_holiday** and **no_change** and the constant **morgan_bros**, the rule:

> accepts(morgan_bros, visa)
>   if public_holiday and no_change(morgan_bros) (1)

would mean that Morgan Brothers accepts VISA cards if it is a public holiday and Morgan Brothers is out of change. If **public_holiday** and **no_change** are listed in our domain database, then this rule will allow us to answer a certain question about the acceptance of credit cards. For a rule to answer a class of questions, it needs to contain variables, indicated by letters like X and Y, to denote arbitrary individuals. Thus, given suitable interpretations of predicates like **accepts** and **credit_card**, the rules:

> accepts(X, Y) if credit_card(Y) and registered(X, Y) (2)
> can_pay_with(X, Y, Z) if customer(X) and accepts(Y, Z) (3)

say that for any individuals X and Y, X accepts mode of payment Y if Y is a type of credit card and X is registered with the Y scheme. Also, for any individuals X, Y and Z, if X is a customer, they can pay Y with mode of payment Z if Y accepts Z. Using these inference rules, a QA system with a database containing information about credit card schemes and people registered with them could answer questions about acceptance and payment.

It is important to note that our Prolog-like language for inference rules is incomplete in many ways and represents a very restricted part of predicate calculus. For instance, it only allows us to write rules that have simple facts as their conclusions; it does not allow negative conditions in rules and it does not allow rules to introduce, by the use of function symbols, objects that have not been encountered before. Nevertheless, this small subset will suffice for the main points that we wish to make. For a question answerer, the limitation on conclusions of rules means that an inference system using this restricted language could be introduced at the 'bottom level' of query evaluation, but could not be used to answer whole DBQ queries – complex DBQ formulae would need to be reduced to simple predications before the inference system could be of any use.

When using an inference system there are two main options for how the DAG of formulae that links the conclusion to the axioms is constructed. In *forwards* (or data-directed) *inference*, the DAG is constructed starting from the axioms and (hopefully) heads towards the desired conclusion. That is, the inference system searches through all possible things that follow from what it knows, intending that some desired conclusions will be among them. The way this is often organized computationally is for the system always to infer all consequences of the facts it is given (that is, to perform all possible sequences of applications of inference rules) and then to record them somewhere. So then, seeing if a goal follows simply involves looking to see whether it is in the set of facts. On the other hand, when new information is added to the set of facts, a great deal of activity may be generated to discover all new consequences. If there are infinitely many consequences, of course, the system will never finish adding the new information. In a forwards inference system, a rule of the form:

A if B and C and D ...

is interpreted to mean 'if B, C, D, ... have been shown to be true, then add A to the set of facts'. This is very similar to the basic idea of bottom-up parsing, where the rule would be read as 'if you have found a B, followed by a C, followed by a D, ... then record the fact that you have found an A'. Thus, a forwards inference system usually operates by accepting a set of facts, inferring all possible conclusions from them and announcing whenever one of the set of goals is inferred to be true. For instance, if we have the last two rules and already know that:

credit_card(visa)
credit_card(mastercard)

customer(j_dore)

then if we discover the new information that:

registered(morgan_bros, visa)

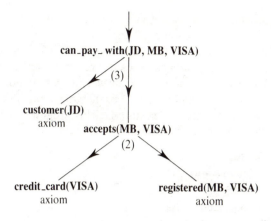

Figure 9.3   Example proof.

then we are entitled to conclude:

accepts(morgan_bros, visa)

by rule (2) (with X being Morgan Brothers and Y being VISA) and:

can_pay_with(j_dore, morgan_bros, visa)

by rule (3) (with X being Jean Dore, Y being Morgan Brothers and Z being VISA). The DAG supporting this proposition is as shown in Figure 9.3. If we have previously announced an interest in the can_pay_with relation, we would expect the system to tell us about the new facts that it has inferred. Otherwise, we would expect it simply to store them away in the hope that they will eventually contribute to inferences that we are interested in.

Although forwards inference is useful in other contexts, it is not attractive for our QA system, because we do not want to explicitly store or explore every true case of every relation just in case it is asked about in a question. We require a more directed approach that focuses on what might be useful for the question at hand. In *backwards* (or goal-directed) *inference*, the DAG of formulae is constructed by starting at the desired conclusion and then heading backwards towards the axioms. In such a framework, no inferencing occurs until a goal is presented to the system. Then the system reasons backwards, reducing the thing it is trying to show to a set of (hopefully, simpler) subgoals. These subgoals are then themselves reduced to simpler goals, until we reach goals that directly match axioms. Thus, in a backwards inference system, a rule of the form:

A if B and C and D ...

is interpreted to mean 'if you wish to show **A**, try showing **B**, **C**, **D**, ...'. This is very similar to the basic idea of top-down parsing, where the rule wouldbe read as 'if you wish to find an **A**, try finding a **B**, followed by a **C**, followed by a **D**, ...'. Thus, a backwards inference system usually operates by accepting a sequence of goals and answering yes or no, according to whether it can show that they are true. For instance, consider the situation where again we have the three rules stated earlier, together with a database containing, among other things, the following facts:

> credit_card(visa)
>
> credit_card(mastercard)
>
> customer(j_dore)
>
> registered(morgan_bros, visa)
>
> registered(jones_inc, visa)

Imagine that the QA system is asked by Jean Dore 'Who can I pay with VISA?' and manages to translate it into the following DBQ formula:

> (all _x (can_pay_with j_dore _x visa) (printout_x))

Evaluation of this query, using the algorithm we described in Section 9.2, involves enumerating all true instances of the formula:

> (can_pay_with j_dore _x visa)
>   (in standard logic, **can_pay_with(j_dore, X, visa)**)

collecting the possible substitutions for **X** and printing them out. Using backwards inference, the system would attempt to construct a DAG with a formula like this at the start. There is only one inference rule (3) that could be used to justify this formula, and so the start of the DAG must look as shown in Figure 9.4(a). Now, the **customer** formula is an axiom, and so only the **accepts** needs justification. Again, only one inference rule is applicable. This introduces an axiom and another formula to be justified, which is illustrated in Figure 9.4(b). Now, the **registered** formula can be matched against facts in the database in two ways. If we choose **X** to be Morgan Brothers, then we can get a complete proof for **can_pay_with(j_dore, morgan _bros, visa)**, whereas if we choose **X** to be Jones Incorporated, then we get a proof of **can_pay_with(j_dore, jones_inc, visa)**. There are thus two possible proofs and two answers to be printed out, as shown in Figure 9.4(c) and (d).

Of the two inference techniques we have considered, forwards inference is probably the more useful if we wish to have a system that responds rapidly to changes in its knowledge and is able to detect one of a large number of possible unusual events. On the other hand, backwards inference is more directed, and so is more appropriate for a system that knows what it is trying to do. As we will see in subsequent sections, however, logical inference is not as straightforward as these simple examples might suggest.

(a)

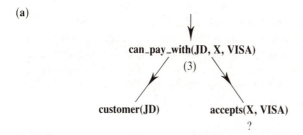

(b)

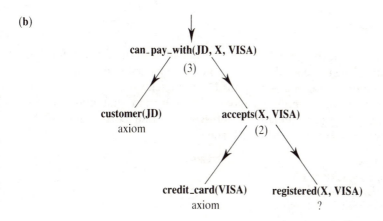

(c)

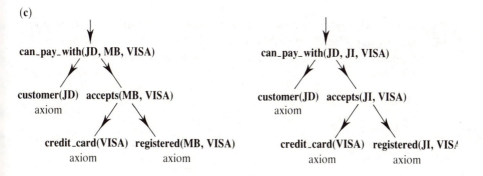

Figure 9.4 Stages in the construction of a proof.

9.4   Implementing backwards and forwards inference

lib bckinfer is a program for doing backwards inference using a LISP adaptation of our rule notation. We will assume that a rule is represented by a list whose first element is the conclusion and whose remaining elements are the conditions. Each such element will be a simple proposition represented in the same way as in the DBQ language. Thus, for instance, here is the LISP version of one of the rules about credit cards:

> ((accepts _x _y) (credit_card _y) (registered _x _y))

A rule that has no conditions will then be simply a list with one element, for instance:

> ((credit_card visa))

We will assume that the global variable infrules will hold the list of inference rules that are going to be used. An example of such a list is given in lib airdb2.

The function back_infer is responsible for backwards inference. It is provided with a single inference goal, a proposition that may contain variables, and it returns the list of substitutions that correspond to the inferrable instances of the goal. For instance:

```
(setq infrules
 '(((employs velsoft (c smith)))
   ((employs mobtek (j martin)))
   ((employs velsoft (s redding)))
   ((employs singco (p butcher)))))
(back_infer '(employs velsoft _x))
(((_X (S REDDING)) ()) ((_X (C SMITH)) ()))
```

The core of back_infer is the following loop, which deals with each inference rule rule in turn, collecting together the substitutions for successful proofs of the goal using that rule. The variable substs is here used as the repository for that collection.

```
(defun back_infer (goal)
  ...
    (let ((substs ()))
       (dolist (rule infrules substs)
          (setq substs
             (append
                (solutions_using_rule goal rule)
                substs))))))
```

solutions_using_rule is responsible for trying to prove the goal using the rule it is provided with. The rule can only be of any use if its conclusion is about the same predicate as the predicate of the goal. It can also only be useful if the goal unifies with the conclusion, yielding a substitution headsubst:

```
(defun solutions_using_rule (goal rule)
  (let ((substs ()))
    (if (and
          (equal (caar rule) (car goal)) ; check same predicate
          (equal (length (car rule)) (length goal))) ; check same no of args
      (let*
        ((newrule (rename rule))
         (headsubst (termunify goal (car newrule))))
        (if headsubst ; check that conclusion of rule matches goal
          (dolist
            (bodysubst
              (back_infer_all
                (apply_subst headsubst (cdr newrule))))
            (setq substs
              (cons
                (compose_substs headsubst bodysubst)
                substs))))))
    substs))
```

If the unification succeeds, headsubst is applied to the body of the rule (the list of conditions). This modified rule body is then sent to back_infer_all, which returns the set of additional substitutions that have to be applied to make true instances of the conditions. The substitutions that result from composing these with headsubst then contribute to the results of solutions_using_rule. For instance, in the following, the binding for _x (velsoft) comes from the first unification, while the binding for _y comes from the satisfaction of the subgoals ((good_worker _x)):

```
(setq infrules
  '(((employs velsoft _x) (good_worker _x))
    ((good_worker (c smith)))
    ((good_worker (s redding)))))
(trace back_infer back_infer_all)
(back_infer '(employs _x _y))
>BACK_INFER (EMPLOYS _X _Y)
!>BACK_INFER_ALL ((GOOD_WORKER _Y))
...
!<BACK_INFER_ALL (((_Y (S REDDING)) ()) ((_Y (C SMITH)) ()))
<BACK_INFER (((#:_0 _Y) (_X VELSOFT) () (_Y (C SMITH)) ())
             ((#:_0 _Y) (_X VELSOFT) () (_Y (S REDDING)) ()))
(((#:_0 _Y) (_X VELSOFT) () (_Y (C SMITH)) ())
 ((#:_0 _Y) (_X VELSOFT) () (_Y (S REDDING)) ()))
```

Note that the variable that prints out as #:_0 is the _x in the use of the first inference rule, which is unified with _y in the goal. The inference rule has to be renamed so that the _x in the use of the rule can be distinguished from the _x in the original goal.

back_infer_all simply takes a list of goals and calls back_infer on them. For each solution of the first goal, it applies that substitution to the rest and then works on the rest. The results from back_infer_all come from composing the substitutions that are obtained from the individual goals.

```
(defun back_infer_all (goals)
  (if (null goals)
    (list empty_subst)
    (let ((substs ()))
      (dolist (subst1 (back_infer (car goals)))
        (dolist (subst2 (back_infer_all (apply_subst subst1 (cdr goals))))
          (setq substs
            (cons
              (compose_substs subst1 subst2)
              substs))))
      substs)))
```

lib forinfer implements a simple forwards inference system, with the main function for_infer. for_infer takes a simple proposition, which is assumed to contain no variables, and adds it to the database of inference rules. If the presence of this new fact makes any inference rules apply in new ways, then the conclusions of those rules are also added to the database. This may cause more rules to run, and so on. The function keeps track of the assertions it still has to add in a list to_add, which is much like the agenda in a chart parser:

```
(defun for_infer (assertion)
  (let ((to_add nil))
    (if (null (fifind assertion))
      (setq to_add (list assertion))
      (setq to_add nil))
    (do
      ((assert (car to_add) (car to_add)))
      ((null to_add))
      (setq to_add (cdr to_add))
      (princ "Adding ") (princ assert) (terpri)
      (setq infrules (cons (list assert) infrules))
      (dolist (new (consequences assert))
        (if (and
              (null (fifind new))
              (not (member new to_add :test #'equal))
              (not (equal new assert)))
          (setq to_add (cons new to_add)))))))
```

The core of for_infer is the function consequences, which returns all the immediate logical consequences of a new fact assert. Each new assertion in the list returned by consequences will in general be placed on the to_add list, but this only happens if the assertion is not already in the database and if it is not already a member of to_add or (by some chance) the original assertion. The first of these is checked by the function fifind, which is just like back_infer, except that it only looks at facts (not rules) in the database. The second is done simply using member, with the relevant test being the function equal, rather than the default eql, because eql will not succeed if it is given two different lists with the same elements. Here is the definition of consequences:

```
(defun consequences (assert)
  (let ((results ()))
    (dolist (infrule infrules)
      (dolist (pattern (cdr infrule))
        (if (and
              (equal (car pattern) (car assert))
              (equal (length pattern) (length assert)))
          (let ((subst1 (termunify assert pattern)))
            (if subst1
              (dolist
                (subst2
                  (find_all (apply_subst subst1
                    (remove pattern (cdr infrule)))))
                (setq results
                  (cons
                    (apply_subst (compose_substs subst1 subst2) (car infrule))
                    results)))))))))
    results))
```

The function looks through all the inference rules and, for each one, tries to unify the new fact with each condition (pattern) in turn. If it manages to do this, it tries to find instances of all the other conditions in the database. The function find_all is just like back_infer_all, except that it only looks for facts; it does not use any inference rules that themselves have conditions. For each way that these other conditions can be satisfied, there is an appropriate substitution and this (subst2), together with the substitution obtained by unifying with the original condition (subst1), determines the instance of the rule conclusion that has now been inferred to be true.

Exercise 9.7 Set up a database of facts and rules involving jobs in your institution (or use lib airdb2, or adapt lib europe). Get lib bckinfer to answer questions such as the following:

(a)   What jobs are more senior than project manager?

(b)   Does any manager supervise a programmer?

(c)   Is there a manager more senior than Jones?

(d)   What committees do both the Vice-Chancellor and the Rector belong to?

You will probably find it useful to write a simple front end to the backwards inference program, such as:

```
(defun test ()
   (loop
      (let ((goal (read)))
         (dolist (subst (back_infer goal))
            (print (apply_subst subst goal))))))
```

[*easy*]

Exercise 9.8   Use lib bckinfer to provide the database retrieval component of lib dbq. To do this, you need to redefine retrieve_all in lib dbq so as to call back_infer. Build a combined program which builds DBQ formulae from simple natural language inputs (using lib fburecog), translates the DAGs into the compact representation (using lib termify) and then submits them to the enhanced query evaluation.   [*intermediate*]

Exercise 9.9   It is possible to encode simple grammars straightforwardly as inference rules. For instance, given predicates as follows:

(S _s1 _s2)   – the string of words _s1 starts with a sentence, and _s2 is the string of words left afterwards.

(NP _s1 _s2) – the string of words _s1 starts with a noun phrase, and _s2 is the string of words left afterwards.

we can write inference rules such as the following:

((S _s1 _s3) (NP _s1 _s2) (VP _s2 _s3))

Lexical items can be introduced by inference rules like the following:

((Noun (dog _x) _x))

This is the basic idea behind *definite clause grammars* in logic programming. Write a mini-grammar in this way, and find solutions to inference goals such as:

(back_infer '(S _s ()))

(It would be best to use the test function defined above.) Why are the generated sentences in nested lists, rather than simple lists? What alterations to the representation (and to operations like unification) would avoid this problem? As a generator of sentences, does the program work breadth first or depth first? Top down or bottom up? When will it get into infinite loops and how could these be avoided?   [*intermediate*]

Exercise 9.10   Extend the grammatical inference rules of the last exercise so that the parse trees of the generated sentences are returned.   [*intermediate*]

Exercise 9.11   lib families provides a rule base about family relationships. Load this library and interact with lib forinfer by telling it the details of your own family. Inspect the output carefully and check that (a) it makes all the inferences that you would expect it to, and (b) that it does not make any inferences that it should not be making. If problems of either kind arise, try to eliminate them by augmenting or modifying the rules in lib families. Are there problems which cannot be fixed simply by changing the rules? You may find it useful to have a front end function to for_infer, defined as follows:

```
(defun test ()
    (loop (for_infer (read))))
```

[*easy*]

Exercise 9.12   The rules in lib families presuppose a very conservative view of family life – remarriage and illegitimacy, for example, are not countenanced. Try and modify them to reflect reality, and, in particular, introduce step-relations (step-daughter, step-father, and so on).   [*easy*]

Exercise 9.13   Can you implement a parser that works similarly to a chart parser by using a forwards inference system of this kind? The fundamental rule of chart parsing would look something like the following as an inference rule:

```
((arc _start _subfinish _goal (_found (_subgoal _subfound)) _rest)
 (arc _substart _subfinish _subgoal _subfound ())
 (arc _start _substart _goal _found (_subgoal _rest)))
```

and a top-down chart parser would also have rules like the following, which embody the top-down rule in conjunction with phrase structure rules VP → V NP and VP → V:

```
((arc _s1 _s1 VP () (V (NP ())))
 (arc _s _s1 _g _f (VP _r)))

((arc _s _s VP () (V ()))
 (arc _s _s _g _f (VP _r)))
```

[*hard*]

9.5   The pathological nature of logical inference

It is important to note that both forwards and backwards inference involve searching in the process of ascertaining whether a goal is true. In forwards inference, a search must be made through all the consequences of the available facts to see if the goal belongs there. Some of these consequences will be quite irrelevant to the goal. In backwards inference, a search must be made through all possible ways in which the rules can be used to establish the goal as a conclusion. Some of these ways will be unsuccessful, because relevant conditions cannot be shown to be true.

One particular danger is that, given a particular set of facts and rules, the inference search space may be infinite, and the inference system may never terminate and tell us that a goal can or cannot be shown to be true. For instance, consider the use of the following information by a backwards inference system:

> **human(X) if human(Y) and mother(X, Y)**
> **human(beryl)**
>
> **mother(petunia, beryl)**

If we ask such a system to find all possible humans, using the first rule the system will generate a subgoal essentially identical to the original goal – to find a human X, it will seek to find a human Y. Of course, the use of this rule will be safe if the system has always found an example of X and Y in a **mother** relation before embarking on the recursive subgoal, which relies, of course, on **mother** terminating nicely. But, unless we give it this hint, or write the rule in a specific order using knowledge about how the inference system works, there is nothing to stop the system getting into an infinite loop. This particular problem is very similar to the left recursion problem that we encountered in Chapter 5 with top-down parsers. If we try to introduce checks to catch infinite loops, we are liable to cut out valid parts of the search space. For instance, it is quite reasonable to find a human by finding another human who is one of their parents. This is how we would establish that Petunia was a human. If we were not allowed to have 'looking for a human' as a subgoal of 'looking for a human', we could not show this (given our premises).

If we have a logical language that allows function symbols, the kinds of infinite loops that are possible can be much more subtle. For instance, given the rules:

> **human(X) if human(mother_of(X))**
> **human(mother_of(mother_of(petunia)))**

a backwards inference system, asked to find a human X could use the first rule to generate a subgoal that was the same except that X was replaced by mother_of(X). We can thus get an infinite sequence of subgoals:

```
human(X)
  human(mother_of(X))
    human(mother_of(mother_of(X)))
      human(mother_of(mother_of(mother_of(X))))
        ...
```

As it happens, the third of these matches the information about Petunia, but there is no way in general that we can tell how many of these subgoals might be relevant.

The situation with a forwards inference system is, unfortunately, no better. Consider the following information, where richer(X, Y) means that X is richer than Y:

```
richer(X, Z) if richer(X, Y) and richer(Y, Z)
richer(pickens, boesky)
richer(boesky, icahn)
richer(icahn, hunt)
```

and imagine what happens when we add richer(hunt, iacocca). As expected, the system will infer for each person that they are richer than Iacocca (even if this is not true in the real world). But some things can be inferred in more than one way:

```
richer(pickens, iacocca) because
  richer(pickens, boesky) and richer(boesky, iacocca)
richer(pickens, iacocca) because
  richer(pickens, icahn) and richer(icahn, iacocca)
richer(pickens, iacocca) because
  richer(pickens, hunt) and richer(hunt, iacocca)
```

Moreover, a given fact can be used in many ways to prove something else. For instance, richer(icahn, iacocca) can be used to prove richer(boesky, iacocca) and richer(pickens, iacocca). We have to be careful to avoid infinite loops where we repeatedly rederive and add the same fact to the database.

In an example like this, we can check for loops quite simply, but once again function symbols produce problems. Consider the following statements about geometry, where p1 is a point and, given any two points, there is a point half_way between them:

```
point(half_way(X, Y)) if point(X) and point(Y) and different(X, Y)
different(half_way(X, Y), X)
different(half_way(X, Y), Y)
point(p1)
```

If we add the facts **point(p2)** and **different(p1, p2)**, then we get an infinite set of consequences including:

```
point(half_way(p1, p2)))
point(half_way(half_way(p1, p2), p2)))
point(half_way(half_way(half_way(p1, p2), p2), half_way(p1, p2))))
point(half_way(half_way(half_way(half_way(p1, p2), p2), half_way(p1, p2)),
      half_way(half_way(p1, p2), p2))))
```

As in the **mother** example, there is no straightforward way, given an arbitrary set of other rules, to determine just which of these are going to be of any use for productive inferences.

It is not just infinite loops that worry the computational linguist (and expert system designers, theorem provers, game programmers, and the like) in general it is just any large search spaces. And these are inevitable if we are to encode any reasonable amount of real-world knowledge in logic. For instance, if we wish to find out whether Morgan Brothers is registered with VISA, we might decide to find out whether Morgan Brothers is considered credit worthy. This might involve considering the income and expenditure of the company over the last year, looking for instances where the company may have been in trouble. Or it might involve considering what customers Morgan Brothers has had recently, or the reputations of the directors of the company, and so on. Each of these possibilities could involve a substantial search among possible proofs without any guarantee of success. And any proof procedure that works purely mechanically from the rules, without any special domain-dependent strategies, is bound to waste a lot of time and cannot be relied upon to generate answers in a reasonable time.

The computational intractability of logical inference is underlined by the formal result that theorem proving in the full predicate calculus is *undecidable*. This means that there *cannot* be a computer program which, given an arbitrary set of axioms and a desired conclusion:

- Prints out 'yes' if the conclusion follows from the axioms.
- Prints out 'no' if the conclusion does not follow from the axioms.
- Always finishes running, printing 'yes' or 'no' as above.

What is it about logic that leads us to this predicament? The trouble is that in choosing logic as a meaning representation language we are choosing a language that makes very weak claims about what the world is like. So, it is not surprising that logic can only provide relatively weak and general inference techniques. For instance, using standard logic commits us to not much more than the following statements:

- The world consists of objects and relations – although we do not know what these are.

- A logical statement is either true or false – although it may be difficult to work out which.

- Logical inference is monotonic – new information may lead to new inferences, but it cannot invalidate earlier ones – although we do not know how to carry out inferences without combinatorial search and infinite loops.

- The logical operators and quantifiers (**all, and, exists, not, or**) are sensible ways to construct complex statements about the world.

How can we solve this problem with uniform proof procedures? One strategy is to investigate ways in which domain-dependent information can be used to guide a uniform proof procedure to make it more intelligent. Alternatively, we may wish to use restrictions of standard logic, where inferences are more computationally feasible. Another possibility is to use other logics, when non-standard rules of inference are required.

We mentioned earlier the problem caused by the fact that even though inferential search spaces may not be infinite they can still be unmanageably large if we encode all our world knowledge simply as logical rules. When a human being has to reason about the world, he or she does not seem to take into account all the factors that might conceivably be relevant – somehow the context focuses the attention in a useful way. It is therefore plausible to design ways of organizing logical rules and restricting their *visibility* to the reasoner, so that it spends less time on dead ends. Such an approach, if it is only based on heuristics, is liable to adversely affect the ability of the inference system to produce all the logically valid consequences, unfortunately.

Restricting inferential visibility is one of the principles behind the ideas of frames (which we first mentioned in Chapter 1) and one of the motivations for the object-oriented programming paradigm that exploits the notion of frame. A *frame* can be thought of as a collection of inference rules that have a common condition. For instance, if we are in a context where we are talking about automobiles, then it might be sensible to make the following information about automobiles and their attributes immediately accessible:

automobile(X) if vehicle(X) and number_of_wheels(X, 4)
and less(weight_of(X), 100Kg)
and human(owner_of(X))

vehicle(X) if automobile(X)

number_of_wheels(X, 4) if automobile(X)

less(weight_of(X), 100Kg) if automobile(X)

human(owner_of(X)) if automobile(X)

Similarly, since **automobile** involves the concept of **person**, we might in certain circumstances (for instance, when we need to know about the owner) make a similar set of inference rules about humans and their attributes immediately accessible. The organization of inference rules into larger chunks is one way in which domain-dependent knowledge can be used to control inference.

9.6 Primitives and canonical forms

In a given domain, it may frequently occur that two logical expressions that are equivalent in terms of truth conditions are not equivalent in terms of form. For instance, if buy(X, Y, Z) means 'X buys Y from Z' and sell(X, Y, Z) means that 'X sells Y to Z', then both of the following are true:

> buy(X, Y, Z) if sell(Z, Y, X)
>
> sell(X, Y, Z) if buy(Z, Y, X)

and hence, for instance, the following statements are equivalent, even though they look different:

> buy(hilton, sheraton, itt)
>
> sell(itt, sheraton, hilton)

It would be wasteful if, every time we wished to infer something about buy, we had to try inferring the equivalent statement in terms of sell (and vice versa). So, it makes sense to abandon using one of the predicates and express everything in terms of the other instead.

Sometimes the use of a predicate will be equivalent to a combination of other uses of predicates:

> bankrupt(X) if in_debt(X) and no_money(X)
>
> in_debt(X) if bankrupt(X)
>
> no_money(X) if bankrupt(X)

In this case, we might decide that bankrupt is to be abandoned and phrase all bankrupt statements in terms of in_debt and no_money instead. If, by appropriately transforming our logical expressions in these kinds of ways, we are able to guarantee that logically equivalent expressions are equivalent in form, then we have found a *canonical form* for logical expressions. Having a canonical form can be of great benefit. For instance, it enables a question–answering system to cope with paraphrases very easily:

> *User*:   ITT sold Sheraton to Hilton.
> *System*:   OK
> .
> .
> .
> *User*:   (Is it the case that) Hilton bought Sheraton from ITT?
> *System*:   YES

One kind of canonical form involves the translation of a logical expression into an equivalent one that only uses predicates from a fixed set of *primitive predicates*. Primitive predicates are predicates whose meaning cannot be expressed using combinations of other predicates. For instance, in a question–answering system about company employees, we would probably take **male** and **female** to be primitives; in an expert system on genetics, one probably would not. Whether a predicate is primitive or not thus depends very much on the domain of application and the range of relations that arise in that domain.

Note that there can be canonical forms that do not involve primitives, and there can be primitive-based systems that do not provide canonical forms. For instance, imagine a canonical form where either **buy** was translated into **sell** or vice versa, depending on some contextual factor. Also, imagine a system that provided several, equivalent but different, translations of a formula in terms of primitives.

One approach to translating complex relations or events into a representation by primitives involves representing the type of a relation or event separately from the objects involved in it. In restricted domains, the ways in which objects can be related to events may generalize across types of events, and so it may be productive to decompose the representation in a way that makes this explicit. For instance, the following sentences:

> The space shuttle flew to Los Angeles.   (1)
>
> The apprentice moved the cylinder into the chamber.   (2)
>
> The plasma arrived at the hospital.   (3)

all seem to be talking about kinds of motion, with emphasis on the destinations of the moved objects. There are certain general inferences that we can make concerning objects and their destinations, regardless of the type of motion that gets them there. For instance, we know that an object is at a given place if it has just finished a motion with that place as its destination. We also know that shortly before the end of the motion, the object must have been somewhere else. Similarly, it is possible to have sentences that describe motion where the emphasis is on where the moving objects come from:

The space shuttle took off from Cape Kennedy.	**(4)**
The apprentice took the cylinder out of the chamber.	**(5)**
The plasma left the hospital.	**(6)**

Again, there are general inferences that we can make about objects and where they start off, regardless of the type of motion. Here is one way we could represent the information in (1) to (6) which makes explicit their similarities and differences:

fly_event(ev1)	moved_object(ev1, ss1)	destination(ev1, la)	**(1)**
move_event(ev2)	moved_object(ev2, cy1)	destination(ev2, ch1)	**(2)**
travel_event(ev3)	moved_object(ev3, pl1)	destination(ev3, ho1)	**(3)**
fly_event(ev4)	moved_object(ev4, ss1)	source(ev4, ck)	**(4)**
move_event(ev5)	moved_object(ev5, cy1)	source(ev5, ch1)	**(5)**
travel_event(ev6)	moved_object(ev6, pl1)	source(ev6, ho1)	**(6)**

The advantage of this kind of representation is that we could phrase inference rules in terms of the very general predicates employed. For instance, the rule:

at(X, Y, Z)
    if moved_object(E, X) and destination(E, Y) and finishing_time(E, Z)

expresses the fact that an object X is at location Y at time Z if there is an event E that moves object X to Y and the time Z is the same as the time when E finishes. If we did not translate event representations into such small pieces, we would have to formulate such an inference rule again and again for different types of events. The question naturally arises as to how general are relations like **moved_object** and **destination**. For how many verbs can we decompose the meanings into such pieces? How many such 'deep cases' (primitive conceptual roles) are there? Some relations between objects and events (for example, the notion of **agent**) seem to be very generally useful, but it is not clear that there are many others.

    If we wish to use canonical forms for the meanings of natural language sentences, we have a choice as to where the canonicalization actually takes place. One possibility is that the semantics associated with lexical items is expressed directly in terms of primitives. For instance, we might say that a use of the word 'bankrupt' gives rise to two logical expressions of the form **in_debt(X)** and **no_money(X)**. Alternatively, we might have a logical predicate **bankrupt** that corresponds directly to the English word sense, together with inference rules:

in_debt(X) if bankrupt(X)

no_money(X) if bankrupt(X)

which are used in a forwards direction. One advantage of the latter is that, if there are actually some subtle inferences about **bankrupt** that cannot be made in terms of **in_debt** and **no_money** (for example, those to do with the special legal status of a bankrupt individual), then those special cases can still be handled, even though the bulk of inferences will be phrased in terms of the more primitive predicates.

Exercise 9.14 Using a small set of primitive predicates such as ingest, expel, solid, mouth and gas, decompose the meanings of as many verbs as you can that are concerned with the movement of physical material into and out of animal bodies. Formulate your analyses as inference rules to run in the context of lib forinfer. How might the inference system detect if an incorrect word sense for a word like 'coke' is chosen in a context like the following:

Kim gulped the coke.

Kim snorted the coke.

[*intermediate*]

9.7   Inheritance and defaults

Information about the properties and attributes of an individual can often be obtained by considering the classes that the individual belongs to. Thus, we know that Clark Kent has an notebook because he is a reporter, that he has two arms because he is a human being, and that he is warm blooded because he is a mammal. In general, it will be more economical, in terms of the number of facts and rules needed, to express information at the level of classes (mammals are warm blooded) rather than in terms of individuals (Clark Kent is warm blooded, Lois Lane is warm blooded, ...), where this is possible. In addition, it will also be more economical to express general information about how the world divides up into classes of objects (all humans are mammals) than to specify all the classes an individual belongs to (Clark Kent is a reporter, Clark Kent is a human, Clark Kent is a mammal, ...). Thus, rules of the following general form are likely to be

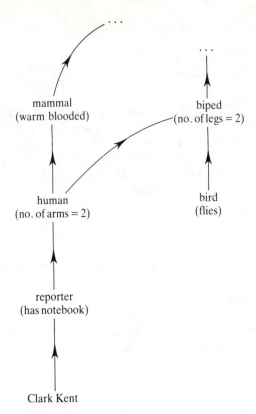

Figure 9.5   Simple semantic network.

especially useful in a system for reasoning about the world:

> **human(X) if reporter(X)**
>
> **mammal(X) if human(X)**
> **biped(X) if human(X)**
> **biped(X) if bird(X)**
> **number_of_legs(X, 2) if biped(X)**
>
> **has_notebook(X) if reporter(X)**
>
> **number_of_arms(X, 2) if human(X)**
> **warm_blooded(X) if mammal(X)**

Facts and rules of the first kind describe the hierarchy of individuals and classes that make up the world (often called an 'isa-hierarchy'). Rules of the second kind express how various attributes and properties follow from class memberships. It is convenient to draw the isa-hierarchy as a directed graph and attach information of the second kind to the classes it applies to. The result is often called a *semantic network*. Thus, the foregoing information would correspond to the semantic network shown in Figure 9.5.

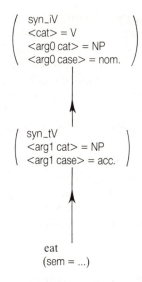

$$\left(\begin{array}{l}\text{syn\_iV} \\ \text{<cat>} = \text{V} \\ \text{<arg0 cat>} = \text{NP} \\ \text{<arg0 case>} = \text{nom.}\end{array}\right)$$

$$\left(\begin{array}{l}\text{syn\_tV} \\ \text{<arg1 cat>} = \text{NP} \\ \text{<arg1 case>} = \text{acc.}\end{array}\right)$$

eat
(sem = ...)

Figure 9.6   Inheritance network for lexical items.

Various work has been done exploiting this network metaphor directly in a computational way. Given the network outlined here, for instance, we can find out how many arms Clark Kent has by searching up the isa-hierarchy (following the arrows) until we find a class to which there is **number_of_arms** information attached. This is a very directed inference process (although still potentially involving search) as compared to the kinds of general backwards inference that we have considered. Implementing special mechanisms to perform these kinds of inferences efficiently may be effective, but it is an open problem to what extent a natural language processing system can make do with only these limited class-based inferences.

Our use of macros in lexical entries was very much in the spirit of organizing information around hierarchies of classes. For instance, we can think of the definitions:

```
Macro syn_iV:
    <cat> = V
    <arg0 cat> = NP
    <arg0 case> = nom.
Macro syn_tV:
    syn_iV
    <arg1 cat> = NP
    <arg1 case> = acc.
Lexeme eat:
    syn_tV.
```

as introducing the inheritance network shown in Figure 9.6.

In our treatment of the lexicon, macros were treated as abbreviations to be expanded at the time a word is looked up. Such a strategy was feasible because the total amount of information associated with a given lexical item was small. If we were representing a reasonable amount of information about humans and reporters, however, we could not carry out such an expansion every time we wanted to retrieve information about a particular human being. Instead we would need to adopt a strategy where the information was looked up only when required, for example for use in a unification.

As well as providing a way of organizing a large amount of information about the world, class membership can also be the basis of efficient detection of anomaly. If we know what kinds of objects can participate in what relations, this gives us a crude way of screening information. Consider, for instance, the problem of understanding the following sentence:

A bat perched on the wall.

where 'bat' may refer to a kind of flying mammal or a wooden implement (used, perhaps, for playing cricket or baseball, or for rioting). We can encode relevant information about chiropterans, perching, baseball bats, cricket bats and the classes of objects associated with them as the following rules for a forwards inference system:

animal(X) if perch(X, Y)
animate(X) if animal(X)
animal(X) if chiropteran(X)

chiropteran(X) if flying_bat(X)

inanimate(X) if cricket_bat(X)
inanimate(X) if baseball_bat(X)

contradiction if animate(X) and inanimate(X)

If we then choose the chiropteran sense for 'bat' and add the information:

flying_bat(bat28)
perch(bat28, wall06)

then the inference process will simply infer that **bat28** is an animal and animate. No contradiction will arise. Chiropterans cannot perch, of course, they can only hang, but our knowledge base does not include this subtlety. If we then choose one of the other two senses for 'bat' and add the information:

baseball_bat(bat29)
perch(bat29, wall07)

then the inference process will correctly produce **contradiction** and we will know that something has gone wrong. In practice, as we have seen, this kind of anomaly detection is normally performed by a process more like type checking. That is, the lexical entry for a verb like 'perch' would contain information that stated that its subject must be a phrase referring to an animal. This will then be checked by looking at class markers in the definition of the relevant noun word sense. In Chapter 8, we saw how such checking could be built into unifications performed during parsing. Such a technique is a clear example of optimizing a restricted kind of inference that is useful in NLP. On the other hand, the optimization requires that the acceptability of phrases can be determined solely from properties of the individual words. A more general inferential approach, as sketched here, would be capable of taking into account information from the context as well as information in lexical entries. Thus, it might be able to detect the anomaly of:

It perched on the wall.

ir. a context where 'it' could only refer to an object already known to be a baseball bat. We will consider the use of background information further in Chapter 10.

Another feature that semantic network systems offer is indexing of information by the objects involved, rather than the relations. Many logic-based systems organize their information around the relations involved, so that, for instance, all the rules that would enable us to conclude things about **number_of_arms** are kept in one place, all the rules about **warm_blooded** are kept somewhere else, and so on. In addition, there is an efficient way of going from the name of a relation to the bundle of information about it. This is convenient if we want to answer inference questions like 'Who is warm blooded?' because all the relevant information is conveniently grouped together and accessible, but it is not a suitable organization if we want to answer questions like 'What do you know about Mayumi?'. The idea of organizing information around objects is the basis of the object-oriented programming paradigm mentioned previously.

Many people have claimed that 'common sense inference' is not the same as logical inference and that intelligent systems should therefore not be constructed on a strictly logical model. For instance, we can write a rule:

black(X) d_if crow(X)

to express the fact that crows are usually black (by default, X is **black** if X is a **crow**) and use it in inferences as if d_if were if. But we must remember that d_if is not really synonymous with the if of standard logic (which logicians call 'material implication') and that, unless we are careful, our putatively logical language will have no clear semantics. From a practical point of view, we must ensure that systems built in this way can cope with the inconsistencies that arise – for instance, when a given bird can be seen to be brown, say, but 'proved' to be black.

Plausible inferences can be thought of as inference rules that hold by default. Unless we have information to the contrary, it is reasonable, and practically useful, to assume that if something is a crow, then it is black. But if we have special information – for instance, that it is an albino crow – then it may be wrong to use the rule. Another way of looking at this starts from the premise that we frequently need to assume that we have complete information about some property – for instance, being a non-black crow. On this view, we must maintain that if there were any non-black crows, then we would explicitly know about them. Using the default inference rule, then, amounts to assuming that the set of non-black crows is as small as it can be consistent with our other knowledge.

Semantic network systems have traditionally implemented a kind of default inference by allowing information specified directly about an entity to override information that the entity might inherit.

Exercise 9.15   Modify the lexical look-up programs presented in Chapter 7 to produce a program with the following characteristics. Given a lexeme and a single feature name (for example, cat), the program returns the value for the lexical entry, expanding macros only as necessary to get this value. You can make some very restrictive assumptions for this. For instance, you can assume that the values of such features are always atomic (not complex DAGs) and that lexical entries never specify sharing between different values. Your program, although it will not handle lexical entries of the complexity that we have presented, will capture the essence of reasoning in terms of classes and inheritance.   [*hard*]

Exercise 9.16   Provide the program developed in the last exercise with lexical entries for classes like 'human', 'man', 'manager' and 'manageress'. Represent the information that managers and manageresses belong to a common subclass of humans and also belong to the class of men and women, respectively. Your program should be able to answer questions like 'Is Jones's job managerial?' and 'Is Dore entitled to maternity leave?', where Jones and Dore are particular individuals, also represented as lexical entries. What extensions to the program would be necessary to represent the information that the immediate superior of a manager is a manager, that Smith's immediate superior is a woman, that a manager's secretary is the same as their department secretary?   [*hard*]

Exercise 9.17   All irregular lexemes are regular in some respect. Most are just like regular lexemes, except that they deviate in one or two parts of the paradigm. Our lexical representation language, however, provides no natural way of saying 'this lexeme is wholly regular except for this form'. By the use of macros, we can describe how most of the information about a lexeme is *inherited* from a prototype regular lexeme (for example, a regular verb), but we cannot specify *default inheritance*, where information is only inherited if it is not explicitly overridden in the lexical entry. Explore the possibility of adding default inheritance machinery to the lexical representation language of Chapter 7 to overcome this expressive weakness. Can this be done by simply changing the intended interpretation of lexical macro definitions? Can such default machinery be usefully extended in its application to the syntactic and semantic components of a lexical entry?   [*hard*]

9.8   A simple semantic network in LISP

Implementing a simple semantic network in LISP is straightforward. Entities can be represented by symbols and attributes by properties on their property lists. Two functions, attr and isa, will prove useful for setting up networks:

```
(defun attr (entity attribute value)
   (setf (get entity attribute) value))

(defun isa (entity1 entity2)
   (setf (get entity1 'isa)
      (cons entity2 (get entity1 'isa))))
```

The function attr allows us to stipulate what value particular attributes have for particular entities; we will make no distinction between individuals and classes in our system – they both count as entities. Where an attribute is a property that an entity may or may not have, we just use the values yes and no accordingly. Procedure isa allows us to specify that one entity (entity1) comes directly below another (entity2) in the isa-hierarchy. We use the property isa to store for an entity, the list of entities that come directly above it in the hierarchy, which is why the isa function adds the second entity provided to the list of entities already recorded under the property. Here is a sequence of function calls resulting in the establishment of an example semantic network representing information about the membership of an organization:

```
(attr 'club_member 'sex 'male)
(attr 'club_member 'over_50 'yes)
(attr 'club_member 'citizenship 'US)

   (isa 'associate 'club_member)
(attr 'associate 'associate_member 'yes)
(attr 'associate 'citizenship 'non_US)
```

```
(isa 'life_member 'club_member)
(attr 'life_member 'life_member 'yes)
(attr 'life_member 'over_50 'no)

(isa 'kim 'associate)
(attr 'kim 'over_50 'no)

(isa 'jean 'associate)
(attr 'jean 'sex 'female)
(attr 'jean 'citizenship 'US)

(isa 'mayumi 'life_member)
(attr 'mayumi 'sex 'female)
(attr 'mayumi 'over_50 'yes)
(attr 'mayumi 'citizenship 'non_US)

(isa 'beryl 'life_member)
(attr 'beryl 'sex 'female)
```

We can now define a function get_attr to retrieve the correct value of a given attribute for a given entity, using inherited information if necessary. This function, together with the example network code, appears in lib inherits.

```
(defun get_attr (entity attribute)
  (catch 'got_one
    (if (get entity attribute)
        (throw 'got_one (get entity attribute))
      (dolist (e1 (get entity 'isa))
        (let ((x (get_attr e1 attribute)))
          (if x
              (throw 'got_one x)))))
    nil))
```

Notice that because of the order of the if clauses in this function, an attribute value specified locally for an entity will always be chosen over values obtained through inheritance. So, inherited information is interpreted as default information that can be explicitly overridden locally. get_attr returns nil if there is no value specified for the attribute, and this fact is used to determine for each entity e1 immediately above the original entity entity in the hierarchy whether a value can be obtained by inheritance from that entity. Here is an exhaustive listing of the conclusions (about Kim, Jean, Mayumi and Beryl) that can be drawn from this new example network, under the intended default inheritance interpretation:

> Kim is an associate member.
> The sex of Kim is male.
> Kim is not over 50.
> The citizenship of Kim is non-US.
>
> Jean is over 50.
> Jean is an associate member.
> The sex of Jean is female.
> The citizenship of Jean is US.

Mayumi is over 50.
Mayumi is a life member.
The citizenship of mayumi is non-US.
The sex of Mayumi is female.

Beryl is a life member.
The citizenship of Beryl is US.
The sex of Beryl is female.
Beryl is not over 50.

Notice that for the results of the program to make sense, the semantic network must be set up so that at most one value can be found for each entity and attribute. For this, we require that if an entity has an attribute specified by more than one ancestor, then one of those ancestors is itself an ancestor of the other. Moreover, we require that no entity is associated locally with more than one value for a given attribute.

Exercise 9.18 Code up some encyclopaedic information about plants or animals (or any appropriate domain in which you have an interest) as a network that can be interpreted by the code in lib inherits. Check that the theorems you can derive from it are what you expect. How might your example network be used to assist in disambiguation, say?   [*easy*]

Exercise 9.19 Interface a semantic network to lib dbq to replace a database for some predicates. You will need to redefine the function retrieve_all in lib dbq to call get_attr for predicates whose definitions involve semantic net attributes. For instance, here is one way to deal with goals involving predicates (citizenship _x _y) and (female _x):

```
...
(if (equal (car goal) 'citizenship) ; (citizenship _x _y)
  (let ((subst
          (termunify
            (get_attr (cadr goal) 'citizenship)
            (caddr goal))))
    (if subst
      (list subst)
      NO))
  (if (equal (car goal) 'female) ; (female _x)
    (if (equal (get_attr 'sex (cadr goal)) 'yes)
      YES
      NO)))
...
```

How can this approach be extended to cover predicates like (club_member _x) which depend on class membership? How could it be extended to deal with goals like (club_member _x) and (female _x) in cases where _x has not yet been given a value?   [*intermediate*]

Exercise 9.20   Allow multiple inheritance by changing the definition of get_attr so that:

(a)   the value associated with the closest ancestor wins, and

(b)   an error is reported if two equally close values for an attribute turn out to be available.

Provide a suitable example network and examine its behaviour under the revised interpretation.   [*hard*]

> ## SUMMARY
>
> - Inference plays a key role in NLP.
>
> - Non-trivial question answering involves inference.
>
> - DBQ expresions can be evaluated against a database.
>
> - Forwards inference is driven by the available premises.
>
> - Backwards inference is driven by the desired conclusion.
>
> - Full logical inference may never terminate.
>
> - Inheritance networks provide efficient but restricted inference.

Further reading

Natural language question–answering systems go back a quarter of a century now. Many of the classic papers on the topic can be found in Grosz *et al.* (1986), while descriptions of a range of 1970's systems are contained in Bolc (1980).

Databases and DBQ languages constitute an important area of computer science, for which Ullman (1982) and Maier (1983) are standard texts. Gray (1984) provides a readable overview, as well as covering other topics relevant to the present chapter. The logic-oriented approach to databases is pursued under the rubric of 'deductive databases' and representative work is compiled in Gallaire and Minker (1978) and Minker (1988).

Genesereth and Nilsson (1987) and Ramsay (1988) provide thorough textbook introductions to the role of logic and the nature of inference in an AI context. More advanced recent material on theorem proving can be found in Gallier (1986) and Wos *et al.* (1984). Bundy (1983) presents a very clear account of a range of automatic theorem-proving methods, as applied to the computer modelling of mathematical reasoning.

Semantic primitives have their linguistic origins in Katz and Fodor (1963), although their binary-feature based approach was soon to be usurped by the predicate-plus-arguments approach to primitivies adopted by McCawley (1970). The best-known use of primitives in an NLP system is that of Schank (1972) who uses 'deep cases' in the primitive-based representation scheme conceptual dependency. Useful, although partisan, discussions of the issues raised by the use of such primitives are to be found in Wilks (1977, 1987). The notion of deep cases originates with Fillmore (1968), and Bruce and Moser (1987) provide a valuable survey of case-based systems in NLP systems.

There are useful sections on semantic networks, forwards inference systems, semantic primitives and frames in Barr and Feigenbaum (1981, Chapter III), and similar, although more up-to-date, material on such topics is to be found in Shapiro (1987). Classic papers on many topics touched on in this chapter, including frames, semantic networks, default inheritance and the modes of inference appropriate to NLP, are bound together in Brachman and Levesque (1985). Ginsberg (1987), an overlapping, but more specialist collection on default inference, also contains much relevant material. Brief introductions to default and non-monotonic reasoning are to be found in Nutter (1987) and Perlis (1987). Extending semantic networks to cover more than the simple examples covered here is not a simple matter, and unclarities and inadequacies of early semantic net systems are well discussed in papers by Woods and Brachman in the Brachman and Levesque collection. Etherington (1988) and Touretzky (1986, 1987) comprise two monograph length and one encyclopedia-entry length discussions of semantic networks and default inheritance. The relevance of the latter to descriptive issues in linguistics and NLP is the subject of Gazdar (1987).

CHAPTER 10

PRAGMATICS

So far in this book, we have been concerned with the processing of language in terms of morphology, syntax and compositional semantics. We have seen that at each of these levels well-formedness constraints on natural language utterances can be formulated and that each mapping between levels is subject to particular kinds of ambiguities. In general, well-formedness constraints at a particular level can help resolve ambiguities in mappings from other levels. This chapter deals with the pragmatic level of NLP, where linguistic utterances are viewed in the context of extended discourses and the wider concerns of the participants. As at the other levels, we can attempt to formalize what is and what is not a plausible pragmatic interpretation of an utterance in some context. Also as before, we find particular kinds of ambiguities arising when we try to map from semantic representations to pragmatic interpretations and vice versa.

To start with, we will focus on aspects of noun phrases, which illustrate some of the classic pragmatic problems in language understanding and allow us to examine some of the computational ideas that have been used in attempts to solve them. Then we turn to the relation between discourse and planning, and show how AI theories of plan construction and plan recognition have been exploited in approaches to language generation and discourse understanding in NLP.

10.1   Ambiguity and levels of language processing

Despite radical oversimplification, the following table gives one a sense of
the layers of analysis required by NLP, and the types of ambiguity they
give rise to:

Level	Well-formedness constraints	Types of ambiguity
Morphological analysis	Rules of inflection and derivation	Analysis: structural, morpheme boundaries, morpheme identity
Syntactic analysis	Grammar rules	Analysis: structural, word category
Semantic interpretation	Selectional restrictions	Analysis: word sense, quantifier scope Generation: synonymy
Pragmatic interpretation	?Principles of cooperative conversation?	Analysis: ?pragmatic function? Generation: ?realization of pragmatic function?

The fact that the mappings between structures at the different levels are
not one to one is probably the major problem in NLP. In natural language
analysis, the aim is to relate a sentence to a set of possible pragmatic
interpretations. In language generation, it is to select among the possible
sentences that may (best) realize a given pragmatic goal. Figure 10.1 shows
the layers of analysis required by NLP, but of course such a diagram should
not be taken too literally as a recipe for building a computational NLP
system. As we have seen, for instance, there is no reason why the building
of semantic representations should not actually be interleaved with the
discovery of syntactic structure. Moreover, we do not have to interpret
well-formedness constraints as an absolute filter on possible representations – in actual language use we are fairly happy to use language in sloppy
and novel ways, even though we generally *prefer* to pick interpretations
that do not deviate too much from the normal. The advantage of a
conceptual model of language processing, like the one depicted in Figure
10.1, is that it gives us a basis for classifying the different kinds of knowledge required, and problems faced, by a natural language processor.

It is unfortunate that, as we move down the figure, it becomes less
and less clear what the appropriate representations should be at the different levels, and how we can encode well-formedness constraints. In
particular, there is still no satisfactory theory of the kinds of pragmatic
functions that linguistic utterances can have or of quite what is involved in

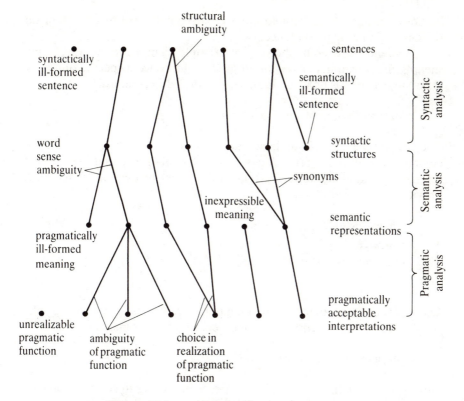

Figure 10.1   Layers of analysis required by NLP.

cooperative conversation. This chapter attempts to give a flavour of current computational thinking about these topics.

10.2   Semantic and pragmatic roles of noun phrases

The canonical function of a singular noun phrase in a sentence is, roughly speaking, to draw the attention of the hearer to some object in the world that is relevant to the current conversational situation. However, such a generalization masks the fact that there are many ways in which this function can be performed. Philosophers of language have made a number of important distinctions concerning the use of noun phrases. The unfortunate thing from a computational point of view is that the function of a noun phrase in a sentence may well be ambiguous or underdetermined. This section gives some idea of the range of functions that a noun phrase may assume. The possible functions will be illustrated by examples, but it must be borne in mind that, without context, it is often hard to force a given reading within a single sentence.

An indefinite noun phrase – for example, 'a new automobile', 'some sheep', 'five accountants' – is often used to introduce a specific object or set of objects that is believed to be new to the addressee, as in:

> Mayumi has bought *a new automobile*.

The natural way for an understander to deal with such a noun phrase computationally is to create a new internal symbol to denote the object referred to and to add to the current world model whatever information is provided about that object:

> automobile(g123)
> new(g123)
> owns(mayumi, g123)
> ...

On the other hand, an indefinite noun phrase can be used in a non-specific sense to provide a description of an object that may or may not exist:

> Mayumi wants to buy *a new XJE*.

Non-specific indefinite noun phrases frequently occur in so-called opaque contexts, where a verb like 'believes', 'wants' or 'hopes' introduces a description that may not correspond straightforwardly with anything in the real world.

Indefinite noun phrases can also be used generically to talk about whole classes of objects, rather than particular objects, as in:

> *A new automobile* typically requires repair twice in the first 12 months.

Verbs like 'be' and 'become' can appear with noun phrase complements, and in such a context an indefinite noun phrase can be seen as simply a convenient way of collecting together one or more properties:

> That heap of twisted metal is *a new automobile*.
> The Macho GTE XL is *a new automobile*.

Definite noun phrases can be used in ways that are fairly similar to the uses of indefinites. For instance, the following sentences illustrate simple referential and generic uses, respectively:

> Mayumi disliked *the new XJE she had bought*.
> *The jaguar* is a relative of *the leopard* that is found in South America.

An attributive use of a definite noun phrase is rather similar to a non-specific use of an indefinite noun phrase. Such a phrase is used, not to refer to a particular known individual, but to indicate an individual by a description that they satisfy. Thus, faced with a wrecked vehicle whose brakes have failed, thanks to a glaring design fault, but whose maker is unknown, it would be quite sensible to say:

> *The manufacturer of this automobile* should be indicted.

In such a context, the example illustrates the attributive usage, but we can readily imagine a context in which, say, speaker and addressee were standing next to a perfectly sound model manufactured by a company of crooks, and the definite noun phrase simply got interpreted referentially.

Pronouns permit references back to entities that have been introduced by previous noun phrases in a discourse. Thus, in the passage:

> Mayumi bought *an old XJE* at the auction.
> *It* had rather a high mileage.

it is natural to take 'it' to mean the automobile mentioned in the first sentence. It is quite possible, however, for a pronoun to correspond to a non-referential noun phrase:

> Mayumi wanted to buy *a centaur*.
> She planned to enter *it* for the Derby.

Here, the most natural interpretation has 'it' corresponding to the centaur that Mayumi wanted to buy, even though there is no real-world object for either noun phrase to refer to.

It is also possible for a pronoun to behave more like a logical variable, in which case it cannot be said to have the same referent as a preceding noun phrase:

> *No male driver* admits that *he* is incompetent.

Plainly, we do not wish to claim that 'no male driver' refers to some entity and that 'he' refers to that same entity.

Finally, a pronoun may be used to refer to something that is available from the context of the utterance, but has not been explicitly mentioned before. For instance, if two people have spotted a group of colleagues who always arrive late, one might well remark to the other:

> Here *they* come, late again!

The examples so far have all involved statements. In questions and commands, indefinite noun phrases are often read non-specifically rather than specifically, being interpreted as descriptions of objects that the addressee is supposed to identify as part of the question–answering or command–obeying process:

> Is her automobile in *a parking place near the exit*?
> Put her automobile into *a parking place near the exit*!

This section has laid out part of the space of possible noun phrase functions, and the problem facing a computational model of language understanding is immediately apparent. How are we to determine how noun phrases are being used and, where they are references to previously available objects, what their referents are? Very occasionally, the syntax provides a clue, as in the case of an indefinite noun phrase following the verb 'be', but for the most part only knowledge of the context and subject matter enables the addressee to determine the function of noun phrases. In this and following sections, we will look at some of the ideas that have been used for applying such knowledge to this task. We must, however, point to the limited range of noun phrases that has actually been dealt with in computer models of language. Almost all language-understanding systems assume that definite noun phrases and pronouns are simply referential, and that indefinite noun phrases are specific (or non-specific in the cases of questions and commands). Even given this simplification, the problems of dealing with noun phrases in non-trivial contexts are considerable, and we will look at some of these in the following sections.

10.3   Given versus new information

If for the moment we restrict our attention to simple declarative sentences, we can sometimes make a useful distinction between two kinds of information that may be provided by linguistic structures. The canonical objective of uttering a declarative sentence is to convey *new* information that the addressee is not already aware of. For addressees to attach this information to their existing knowledge, the speaker or writer may also convey a certain amount of *given* information that the addressee already knows. For instance, in:

> It was *a new automobile* that Maria bought when she got home.

the addressee is likely to know that Maria bought something when she got home, this being the old or given information. The new information conveyed by the utterance of such a sentence is the characterization of the object bought. Linguists and philosophers sometimes say that the fact that Maria bought something is *presupposed* by the utterance of the example sentence given.

How is the given–new distinction relevant to the interpretation of noun phrases? Assuming that conversation is taking place with a partner who wishes to be helpful, the addressee might hope that given and new information will be marked in some way and that information marked as given will indeed correspond to information already present in what the speaker believes the hearer knows. Thus, if a computer system can correctly identify the information that is given, it can check that that information really is consistent with its background knowledge and can make the necessary disambiguations to force it to be so. Moreover, if the new information is also clearly marked, the system can respond by adding this to its model of the world. For instance, in the foregoing example, 'she' might in principle refer to Mayumi who was mentioned in the previous sentence, say. But if only one of Mayumi and Maria is known to be going home, then that person is likely to be the referent of the pronoun. Indeed, if that person is not the referent, then it is plausible to argue that the sentence is inconsiderately or carelessly phrased.

Definite–indefinite marking is a clue to given–new status. For instance, when reading the following:

> *The sales manager* employed *a foreign distributor*.

we would expect (without any context to tell us otherwise) the sales manager to have already been introduced into the conversation (or to be known about in the context), whereas the foreign distributor is probably someone only being introduced for the first time. If 'the sales manager' is interpreted as providing given information, checking to see whether it is appropriate involves looking to see whether there is a sales manager in the current context. Unfortunately, definite noun phrases do not always convey entirely given information. In the following:

> *Mayumi Yokozawa* arrived at London Heathrow yesterday.
> *The successful automobile sales manager with an unbeaten US quota busting record* seemed tired after her flight.

the definite noun phrase does refer back to a previously mentioned person (Mayumi), but is generally conveying new information about her.

If we can identify the given information provided by a sentence, we can use it to constrain the sets of possible referents for noun phrases. In the sentence about Maria's new purchase, 'she' had to refer to somebody who was going home; in the sentence about the sales manager, the subject noun phrase had to refer to someone who was a sales manager. As already indicated, such a noun phrase presupposes the existence of a uniquely identifiable sales manager in the context. If there are ambiguous noun phrases in a sentence, it may well be worthwhile extracting the presuppositions to provide extra constraints. Indeed, it may even be worth looking for further, implicit, presuppositions that are required for the new information to make sense. For instance, it would be incoherent to say that something is an automobile if it was already known that it was a man or a robot; likewise it would be incoherent to say that something was inside itself. The checking of such presuppositions can be achieved by forwards inference rules that are on the look out for contradictions. For instance, if we had the following forwards inference rules:

> vehicle(X) if automobile(X)
>
> number_of_legs(X, 2) if man(X)
> number_of_legs(X, 2) if robot(X)
>
> contradiction if vehicle(X) and number_of_legs(X, 2)
>
> different(X, Y) if in(X, Y)
>
> contradiction if different(X, X)

we would immediately notice a contradiction when we tried to add the new information about the following erroneous pronoun referents:

> A *robot* demonstrated the Macho GTE XL.
> *It* is an automobile.
> (* "it" → a robot)
>
> A toolkit is provided with *the automobile*.
> *It* is in the automobile.
> (* "it" → the automobile)

Another way to check such presuppositions is via backwards inference. In this case, every time we are about to add some new information to the knowledge base we must check that it is consistent with what we already know. Sufficient rules for consistency might include the following:

> consistent(automobile(X)) if vehicle(X) and ...
> consistent(in(X, Y)) if different(X, Y) and ...

Rules about consistency will need to take into account the order in which we are likely to receive information about objects. It is possible that we will find out what kind of thing an object is, such as whether it is a vehicle, before we find out that it is an automobile, for instance. Then, we can expect to establish the consistency of being an automobile with what we already know by means of the first rule. But if we were told about an object being an automobile before we were told what kind of object it was, the first rule would not suffice to establish consistency. Such consistency rules are not really expressing generalizations about the world, but are heuristic metalogical rules indicating special cases where new information is unlikely to contradict what is already known. The advantage of using them is that they can produce candidate referents, rather than simply cause us to reject erroneous referents.

Rather than explicitly reason in terms of consistency, it is more efficient to directly compute a set of propositions that should be true for a sentence to make sense. We can then reject (or disprefer) possible interpretations that do not support the truth of these presuppositions. This idea is illustrated by the following small grammar for a variant of the carpentry domain introduced in Chapter 8. When a carpenter is giving an instruction to an apprentice, in general there will be shared knowledge about most of the objects and relations involved. So, we can make a simplifying assumption that the semantic representation of such a natural language instruction involves a desired action together with a set of presuppositions. In general, it will be necessary to determine which objects in the world the action is to operate on; the possibilities can be restricted to those that allow the presuppositions to be true.

Here are some rules for a simple carpentry grammar. The initial category IMP(erative) has two features associated with it, sem(antics) and pre(suppposition), for holding the representation of the desired action and the presuppositions. Both of these are represented as DAGs in the same way as in Chapter 8.

EXAMPLE: Carpentry grammar with presuppositions

```
Rule
  IMP → V NP PP:
    <V p> = <PP p>
    <V arg1> = <NP referent>
    <V arg2> = <PP arg1>
    <IMP sem> = <V sem>
    <IMP sem arg0> = addressee
    <IMP pre connective> = and
    <IMP pre prop1> = <V pre>
    <IMP pre prop2 connective> = and
    <IMP pre prop2 prop1> = <NP pre>
    <IMP pre prop2 prop2> = <PP np_pre>.
Rule
  NP → DET N:
    <NP pre> = <N pre>
    <NP referent> = <N referent>.
```

Rule
NP1 → NP2 PP:
    <NP1 cat> = NP
    <NP2 cat> = NP
    <NP1 referent> = <NP2 referent>
    <NP1 referent> = <PP arg0>
    <NP1 pre connective> = and
    <NP1 pre prop1> = <NP2 pre>
    <NP1 pre prop2 connective> = and
    <NP1 pre prop2 prop1> = <PP p_pre>
    <NP1 pre prop2 prop2> = <PP np_pre>.

Rule
PP → P NP:
    <PP arg0> = <P arg0>
    <PP arg1> = <NP referent>
    <PP arg1> = <P arg1>
    <PP p> = <P p>
    <PP np_pre> = <NP pre>
    <PP p_pre> = <P pre>.

The idea here is that IMP accumulates its sem directly from that of its main verb – the subcomponents of sem will be filled in by features from the associated noun phrases, as before. pre is, however, accumulated from propositions obtained from several places: the main verb may yield presuppositions that ensure that it is being used sensibly; a noun phrase may yield presuppositions that ensure that a suitable object exists in the world; and a prepositional phrase may yield presuppositions that must be true for the phrase to be appropriately used in the context. In fact, we divide the presuppositions arising from a use of a prepositional phrase into two sets: those that arise from the noun phrase, called the <np_pre>, and those that arise from the use of the preposition, called the <p_pre>. To make things clearer, here are some lexical entries that would go with the foregoing rules:

Word put:
    <cat> = V
    <p> = in
    <sem predicate> = put_in
    <sem arg1> = <arg1>
    <sem arg2> = <arg2>
    <pre predicate> = fit_in
    <pre arg0> = <arg1>
    <pre arg1> = <arg2>.

Word in:
    <cat> = P
    <p> = in
    <pre predicate> = in
    <pre arg0> = <arg0>
    <pre arg1> = <arg1>.
Word washer:
    <cat> = N
    <pre predicate> = washer
    <pre arg0> = <referent>.
Word box:
    <cat> = N
    <pre predicate> = box
    <pre arg0> = <referent>.
Word it:
    <cat> = NP
    <pre predicate> = true.

The first entry covers a particular sense of the verb 'put' that subcategorizes for a following noun phrase and prepositional phrase with preposition 'in', as in 'put the washer in the box'. The semantics of such a construction is that the predicate put_in is to be applied to the addressee and the two objects involved. In addition, this action will only be appropriate if the first object fits into the other – predicate fit_in. So, if X and Y are the two objects involved, the verb contributes the following (in a rather informal notation):

    <sem> = **put_in(addressee, X, Y)**
    <pre> = **fit_in(X, Y)**

If the command were 'put the washer in the box', then there would also be presuppositions arising from the two noun phrases. Thus, the final representation of imp would be:

    <sem> = **put_in(addressee, X, Y)**
    <pre> = **fit_in(X, Y) and washer(X) and box(Y)**

or, as a DAG, as shown in Figure 10.2.

If we wish to interpret the command in a context, we need to find values of X and Y to determine what is to be put into what. The computed presuppositions can be used as a basis for looking for possible candidates, or can be used to ensure that values chosen by some other method are reasonable. Note that the conditions expressed are conditions on objects in the world (or, at least, the machine's representation of the world), not on linguistic objects. With techniques like selectional restrictions, we attempt to capture certain semantic well-formedness conditions in terms of

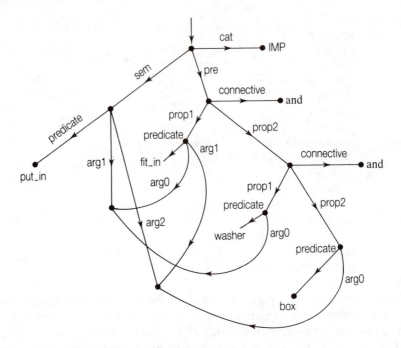

Figure 10.2 'put the washer in the box'.

properties of words. Some of the constraints that we can capture with presuppositions could be partially dealt with in a similar way. For instance, for X to fit in Y, Y must be a container: it can be easily verified that 'the box' must denote a container because the word 'box' always denotes a property that only holds of containers. On the other hand, with presuppositions we are also able to capture real-world constraints that elude selectional restrictions. For instance, it is not true that every object X will fit in every container Y. First of all, X has to be smaller then Y; secondly, Y must not already have too much in it; and so on. Thus, this use of presuppositions is significantly more powerful than the use of selectional restrictions.

In practice, the formulation of presuppositions often takes into account the fact that a human addressee can make simple inferences. Consider the following examples:

> Mary has two children, one male, one female.
> *The daughter* is just starting a career as an accountant.

> Jan bought a car from a secondhand dealer.
> *The roof* was slightly scratched.

If we wish our computational models of language understanding to make sense of such sentences, then we must provide them with appropriate rules of inference. For instance, a female child is the same as a daughter:

> **daughter(X) if daughter(X, Y)**
> **daughter(X, Y) if female(X) and child(X, Y)**

For the second example, we require an inference rule that infers the existence of an object (the roof) that has not been explicitly mentioned. We can express this in logic by using a function symbol:

> **roof(roof_of(X)) if vehicle(X)**

Such a rule will enable us to infer that if **veh129** is a vehicle, then there is an object **roof_of(veh129)** which is a roof. Used forwards, it will automatically create roof objects whenever vehicles are introduced. Used backwards, it will introduce roofs of vehicles as necessary to satisfy an inferencing goal.

Our discussion of the given–new distinction and presuppositions has been largely from the point of view of the language understander. Of course, a considerate natural language generation system needs to address the·problems that an understander has. A plausible strategy is for such a system always to provide explicitly enough given information (in a definite description) to distinguish a phrase's referent from all other objects that it might be confused with.

Exercise 10.1 lib presupp contains a LISP version of the simple carpenter's grammar that explicitly computes presuppositions. It also contains some example inference rules that capture the characteristics of a particular tiny carpentry domain:

```
(setq infrules
  '(((manipulate _x) (screw _x))
    ((manipulate _x) (washer _x))
    ((fit_in washer1 hole1))
    ((fit_in screw2 hole1))
    ((fit_in _x box1) (screw _x))
    ((fit_in _x box1) (washer _x))
    ((fit_on _x _y) (washer _x))
    ((on washer1 screw1))
    ((screw screw1))
    ((screw screw2))
    ((washer washer1))
    ((hole hole1))
    ((box box1))
    ((true _x))))
```

Construct a program which, given a sentence:

(a)   syntactically analyzes it according to the lib presupp grammar (use lib fburecog),

(b)   converts the pre and sem DAGs into terms (use lib termify),

(c)   uses backwards inference to compute values that satisfy the presuppositions (use lib bckinfer), and

(d)   displays the final interpretations (that is, the possible actions indicated).

Your program should allow for several results arising at each stage (for example, several syntactic analyses, several solutions to the presuppositions). What results does your program obtain for the following sentences?

> Put it in the box!
>
> Put it in the hole!
>
> Put the washer on the screw in the box!
>
> Put the screw in the hole!

[*intermediate*]

10.4   Understanding by prediction

Section 10.3 outlined a simple model for the resolution of definite noun phrases and pronouns. A major drawback with it was, however, that it was a very passive model of understanding. The hope was that referents would be established simply through the verification that each sentence made sense, given the model of the world previously established. This is, of course, a kind of understanding in context, as we would expect the model of the world to change after each sentence is processed. On the other hand, intuitively understanding ought to be a more active process. That is, an understander that is getting something out of a text should be building up predictions or expectations about new information and actively comparing these with successive inputs to resolve ambiguities. On what basis might an understander predict future inputs? We might expect inputs that are related to what has come before, for instance, inputs that elaborate on a theme that has been introduced:

> The apparatus consists of a disc supported by a horizontal plate.
> *It* is heavy and uniform.
>
> The burning of the petrol–air mixture in an engine generates a terrific amount of heat. The circulation of oil around the engine helps to cool *it*.

In the first example, we are told about a disc being supported. In such a context, we are more likely to be told about the weight of the disc rather than the weight of the support; hence, resolving the pronoun 'it'. Thus:

heavy(X) d_if supports(Y, X)   (1)

is a plausible inference rule. In the second example, we are told about the build-up of heat in a mechanical device. Mechanical devices are usually designed to solve such problems, and so we might expect to hear later about how the engine is cooled. Thus, it would be more plausible for the pronoun 'it' to refer to the engine than to the oil. Again, we could formulate a plausible inference rule explaining why we expect to hear about the engine being cooled:

cools(cooling_system(X), X) d_if generates_heat(Y) and at(Y, X)   (2)

Naive models about what kinds of attributes and behaviours commonly go together provide another source of predictions. For instance, in reading:

The leader of the demonstrators was overpowered by one of the policemen. *He* was carrying a banner.

we are more likely to think that the demonstrator was carrying a banner rather than the policeman. But if the second sentence had been 'He was equipped with a riot shield and rubber bullets' a human reader might well decide that the policeman is being talked about, even though it is quite possible in principle that the leader of a group of demonstrators might have such equipment.

How can we use such predictions in practice in a language-understanding system? The idea is to try to construct a proof of (perhaps part of) the information provided in a sentence from the existing world knowledge and plausible inference rules of the kind illustrated. That is, essentially, to treat all information as if it was given and to attempt to satisfy the presuppositions using plausible inference. Consider the first example sentence again, together with a plausible representation for its meaning:

The apparatus consists of a disc supported by a horizontal plate.

component(disc43, apparatus7)
component(plate25, apparatus7)

supports(plate25, disc43)

horizontal(plate25)

The contribution of the second sentence is the following new information:

It is heavy and uniform.

heavy(X)
uniform(X)

where **X** is the referent of 'it'. Now, using the first plausible inference rule we can actually prove an instance of the first assertion:

heavy(disc43)

and so, on the basis of the prediction, we could conclude that **X** is **disc43**. In constructing a proof of the new information, we might start from either the existing database, working forwards searching for a conclusion of the right kind, or we might work backwards from the desired conclusion, looking for ways of establishing it, or we might adopt a mixed strategy of some kind. In general, once we have assembled a reasonably large set of plausible inference rules, we will start finding multiple solutions; for instance, in the example it is perhaps plausible that the plate is heavy because supporting objects have to be strong and strong objects are often heavy. So, we will need a basis for preferring one solution over another. One strategy that has been proposed is to prefer the solution whose proof is shortest. This seems intuitively reasonable, except for the fact that the length of a proof depends as much on arbitrary factors, such as which predicates are used in the representation language, as on any meaningful notion of closeness between axioms and conclusion.

A very simple LISP prediction program is provided by lib predict. The function predict is given a list of assertions that might be derived from an English sentence and adds them to its world model if they are unambiguous and not already predicted. Assertions may contain variables, corresponding to references that need to be resolved, in which case the function uses backwards inference to try and infer instances of the assertions that are already predicted. Facts and plausible inference rules are expected to be put into the global variable infrules, as required by lib bckinfer. The most important part of the function is as follows:

```
(defun predict (assertions)
  (let
      ((substs (back_infer_all assertions)))
      ...
      (if (equal (length substs) 1)
          (progn
              (print '(assertions uniquely predicted))
              (print (apply_subst (car substs) assertions)))
```

That is, if backwards inference yields a unique substitution such that the assertions are predicted, then the corresponding instance of the assertions is displayed. As well as catering for this case, the function handles other possibilities: a ground set of assertions (one containing no variables) that cannot be predicted (these are just added to infrules) and a non-ground set of assertions that either have no predictions or have several predictions (it just warns you about these). The library file comes with a tiny set of example inference rules, based on Exercise 10.2:

```
(setq infrules
 '(((church (church_of _x)) (town _x))
   ((see people _x) (famous _x) (object _x))
   ((object _x) (spire _x))
   ((spire (spire_of _x)) (church _x))))
```

The program can be used by a person simulating the output of a natural language front end, providing lists of assertions in the order they might be generated from a text:

```
(loop (predict (read)) (terpri))
((town morton_underwell))
(ASSERTIONS NOT PREDICTED BUT UNAMBIGUOUS)
((spire _x))
(ASSERTIONS UNIQUELY PREDICTED)
((SPIRE (SPIRE_OF (CHURCH_OF MORTON_UNDERWELL))))
((famous (spire_of (church_of morton_underwell))))
(ASSERTIONS NOT PREDICTED BUT UNAMBIGUOUS)
((see people _x))
(ASSERTIONS UNIQUELY PREDICTED)
((SEE PEOPLE (SPIRE_OF (CHURCH_OF MORTON_UNDERWELL))))
```

In this example, the prediction program is able to predict the existence of the spire on the church in Morton Underwell, and is able to predict that it is this, rather than the church or the town, that people probably come to see.

Exercise 10.2   Discuss plausible inference rules that would predict the likely referents for pronouns in the following passage from a guide book:

> Morton Underwell is a quiet town at the end of the Treville valley. The parish church is well known for its angled spire. People come from miles around to see it. It was built in Norman times and partially destroyed in the war. Victor Grisman, the famous violinist, was born where the present vicar lives. His father was a wealthy landowner. He died when he was only 8. A museum has been set up in his memory. It is open every weekday.

[intermediate]

Exercise 10.3 Further develop the set of inference rules provided with lib predict and produce a complete simulation of the processing of the Morton Underwell example. You will find that you cannot, in general, present all the information from a given sentence at once, because some of it will be genuinely unpredicted. In addition, if you attempt to deal with sentences with a noun phrase indicating a new object, you will have to decide whether to present the assertions with a variable standing for this object, if the existence of the object might be predicted, or with a new name standing for this object, if the existence of the object should not be predictable. What kinds of improvements to the program would enable it to handle cases like this more automatically?   [*intermediate*]

Exercise 10.4 Extend the set of inference rules developed for the last exercise, so that the program comes up with alternative possibilities for referents. Extend lib bckinfer so that with each substitution it returns the number of proof steps required. Extend lib predict so that it picks the substitution resulting from the shortest proof.   [*hard*]

10.5   More controlled versions of prediction

In using a general inference technique for prediction, we will suffer from the general combinatorial explosion associated with logical inference. One trouble with the method is that the inferences are not sensitive to the order in which material is presented. So, in the example about the apparatus, our inference system will still be prepared to infer that the disc is heavy, long after the discourse has finished with that particular object. Often, we would expect to hear about something as central as the weight of a physical object soon after the object is first introduced, but intuitions about this are not strong. One situation where we have stronger expectations about the order and timing of natural language inputs is when the actions of human agents are being described. Human actions are frequently stereotyped and, fortunately, the default strategy in natural language descriptions is to describe them in temporal order. For instance, if a customer C orders an automobile A from a dealer D, then we might expect the same dealer to deliver that automobile to that customer some time later:

delivers(D, A, C) d_if orders(C, A, D)

Because of this expectation, we might expect in an example like:

> *Lee* ordered *an XJE* from *the dealer*.
> He thought the engine attractive.
> *She* delivered *it* to *him* the following weekend.

to correctly understand the third sentence, even though it contains three ambiguous pronouns. But we might also expect that in an extended version of the example:

> *Lee* ordered *an XJE* from *the dealer*.
> He thought the engine attractive.
> But when he drove to work in it he found it very uncomfortable.
> His mother bought him a hat for his birthday.
> *She* delivered *it* to *him* the following weekend.

the pronouns would be resolved differently. This is because Lee's driving the automobile to work would normally happen after its delivery, and so after that point in the text we no longer have that expectation. A special technique, called *script application*, has been devised to deal with such temporally ordered predictions more efficiently. The idea is to encapsulate a sequence of actions that belong together into a script:

```
script automobile_buying:
   <{customer(C), automobile(A), dealer(D), garage(G)},
      <
      goes(C, G),
      test_drives(C, A),
      orders(C, A, D),
      delivers(D, A, C),
      drives(C, A)
      >>
```

At some point in the text, an understanding system will decide that a given script is appropriate; in general, a script expresses a sequence of actions with some purpose, and so this script might be suggested by a sentence like 'Lee wanted to have a new automobile'. This is called *cueing* the script. Once a script is cued, the system keeps track of how far through the sequence the text has got, and also of what values are currently associated with the objects involved in the script. All the actions *after* the current point in the script (but not those before) are then predicted to be possible inputs.

We can easily represent a basic script as a list of propositions in LISP, with the first element being a summary of the script and the subsequent elements being the expected actions, in order. Here are a couple of scripts represented this way: the automobile-buying script shown and a hat-buying script:

```
((auto_buy _Customer _Auto1 _Auto2 _Driver _Garage)
 (goes _Customer _Garage)
 (test_drives _Customer _Auto1)
 (orders _Customer _Auto2 _Driver)
 (delivers _Driver _Auto2 _Customer)
 (drives _Customer _Auto2))
```

```
((hat_buy _Customer _Hat _Assistant _Store)
 (goes _Customer _Store)
 (tries_on _Customer _Hat)
 (buys _Customer _Hat _Assistant)
 (delivers _Assistant _Hat _Customer)
 (wears _Customer _Hat))
```

lib scripts implements a simple script applier in LISP. It differs from actual script appliers, in that it expects to be given the set of propositions from a whole text, rather than having to work out plausible scripts at the end of each sentence. Moreover, it incorporates no special mechanism for script cueing, since each script is assumed to be potentially applicable.

script_match expects to be given a list of propositions, expressing a sequence of actions described in a particular order. As with lib predict, these may contain variables. The program goes through all the scripts in the global list scripts and sees which of them predicts the sequence of described actions. As soon as it finds one, it assumes that it is the only such script and prints out the header and complete set of predicted actions for the script, making use of whatever information about the objects involved it can obtain from the propositions provided. Here is an example of the function in use:

```
(script_match '((goes Jan Smiths)
                (tries_on _x hat45)
                (wears _y _z)))

((HAT_BUY JAN HAT45 _ASSISTANT SMITHS)
 (GOES JAN SMITHS)
 (TRIES_ON JAN HAT45)
 (BUYS JAN HAT45 _ASSISTANT)
 (DELIVERS _ASSISTANT HAT45 JAN)
 (WEARS JAN HAT45))
```

In this example, the program is given a list of propositions that might arise from a text like the following:

> Jan went to Smiths. He tried on a bowler hat. He wore it to his brother's wedding.

The program has decided that a hat_buy script is applicable to this sequence of actions. In doing so, it has obtained the referents of three pronouns. Although the example text only mentions three actions, the script indicates that in fact five actions took place, including Jan buying the hat and it being delivered to him. Some of these actions involve the unmentioned salesperson _Assistant, about whom nothing else is known.

script_match goes through each script in turn, determining all ways that that script might match the sequence of events in the story. Each possible way is represented by a substitution, which assigns values to the variable symbols in the script. script_match takes the first such substitution that it can find and returns the result of applying it to the relevant script:

```
(defun script_match (story)
  (dolist (script scripts nil)
    (let ((predictions (cdr script)))
      (let (
              (substs (predict_all_ways predictions story empty_subst)))
        (if substs
            (return (apply_subst (car substs) script)))))))
```

predict_all_ways tries all ways of matching the predictions of a script with a story. It returns a list containing the relevant substitutions for all these successes. It works by recursing down the list of events in the story, at each point passing down the remaining predictions of the script and the substitution obtained so far:

```
(defun predict_all_ways (predictions story current_subst)
  (if (null story)
      (list current_subst)
      (let ((event (car story)) (successes ()))
        (do (
              (restpredictions (cdr predictions) (cdr restpredictions))
              (predict (car predictions) (car restpredictions)))
            ((null predict) successes)
          (let ((subst (termunify event predict)))
            (if subst
                (setq successes
                      (append
                        (predict_all_ways
                          (apply_subst subst restpredictions)
                          (apply_subst subst (cdr story))
                          (compose_substs subst current_subst))
                        successes)))))))))
```

If predict_all_ways ever gets to the point when the story is exhausted (the if case), it can simply indicate success by returning the current substitution. Otherwise it looks through the predictions provided, looking for one that matches (by termunify) the first event in the story. For each way that this can be done, it recursively calls predict_all_ways, with the rest of the story, the predictions that follow the found prediction and a modified current substitution. Each of these arguments is suitably modified to take into account the substitution subst that results from unifying the event with the prediction. The result returned will then be the result of concatenating the lists of substitutions returned by these recursive calls; this final list is kept in the variable successes.

Exercise 10.5 Add at least two more examples to the list scripts and try out the program on a range of action sequences. [*easy*]

Exercise 10.6 Specify the changes that would be necessary to the program to allow scripts to specify alternative sequences of actions – for instance, a hat may be simply taken home by the customer, rather than be delivered. [*intermediate*]

Exercise 10.7 If there were hundreds, or thousands, of possible scripts, how could the program be modified to limit the number it has to actively consider? [*hard*]

Exercise 10.8 What happens if one of the program's inputs is not expected in a script that predicts everything else? How could the program be modified to choose the script that predicts the highest number of the input propositions? [*hard*]

Exercise 10.9 What changes to the program would be necessary to allow it to interpret sentences one by one, rather than it having to wait until the whole sequence of inputs is available? [*hard*]

Exercise 10.10 What changes would be necessary to enable a script to specify extra conditions on the objects taking part in expected propositions? For instance, with the following augmented scripts:

```
(setq scripts
 '(((auto_buy _Customer _Auto1 _Auto2 _Driver _Garage)
   ((person _Customer)
    (auto _Auto1)
    (auto _Auto2)
    (person _Driver)
    (garage _Garage))
   (goes _Customer _Garage)
   (test_drives _Customer _Auto1)
   (orders _Customer _Auto2 _Driver)
   (delivers _Driver _Auto2 _Customer)
   (drives _Customer _Auto2))
  ((hat_buy _Customer _Hat _Assistant _Store)
   ((person _Customer)
    (hat _Hat)
    (person _Assistant)
    (shop _Store))
   (goes _Customer _Store)
   (tries_on _Customer _Hat)
   (buys _Customer _Hat _Assistant)
   (delivers _Assistant _Hat _Customer)
   (wears _Customer _Hat))))
```

where the second component specifies restrictions to be satisfied by the objects, it would be possible to determine that (goes Jan Sears) could only be an action in the second script, if Sears is known to be a store but not a garage. [*hard*]

10.6 Problems with prediction

There are many unsolved problems associated with script application. For instance, it is unclear how we should decide exactly what should belong and what should not belong to a script. It is often uncertain exactly when a particular script should be cued and, once it has been cued, how long it should remain under consideration when none of its predicted actions have appeared for a time. In addition, it is not obvious what should happen when several cued scripts claim to predict different instances of an input proposition.

Another technical problem with prediction in general is that the plausible inference rules used may well suggest the existence of objects not explicitly mentioned in the text. For instance, the rule about the engine in Section 10.2 implies the existence of an object cooling_system(X) for any object X which is hot. Sometimes the same object may be given different names by different rules. And sometimes the name given to an object by a rule will be different from the name we assign it as the referent of a noun phrase. This can be a problem because inference systems frequently make the *unique name assumption*; that is, the assumption that different names denote different objects. So, if we are trying to find out information about an object using one name, we will not find it if the information is stored under the other name. Consider, for instance, the following short passage:

> The burning of the petrol–air mixture in the engine generates a terrific amount of heat. A large pipe leads cold water through the engine to keep the main tank full. The pipe also serves to cool it.

The first sentence introduces a new object – a hot engine, engine83, say. On the basis of the plausible inference rule given earlier we expect there to be another object cooling_system(engine83). The second sentence introduces a pipe that for the moment seems completely new, and we are likely to assign it a new name, pipe45, say. If we are to correctly disambiguate the pronoun in the third sentence by the use of our rule, however, we have to satisfy the following from our world-model and plausible inference rules:

pipe(X) and cools(X,Y)

We cannot do this unless we realize that pipe45 and cooling_system(engine83) might in fact be the same thing. An inference system supporting prediction thus needs to be able to hypothesize equality between seemingly different objects and, if this hypothesis is borne out, to subsequently use the equality to facilitate other inferences.

Is there any way we can formalize what is going on in the seemingly rather *ad hoc* technique of prediction? We might be able to think of the plausible inference rules as default rules, which can be expected to hold unless their conclusions are explicitly contradicted in the text. The task of the prediction mechanism is, at any stage, to build a particular kind of model of the situation being described which is consistent with, but possibly more explicit than, the information actually provided. In this model, we prefer there to be as few different true facts and objects in the world as possible. Thus, a given default rule might be used if it enabled us to conclude that two objects or facts are the same. Otherwise, we will guess that the conclusion of the rule is false, and so the rule does not apply. But such a crude sketch conceals the immense problems in properly understanding default inference systems, let alone the problem of relating techniques used in NLP to them.

10.7   Using discourse structure

In the previous sections, we modelled referential pronouns as objects for which very few constraints were known to hold. When the pronoun 'it' is used, however, we do typically know more than merely that the object referred to is either a baby or non-human. It is certainly not the case that all known babies and non-human objects are equally good candidates for the referent. Thus, for instance, in using this pronoun we are unlikely to be referring to an object that we have never talked about before; rather, in general, we are likely to be referring to an object that we have mentioned quite recently. The principles just stated amount to an assertion that the position of a pronoun in a discourse may influence the way it is interpreted. There are unwritten conventions about when an object can be referred to by a pronoun and a considerate speaker will keep to these, to make the addressee's job easier. In general, the structure of the discourse may indeed affect the interpretation of various kinds of potentially ambiguous or referentially underdetermined expressions. If we can determine how this happens, it may enable the possibilities considered in the various inferential approaches to ambiguity resolution to be considerably restricted.

Within sentences, certain grammatical constructions constrain the interpretation of pronouns. For instance, in:

The robot washed *it*.

it is not possible for 'it' to be referring to the robot, since such a reference would require the use of the reflexive pronoun 'itself'. But how can the previous sentences affect the possibilities for a pronoun referent? One simple approach that has been taken is to assume that objects can be referred to by a pronoun with a likelihood that increases with the proximity of a previous noun phrase referring to the same object. So, if we keep a 'history list' of the objects that have been referred to, in the order in which the noun phrases have appeared, we can use this list as an initial candidate cohort, with items later in the list preferred to those earlier, ceteris paribus.

Mayumi went to visit Martin yesterday	[Mayumi,
	Martin,
He was trying to find Maria	Martin,
	Maria,
She ...	???, ...]

Using the history list approach for this example, Maria would be the preferred candidate for the referent of 'she', with Martin next and Mayumi last. Of course, Martin can be eliminated for reasons of probable sex. Such an approach is obviously rather crude, but is of some help if used in conjunction with other devices to help in pronoun disambiguation. More sophisticated techniques use a model of 'local focus' and attempt to characterize the ways in which focus can change between adjacent sentences and the ways in which grammatical constructions facilitate these changes. According to such models, the use of pronouns and abbreviated referring phrases correlates with which items are in focus – for instance, pronouns tend to indicate items in focus. A language-understanding system can use this correlation to produce a preference order among the alternative elements that might be in focus in a given sentence. A language-generation system can use the correlation as the basis of deciding whether to pronominalize or not in producing a description to identify an object.

One reason why the simple history list idea does not work well is the fact that discourses appear to have a non-trivial structure above the sentence level and that patterns of referring reflect this. A classic example, due to Barbara Grosz, involves two humans, E and A, talking while one assembles an air compressor:

E: Good morning. I would like you to reassemble the compressor. **(1)**
...

E: I suggest you begin by attaching the pump to the platform. **(2)**
...

E: Good. All that remains then is to attach the belt housing cover to the belt housing frame. **(3)**
...

A: All right, the belt housing cover is on and tightened down. **(4)**

E: Fine. Now let's see if *it* works. **(5)**

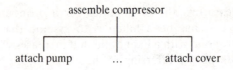

Figure 10.3 Structure of an assembly task.

Grosz argues that the pronoun 'it' in (5) refers back to the compressor, last mentioned in (1), even though 30 minutes and 60 utterances have passed between the two sentences. If she is right, the organization of the discourse seems to reflect the structure of the assembly task, which can be shown as a tree, as in Figure 10.3. The pattern of the discourse is here analogous to a depth-first, left-right traversal of the task tree, at each point discussing the task associated with the current node. This is hardly surprising, given the outside constraints on how the assembly is done. Hence, we would expect the conversation, at the end of the discussion of the attachment of the belt housing cover, to pop up to the topic of the top node. Thus, although utterances (4) and (5) might seem a very long way from utterance (1) in terms of the amount of intervening text, in terms of how the topic of conversation is likely to move around, utterance (4), and hence utterance (5), is very close to utterance (1). Researchers in this area hope that uncovering the hierarchical structure of a discourse might enable an under-standing program to narrow down the parts of the subject material (the 'focus spaces') where referents may be found. It can perhaps also restrict the range of inferences that are investigated in the search for possible referents.

Especially with dialogues, many investigators have been tempted to assign category labels to segments of discourse, rather than just assign a hierarchical structure. For instance, the following dialogue:

A: I really think the automobile needs servicing.

B: But we only had it done recently.

A: No, not for two years ... .
Incidentally did you hear that gas prices are about to double?

B: OK ...
but we have not had any problems recently.

A: My mother has hers done every year.

B: I refuse to spend any more money on this jalopy.

might provoke a hierarchical analysis in terms of the following labels (one for each line):

A: Statement

B: Challenge

A: Challenge
                 Interruption

B: Concession
             Challenge

A: Support

B: Rejection

There would seem to be obvious constraints on the order in which these putative conversational moves can be made. Thus, for instance, we might claim that a challenge cannot be made before the statement that it challenges; or that a concession must terminate the discussion of a subsidiary point, and thus cause the main issue to be resumed. In addition, researchers in this tradition have hoped to account for certain punctuation words, like 'OK' and 'but', in terms of the information they provide about this structure. If it were to exist, a grammar of possible conversation structures would be a useful tool for a language-understanding program, in that it could form the basis of making or constraining predictions about future natural language inputs.

Discourse structure may be a partial key to other ambiguity problems apart from reference. A domestic HAL (the eavesdropping computer in the film '2001') would have great trouble with the example automobile dialogue, and we might hope that knowledge of the constraints on conversational structure would help it. For instance, the statement about the mother having 'hers done' would certainly be hard to interpret if it was not seen as a statement supporting the main issue. In a language-generation system, we are free to determine the discourse structure ourselves to some extent, but, to be fair to the addressee, we should make use of all possible devices (for instance, punctuation words) to signal it clearly.

This section has summarized a line of research that attempts to characterize the syntax of discourses and how patterns of pronominalization (and such like) reflect this. Unfortunately, such research, while it may provide quite complex criteria for how a discourse might develop according to the structure of the previous discourse, fails to account for why, in an actual situation, a discourse goes one way rather than another. And it leaves open the question as to how a general category, like 'challenge', will be instantiated or recognized. Thus, it claims to lay out a grammar of options but does not tell a language generator which one to take at any given point, nor how to realize the option chosen, and it fails to provide a lexicon of options that a language interpreter could use as the basis for an attempt to parse the discourse in terms of the units provided by the grammar. It is also clear that there could be no such lexicon. A word like 'sins' in English is either the third-person singular present tense verb form or the plural noun form. There are no other possibilities. But 'it's cold in here', given the right context, can constitute virtually any kind of discourse act: an answer, a complaint, a question, a statement, an explanation, a challenge, and so on. The lexicon of words provides vital information for the syntax of sentences. But a lexicon of sentences could provide almost nothing by way of information for an attempted syntax of discourse.

10.8   Language generation as a goal-oriented process

One way to make sense of why a discourse sometimes goes one way and sometimes goes in another is to consider the plans and goals of the speakers. Spoken and written utterances are actions and actions, in general, are performed as a result of plans to achieve goals. So, the following is a simple model of linguistic communication. A speaker with a given goal produces a plan to achieve it and executes this plan by performing a number of actions, some of which may be linguistic actions. In organizing a linguistic action, speakers generally use what discourse and sentence-structuring techniques the language makes available for encoding their intentions perspicuously. The addressee, who is able to detect these structures, decodes them to get an impression of the speaker's goal and plan, and responds helpfully (or otherwise, if they do not agree with the addressee's own goals). On this view, the syntax of discourse, such as it is, is epiphenomenal and plays (at most) a subordinate role to the activity that drives the discourse.

The development of planning systems has been an important area of AI since the early 1970s and it is an area where a great deal of progress has been made. Most AI planning systems regard plans as being composed of sequences of instances of operators. An *operator* is a representation of a type of action, and associated with an operator are preconditions – things that must be true before the action can be done – and effects – things that the action makes true or false. Here are possible operators for move and request actions:

> Operator:
>   move(Agent, Source, Destination)
>
> Preconditions:
>   at(Agent, Source)
>   want(Agent, move(Agent, Source, Destination))
>
> Effects:
>   not at(Agent, Source)
>   at(Agent, Destination)

Operator:
  request(Speaker, Addressee, Action)

Preconditions:
  can_do(Addressee, Action)

  channel(Speaker, Addressee)

  want(Speaker, request(Speaker, Addressee, Action))

Effects:
  believe(Addressee, want(Speaker, Action))

A **move** action involves an **Agent** and two places, **Source** and **Destination**. For a person to move intentionally from **Source** to **Destination**, they must initially be at **Source**, and they must actually want to move. As a consequence of the action, they are no longer at **Source**, but are at **Destination**. Similarly, three things are involved in a **request** action: a **Speaker**, an **Addressee** and a requested **Action**. For a satisfactory request to take place, the **Addressee** must be able to do the action and the **Speaker** has to want to make the **Request**. In addition, there must be some kind of communication channel between the **Speaker** and the **Addressee**. The only immediate consequence of the **Request**, and it being recognized as such, is that the **Addressee** believes that the **Speaker** wants the action to take place.

Usually, to produce a plan that achieves some goal (makes some state of affairs true), an AI planning system looks for an instance of an operator that, if executed, would achieve the goal. It then recursively plans to make the preconditions of that operator instance true. So, our **request** operator would be useful in a plan that required someone to believe that someone else wants something, either as its main goal or as a subgoal introduced during the planning to achieve some other main goal. A successful plan is a partially ordered network of operator instances, where the preconditions of each operator are guaranteed to be satisfied before it is to be executed, and where the main goal is guaranteed to be true after the execution of the last action. This is illustrated in Figure 10.4.

The **request** operator is concerned with the external relation between utterances and what intelligent agents do to satisfy their goals. Of course, if one takes the planning metaphor seriously, there should be a principled way of realizing requests and the like as sequences of actions that cause actual sentences to be uttered. For this, we need to invoke the notion of *hierarchical planning*. Hierarchical planning arises when some actions are initially planned at a high level of abstraction. Then, each action in the plan is expanded into a network of simpler actions that make it up – but note that there may be several alternative expansions to be explored. At this point, the organization of the plan may have to be altered ('criticized') to account for interactions between parts of what were previously unanalyzed primitive actions. Then, the actions in this expanded plan are themselves

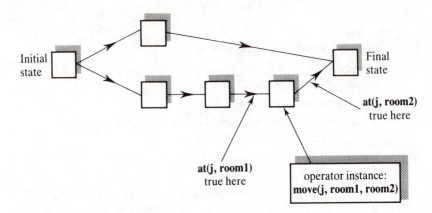

Figure 10.4 A plan.

expanded into smaller actions and new interactions are corrected. This process continues until a level of abstraction is reached that suffices for the current task, as illustrated in Figure 10.5.

Here is one possible hierarchy of levels at which planning could take place in the generation of an utterance:

Illocutionary acts
request, statement, suggestion, question, ...

Sentence realization acts
actions corresponding to the realization of imperative, declarative or interrogative syntax, choice of overall intonation contour, ...

Phrase realization acts
formulating an NP as 'the door', 'that door',

Word realization acts
producing 'don't' for 'do not', 'eaten' as the passive form of 'eat', ...

Illocutionary acts like requesting typically involve making a choice of sentence type and structure. Often, a request can be realized as any of the three main sentence types, for instance:

Can you close the door?
Close the door!
You will now close the door.

The action of uttering any one of these sentence types involves uttering smaller phrases, which may involve uttering yet smaller phrases. Typically, there will be a number of layers of phrase realization actions in the abstraction hierarchy between an illocutionary act and a set of basic linguistic realization acts (involving words, sequencing, intonation and punctuation) that it can expand into.

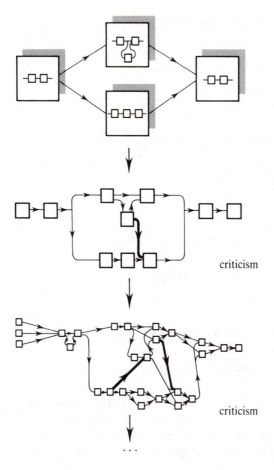

criticism

criticism

. . .

Figure 10.5   Hierarchical planning.

In general, the effect of illocutionary acts, such as requesting, involves changes in the beliefs of the addressee, and the planning of such actions needs to take beliefs into account. In reasoning about beliefs, a speaker may need to distinguish between his or her own beliefs, those of the addressee, the addressee's beliefs about the speaker's beliefs, the speaker's beliefs about the addressee's beliefs about their own beliefs, and so on. As an illustration of how a planning system might reason about appropriate illocutionary acts, here is a simple example, based heavily on the work of Philip Cohen but considerably simplified. To reproduce the elements of Cohen's model, we first need to split up the preconditions of operators, distinguishing can_do preconditions from **want** preconditions. The idea is that, for the action to take place, the action must be physically possible, and in addition the relevant person must actually want to do the action. So, here are our new versions of the **move** and **request** actions:

Operator:
  move(Agent, Source, Destination)

can_do preconditions:
  at(Agent, Source)

want preconditions:
  want(Agent, move(Agent, Source, Destination))

Effects:
  not at(Agent, Source)
  at(Agent, Destination)

Operator:
  request(Speaker, Addressee, Action)

can_do preconditions:
  can_do(Addressee, Action)

  channel(Speaker, Addressee)

want preconditions:
  want(Speaker, request(Speaker, Addressee, Action))

Effects:
  believe(Addressee, want(Speaker, Action))

Now, imagine that we have a small world containing two agents, Sue and Alan, and two places, inside and outside of a given room. Sue and Alan are both initially in the room, but Sue wants Alan to go out. What should Sue do? Here is a possible description of the relevant world:

channel(Sue, Alan)

at(Alan, inside)
at(Sue, inside)

Intuitively, the answer is that Sue should request Alan to go out, using the **request** operator, and that Alan will then go out, using the **move** operator. But how can Sue establish that such a sequence of actions will actually work as intended? It is necessary to construct a proper plan. First of all, the goal of the plan is the following state of affairs:

at(Alan, outside)

Looking at the definition of the **move** operator, we can see that the instance **move(Alan, inside, outside)** will achieve the desired effect. Sue must therefore

ensure that the preconditions of this action are made true. The preconditions are:

> can_do preconditions:
>   at(Alan, inside)
>
> want preconditions:
>   want(Alan, move(Alan, inside, outside))

The can_do precondition is all right, but we do not initially have Alan
wanting to move. This is what the request action might be useful for. The
request operator, unfortunately, only gets the addressee to believe that the
speaker wants some action to take place. This is quite reasonable, because
asking someone to do something does not guarantee that they will actually
do it. So, we need to consider some other action that will bridge the gap. In
general, to have someone adopt your wants as theirs requires setting up a
cooperative relation, and we will not go into what this might involve.
Instead, we will assume an operator cause_to_want:

> Operator:
>   cause_to_want(Speaker, Addressee, Action)
>
> can_do preconditions:
>   can_do(Addressee, Action)
>   believe(Addressee, want(Speaker, Action))
>
> want preconditions:
>   <none>
>
> Effects:
>   want(Addressee, Action)

Unlike the previous operators, cause_to_want has no want preconditions.
This means that we can think of the action 'just happening' as soon
as it is enabled, without anyone having to actually do anything. Now, to
achieve want(Alan, move(Alan, inside, outside)), Sue can plan to have
cause_to_want(Sue, Alan, move(Alan, inside, outside)) take place. For this to be
all right, the preconditions must be made true. Firstly, Alan has to be able to
do the move action. Secondly, Alan must believe that Sue wants him to
move. This can be achieved by a request action, whose preconditions are
already true. The plan that has been built is shown in Figure 10.6.

    Now, although this might already seem a lot of work to decide to
make a simple request, we have in fact skirted around a number of
important issues. In particular, our representation has not been explicit
about all the beliefs of the agents. For Sue to plan to get Alan to move, it is
Sue who must know that Alan is able to move and that Alan is in the room. In
addition, Sue must believe that Alan knows that he is able to move and
that Alan knows where he is. We have skirted around such issues by

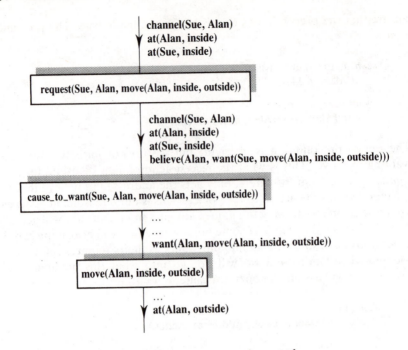

Figure 10.6   Plan to get Alan outside.

assuming that the facts about certain predicates, like **at**, **channel** and **can_do**, are universally known. Without this assumption, the plan is not valid. Of course, not all predicates are universally known – indeed, the whole point of this plan is that Sue's desires are not initially known to Alan.

Here is another example. Initially, there are two agents, Sue and Ann, with a communication channel between them. Ann knows the combination of a particular safe:

> **channel(Sue, Ann)**
> **channel(Ann, Sue)**
>
> **knows_ref(Ann, combination)**

Sue's objective is to know the combination herself:

> **knows_ref(Sue, combination)**

This time, the operator **inform_ref** is applicable. It involves one agent telling the other the value associated with some predicate, the predicate here being the combination of the safe:

Operator:
    inform_ref(Speaker, Addressee, Predicate)

can_do preconditions:
    knows_ref(Speaker, Predicate)
    channel(Speaker, Addressee)

want preconditions:
    want(Speaker, inform_ref(Speaker, Addressee, Predicate))

Effects:
    knows_told_ref(Addressee, Speaker, Predicate)

Now, if Sue plans to have inform_ref(Ann, Sue, combination) executed, the result of this will be only knows_told_ref(Sue, Ann, combination) – Sue will know the value that she has been told by Ann, but will not necessarily be sure that this is the correct value. As before, we need a special action that will transform this into Sue knowing the value, as follows:

Operator:
    convince_ref(Speaker, Addressee, Predicate)

can_do preconditions:
    knows_told_ref(Speaker, Addressee, Predicate)

want preconditions:
    <none>

Effects:
    knows_ref(Speaker, Predicate)

A complete plan, using the operators presented, is shown in Figure 10.7.
    Although these have both been very simple examples, the operators used seem to have some generality, and there is a real possibility that the generation of natural language utterances, at least at the illocutionary act level, might be planned by a computer system in the same way as it plans other actions in the world. Whether the notion of planning can be extended productively to the more detailed levels of linguistic realization is, however, still a relatively unexplored issue.
    lib plan implements a simple planner that can develop plans such as these two examples. Operators are represented in LISP as lists with four elements: the name of the operator, the can_do preconditions, the want preconditions and the effects. All but the first of these are lists of

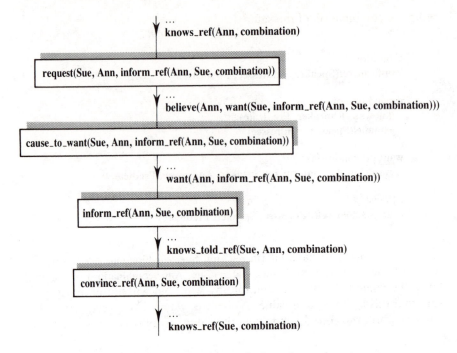

Figure 10.7   Plan for Sue to find out the combination.

propositions, so that we can express multiple preconditions and effects.
Here is our request operator in this notation:

```
((request _speaker _addressee _act)
  ((can_do _addressee _act) (channel _speaker _addressee))
  ((want _speaker (request _speaker _addressee _act)))
  ((believe _addressee (want _speaker _act))))
```

The program assumes that the global variable operators holds the list of all
the operators that it can use in forming plans, and it assumes that the initial
state of the world is represented in infrules, as required for lib bckinfer. Although
the planner plays the part of a particular agent in building the plan, and
therefore reasons within the beliefs of that agent, for convenience we will
express the world model in an impartial way, with all belief contexts
explicitly spelled out. Moreover, in presenting goals to the planner, we will
omit the (believe agent ...) that should surround each one. Of course, if the goals
involve predicates about which there is universal knowledge, then there is
no distinction anyway. So, here is an example of lib plan being used.
The function plan returns a list of action names, representing the sequence

of actions that should be performed (in the order given) to achieve the goal.

```
(setq infrules
 '(((channel sue alan))
   ((at alan inside))
   ((at sue inside))
   ((believe sue (wants alan (move sue inside outside))))))
(plan 'sue '((at alan outside)))

(TRYING DEPTH 0)
(TRYING DEPTH 1)
(TRYING DEPTH 2)
(TRYING DEPTH 3)
(TRYING DEPTH 4)
((INFORM SUE ALAN (WANT SUE (MOVE ALAN INSIDE OUTSIDE)))
 (CONVINCE SUE ALAN (WANT SUE (MOVE ALAN INSIDE OUTSIDE)))
 (CAUSE_TO_WANT SUE ALAN (MOVE ALAN INSIDE OUTSIDE))
 (MOVE ALAN INSIDE OUTSIDE))
```

Planning involves search, and the program uses the same technique as the simple recognizers of Chapter 5 to implement a depth-first search. That is, the top function plan calls another function, called plan_next, which, through its arguments, is given a complete description of a state in the planning process. Corresponding to each way of extending this state to a state that may be closer to a complete plan, plan_next calls itself recursively with the arguments expressing the new state. Thus, as with the recognizers, the search tree is echoed precisely in the calling tree of the program. A state of the planning process is represented by five different values:

(1) agent – the agent who is doing the planning.

(2) goals – the list of goals that still need to be made true, expressed without an explicit (believe agent...).

(3) actions – the list of actions that are planned to be executed, once the current goals have been made true.

(4) currentsubst – a substitution that expresses extra information about actions and goals, which has been obtained since they were originally formulated.

(5) depth, which we will discuss later.

If plan_next is ever called with goals as an empty list, then the planning is terminated and the list of actions accumulated at this point is returned as the plan. Otherwise, plan_next takes the first element of goals, goal, to work on.

The first main possibility to investigate is whether goal is already true. try_already_true is responsible for attempting to infer that the goal is already true and continuing planning from there if so. The other main possibility is that some action is necessary to make goal true. try_to_make_true is responsible for finding an action that would make the goal true and then planning for the preconditions of that action to be true:

```
(defun plan_next (agent goals actions currentsubst depth maxdepth)
  (if (null goals)
    (throw 'plan (apply_subst currentsubst actions))
    (if (> depth maxdepth)
      nil
      (let ((goal (apply_subst currentsubst (car goals))) (othergoals (cdr goals)))
        ...
        (progn
          (try_planners_own agent goal othergoals actions
            currentsubst depth maxdepth)
          (try_already_true agent goal othergoals actions
            currentsubst depth maxdepth)
          (try_to_make_true agent goal othergoals actions
            currentsubst depth maxdepth))))))
```

Since we are planning from the point of view of a particular agent, to see whether a goal is already true, we actually need to test whether the agent believes that it is true, unless the goal involves a predicate that is universally known. For each possible way that a true instance of the goal can be found, plan_next is called recursively with the rest of the goals and with a substitution that reflects any extra information obtained through finding the goal in the world model:

```
(defun try_already_true (agent goal goals actions currentsubst depth maxdepth)
  (let ((dbgoal
          (if (member (car goal) universal_knowledge)
            goal
            (list 'believe agent goal))))
    (dolist (subst (back_infer dbgoal))
      (plan_next agent goals actions
        (compose_substs subst currentsubst) depth maxdepth))))
```

Finally, try_to_make_true looks for an operator that could achieve the goal by one of its effects e. For each such operator, it tries planning to achieve the preconditions (can_dos and wants), again giving the recursive call to plan_next an augmented substitution which reflects the information obtained by matching goal with e.

```
(defun try_to_make_true (agent goal goals actions currentsubst depth maxdepth)
   (dolist (operator operators)
      (let ((o (rename operator)))
         (dolist (e (cadddr o)) ; the effects of the operator
            (let ((subst (termunify goal e)))
               (if subst
                  (plan_next agent (append (cadr o) (caddr o))
                     (cons (car o) actions)
                     (compose_substs subst currentsubst)
                     (1+ depth) maxdepth)))))))
```

Depth-first search is actually a bad search strategy for planning, because there are usually infinitely many ways of achieving a given goal and arbitrarily long plans to investigate. For instance, if Sue wants Alan to move out of the room, she could simply make a request, go out of the room and make the request, go out of the room, come back into the room and make the request, and so on. Depth-first search is unlikely to find the best plan, which is probably the shortest plan, and is liable to get into infinite loops trying to generate longer and longer plans. Because of this problem, the plan program uses a modified depth-first strategy as follows. Each time plan_next is called, a depth argument records how many actions are already in the actions list. Another argument maxdepth imposes a limit on how many actions are allowed in a plan, and any call to plan_next having a depth value already greater than this automatically returns without any solutions. The top level function plan first of all calls plan_next with maxdepth equal to 0, then with maxdepth equal to 1, then with maxdepth equal to 2, and so on, until a solution is found. Although this approach, known as *iterative deepening*, involves a lot of duplicated work, it does ensure that the program finds a shortest plan and does not get into infinite loops.

Although we have now covered the main part of the program, the program also deals with various special cases. For instance, to achieve (can_do <agent> <action>), it looks up the can_do preconditions for <action> and tries to achieve these. The planner also knows explicitly about the predicates concerning which there is universal knowledge.

The program implemented in lib plan is a restricted planner in the following way: it chains backwards from the desired goal to an action that will achieve that goal; then it looks for an unsatisfied precondition of that action and finds an action that will make that precondition true; then it looks for an unsatisfied precondition of that action; and so on, until an action is reached, all of whose preconditions are initially true. It then stops. At this point, the list of actions it has chained through gives a rough idea of a sequence of actions to be performed, but there is no guarantee that any but the first of these can actually be performed. It is quite possible, for instance, that a remaining unsatisfied precondition of one of the actions cannot be made true in any way. Or that for some reason one of the effects of carrying out one of the actions is to make one of the other actions impossible. The key feature of a planning system that this program lacks is the ability to reason properly about changes in the world that result from performing an action and how these interact with the preconditions and effects of other planned actions.

Exercise 10.11 Would it be possible to implement a planner by providing appropriate rules for an inference system? What are the relative complexities of planning and inference?   [*hard*]

Exercise 10.12 Consider the following redefinition of the **request** operator:

Operator:
   request(Speaker, Addressee, Action)

can_do preconditions:
   can_do(Addressee, Action)
   channel(Speaker, Addressee)

want preconditions:
   want(Speaker, done(Addressee, Action))

Effects:
   believe(Addressee, done(Speaker, request(Speaker, Addressee, Action)))
   believe(Speaker, done(Speaker, request(Speaker, Addressee, Action)))

Can this achieve everything achieved by the earlier definition? Is it preferable? What needs to be said about the **done** predicate?   [*intermediate*]

Exercise 10.13 lib plan comes with a set of operators that includes inform and convince, as well as the operators presented in the text. Use the program, with and without request included in the set of operators, to solve the examples given in the text and also the following example:

> There are three agents, Sue, Alan and Ann. Ann knows the combination of the safe, but nobody else does. Sue can communicate with Alan, and Alan can communicate with Ann, but Sue and Ann cannot communicate directly. Sue wants to know the combination. What should she do?

[*intermediate*]

10.9   Language understanding and plan recognition

We have discussed the planning view of language largely from the point of view of the speaker. But successful communication will only normally take place if the addressee is able to recognize the plans behind the speaker's utterances. Only then will the addressee be able to give genuinely cooperative responses and sensibly anticipate future utterances. The process of plan recognition is unfortunately relatively poorly understood. Nonetheless, it is a task of quite general usefulness. Plan recognition is obviously relevant in a conversational context, where one language user is trying to make sense of the utterances of another. It is also vital for the understanding of narratives about intelligent agents, such as:

> Sue Ellen wanted to take over El Paso Oil.
> She asked her secretary to call her banker.

Recognizing the (obvious-only-to-us) connections between such statements and making sensible predictions about what is likely to come next is vital for understanding, and any mechanism for doing this will largely subsume the very simple ideas for anticipating stereotyped sequences of events that we discussed earlier. In particular, if we observe or are told about an action, we can expect that the agent may have, as a goal, one of the effects of the action, and we can predict the occurrence of actions that have such effects as their preconditions. If we are told about an agent's unachieved goal, we can predict that the agent may perform actions that lead towards that goal being achieved.

There is a close similarity between hierarchical plan operators and phrase structure grammar rules, and plan recognition is in many ways akin to parsing. For instance, the hierarchical relations between certain operators can be fairly easily expressed by phrase structure rules:

```
Rule
    company_takeover → raise_funds buy_shares call_agm.

Word mortgage_property:
    <cat> = raise_funds.
Word sell_shares:
    <cat> = raise_funds.
```

One can also capture to a certain extent preconditions and effects of operators by adding features to the rules:

```
Rule {takeover}
    company_takeover → raise_funds buy_shares call_agm:
        <raise_funds resources before> = <company_takeover resources before>
        <raise_funds resources after> = <buy_shares resources before>
        <buy_shares resources after> = <call_agm resources before>
        <call_agm resources after> = <company_takeover resources after>.
```

```
Word mortgage_property:
    <cat> = raise_funds
    <resources before shares> = <resources after shares>
    <resources before funds> = low
    <resources after funds> = high
    <resources before property> = owned
    <resources after property> = loaned.
```

Exercise 10.14 Express some example planning operators in this notation and use a recognizer or parser to recognize simple plans, such as:

mortgage_property buy_shares call_agm

If you use a bottom-up chart parser, then you should be able to give partial sequences of actions, such as:

mortgage_property buy_shares

and read off from the chart hypotheses about what plans the actions might be part of. [*intermediate*]

SUMMARY

- Pragmatics concerns context-dependent aspects of utterance meaning.

- NPs have many different pragmatic functions.

- Utterances convey both given and new information.

- Given information is presupposed.

- Prediction can be used to fill in missing information.

- Scripts provide a very controlled form of prediction.

- Discourse structure can help to determine referents.

- Language generation involves planning to achieve goals.

- Language understanding involves recognizing the speaker's plan.

Further reading

This chapter fails to do justice to many aspects of pragmatics which NLP work has yet to come to grips with. Levinson (1983) provides an invaluable introduction to these, as well as providing much extra material on topics that this chapter has touched on, such as presupposition, speech acts and conversational sequencing. Leech (1983) provides an alternative perspective on a largely overlapping set of topics. From an NLP perspective, the only text with substantial coverage of pragmatic issues is Allen (1987, Part III), although Charniak and McDermott (1985, Chapter 10) and Tennant (1981, Chapter 7) contain useful material. The majority of the papers in Joshi *et al.* (1981) are relevant to one or more of the topics considered here, as are those in Grosz *et al.* (1986, Sections III, IV and V). For a cognitive science perspective on the area, see Johnson-Laird (1983, Chapter 14).

Partee (1970) outlines many of the problems connected with noun phrase interpretation that have preoccupied formal semantics researchers since the late 1960s – see, for example, Heny (1981), for a representative collection. One of the most promising recent developments in this connection is discourse representation theory (Kamp 1981) which has been investigated in an NLP context by Bartsch (1987), Hess (1987), Johnson and Klein (1986), Pinkal (1986), and Wada and Asher (1986). Mellish (1985) is a monograph largely devoted to the NLP problems that noun phrase interpretation gives rise to, and Hawkins (1978) is an invaluable source of data and discussion of the many subtle distinctions that are involved in such interpretation.

The treatment here of the given–new distinction and of the manner in which phrases inherit the presuppositions of their parts, known as the *projection problem*, concentrates on NLP concerns at the expense of glossing over many of the subtleties inherent in the phenomena. Van der Sandt (1988) gives a comprehensive account of the relevant facts, the previous literature and the problems, and offers an interesting new solution to the projection problem. Other relevant recent work includes Horton and Hirst (1988), Mercer and Reiter (1982), Mercer and Rosenberg (1984), and Mercer (1988).

Early versions of prediction can be found in Charniak (1973), Wilks (1975), and Schank and Rieger (1974). The original script applier program, SAM, is described in Cullingford (1981), but the version here is based more on the cut-down program Micro SAM presented in Schank and Riesbeck (1981). Dyer *et al.*(1987) provide an extended discussion of this line of work, together with plenty of further leads into the literature. See Charniak and Goldman (1988) for a state-of-the-art application of unification techniques to noun phrase referent determination via scripts.

A useful survey of work done in discourse understanding is provided by Scha *et al.* (1987). The compressor reassembly example is to be found in Grosz (1977), while Grosz and Sidner (1986) provide a more recent perspective on similar data, and Hajicôvá and Sgall (1985) look at the problem of focus identification. The role of focus in language generation provides a major theme for McKeown (1985).

Critiques of syntactic approaches to conversation and discourse are provided by Levinson (1981) and Garnham (1983), respectively. An early AI attempt to make sense of conversations in terms of the participants' purposes is reported in Power (1979). And one of the first workers to use plan recognition in NLP was Wilensky, who documents a number of approaches in Wilensky (1983). The action-planning approach to speech acts originates with papers such as Allen and Perrault (1980/1986), Allen (1983), and Cohen and Perrault (1979). In subsequent work, Cohen and Levesque (1985) have argued persuasively for eliminating the primitive status of acts such as requesting in favour of an analysis in terms of a logic of rational communication. Cohen (1984) provides a link between the action-planning work and the issues that arise in determining noun phrase referents, discussed earlier. Appelt (1985) and Houghton (1989) are monographs devoted to the planning approach to language generation. Other approaches to language generation are discussed by McDonald (1983) and Mann (1983).

APPENDIX

CODE LISTING

A.1 Introduction

The programs discussed in the text have been organized as a set of library files that can be loaded independently. A library file has a name that ends with .lsp and is generally referred to by the part of its name preceding this suffix. The code assumes the existence of two functions, uses and lib, which load the library file with a given name (expressed as a symbol). uses differs from lib, in that lib will always load the file, whereas uses will only load the file if it has not already been loaded. The definitions of lib and uses need to be installation dependent and ideally should be made immediately available to users of this material whenever they run LISP (LISP systems often provide such a facility, but in an implementation-dependent way). For concreteness, here is one possible set of definitions, which have been used on a machine running the UNIX operating system:

```
(defun lib (file)
  (load
    (concatenate 'string
      "$CLBOOK/Lisp/lib/"
      (string-downcase (symbol-name file))
      ".lsp"))
  (setf (get file 'loaded) t))

(defun uses (file)
  (cond
    ((get file 'loaded) t)
    (t (lib file))))
```

This definition of lib assumes that the library files have been stored in the directory '$CLBOOK/Lisp/lib'. It simply concatenates that directory name, the name provided and the .lsp suffix, loading the file with the resulting name. lib and uses use the loaded entry on a symbols property list to record whether the library file of that name has been loaded or not.

Using lib and uses, each library file makes sure that, when it is loaded, any other library files required are also automatically loaded. This is why most of the files start with commands like:

```
(uses 'subst)
```

A.2   Brief Description of some Common LISP facilities

Not all textbooks cover every single system function and special form provided by
Common LISP. For completeness, we describe below every feature of Common
LISP that we use in the library programs but which is omitted by either Touretzky
(1984) or Winston and Horn (1984).

A.2.1   Numbers

- (+ *number number*) – returns the sum of the two numbers.
- (– *number number*) – returns the difference of the two numbers.
- (' *number number*) – returns the product of the two numbers.
- (1+ *number*) – is the same as (+ *number* 1).
- (min *number number*) – returns the smaller of the two numbers.
- (random *integer*) – returns a random non-negative integer (whole number) less
  than the integer provided

A.2.2   Lists

- (butlast *list n*) – returns a list with the same elements as
  list, but omitting the last *n* elements (*n* is assumed
  to be 1 if it is not explicitly provided).
- (consp *object*) – tests whether its argument is a non-empty list.
- (ldiff *list sublist*) – returns the list of elements of *list* that
  appear before *sublist* (which must be a sublist of *list*).
- (nth *n list*) – returns the nth element of *list*
  (elements being numbered from 0 upwards).
- (second *list*) – the same as (nth 1 *list*).
- (nthcdr *n list*) – returns the result of applying cdr *n*
  times on *list*.
- (remove *item list*) – returns the same list as *list*,
  but with all occurrences of *item* removed.
- (getf *list indicator*) – *list* must be a property list
  (a list of alternating indicators and values). This function returns
  the value in *list* that occurs after *indicator*.

A.2.3   Strings, symbols and characters

- (char *string n*) – returns the nth character in *string*
  (characters being numbered from 0 upwards).
- (symbol-name *symbol*) – returns the print name of a symbol (a string).
- (symbolp *item*) – tests whether its argument is a symbol.
- (gensym *string*) – returns a completely new symbol whose print name
  has the given string as prefix.

A.2.4   Iteration

(dolist (*var list result*).*body*)

This causes the code in *body* to be executed repeatedly, with the variable *var* being bound to the successive elements of the list obtained by evaluating *list*. The result returned is the result of evaluating *result* (or is nil, if there is no result specified).

(do' ((*var1 init1 step1*) ...) (*end-test.result*).*body*)

This behaves exactly like do, except that the bindings of the variables are established in sequence, rather than in parallel. This means that the *init* and *step* expressions can make use of variables appearing earlier in the form. In addition, the step assignments are performed in sequence.

(loop *body*)

This causes the given *body* to be repeatedly evaluated. The repetition goes on indefinitely. Such a program will only terminate if the loop construct is exited via a construct like return or throw.

A.2.5   Errors

(error *string*)
(error *string item*)

Evaluating either of these forms causes an error to be signalled, with *string* printed out as an explanatory message. In the second case, *item* is also printed out, to appear in the message at the place marked by '~S' in *string*.

A.2.6   Other macros and special forms

(let' ((*var1 value1*) ...).*body*)

This form behaves exactly like let, except that the bindings of the variables are established in sequence, rather than in parallel. This means that the *value* expression can make use of variables appearing earlier in the form.

(catch *tag.body*)
(throw *tag result*)

The evaluation of a catch special form proceeds exactly as the evaluation of its *body*, unless a throw special form with the same *tag* is evaluated during that process. If this happens, the evaluation of the catch is prematurely aborted, and the catch form returns the *result* value specified in the throw.

(case *form* (*value1 . body1*) ... (*valuen.bodyn*))

This causes a different *body* to be evaluated, depending on the result of evaluating *form*. In this construction, the appropriate pieces of code are placed after the (implicitly quoted) values of *form* that they are applicable to. The special value 'otherwise' indicates a body to be evaluated if the result is not one of the other values specified.

>   (setf (get *symbol key*) *value*)

This form is used to assign *value* to the entry in *symbol*'s property list with the appropriate key; in other versions of LISP, this is achieved by a function called putprop.

A.2.7   Macro character sequences

The following macro sequences are used in the programs:

>   #\

is used to indicate a character with a given printed form. For instance #\a is a character that prints as 'a'.

>   #'

#'x is an abbreviation for (function *x*). If *x* is a symbol, it is used to get the functional value of that symbol; if *x* is a lambda expression, for the examples considered here, it behaves just like ordinary '.

>   #:

Symbols created by gensym are printed out preceded by this prefix. This indicates that the symbols are *uninterned*; that is, if such symbols are read in, multiple occurrences of the same name will give rise to different symbols.

The backquote acts like a normal quote, except that within the following expression a , unquotes the expression following it. Moreover, a ,@ causes the following expression, unquoted, to be evaluated as a list and its elements spliced into the constructed list, instead of the list being inserted as a single element.

A.3   Index of library files

This section lists the library files, the chapter reference, in [ ], and the contents of the file.

A.4   Index of procedures defined

This section lists the procedures defined, their chapter reference and their file of definition.

try_already_true	[10]	plan.lsp
try_planners_own	[10]	plan.lsp
try_to_achieve_can_do	[10]	plan.lsp
try_to_make_true	[10]	plan.lsp
unify	[4]	randgen.lsp
unify	[4]	randtree.lsp
unify	[7]	dagunify.lsp

A.5   Code listings

The following code listings are in alphabetical order of filenames.

```
;;; airdb1.lsp [Chapter 9] Example database about airline companies


;;; (located COMPANY COUNTRY)
;;; (bought COMPANY COMPANY)
;;; (subsidiary COMPANY COMPANY)

(defvar database)

(setq database
 '((located Air_Cal US)
   (located American_Airlines US)
   (located British_Airways England)
   (located British_Caledonian England)
   (located Cambrian_Airways Scotland)
   (located Carl_Icahn US)
   (located Continental US)
   (located Delta US)
   (located Eastern_Airlines US)
   (located Empire US)
   (located Frontier US)
   (located Hughes_Airwest US)
   (located National_Airlines US)
   (located Northwest US)
   (located Ozark US)
   (located Pan_Am_Pacific US)
   (located Pan_Am US)
   (located People_Express US)
   (located Piedmont US)
   (located Republic US)
   (located Scotair Scotland)
   (located Scottish_Airways Scotland)
   (located Texas_Air US)
   (located Trans_World_Airlines US)
   (located US_Air US)
   (located United_Airlines US)
   (located Virgin_Airways England)
   (located Western US)
```

```
(bought American_Airlines Air_Cal)
(bought British_Airways British_Caledonian)
(bought Carl_Icahn Trans_World_Airlines)
(bought Delta Western)
(bought Northwest Republic)
(bought Pan_Am National_Airlines)
(bought People_Express Frontier)
(bought Piedmont Empire)
(bought Republic Hughes_Airwest)
(bought Texas_Air Continental)
(bought Texas_Air Eastern_Airlines)
(bought Texas_Air People_Express)
(bought Trans_World_Airlines Ozark)
(bought United_Airlines Pan_Am_Pacific)
(bought US_Air Piedmont)

(subsidiary Scotair British_Caledonian)
(subsidiary Scotair British_Airways)
(subsidiary Cambrian_Airways British_Airways)
(subsidiary Scottish_Airways British_Airways)))
```

```
;;; airdb2.lsp [Chapter 9] Example rule base about airline companies
```

```
;;; (located COMPANY COUNTRY)
;;; (bought COMPANY COMPANY)
;;; (subsidiary COMPANY COMPANY)
;;; (airline COMPANY)
;;; (uk_based COMPANY)
;;; (us_based COMPANY)
;;; (subsidiary COMPANY)

(defvar infrules)

(setq infrules
 '(((located Air_Cal US))
   ((located American_Airlines US))
   ((located British_Airways England))
   ((located British_Caledonian England))
   ((located Cambrian_Airways Scotland))
   ((located Carl_Icahn US))
   ((located Continental US))
   ((located Delta US))
   ((located Eastern_Airlines US))
   ((located Empire US))
   ((located Frontier US))
   ((located Hughes_Airwest US))
   ((located National_Airlines US))
   ((located Northwest US))
   ((located Ozark US))
   ((located Pan_Am_Pacific US))
```

```
((located Pan_Am US))
((located People_Express US))
((located Piedmont US))
((located Republic US))
((located Scotair Scotland))
((located Scottish_Airways Scotland))
((located Texas_Air US))
((located Trans_World_Airlines US))
((located US_Air US))
((located United_Airlines US))
((located Virgin_Airways England))
((located Western US))

((bought American_Airlines Air_Cal))
((bought British_Airways British_Caledonian))
((bought Carl_Icahn Trans_World_Airlines))
((bought Delta Western))
((bought Northwest Republic))
((bought Pan_Am National_Airlines))
((bought People_Express Frontier))
((bought Piedmont Empire))
((bought Republic Hughes_Airwest))
((bought Texas_Air Continental))
((bought Texas_Air Eastern_Airlines))
((bought Texas_Air People_Express))
((bought Trans_World_Airlines Ozark))
((bought United_Airlines Pan_Am_Pacific))
((bought US_Air Piedmont))

((subsidiary Scotair British_Caledonian))
((subsidiary Scotair British_Airways))
((subsidiary Cambrian_Airways British_Airways))
((subsidiary Scottish_Airways British_Airways))

((airline Airline) (located Airline _x))

((uk_based Airline) (located Airline England))
((uk_based Airline) (located Airline Scotland))
((us_based Airline) (located Airline US))
((subsidiary Airline) (subsidiary Airline _x))
((subsidiary Airline1 Airline2) (bought Airline2 Airline1))))
```

```
;;; airlines.lsp [Chapter 8] PATR grammar, with semantics, for question answering
```

```
;;; extracting the useful information from a dag
```

```
(defun category (d subst)
    (find_feature_value 'sem d subst))
```

```
;;; building a parse tree - just keep the head category

(defun tree (cat subtrees) cat)

(setq lexical_rules
  '((Word (Delta)
          (cat) = NP
          (referent) = TWA
          (sem) = (hole))
    (Word (is independent)
          (cat) = VP
          (sem predicate) = independent
          (sem arg0) = (arg0))
    (Word (took over)
          (cat) = TV
          (sem predicate) = took_over
          (sem arg0) = (arg0)
          (sem arg1) = (arg1))
    (Word (airline)
          (cat) = N
          (sem predicate) = airline
          (sem arg0) = (referent))
    (Word (hotel chain)
          (cat) = N
          (sem predicate) = hotel_chain
          (sem arg0) = (referent))
    (Word (every)
          (cat) = Det
          (sem quantifier) = all)
    (Word (each)
          (cat) = Det
          (sem quantifier) = all)
    (Word (an)
          (cat) = Det
          (sem quantifier) = exists)
    (Word (a)
          (cat) = Det
          (sem quantifier) = exists)
    (Word (who)
          (cat) = NP
          (sem quantifier) = all
          (sem restriction) = (hole)
          (sem body action) = printout
          (sem body arg0) = (sem variable)
          (sem variable) = (referent))))


(setq rules
  '((Rule (S -> NP VP)
          (S cat) = S
          (NP cat) = NP
          (VP cat) = VP
          (S sem) = (NP sem)
          (NP hole) = (VP sem)
          (NP referent) = (VP arg0))
```

```
(Rule (VP -> TV NP)
      (VP cat) = VP
      (TV cat) = TV
      (NP cat) = NP
      (VP sem) = (NP sem)
      (NP hole) = (TV sem)
      (TV arg0) = (VP arg0)
      (TV arg1) = (NP referent))
(Rule (NP -> Det N)
      (NP cat) = NP
      (Det cat) = Det
      (N cat) = N
      (NP sem quantifier) = (Det sem quantifier)
      (NP sem variable) = (NP referent)
      (NP sem restriction) = (N sem)
      (NP sem body) = (NP hole)
      (N referent) = (NP referent))))
```

```
;;; atnarcs1.lsp [Chapter 3] Example ATN

(setq networks
 '((S
    ((Registers (pps auxs mood mainverb arg0 arg1))
     (Initial (0)        t ((setq pps ()) (setq auxs ())))
     (Final (3)          t ((list mood
                                   (append
                                    (list mainverb
                                       (list (quote arg0) arg0)
                                       (list (quote arg1) arg1)
                                    )
                                    pps))))
     (From 0 to 1 by NP  t ((setq arg0 star) (setq mood (quote add))))
     (From 1 to 2 by V   t ((setq mainverb star)))
     (From 2 to 2 by V   t ((setq auxs (cons mainverb auxs))
                              (setq mainverb star)))
     (From 2 to 3 by NP  t ((setq arg1 star)))
     (From 2 to 3 by |#| t ((setq arg1 ())))
     (From 3 to 3 by PP  t ((setq pps (cons star pps))))))
   (NP
    ((Registers (res))
     (Initial (0)        t ())
     (Final (1)          t (res))
     (From 0 to 1 by PN  t ((setq res star)))))
```

```
(PP
    ((Registers (p arg))
     (Initial (0)              t ())
     (Final (2)                t ((list p arg)))
     (From 0 to 1 by P         t ((setq p star)))
     (From 1 to 2 by NP   t ((setq arg star)))))))

(setq abbreviations
 '((PN abbreviates john mary susan peter)
   (P abbreviates with behind)
   (V abbreviates will see)))
```

```
;;; atnarcs2.lsp [Chapter 3] Extended ATN
```

```
(setq networks
 '(
 (S
    (
     (Registers (pps auxs mood mainverb arg0 arg1))
     (Initial (0)              t          ((setq pps ()) (setq auxs ()) (setq hold())))
     (Final (3) (null hold)               ((list mood
                                                (append
                                                    (list mainverb
                                                        (list (quote arg0) arg0)
                                                        (list (quote arg1) arg1)
                                                    )
                                                    pps))))
     (from 0 to 4 by V     t    ((setq mainverb star)))
     (From 4 to 2 by NP    t    ((setq arg0 star) (setq mood (quote search))))
     (From 0 to 1 by NP    t    ((setq arg0 star) (setq mood (quote add))))
     (From 1 to 4 by V     (equal arg0 (quote ?))
                                ((setq mainverb star) (setq hold t)))
     (From 1 to 2 by V     t    ((setq mainverb star)))
     (From 2 to 2 by V     t    ((setq auxs (cons mainverb auxs))
                                 (setq mainverb star)))
     (From 2 to 3 by NP    t    ((setq arg1 star)))
     (From 2 to 3 by |#|   t    ((setq arg1 nil)))
     (From 3 to 3 by PP    t    ((setq pps (cons star pps))))))
 (NP
    (
     (Registers (res))
     (Initial (0)              t          ())
     (Final (1)                t          (res))
     (From 0 to 1 by WH t    ((setq res (quote ?))))
     (From 0 to 1 by PN t    ((setq res star)))
     (From 0 to 1 by |#| hold    ((setq res (quote ?)) (setq hold nil)))))
```

```
(PP
  (
    (Registers (p arg))
    (Initial (0)            t        ())
    (Final (2)              t        ((list p arg)))
    (From 0 to 1 by P       t        ((setq p star)))
    (From 1 to 2 by NP      t        ((setq arg star)))))))
(setq abbreviations
 '(
   (PN abbreviates john mary susan peter)
   (P abbreviates with behind)
   (V abbreviates will see)
   (V abbreviates who what)))
```

```
;;;; atnrecog.lsp [Chapter 3] Parsing using an ATN
```

```
(uses 'fstape)      ;; for tape-moving functions
(defvar networks)
(defvar abbreviations)

;; Accessing portions of networks

(defun initial_nodes (net)
   (nth 1 (assoc 'Initial net)))

(defun initial_tests (net)
   (nth 2 (assoc 'Initial net)))

(defun initial_actions (net)
   (nth 3 (assoc 'Initial net)))

(defun final_nodes (net)
   (nth 1 (assoc 'Final net)))

(defun final_tests (net)
   (nth 2 (assoc 'Final net)))

(defun final_actions (net)
   (nth 3 (assoc 'Final net)))

(defun transitions (net)
   (cddr net))

(defun trans_node (transition)
   (getf transition 'From))

(defun trans_newnode (transition)
   (getf transition 'to))
```

```
(defun trans_label (transition)
   (getf transition 'by))

(defun trans_tests (transition)
   (nth 6 transition))

(defun trans_actions (transition)
   (nth 7 transition))

(defun get_network (name)
   (cadr (assoc name networks)))

(defun regs_used (net)
   (nth 1 (assoc 'Registers net)))

(defun initial_regs (net)
  (list
    (regs_used net)
    (mapcar #'not (regs_used net))))

;;; Stack accessing

(defun stacked_networkname (stack)
   (nth 0 (car stack)))

(defun stacked_node (stack)
   (nth 1 (car stack)))

(defun stacked_regs (stack)
   (nth 2 (car stack)))

(defun stacked_tests (stack)
   (nth 3 (car stack)))

(defun stacked_actions (stack)
   (nth 4 (car stack)))

;;; Top level of ATN interpreter

(defun atn_recognize (networkname tape)
  (catch
    'atn
    (let* (
       (network (get_network networkname))
       (regs_hold
         (doactions (initial_regs network) (initial_actions network) () ())))
      (dolist (initialnode (initial_nodes network))
        (atn_recognize_next
          networkname initialnode tape () (car regs_hold) (cadr regs_hold)))

;;; tape moving
(defun atn_recognize_move (label tape)
   (recognize_move label tape))

;;; Try all ATN traversals starting at a given node

(defun atn_recognize_next (networkname node tape stack regs hold)
  (if (member node (final_nodes (get_network networkname)))
    (atn_recognize_pop networkname tape stack regs hold))
```

```
(dolist (transition ((transitions (get_network networkname)))
  (if (equal (trans_node transition) node)
    (let ((label (trans_label transition))
      (newnode (trans_newnode transition)))
      (if (get_network label)
        ;; interpret label as network name
        (atn_recognize_push label networkname transition tape stack regs hold))
        ;; interpret label as symbol/abbreviation
        (atn_recognize_traverse label networkname transition tape stack regs hold)))))


(defun atn_recognize_pop (networkname tape stack regs hold)
  (if (dotests regs (final_tests (get_network networkname)) hold nil)
    (let (
      (star_newhold)
        (dopopactions regs (final_actions (get_network networkname)) hold nil)))
      (if (and (null stack) (null tape))
        ;; end of top-level network
        (throw 'atn (car star_newhold))
        (if (and stack
          ;; end of subsidiary network
          ;; do tests at end of original PUSH
          (dotests
            (stacked_regs stack)
            (stacked_tests stack)
            (cadr star_newhold)            ; hold
            (car star_newhold)))           ; star (result of POP)
          ;; execute actions at end of original PUSH
          (let ( (newregs_newhold
                  (doactions
                    (stacked_regs stack)
                    (stacked_actions stack)
                    (cadr star_newhold))))  ; hold
                  (car star_newhold))))     ; star
            ;; proceed in original network, using stacked values
            (atn_recognize_next
              (stacked_networkname stack)
              (stacked_node stack)
              tape
              (cdr stack)
              (car newregs_newhold)
              (cadr newregs_newhold)))))))))


(defun atn_recognize_push (label networkname transition tape stack regs hold)
  (let ((newnet (get_network label)))
    ;; try tests at start of proposed network
    (if (dotests (initial_regs newnet) (initial_tests newnet) hold nil)
      ;; execute actions at start of new network
      (let ((newregs_newhold
        (doactions
          (initial_regs newnet)
          (initial_actions newnet)
          hold
          nil)))
```

```
      ;; explore from all initial nodes
      (dolist (initialnode (initial_nodes newnet))
        (atn_recognize_next
          label
          initialnode
          tape
          (cons              ; new value of stack
            (list
              networkname                 ; network
              (trans_newnode transition)  ; destination node
              regs                        ; registers
              (trans_tests transition)    ; post tests
              (trans_actions transition)  ; post actions
              )
            stack)
          (car newregs_newhold)
          (cadr newregs_newhold)))))))

(defun atn_recognize_traverse (label networkname transition tape stack regs hold)
  ;; try moving the tape
  (dolist (newtape (recognize_move label tape))
    ;; set the star register
    (let ((star (diff_tape newtape tape)))
      ;; try the arc tests
      (if (dotests regs (trans_tests transition) hold star)
        (let (
          (newregs_newhold
            ;; execute the arc actions
            (doactions
              regs
              (trans_actions transition)
              hold
              star)))
          ;; continue from the destination node
          (atn_recognize_next
            networkname
            (trans_newnode transition)
            newtape
            stack
            (car newregs_newhold)
            (cadr newregs_newhold)))))))

(defun diff_tape (newtape oldtape)
  (if (equal newtape oldtape)
    '()
    (car oldtape)))

;;;; Actions and Tests

(defun dopopactions (regs expr hold star)
  (apply
    `(lambda ,(cons 'star (cons 'hold (car regs)))
      (list
        (let () ,@expr)
        hold))
    (cons star (cons hold (cadr regs)))))
```

```
(defun doactions (regs actions hold star)
  (apply
    `(lambda ,(cons 'star (cons 'hold (car regs)))
      ,@actions
      (list
        (list (quote ,(car regs))
          (list ,@(car regs))) hold))
    (cons star (cons hold (cadr regs)))
    )
)

(defun dotests (regs tests hold star)
  (apply
    `(lambda ,(cons 'star (cons 'hold (car regs)))
      ,tests)
    (cons star (cons hold (cadr regs)))
    )
)
```

```
;;; bckinfer.lsp [Chapter 9] Backwards inference engine
```

```
;;; N.B. NOT uses negation by failure

(uses 'subst)
(uses 'tunify)

(defvar infrules)
(defparameter YES (list empty_subst))

(defun back_infer (goal)
  (if (equal (car goal) 'and)
    (back_infer_all (cdr goal))
    (if (equal (car goal) 'true)
      (list YES)
      (if (and (equal (car goal) 'not) (equal (length goal) 2))
        (if (back_infer (cadr goal))
          nil
          (list YES))
        (let ((substs ()))
          (dolist (rule infrules substs)
            (setq substs
              (append
                (solutions_using_rule goal rule)
                substs)))))))))
```

```
(defun solutions_using_rule (goal rule)
  (let ((substs ()))
    (if (and
        (equal (caar rule) (car goal)) ; check same predicate
        (equal (length (car rule)) (length goal))) ; check same no of args
      (let*
        ((newrule (rename rule))
         (headsubst (termunify goal (car newrule))))
        (if headsubst ; check that conclusion of rule matches goal
          (dolist
            (bodysubst
              (back_infer_all
                (apply_subst headsubst (cdr newrule))))
            (setq substs
              (cons
                (compose_substs headsubst bodysubst)
                substs))))))
    substs))

(defun back_infer_all (goals)
  (if (null goals)
    (list empty_subst)
    (let ((substs ()))
      (dolist (subst1 (back_infer (car goals)))
        (dolist (subst2 (back_infer_all (apply_subst subst1 (cdr goals))))
          (setq substs
            (cons
              (compose_substs subst1 subst2)
              substs))))
      substs)))
```

```
;;; bubrecog.lsp [Chapter 5] Bottom-up, breadth-first recognition for a CF-PSG
```

```
(defvar rules)

;;; as in burecog

(defun rewrite (string LHS RHS)
  ;; returns a new string if the rule can rewrite it – or nil
  (if (null RHS)                    ; successful rewrite
    (cons LHS string)
    (if (null string)              ; end of string
      nil
      (if (equal (car string) (car RHS))
        (rewrite (cdr string) LHS (cdr RHS))
        nil))))                    ; rule does not match

(defun recognize (string)
  (do ((alternatives (list string))) ((null alternatives))
    (setq alternatives (next_states_list alternatives))))
```

```lisp
;;;; Given a list of states, append the next states from all
;;;; of them
(defun next_states_list (list)
  (if (null list)
    '()
    (append
      (next_states (car list))
      (next_states_list (cdr list)))))

;;;; Given a single state, make the list of next states
(defun next_states (string)
  (if (equal (length string) 1)
    (print (car string)))
  (do (
    (left () (append left (list (car remaining))))
    (remaining string (cdr remaining))
    (results ()))
    ((null remaining) results)       ; do until end of string
    (dolist (rule rules)
      (let ((newstring (rewrite remaining (car rule) (cdr rule))))
        (if newstring
          (setq results (cons (append left newstring) results)))))))
```

```lisp
;;;; buparse1.lsp [Chapter 5] Bottom-up parsing for a CF-PSG
```

```lisp
(defvar parses)
(defvar rules)
(defun initial_segment (goals string)
  ;; returns nil or a list (needed others)
  (do*
    (
    (restgoals goals (cdr restgoals))
    (needed nil (append needed (list (car reststring))))
    (reststring string (cdr reststring)))
    ((not (rule_item_match restgoals reststring))
    (if (null restgoals)
      (list needed reststring)
      nil))))

;;;; does the first item of a list of goals match
;;;; the first item in a string?
(defun rule_item_match (goals string)
  (and goals
    (or
      (and
        (consp (car goals))    ; category
        (consp (car string))   ; tree
        (equal (caar goals) (caar string)))
      (and
        (atom (car goals))     ; word
        (equal (car goals) (car string))))))
```

```
(defun next (string)
  (if (equal (length string) 1)
    (setq parses (cons (car string) parses))
    (do
      (
        (left nil (append left (list (car tape))))
        (tape string (cdr tape)))
      ((null tape))            ; do until end of tape
      (dolist (rule rules)
        (let ((needed_others (initial_segment (cdr rule) tape)))
          (if (null needed_others)
            nil                  ; rewrite failed
            (next (append left (list (cons (caar rule) (car needed_others))) (cadr needed_others)))))))))

(defun parse (string)
  (setq parses nil)
  (next string)
  parses)
```

```
;;;; buparse2.lsp [Chapter 5] Bottom-up parser CF-PSG with less redundancy
```

```
(defvar parses)
(defvar rules)

(defun next (string pos)
  (if (equal (length string) 1)
    (setq parses (cons (car string) parses))
    (do
      (
        (left nil (append left (list (car tape))))
        (len (length string) (- len 1))
        (newpos pos)
        (tape string (cdr tape)))
      ((null tape))                 ;; do until end of tape
      (setq newpos (min len newpos))
      (dolist (rule rules)
        (let ((needed_others (initial_segment (cdr rule) tape)))
          (if (and needed_others (< (length (cadr needed_others)) pos))
            (next (append left (list (cons (caar rule) (car needed_others)))
              (cadr needed_others)) newpos))))
      (if (atom (car tape))
        (setq tape nil)))))         ; quit loop

(defun initial_segment (goals string)
  ;; returns nil or a list (needed others)
  (do*
    (
      (restgoals goals (cdr restgoals))
      (needed nil (append needed (list (car reststring))))
      (reststring string (cdr reststring)))
```

```
    ((not (rule_item_match restgoals reststring))
    (if (null restgoals)
       (list needed reststring) nil))))

  ;;; does the first item of a list of goals match
  ;;; the first item in a string?

  (defun rule_item_match (goals string)
  (and goals
    (or
      (and
        (consp (car goals))        ;; category
        (consp (car string))       ;; tree
        (equal (caar goals) (caar string)))
      (and
        (atom (car goals))         ;; word
        (equal (car goals) (car string))))))

(defun parse (string)
  (setq parses nil)
  (next string (length string))
  parses)
```

```
;;; burecog.lsp [Chapter 5] Bottom-up recognition for a CF-PSG
```

```
(defun next (string)
  (if (equal string '((S)))
    (print '(yes))
    (do
      (
       (left nil (append left (list (car tape))))
       (tape string (cdr tape)))
      ((null tape))                          ; do until end of tape
      (dolist (rule rules)
        (let ((newstring (rewrite tape (car rule) (cdr rule))))
        (if (null newstring)
          nil                               ; rewrite failed
          (next (append left newstring))))))))

(defun rewrite (string LHS RHS)
  ;; returns a new string if the rule can rewrite it – or nil
  (if (null RHS)                            ; successful rewrite
    (cons LHS string)
    (if (null string)                       ; end of string
      nil
      (if (equal (car string) (car RHS))
        (rewrite (cdr string) LHS (cdr RHS)) nil))))     ; rule does not match
```

```
;;; cfpsgram.lsp [Chapter 4] Example context-free grammar in list format
```

```
(defvar rules)

(setq rules
  '(((S) (NP) (VP))
    ((VP) (V))
    ((VP) (V) (NP))
    ((V) died)
    ((V) employed)
    ((NP) nurses)
    ((NP) patients)
    ((NP) Medicenter)
    ((NP) Dr Chan)))
```

```
;;; chart.lsp [Chapter 6] Simple chart parser
```

```
;;; This file contains code for both top-down and bottom-up
;;; but the former is commented out

(defvar chart)
(defvar agenda)

;; an edge is a list of 5 elements :
;;      start finish label found tofind
(defun start (edge)
  (nth 0 edge))

(defun finish (edge)
  (nth 1 edge))

(defun label (edge)
  (nth 2 edge))

(defun found (edge)
  (nth 3 edge))

(defun tofind (edge)
  (nth 4 edge))

;;; add an edge to the chart, recording any new edges that may need
;;; to be added as a consequence

(defun add_edge (edge)
  (setq chart (cons edge chart))
  (if (null (tofind edge))                    ; added edge is inactive
    (progn
      (dolist (chartedge chart)
        (if (not (null (tofind chartedge)))   ; look for active edge
          (check_and_combine chartedge edge)))
      (inactive_edge_function edge))
```

```
      (progn                                ; otherwise added edge is active
        (dolist (chartedge chart)
          (if (null (tofind chartedge))          ; look for inactive edge
            (check_and_combine edge chartedge)))
        (active_edge_function edge))))

;;; try to combine an active and inactive edge
;;; using the fundamental rule
;;; add a new edge to agenda if these can combine

(defun check_and_combine (active_edge inactive_edge)
  (if
    (and
      (equal (start inactive_edge) (finish active_edge))
      (equal (label inactive_edge) (car (tofind active_edge))))
    (agenda_add
      (list                                ; new edge
        (start active_edge)
        (finish inactive_edge)
        (label active_edge)
        (append (found active_edge)
          (list
            (tree (label inactive_edge) (found inactive_edge))))
        (cdr (tofind active_edge))))))

;;; initialize the chart (bottom-up version)

(defun initialize_chart (goal string)
  (do* (
    (vertex 0 (+ vertex 1))
    (remaining string (cdr remaining))
    (word (car string) (car remaining)))
    ((null word))
    (agenda_add
      (list
        ;; (start finish label found tofind)
        vertex (+ 1 vertex) word nil nil))))

;;; top level function

(defun chart_parse (goal string)
  (setq agenda nil)
  (setq chart nil)
  (initialize_chart goal string)
  (do
    ( (edge (car agenda) (car agenda)) )
    ((null agenda))                        ;; do until agenda empty
    (setq agenda (cdr agenda))
    (add_edge edge))                       ;; add and combine edge with chart
  (let ((parses ()))
    (dolist (edge chart parses)
      (if (and
        (equal (start edge) 0)
        equal (finish edge) (length string))  ; end of string
        (equal (label edge) goal)           ; recognizes goal
        (null (tofind edge)))               ; edge complete
```

```
            (setq parses
              (cons
                (tree goal (found edge))        ; parse tree
                parses))))))
;;; bottom up parsing functions
(defun inactive_edge_function (edge)
  (dolist (rule rules)
    (if (equal (label edge) (cadr rule))        ; the first daughter in the rhs
      (agenda_add
        (list
          (start edge) (start edge) (car rule) nil (cdr rule))))))
(defun active_edge_function (edge) t)
;;; depth first search
(defun agenda_add (edge)
  (if  (or
        (already_in edge agenda)                ; left recursion check
        (already_in edge chart))
      nil                                        ; do not add to agenda
      (setq agenda (cons edge agenda))))         ; add to front of agenda
(defun already_in (edge edgelist)
  (member edge edgelist :test #'equal))
;;; building parse trees
(defun tree (cat subtrees)
  (if (consp cat)
    (cons (car cat) subtrees)
    cat))
;;; top down functions (commented out)
;;; remove the '(consp' line and the one marked below to release
;;; the top-down code
(consp '(
(defun inactive_edge_function (edge) t)
(defun active_edge_function (edge)
  (add_rules_to_expand (car (tofind edge)) (finish edge)))
(defun add_rules_to_expand (goal vertex)
  (dolist (rule rules)
    (if (equal goal (car rule))                  ; the lhs of the rule
      (agenda_add
        (list vertex vertex (car rule) nil (cdr rule))))))
(defun initialize_chart (goal string)
  (do* (
    (vertex 0 (+ vertex 1))
    (remaining string (cdr remaining))
    (word (car string) (car remaining)))
    ((null word))
    (agenda_add
      (list
        ;; (start finish label found tofind)
        vertex (+ 1 vertex) word nil nil    )))
  (add_rules_to_expand goal 0))
))      ;; remove this line to release the top-down code
```

```
;;; dagunify.lsp [Chapter 7] Unification for DAGs

(uses 'subst)

;;; This library file provides the following utilities for operating
;;; on dags:

;;;(get_value feature dag subst1) returns (value subst2)
;;;(combine_values value1 value2 substitution1) returns substitution2/nil;
;;;(find_feature_value feature dag substitution) returns value/'ANY;
;;;(unify dag1 dag2) returns substitution/nil;
;;;(simplify_features subst dag1) returns dag2;
;;;(put_value_in (feature value) dag subst1) returns (subst2 remainder_dag)

;;; Unification

(defun unify (dag1 dag2)
  (combine_values dag1 dag2 empty_subst))

(defun combine_values (dag1 dag2 substitution)
  (let* (
    (realdag1 (lookup_subst dag1 substitution))
    (realdag2 (lookup_subst dag2 substitution)))
   (if (equal realdag1 realdag2)
    substitution
    (if (isvar realdag1)
      (add_subst realdag1 realdag2 substitution)
      (if (isvar realdag2)
        (add_subst realdag2 realdag1 substitution)
        (if (and (listp realdag1) (listp realdag2))
          ;; make sure that everything in dag1 is in dag2
          (do
            ((subst substitution))
            ((isvar realdag1)
             ;; finally put the rest of dag2 at the end of dag1
             ;; (as long as subst is not nil)
             (and subst (add_subst realdag1 realdag2 subst)))
            (let* (
              (feature (caar realdag1))
              (value (lookup_subst (cadar realdag1) subst)))
             (if (equal feature '&)
               (setq realdag1 value)
               (let (
                 (subst_dag2 (put_value_in (list feature value) realdag2 subst)))
                (setq realdag2 (cadr subst_dag2))
                (setq subst (car subst_dag2))
                (setq realdag1 (cdr realdag1))
                (if (null subst) (return nil))))))
          nil))))))

;;; Go through a dag and add the feature-value pair in FPAIR,
;;; adding to the substitution substitution
;;; if necessary. This function returns in a list:
```

```
;;;
;;;   a) the new value of substitution
;;;   b) the rest of the dag
;;;       (i.e. everything except that one feature-value pair)

(defun put_value_in (fpair dag substitution)
  (let*
    ((realdag (lookup_subst dag substitution)))
    (if (consp realdag)
      (let ((value (assoc (car fpair) realdag)))
        (if value
          ;; dag already has a value for that feature
          (list
            (combine_values (cadr value) (cadr fpair) substitution)
            (delete_feature_entry (car fpair) realdag))
          ;; try the continuation entry
          (let (
            (rest (lookup_subst (cadar (last realdag)) substitution))
            (first (butlast realdag)))
            (if (isvar rest)
              ;; continuation is empty
              (let ((newrest (newvar)))
                (list
                  (add_subst rest (list fpair (list '& newrest)) substitution)
                  (append first (list (list '& newrest)))))
              ;; continuation non-empty - recurse
              (let ((subst_rest (put_value_in fpair rest substitution)))
                (list
                  (car subst_rest)
                  (append first (cadr subst_rest))))))))
      (if (isvar realdag)
        ;; variable as dag - add to substitution
        (let ((newrest (newvar)))
          (list
            (add_subst realdag (list fpair (list '& newrest)) substitution)
            (list (list '& newrest))))
        (error "Cannot find feature value in atom ~S" (list (car fpair) dag))))))

;;; delete the entry for a given feature in a dag
;;; (guaranteed to come before the continuation entry)

(defun delete_feature_entry (feature dag)
  (if (equal feature (caar dag))
    (cdr dag)
    (cons (car dag) (delete_feature_entry feature (cdr dag)))))

;;; Get value of a feature, adding to the substitution if necessary
;;; return a list consisting of a value and a new substitution

(defun get_value (feature dag substitution)
  (let* (
    (realdag (apply_subst substitution dag))
    (value (and (consp realdag) (assoc feature realdag))))
    (if value
      (list (cadr value) substitution)
```

```lisp
(if (isvar realdag)
    (let* ((newrest (newvar)) (newvalue (newvar)))
      (list
        newvalue
        (add_subst
          realdag
          (list (list feature newvalue) (list '& newrest))
          substitution)))
    (if (consp realdag)
        (let ((rest (apply_subst substitution (cadar (last realdag)))))
          (if (isvar rest)
              (let* ((newrest (newvar)) (newvalue (newvar)))
                (list
                  newvalue
                  (add_subst
                    rest
                    (list (list feature newvalue) (list '& newrest))
                    substitution)))
              (get_value feature rest substitution)))
        '(() ())))))))

;;; find the value associated with a feature in a dag
;;; return ANY if there is no recorded value

(defun find_feature_value (feature dag substitution)
  (let ((realdag (lookup_subst dag substitution)))
    (if (consp realdag)
      (let
        ((value (assoc feature realdag)))
        (if value
          (lookup_subst (cadr value) substitution)
          (let ((rest (lookup_subst (cadar (last realdag)) substitution)))
            (if (isvar rest)
              'ANY
              (find_feature_value feature rest substitution)))
        ))
      'ANY)))

;;; Version of apply_subst which produces a
;;; new version of a dag which has all the remainders
;;; 'flattened out'

(defun simplify_features (substitution dag)
  (let ((realdag (lookup_subst dag substitution)))
    (if (consp realdag)
      (simplify_features_list substitution realdag)
      realdag)))

(defun simplify_features_list (substitution dag)
  (if (null dag)
    '()
    (if (equal (caar dag) '&)
      (let ((remainder (lookup_subst (cadar dag) substitution)))
        (if (isvar remainder)
          (list (list '& remainder))
          (simplify_features_list substitution remainder)))
```

```
(cons
    (list (caar dag) (simplify_features substitution (cadar dag)))
    (simplify_features_list substitution (cdr dag))))))))
```

```
;;; dbq.lsp [Chapter 9] Database query language evaluator
```

```
;;; N.B. (because of negation as failure) some kinds of
;;; queries return no bindings but only success/failure

(uses 'subst)
(uses 'tunify)
(defvar database)

;;; return a list of substitutions

(defparameter NO nil)
(defparameter YES (list empty_subst))

(defun query (formula)
  (if (listp formula)
    (case (car formula)
      (all
        (process_all
          (cadr formula)            ; x
          (caddr formula)           ; p1
          (caddr (cdr formula))))   ; p2
      (exists
        (process_exists
          (cadr formula)            ; x
          (caddr formula)           ; p1
          (caddr (cdr formula))))   ; p2
      (and
        (process_and
          (cadr formula)            ; p1
          (caddr formula)))         ; p2
      (or
        (process_or
          (cadr formula)            ; p1
          (caddr formula)))         ; p2
      (not
        (process_not
          (cadr formula)))          ; p1
      (true
        YES)                        ; return true
      (printout
        (print (cadr formula)) YES) ; return true
      (otherwise (retrieve_all formula)))
    (retrieve_all formula)))
```

```lisp
(defun process_all (x p1 p2)
  (dolist (subst (query p1) YES)
    (if (equal (lookup_subst x subst) x)
        (error "ALL condition doesnt bind variable ~S" (list x p1)))
    (if (null
          (query
            (apply_subst
              (add_subst x (lookup_subst x subst) empty_subst)
              p2)))
        (return NO))))

(defun process_exists (x p1 p2)
  (dolist (subst (query p1) NO)
    (if (equal x (lookup_subst x subst))
        (error "EXISTS condition doesnt bind variable ~S" (list x p1)))
    (if (query
          (apply_subst
            (add_subst x (lookup_subst x subst) empty_subst) p2))
        (return YES))))

(defun process_and (p1 p2)
  (let ((results ()))
    (dolist (subst1 (query p1))
      (dolist (subst2 (query (apply_subst subst1 p2)))
        (setq results
          (cons
            (compose_substs subst1 subst2)
            results))))
    results))

(defun process_or (p1 p2)
  (append (query p1) (query p2)))

(defun process_not (p1)
  (if (null (query p1))
      YES
      NO))

(defun retrieve_all (formula)
  (let ((results ()))
    (dolist (term database results)
      (let ((subst (termunify term formula)))
        (if subst
            (setq results (cons subst results)))))))
```

;;; disambig.lsp [Chapter 8] PATR grammar showing disambiguation by semantic features

---

;;; This grammar illustrates the use of semantic markers to
;;; reduce the number of parses
;;; E.g. it only produces one analysis of each of the following
;;;   get a screwdriver with a narrow blade
;;;   get a screwdriver with your left hand

```
(setq rules
 '((Rule (VP -> TV NP)
        (VP cat) = VP
        (TV cat) = TV
        (NP cat) = NP
        (TV arg1 type) = (NP type))
  (Rule (VP1 -> VP2 PP)
        (VP1 cat) = VP
        (VP2 cat) = VP
        (PP cat) = PP
        (PP arg0 type) = action)
  (Rule (PP -> P NP)
        (PP cat) = PP
        (P cat) = P
        (NP cat) = NP
        (PP arg0 type) = (P arg0 type)
        (P arg1 type) = (NP type))
  (Rule (NP -> Det NB)
        (NP cat) = NP
        (Det cat) = Det
        (NB cat) = NB
        (NP type) = (NB type))
  (Rule (NP1 -> NP2 PP)
        (NP1 cat) = NP
        (NP2 cat) = NP
        (PP cat) = PP
        (NP1 type) = (NP2 type)
        (PP arg0 type) = (NP2 type))
  (Rule (NB -> N)
        (NB cat) = NB
        (N cat) = N
        (NB type) = (N type))
  (Rule (NB1 -> Adj NB2)
        (NB1 cat) = NB
        (Adj cat) = Adj
        (NB2 cat) = NB
        (NB1 type) = (Adj arg0 type)
        (NB1 type) = (NB2 type))))

(setq lexical_rules
 '((Word (with)
        (cat) = P
        (arg0 type) = action
        (arg1 type major) = physobj
        (arg1 type minor) = instrument)
  (Word (with)
        (cat) = P
        (arg0 type major) = physobj
        (arg1 type major) = physobj
        (arg1 type minor) = component)
  (Word (get)
        (cat) = TV
        (arg1 type major) = physobj)
```

```
(Word (a)
       (cat) = Det)
(Word (your)
       (cat) = Det)
(Word (screwdriver)
       (cat) = N
       (type major) = physobj)
       (Word (hand)
       (cat) = N
       (type major) = physobj
       (type minor) = instrument)
(Word (blade)
       (cat) = N
       (type major) = physobj
       (type minor) = component)
(Word (narrow)
       (cat) = Adj
       (arg0 type major) = physobj)
(Word (left)
       (cat) = Adj
       (arg0 type major) = physobj)))

(defun category (d subst)
   (find_feature_value 'cat d subst))

(defun tree (cat subtrees)
   (cons cat subtrees))
```

```
;;; eng_fre1.lsp [Chapter 2] Simple FST for English–French translation

(defvar eng-fre1)

(setq eng_fre1
 '((Initial (1))
   (Final (5))
   (From 1 to 2 by WH)
   (From 2 to 3 by BE)
   (From 3 to 4 by DET)
   (From 4 to 5 by NOUN)))

(setq abbreviations
 '((WH (where ou))
   (BE (is est))
   (DET (the |#|))
   (NOUN (exit la_sortie) (policeman le_gendarme)
         (shop la_boutique) (toilet la_toilette))))
```

```
;;; eng_fre2.lsp [Chapter 3] Simple PT for English–French translation
```

```lisp
(defvar networks)

(setq networks
 '((S
      ((Initial  (0))
       (Final    (2))
       (From 0 to 1 by NP)
       (From 1 to 2 by VP)))
   (NP
      ((Initial  (0))
       (Final    (2))
       (From 0 to 1 by DET-FEMN)
       (From 1 to 2 by N-FEMN)
       (From 0 to 4 by DET-MASC)
       (From 4 to 2 by N-MASC)
       (From 2 to 3 by WH)
       (From 3 to 2 by VP)))
   (VP
      ((Initial  (0))
       (Final 1 2))
       (From 0 to 1 by V)
       (From 1 to 2 by NP)
       (From 1 to 3 by (that que))
       (From 3 to 2 by S)))))

(setq abbreviations
 '((N-MASC (man homme) (horse cheval))
   (N-FEMN (house maison) (table table))
   (NP (John Jean) (Mary Marie) (Jean Jeanne))
   (DET-MASC (a un) (the le) (this ce))
   (DET-FEMN (a une) (the la) (this cette))
   (V (sees voit) (hits frappe) (sings chante) (lacks manque))
   (WH (who qui) (which qui) (that qui))))
```

```
;;; english1.lsp [Chapter 2] FSTN for a fragment of English
```

```lisp
(defvar english1)

(setq english1
 '((Initial (1))
   (Final (9))
   (From 1 to 3 by NP)
   (From 1 to 2 by DET)
   (From 2 to 3 by N)
   (From 3 to 4 by BV)
   (From 4 to 5 by ADV)
   (From 4 to 5 by |#|)
```

```
     (From 5 to 6 by DET)
     (From 5 to 7 by DET)
     (From 5 to 8 by |#|)
     (From 6 to 6 by MOD)
     (From 6 to 7 by ADJ)
     (From 7 to 9 by N)
     (From 8 to 8 by MOD)
     (From 8 to 9 by ADJ)
     (From 9 to 4 by CNJ)
     (From 9 to 1 by CNJ)))

(setq abbreviations
 '((NP kim sandy lee)
   (DET a the her)
   (N consumer man woman)
   (BV is was)
   (CNJ and or)
   (ADJ happy stupid)
   (MOD very)
   (ADV often always sometimes)))
```

```
;;; english2.lsp [Chapter 3] RTN for a fragment of English
```

```
(defvar networks)
(setq networks
 '((S
       ((Initial  (0))
        (Final    (2))
        (From 0 to 1 by NP)
        (From 1 to 2 by VP)))
   (NP
       ((Initial  (0))
        (Final    (2))
        (From 0 to 1 by DET)
        (From 1 to 2 by N)
        (From 2 to 3 by WH)
        (From 3 to 2 by VP)))
   (VP
       ((Initial  (0))
        (Final (1 2))
        (From 0 to 1 by V)
        (From 1 to 2 by NP)
        (From 1 to 3 by that)
        (From 3 to 2 by S)))))

(setq abbreviations
 '((N woman horse table mouse man)
   (NP Mayumi Maria Washington John Mary)
   (DET a the that)
   (V sees hits sings lacks saw)
   (WH who which that)))
```

```
;;; europe.lsp [Chapter 9] Example database for question answering

;;; (border COUNTRY1 COUNTRY2)
;;; (country COUNTRY POPULATION CAPITAL)

(defvar database)

(setq database
 '((border portugal spain)
   (border spain portugal)
   (border spain andorra)
   (border andorra spain)
   (border spain france)
   (border france spain)
   (border andorra france)
   (border france andorra)
   (border france luxembourg)
   (border luxembourg france)
   (border france belgium)
   (border belgium france)
   (border france germany)
   (border germany france)
   (border france switzerland)
   (border switzerland france)
   (border france italy)
   (border italy france)
   (border belgium netherlands)
   (border netherlands belgium)
   (border luxembourg belgium)
   (border belgium luxembourg)
   (border belgium germany)
   (border germany belgium)
   (border luxembourg germany)
   (border germany luxembourg)
   (border germany switzerland)
   (border switzerland germany)
   (border germany austria)
   (border austria germany)
   (border switzerland austria)
   (border austria switzerland)
   (border switzerland italy)
   (border italy switzerland)
   (border austria italy)
   (border italy austria)
   (country portugal 92 lisbon)
   (country spain 505 madrid)
   (country andorra 1 andorra)
   (country france 547 paris)
   (country belgium 31 brussels)
   (country luxembourg 1 luxembourg)
   (country netherlands 41 amsterdam)
   (country germany 249 bonn)
   (country switzerland 41 berne)
```

```
(country austria 84 vienna)
(country italy 301 rome)))
```

;;; families.lsp [Chapter 9] Inference rules for family relationships

---

```
(defvar infrules)

(setq infrules
 '(((aunt _x _y) (married _x _z) (uncle _z _y))
  ((aunt _x _y) (nephew _y _x) (female _x))
  ((aunt _x _y) (niece _y _x) (female _x))
  ((aunt _x _y) (sibling _x _z) (parent _z _y) (female _x))
  ((brother _x _y) (sibling _x _y) (male _x))
  ((brother_in_law _x _z) (brother _x _y) (married _y _z))
  ((brother_in_law _x _z) (husband _x _y) (sibling _y _z))
  ((child _x _y) (parent _y _x))
  ((child _x _z) (child _x _y) (married _y _z))
  ((child _x _y) (daughter _x _y))
  ((child _x _y) (son _x _y))
  ((cousin _x _y) (cousin _y _x))
  ((cousin _x _y) (parent _z _x) (aunt _z _y))
  ((cousin _x _y) (parent _z _x) (nephew _y _z))
  ((cousin _x _y) (parent _z _x) (niece _y _z))
  ((cousin _x _y) (parent _z _x) (uncle _z _y))
  ((daughter _x _y) (female _x) (child _x _y))
  ((daughter_in_law _x _z) (married _x _y) (son _y _z))
  ((father _x _y) (parent _x _y) (male _x))
  ((father_in_law _x _z) (father _x _y) (married _y _z))
  ((female _x) (aunt _x _y))
  ((female _x) (daughter _x _y))
  ((female _x) (daughter_in_law _x _y))
  ((female _x) (grandmother _x _y))
  ((female _x) (married _x _y) (male _y))
  ((female _x) (mother _x _y))
  ((female _x) (mother_in_law _x _y))
  ((female _x) (niece _x _y))
  ((female _x) (sister _x _y))
  ((female _x) (sister_in_law _x _y))
  ((female _x) (wife _x _y))
  ((grandfather _x _y) (grandparent _x _y) (male _x))
  ((grandmother _x _y) (grandparent _x _y) (female _x))
  ((grandparent _x _z) (parent _x _y) (parent _y _z))
  ((husband _x _y) (wife _y _x))
  ((husband _x _y) (male _x) (married _x _y))
  ((male _x) (brother _x _y))
  ((male _x) (brother_in_law _x _y))
  ((male _x) (father _x _y))
  ((male _x) (father_in_law _x _y))
  ((male _x) (grandfather _x _y))
  ((male _x) (husband _x _y))
```

```
((male _x) (married _x _y) (female _y))
((male _x) (nephew _x _y))
((male _x) (son _x _y))
((male _x) (son_in_law _x _y))
((male _x) (uncle _x _y))
((married _x _y) (married _y _x))
((married _x _y) (husband _x _y))
((married _x _y) (wife _x _y))
((mother _x _y) (parent _x _y) (female _x))
((mother_in_law _x _z) (mother _x _y) (married _y _z))
((nephew _x _y) (aunt _y _x) (male _x))
((nephew _x _y) (uncle _y _x) (male _x))
((niece _x _y) (aunt _y _x) (female _x))
((niece _x _y) (uncle _y _x) (female _x))
((parent _x _y) (child _y _x))
((parent _x _z) (married _x _y) (parent _y _z))
((parent _x _y) (father _x _y))
((parent _x _y) (mother _x _y))
((parent _x _y) (parent _x _z) (sibling _y _z))
((sibling _x _y) (brother _x _y))
((sibling _x _y) (parent _z _x) (parent _z _y) (distinct _x _y))
((sibling _x _y) (sibling _y _x))
((sibling _x _y) (sister _x _y))
((sister _x _y) (sibling _x _y) (female _x))
((sister_in_law _x _z) (sister _x _y) (married _y _z))
((sister_in_law _x _z) (wife _x _y) (sibling _y _z))
((son _x _y) (male _x) (child _x _y))
((son_in_law _x _z) (married _x _y) (daughter _y _z))
((uncle _x _y) (married _x _z) (aunt _z _y))
((uncle _x _y) (nephew _y _x) (male _x))
((uncle _x _y) (niece _y _x) (male _x))
((uncle _x _y) (sibling _x _z) (parent _z _y) (male _x))
((wife _x _y) (husband _y _x))
((wife _x _y) (female _x) (married _x _y))))
```

```
;;; fburecog.lsp [Chapter 7] Bottom-up recognition for PATR grammars
```

```
(uses 'lisppatr)

(defvar rules)
(defvar lexical_rules)
(defvar parses)

(defun next (string pos)
  (if (equal (length string) 1)
    (setq parses
      (cons (category (car string) empty_subst) parses))
```

```lisp
(do (
   (len (length string) (-len 1))
   (left nil (append left (list (car tape))))
   (newpos pos)
   (tape string (cdr tape)))
  ((null tape))
  (setq newpos (min len newpos))
  (if (atom (car tape))
    (progn
      (if (< (length (cdr tape)) newpos)
        (dolist (rule lexical_rules)
          (let ((subst_others (rhs_match tape rule)))
            (if (car subst_others)
              (next
                (append left (cadr subst_others))
                (length (cadr subst_others)))))))
      (setq tape nil)) ; quit loop
    (dolist (rule rules)
      (let* (
        (subst_others (rhs_match tape rule))
        (others (cadr subst_others)))
        (if (and
            (car subst_others)
            (< (-(length others) 1) newpos))
          (next
            (apply_subst
              (car subst_others)
              (append left others))
            (length others)))))))

;;;; return the list of categories recognized

(defun recognize (string)
  (setq parses nil)
  (next string (length string))
  parses
  )
```

```lisp
;;; fchart.lsp [Chapter 7] Chart parser for PATR grammars


;;; A version that does topdown with lexical lookup bottom-up
;;;
(uses 'lisppatr)
(uses 'subsumes)

(defvar rules)
(defvar lexical_rules)
(defvar chart)
(defvar agenda)
(defvar existing_goals)
```

```
;;; existing_goals is used to hold a dag of the form
;;;    ((goal c)(vertex s)(& ...)),
;;; where c is a category and s a starting position
;;; in the chart. The presence of one of these in existing_goals
;;; indicates that we have already tried (topdown) looking for instances
;;; of the specified category starting at the specified position

;; an edge is a list of 5 elements :
;;      start finish label found tofind
(defun start (edge)
   (nth 0 edge))

(defun finish (edge)
   (nth 1 edge))

(defun label (edge)
   (nth 2 edge))

(defun found (edge)
   (nth 3 edge))

(defun tofind (edge)
   (nth 4 edge))

;;; add an edge to the chart, recording any new edges that may need
;;; to be added as a consequence

(defun add_edge (edge)
   (setq chart (cons edge chart))
   (if (null (tofind edge)) ; added edge is inactive
      (progn
         (dolist (chartedge chart)
            (if (not (null (tofind chartedge)))          ; an active edge
               (check_and_combine chartedge edge)))
         (inactive_edge_function edge))
      (progn ; otherwise added edge is active
         (dolist (chartedge chart)
            (if (null (tofind chartedge))                ; an inactive edge
               (check_and_combine edge chartedge)))
         (active_edge_function edge))))

;;; try to combine an active and inactive edge
;;; using the fundamental rule
;;; add a new edge to agenda if these can combine

(defun check_and_combine (active_edge inactive_edge)
   (if (equal (start inactive_edge) (finish active_edge))
      (let ((subst (unify (label inactive_edge) (car (tofind active_edge)))))
         (if subst
            (let (
               (subtrees
                  (append (found active_edge)
                     (list
                        (tree
                           (category (label inactive_edge) subst)
                           (found inactive_edge))))))
```

```lisp
          (agenda_add
            (rename
              (apply_subst subst
                (list                            ;; new edge
                  (start active_edge)
                  (finish inactive_edge)
                  (label active_edge)
                  subtrees
                  (cdr (tofind active_edge)))))))))))
```

`;;; initialize the chart (top-down version)`

```lisp
(defun initialize_chart (goal string)
  ;; add lexical edges
  ;; try each lexical rule in turn on each position in the chart
  ;; this is inefficient
  (do (
    (restwords string (cdr restwords))
    (vertex 0 (+ 1 vertex)))
    ((null restwords))
    (dolist (rule lexical_rules)
      (let ((subst_others (rhs_match restwords rule)))
        (if (car subst_others)                   ; if subst not nil
          (let ((needed (ldiff restwords (cdadr subst_others))))
            (agenda_add
              (list
                vertex
                (+ vertex (length needed))
                (rename (caadr subst_others))
                needed
                nil)))))))
  ;; add goal edge
  (add_rules_to_expand goal 0))
```

`;;; top level function`

```lisp
(defun chart_parse (goal string)
  (setq agenda nil)
  (setq chart nil)
  (setq existing_goals nil)
  (initialize_chart goal string)
  (do
    ((edge (car agenda) (car agenda)))
    ((null agenda))
    ;; do until agenda empty
    (setq agenda (cdr agenda))
    (add_edge edge)
    ;; add and combine edge with chart
    )
  (let ((parses ())) ; find complete parses
    (dolist (edge chart parses)
      (if (and
        (equal (start edge) 0)
        (equal (finish edge) (length string))    ; end of string
        (null (tofind edge))                     ; edge complete
        (unify (label edge) goal))               ; recognizes goal
```

```
        (setq parses
         (cons
          (tree
            (category (label edge) empty_subst)
            (found edge))
          parses))))))

;;; other top-down parsing functions
;;; (no bottom-up operations here)

(defun inactive_edge_function (x) t)

;;; The topdown rule
;;;
;;; The topdown rule is invoked when an edge requiring a next phrase of
;;; category subgoal is added. Now subgoal may be a very general
;;; category and hence not subsumed by any category already recorded in
;;; existing_goals. When subgoal is unified with the LHS of a rule,
;;; however, the result will be more specific and may be subsumed by
;;; an existing goal. So subsumption by an existing goal is tested
;;; after unification with the LHS of a rule. On the other hand, once
;;; all the rules have been through, all ways of finding an instance
;;; of the original subgoal category have been tried, and so
;;; it is this general category that is put into a new entry in
;;; existing_goals

(defun active_edge_function (edge)
  (add_rules_to_expand (car (tofind edge)) (finish edge)))

(defun add_rules_to_expand (goal vertex)
  (dolist (rule rules)
    (let
      ((subst_rhs (lhs_match goal rule)))
      (if (not (null (car subst_rhs)))
        (let* (
          (LHS (apply_subst (car subst_rhs) goal))
          (RHS (cadr subst_rhs)))
          (if (not (subsumed_goal LHS vertex))
          ;; if goal not subsumed, add the new edge,
          ;; renaming so that it can combine with other
          ;; edges from rules using the same variable
          ;; symbols (e.g. edges from the same rule that just
          ;; produced it)
          (agenda_add
            (rename
              (list
                vertex
                vertex
                LHS
                nil
                RHS))))))))
  (record_goal goal vertex))

;;; look to see whether a particular category, or one more
;;; general than it, has been looked for at a given vertex
```

```lisp
(defun subsumed_goal (goal vertex)
  (let ((goaldag
      (list
        (list 'goal goal)
        (list 'vertex vertex)
        (list '& (newvar)))))
    (dolist (g existing_goals nil)
      (if (subsumes g goaldag)
        (return t)))))
```

```
;;; record that a particular category has been searched for
;;; at a given vertex
```

```lisp
(defun record_goal (goal vertex)
  (setq existing_goals
    (cons
      (list
        (list 'goal goal)
        (list 'vertex vertex)
        (list '& (newvar)))
      existing_goals)))
```

```
;;; Add an edge to the agenda. In topdown parsing, the only way that
;;; duplicate edges can be introduced is via the topdown rule (as
;;; long as there are no duplicate edges, the fundamental rule cannot
;;; possibly create any). So for efficiency the checking of duplications
;;; is done in active_edge_function.
```

```lisp
(defun agenda_add (edge)
  (setq agenda (cons edge agenda)))
```

```
;;; featexp.lsp [Chapter 4] Expanding a feature-based grammar into a CF-PSG
```

```
;;; Assume that all the possible features, together with all
;;; their possible values, are declared in the global variable
;;; features:
;;;
;;; (setq features
;;;   '( (cat S NP VP PP AP P N V 0)
;;;      (slash S NP VP PP AP P N V 0)
;;;      (subcat S NP VP PP AP P N V 0)
;;;      (empty yes no)))
```

```lisp
(defvar features)
(defvar varlist)
```

```
;;; expand a rule into all possible instances
```

```lisp
(defun expand_rule (rule)
  (let ((newrule (fillout_rule rule)))
    (subst_values varlist newrule)))
```

```
;;; Produce a variant of a rule where every category simply
;;; lists in order a value for each possible feature.
;;; Entries for features come out in the reverse order to
;;; the order of the global variable features

(defun fillout_rule (rule)
  (setq varlist ())
  (mapcar #'fillout_cat rule))

(defun fillout_cat (cat)
  (let ((results ()))
    (dolist (flist features results)
      (setq results (cons (get_feature_val (car flist) cat) results)))))

;;; for all possible name/value possibilities in the varlist,
;;; print out the appropriate version of the rule

(defun subst_values (varlist rule)
  (if (null varlist)
    (print rule)
    (dolist (val (cdar varlist))
      (subst_values (cdr varlist)
        (subst_value (caar varlist) val rule)))))

;;; produce a new version of a thing (e.g. rule) which has value
;;; substituted for each occurrence of name

(defun subst_value (name val thing)
  (if (equal name thing)
    val
    (if (consp thing)
      (cons
        (subst_value name val (car thing))
        (subst_value name val (cdr thing)))
      thing)))

;;; find the entry in a category for a given feature name.
;;; if the entry is a variable, make sure it is in the varlist.
;;; if there is no entry, introduce a new variable for it

(defun get_feature_val (featname category)
  (let
    ((val
       (if (assoc featname category)
         (cadr (assoc featname category))
         (gensym "_")))
     (possvalues (cdr (assoc featname features))))
    (if (and (symbolp val)
         (equal (char (symbol-name val) 0) # \_)
         (not (assoc val varlist)))
      (setq varlist (cons (cons val possvalues) varlist)))
    val))
```

```
;;; finite.lsp [Chapter 2] Utilities for finite-state networks
```

```
;;; abbreviations
(defvar abbreviations)
```

```
;;; basic network accessing
(defun initial_nodes (network)
;;   returns the list of initial nodes
     (nth 1 (assoc 'Initial network)))
```

```
(defun final_nodes (network)
;;   returns the list of final nodes
     (nth 1 (assoc 'Final network)))
```

```
(defun transitions (network)
;;   returns the list of transitions
     (cddr network))
```

```
;;; the subcomponents of a transition
```

```
(defun trans_node (transition)
   (getf transition 'From))
```

```
(defun trans_newnode (transition)
   (getf transition 'to))
```

```
(defun trans_label (transition)
   (getf transition 'by))
```

```
;;; forinfer.lsp [Chapter 9] Forwards inference engine
```

```
(uses 'subst)
(uses 'tunify)
```

```
(defvar infrules)
```

```
(defun for_infer (assertion)
  (let ((to_add nil))
    (if (null (fifind assertion))
       (setq to_add (list assertion))
       (setq to_add nil))
    (do
      ((assert (car to_add) (car to_add)))
      ((null to_add))
      (setq to_add (cdr to_add))
      (princ "Adding ") (princ assert) (terpri)
      (setq infrules (cons (list assert) infrules))
      (dolist (new (consequences assert))
        (if (and
           (null (fifind new))
           (not (member new to_add :test #'equal))
           (not (equal new assert)))
          (setq to_add (cons new to_add)))))))
```

```
(defun consequences (assert)
  (let ((results ()))
    (dolist (infrule infrules)
      (dolist (pattern (cdr infrule))
        (if (and
            (equal (car pattern) (car assert))
            (equal (length pattern) (length assert)))
          (let ((subst1 (termunify assert pattern)))
            (if subst1
              (dolist
                (subst2
                  (find_all (apply_subst subst1
                      (remove pattern (cdr infrule)))))
                (setq results
                  (cons
                    (apply_subst (compose_substs subst1 subst2) (car infrule))
                    results))))))))
    results))

(defun find_all (goals)
  (if (null goals)
    (list empty_subst)
    (let ((substs ()))
      (dolist (subst (fifind (car goals)))
        (dolist (newsubst (find_all (apply_subst subst (cdr goals))))
          (setq substs (cons (compose_substs subst newsubst) substs))))
      substs)))

(defun fifind (goal)
  (let ((substs ()))
    (dolist (infrule infrules)
      (if (and
          (equal (caar infrule) (car goal))
          (equal (length (car infrule)) (length goal))
          (null (cdr infrule)))
        (let ((newsubst (termunify goal (car (rename infrule)))))
          (if newsubst
            (setq substs (cons newsubst substs))))))
    substs))
```

```
;;; fsbgen.lsp [Chapter 2] Breadth-first generation of sentences from an FSTN
```

```
(uses 'finite)
(uses 'fstape)

(defun generate (network)
  (let ((agenda (generate_initial_states network)))
    (do () ((null agenda)) ; do until agenda empty
      (setq agenda (generate_next_states_list agenda network)))))
```

```
;;; Given a list of states (agenda), append together the next states
;;; that arise from all the individual states

(defun generate_next_states_list (agenda network)
  (if (null agenda)
   '()
   (append
     (generate_next_states (car agenda) network)
     (generate_next_states_list (cdr agenda) network))))

;;; calculate the next states from a given state (node tape)

(defun generate_next_states (node_tape network)
  (if (member (car node_tape) (final_nodes network))
    (print (cadr node_tape)))
  (let ((results '()))
    (dolist (transition (transitions network) results)
      (if (equal (car node_tape) (trans_node transition))
        (dolist (newtape (generate_move (trans_label transition) (cadr node_tape)))
          (setq results (cons (list (trans_newnode transition) newtape) results)))
        '()))))                 ; transition from the wrong node

;;; create a list of initial states, starting within a given network
;;; and with an empty tape

(defun generate_initial_states (network)
  (let ((results '()))
    (dolist (n (initial_nodes network) results)
      (setq results (cons (cons n '()) results)))))
```

```
;;; fsgen.lsp [Chapter 2] Exhaustive generation of sentences from an FSTN
```

```
(uses 'finite)
(uses 'fstape)

(defun generate_next (node tape network)
  ;; prints out sentences
  (if (member node (final_nodes network))
    (print tape)
    (dolist (transition (transitions network))
      (if (equal node (trans_node transition))
        (dolist (newtape (generate_move (trans_label transition) tape))
          (generate_next (trans_newnode transition) newtape network))
        '()))))  ; transition from the wrong node

(defun generate (network)
  ;; generates valid sentences of the given network
  (dolist (initialnode (initial_nodes network))
        (generate_next initialnode nil network))
  t)
```

```
;;; fsrecog.lsp [Chapter 2] Finite-state recognition


(uses 'finite)
(uses 'fstape)

(defun recognize (network tape)
  ;; returns t if sucessfully recognizes tape – nil otherwise
  (catch
    'stop
    (dolist (initialnode (initial_nodes network))
      (recognize_next initialnode tape network))
    nil))                                        ; failed to recognize

(defun recognize_next (node tape network)
  ;; throws t or returns nil
  (if (and (null tape) (member node (final_nodes network)))
    (throw 'stop t)                              ; success
    (dolist (transition (transitions network))
      ;; try each transition of the network
      (if (equal node (trans_node transition))  ; if it starts at the right node
        (dolist (newtape (recognize_move (trans_label transition) tape))
          ;; try each possible new value of tape
          (recognize_next (trans_newnode transition) newtape network))))))
```

```
;;; fstape.lsp [Chapter 2] Tape-moving procedures for finite-state networks
```

```
;;; single tape moving for recognition

;;; recognition

(defun recognize_move (label tape)
  (if (equal label (car tape))
    (list (cdr tape))
    (if (member (car tape) (assoc label abbreviations))
      (list (cdr tape))
      (if (equal label '|#|)
        (list tape)
        '()))))

;;; single tape moving for generation

(defun generate_move (label tape)
  (if (equal label '|#|)
    (list tape)
    (if (assoc label abbreviations)
      (let ((results '()))
        (dolist (word (cdr (assoc label abbreviations)) results)
          (setq results (cons (append tape (list word)) results))))
      (list (append tape (list label))))))
```

```
;;; fstgen.lsp [Chapter 2] Exhaustive generation of sentence pairs from an FSTN
```

```
(uses 'finite)
(uses 'fstape)

(defun generate2 (network)
  (dolist (initialnode (initial_nodes network))
    (generate2_next initialnode '(() ()) network))
  t)

(defun generate2_next (node tape network)
  (if (member node (final_nodes network))
    (print tape))
  (dolist (transition (transitions network))
    (if (equal node (trans_node transition))
      (dolist (newtape (generate2_move (trans_label transition) tape))
        (generate2_next (trans_newnode transition) newtape network)))))
```

```
;;; Tape moving
```

```
(defun generate2_move (label tape)
  (if (listp label)            ;; a pair
    (let ((results '()))
      (dolist (newtape1 (generate_move (car label) (car tape)))
        (dolist (newtape2 (generate_move (cadr label) (cadr tape)))
          (setq results (cons (list newtape1 newtape2) results))))
      results)
    (if (equal label '|#|)
      tape                     ;; no move character
      (if (assoc label abbreviations)
        (generate2_move_list (cdr (assoc label abbreviations)) tape)
        '()))))
```

```
;;; Produce a list of new tapes, given a LIST of labels
```

```
(defun generate2_move_list (labels tape)
  (if (null labels)
    '()
    (append
      (generate2_move (car labels) tape)
      (generate2_move_list (cdr labels) tape))))
```

```
;;; fstrans.lsp [Chapter 2] Finite-state transduction
```

```
(uses 'finite)
(uses 'fstape)
```

```lisp
(defun transduce_move (label tape)
  ;; returns a list of tapes
  (if (listp label)                    ; a pair
    (let ((results '()))
      (dolist (newinput (recognize_move (car label) (car tape)))
        (dolist (newoutput (generate_move (cadr label) (cadr tape)))
          (setq results (cons (list newinput newoutput) results))))
      results)
    (if (equal label '|#|)
      (list tape)
      (if (assoc label abbreviations)
        (transduce_move_list (cdr (assoc label abbreviations)) tape)))))

;;; Produce a list of new tapes, given a LIST of labels

(defun transduce_move_list (labels tape)
  (if (null labels)
    '()
    (append
      (transduce_move (car labels) tape)
      (transduce_move_list (cdr labels) tape))))

(defun transduce_next (node tape network)
  ;; returns nil or throws an output tape
  (if (and (null (car tape)) (member node (final_nodes network)))
    (throw 'stop (cadr tape))
    (dolist (transition (transitions network))
      (if (equal node (trans_node transition))
        (dolist (newtape (transduce_move (trans_label transition) tape))
          (transduce_next (trans_newnode transition) newtape network))
        nil))))              ; transition from wrong node

(defun transduce (network tape)
  (catch
    'stop
    (dolist (initialnode (initial_nodes network))
      (transduce_next initialnode (list tape nil) network))
    nil))
```

;;; inherits.lsp [Chapter 9] Simple semantic net with default inheritance

---

```lisp
(defun attr (entity attribute value)
  (setf (get entity attribute) value))

(defun isa (entity1 entity2)
  (setf (get entity1 'isa)
    (cons entity2 (get entity1 'isa))))

(attr 'club_member 'sex 'male)
(attr 'club_member 'over_50 'yes)
(attr 'club_member 'citizenship 'US)
```

```
 (isa 'associate 'club_member)
(attr 'associate 'associate_member 'yes)
(attr 'associate 'citizenship 'non_US)

 (isa 'life_member 'club_member)
(attr 'life_member 'life_member 'yes)
(attr 'life_member 'over_50 'no)

 (isa 'kim 'associate)
(attr 'kim 'over_50 'no)

 (isa 'jean 'associate)
(attr 'jean 'sex 'female)
(attr 'jean 'citizenship 'US)

 (isa 'mayumi 'life_member)
(attr 'mayumi 'sex 'female)
(attr 'mayumi 'over_50 'yes)
(attr 'mayumi 'citizenship 'non_US)

 (isa 'beryl 'life_member)
(attr 'beryl 'sex 'female)

(defun get_attr (entity attribute)
  (catch 'got_one
    (if (get entity attribute)
      (throw 'got_one (get entity attribute))
      (dolist (e1 (get entity 'isa))
        (let ((x (get_attr e1 attribute)))
          (if x
            (throw 'got_one x)))))
    nil))
```

```
;;; lexicon.lsp [Chapter 7] Example lexical entries
```

```
(uses 'lisppatr)

(setf (get 'mor_regV 'patr_macro)
 '((mor form1 stem) = (mor root)
   (mor form1 suffix) = NULL
   (mor form2 stem) = (mor root)
   (mor form2 suffix) = NULL
   (mor form3 stem) = (mor root)
   (mor form3 suffix) = s
   (mor form4 stem) = (mor root)
   (mor form4 suffix) = ed
   (mor form5 stem) = (mor root)
   (mor form5 suffix) = ed
   (mor form6 stem) = (mor root)
   (mor form6 suffix) = ed
   (mor form7 stem) = (mor root)
   (mor form7 suffix) = ing       ))
```

```lisp
(setf (get 'syn_iV 'patr_macro)
 '((syn cat) = V
   (syn arg0 cat) = np
   (syn arg0 case) = nom))

(setf (get 'syn_tV 'patr_macro)
 '( syn_iV
   (syn arg1 cat) = np
   (syn arg1 case) = acc))
```

;;; Associating lexemes with conditions – we will use the property 'lexicon

```lisp
(defun lookup_conditions (lex)
  (get lex 'lexicon))

(defun set_conditions (lex conds)
  (setf (get lex 'lexicon) conds))
```

;;; example setting up of a lexical entry

```lisp
(set_conditions 'love
 '( (mor root) = love
    (sem) = love2a
    mor_regV
    syn_tV              ))
```

```lisp
(defvar example_wfc)

(setq example_wfc
 '( (word mor form) = (lexeme mor form3)
    (word syn) = (lexeme syn)
    (word syn cat) = V
    (word syn arg0 per) = 3
    (word syn arg0 num) = sing
    (word syn tense) = pres
    (word sem) = (lexeme sem)            ))
```

;;; look up a word in the lexicon

```lisp
(defun lookup_lex (lex)
  (if (lookup_conditions lex)
   (let*
    ((structure (newvar))
     (subst (apply_condition (lookup_conditions lex) structure empty_subst)))
    (if subst
     (apply_subst subst structure)
     (error "Inconsistent lexical entry for word ~S" lex)))
   (error "No lexical entry for word ~S" lex)))
```

;;; apply a WFC to a skeleton word entry and lexeme entry,
;;; returning a full word entry if possible

```lisp
(defun apply_wfc (wfc word lex)
  (let*
   ((structure (list (list 'word word) (list 'lexeme lex)))
    (subst (apply_condition wfc structure empty_subst)))
   (if subst
    (simplify_features subst word)
    nil)))
```

```
;;; lisppatr.lsp [Chapter 7] PATR rules and conditions
```

```
;;; PATR conditions are expressed in lists
;;; An individual condition can be of the form:
;;;        path = value
;;; where path is a list of feature names and value
;;; is either a list of feature names or a simple
;;; symbol or number
;;; An individual condition can also be a single
;;; atom, in which case it is assumed to have a
;;; value for the property patr_macro, which provides
;;; a whole set of conditions for which the atom
;;; is an abbreviation.
;;; Here is an example set of conditions (with
;;; no macros):
;;;
;;;     (((mor form1 stem)  = (mor root))
;;;      ((mor form1 suffix) = s         )
;;;      ((mor form2 stem)  = (mor root))
;;;      ((mor form2 suffix) = NULL      ))
;;;

(uses 'dagunify)


;;; apply_condition is given a set of conditions (e.g. the list
;;; shown above), a dag and a substitution (which may provide
;;; extra information about the dag). It returns a new
;;; substitution (extending the initial one) which, when
;;; applied to the dag will produce a dag that satisfies the
;;; conditions

(defun apply_condition (entry dag subst)
  (if (null entry)
     subst
     (if (consp (car entry))
        ;; path1 = path2
        (let*
          ((end1_subst1 (apply_path (car entry) dag subst))
           (end1 (car end1_subst1))
           (subst1 (cadr end1_subst1)))
          (if subst1
            (let*
              ((end2_subst2 (apply_path (nth 2 entry) dag subst1))
               (end2 (car end2_subst2))
               (subst2 (cadr end2_subst2)))
              (if subst2
                (let ((newsubst (combine_values end1 end2 subst2)))
                  (if newsubst
                    (apply_condition (cdddr entry) dag newsubst)
                    nil))
                nil))
            nil))
```

```
(if (and (symbolp (car entry)) (get (car entry) 'patr_macro))
    ;; macro
    (let
     ((newsubst
        (apply_condition (get (car entry) 'patr_macro) dag subst)))
     (if newsubst
         (apply_condition (cdr entry) dag newsubst)
         nil))
    (error "Illegal PATR entry ~S" entry)))))


;;;; Given a sequence of feature names (a path,
;;;; e.g. (verb arg0 cat)), return the value at the
;;;; end of that path in a given dag. If the dag
;;;; does not yet have that path defined, add to
;;;; the substitution subst so that it is.
;;;; This function returns a list consisting of:
;;;; a) the value at the end of the path
;;;; b) the modified substitution

(defun apply_path (path dag subst)
  (if (null path)
      (list dag subst)
      (if (atom path)
          (list path subst)
          (if (consp path)
              (let ((subst_val (get_value (car path) dag subst)))
                (if (car subst_val)
                    (apply_path (cdr path) (car subst_val) (cadr subst_val))
                    subst_val))
              (error "Ill-formed path ~S" path)))))

;;;; try to match a dag with the LHS of a PATR rule.
;;;; return a list consisting of
;;;;    a) a substitution, or nil
;;;;    b) the list of dags corresponding to the RHS
;;;;
;;;; the substitution returned needs to be applied to
;;;; the LHS and anything that might share variables with it

(defun lhs_match (dag patr_rule)
  (if (member '-> (cadr patr_rule))
      ;; normal rule
      (let* (
        (lhs (caadr patr_rule))
        (rhs (cddadr patr_rule))
        (conditions (cddr patr_rule))
        (bigdag
          (cons
            (list lhs dag)
            (append
              ;; create a feature entry for each RHS name
              (mapcar #'new_feature_entry rhs)
              (list (list '& (newvar)))))))
        (subst (apply_condition conditions bigdag empty_subst)))
```

```
    (if subst
      (list
        subst
        (extract_named_feature_values rhs subst bigdag))
      '(() ()))))
    ;; lexical rule
    (let* (
        (rhs (cadr patr_rule))
        (conditions (cddr patr_rule))
        (subst (apply_condition conditions dag empty_subst)))
      (if subst
        (list subst rhs)
        '(() ())))))

;;; create a new (feature value) list for a named feature

(defun new_feature_entry (name)
  (list name (newvar)))

;;; extract from a dag the values of the named list of
;;; features

(defun extract_named_feature_values (names subst dag)
  (if (null names)
    '()
    (cons
      (simplify_features subst (find_feature_value (car names) dag subst))
      (extract_named_feature_values (cdr names) subst dag))))

;;; try to match a rule, given a list of dags for the RHS. Return a list
;;; containing:
;;;    a) a substitution, or nil
;;;    b) the list of dags corresponding to the LHS and any unused dags
;;; The substitution returned needs to be applied to
;;; the LHS and the RHS

(defun rhs_match (dags patr_rule)
  (if (member '-> (cadr patr_rule))
    ;; normal rule
    (let (
        (lhs (caadr patr_rule))
        (rhs (cddadr patr_rule))
        (conditions (cddr patr_rule)))
      ;; make sure there are enough non-lexical dags
      (if (< (length dags) (length rhs))
        '(() ())
        (let* (
            (dag (newvar))
            (restdags (nthcdr (length rhs) dags))
            (bigdag
              (cons
                (list lhs dag)
                (append
                  (do
```

```
                    ((needed rhs (cdr needed))
                     (available dags (cdr available))
                     (pairs nil
                        (cons (list (car needed) (car available)) pairs)))
                    ((null needed) pairs))
                  (list (list '& (newvar))))))))
           (subst (apply_condition conditions bigdag empty_subst)))
        (if subst
           (list subst (cons (simplify_features subst dag) restdags))
           '(() ())))))
    ;; lexical rule
    (let (
      (rhs (cadr patr_rule))
      (conditions (cddr patr_rule)))
      (if (< (length dags) (length rhs))
        '(() ())
        (let* (
           (restdags (nthcdr (length rhs) dags))
           (useddags (ldiff dags restdags)))
          (if (equal rhs useddags)
             ;; make sure the words are right
             (let* (
                (dag (newvar))
                (subst (apply_condition conditions dag empty_subst)))
               (if subst
                 (list subst (cons (simplify_features subst dag) restdags))
                 '(() ())))
             '(() ()))))))))

;;; make_dag produces a minimal dag that satisfies a set
;;; of conditions

(defun make_dag (conds)
  (let ((dag (newvar)))
    (simplify_features
      (apply_condition conds dag empty_subst)
      dag)))
```

```
;;; patrgram.lsp [Chapter 7] Simple PATR grammar
```

```
(setq rules
   '((Rule  (S -> NP VP)
            (S cat) = S
            (NP cat) = NP
            (VP cat) = VP
            (S slash) = (VP slash)
            (NP slash) = 0)
```

```
     (Rule   (VP -> V X)
             (VP cat) = VP
             (V cat) = V
             (V arg1) = (X cat)
             (V slash) = 0
             (VP slash) = (X slash))

     (Rule   (PP -> P X)
             (PP cat) = PP
             (P cat) = P
             (P arg1) = (X cat)
             (P slash) = 0
             (PP slash) = (X slash))

;;;  (Rule   (X0 -> X1 C X2)
;;;          (X0 cat) = (X1 cat)
;;;          (X0 cat) = (X2 cat)
;;;          (C cat) = C
;;;          (C slash) = 0
;;;          (X0 slash) = (X1 slash)
;;;          (X0 slash) = (X2 slash)
;;;          (X0 arg1) = (X1 arg1)
;;;          (X0 arg1) = (X2 arg1))

     (Rule   (S -> X1 X2)
             (S cat) = S
             (S slash) = 0
             (X1 slash) = 0
             (X1 empty) = no
             (X2 cat) = S
             (X2 slash) = (X1 cat)
             (X2 empty) = no)

     (Rule   (X0 -> )
             (X0 cat) = (X0 slash)
             (X0 empty) = yes)))

(setq lexical_rules
  '((Word (approved)
          (cat) = V
          (slash) = 0
          (arg1) = PP)
    (Word (disapproved)
          (cat) = V
          (slash) = 0
          (arg1) = PP)
    (Word (appeared)
          (cat) = V
          (slash) = 0
          (arg1) = AP)
    (Word (seemed)
          (cat) = V
          (slash) = 0
          (arg1) = AP)
```

```
(Word (had)
      (cat) = V
      (slash) = 0
      (arg1) = VP)
(Word (believed)
      (cat) = V
      (slash) = 0
      (arg1) = S)
(Word (thought)
      (cat) = V
      (slash) = 0
      (arg1) = S)
(Word (of)
      (cat) = P
      (slash) = 0
      (arg1) = NP)
(Word (fit)
      (slash) = 0
      (cat) = AP)
(Word (competent)
      (slash) = 0
      (cat) = AP)
(Word (well - qualified)
      (slash) = 0
      (cat) = AP)
(Word (Dr Chan)
      (slash) = 0
      (cat) = NP)
(Word (nurses)
      (slash) = 0
      (cat) = NP)
(Word (MediCenter)
      (slash) = 0
      (cat) = NP)
(Word (patients)
      (slash) = 0
      (cat) = NP)
(Word (died)
      (arg1) = 0
      (slash) = 0
      (cat) = V)
(Word (employed)
      (arg1) = NP
      (slash) = 0
      (cat) = V)))

(defun category (d subst)
  (let (
    (cat (find_feature_value 'cat d subst))
    (slash (find_feature_value 'slash d subst)))
    (if (equal slash 0)
      cat
      (list cat '/ slash))))
```

```
(defun tree (cat subtrees)
  (cons cat subtrees))
```

```
;;; pdtransd.lsp [Chapter 3] Pushdown transduction

(uses 'finite)
(uses 'fstrans)      ;;; for transduce_move

(defun rtn_transduce_move (label tape)
  (transduce_move label tape))

(defun get_network (name)
  (cadr (assoc name networks)))

(defun rtn_transduce_next (networkname node tape stack)
  (if (member node (final_nodes (get_network networkname)))
    (rtn_transduce_pop tape stack))
  (dolist (transition (transitions (get_network networkname)))
    (if (equal (trans_node transition) node)
      (let ((label (trans_label transition))
            (newnode (trans_newnode transition)))
        (if (get_network label)
          ;; interpret label as network name
          (rtn_transduce_push label networkname newnode tape stack))
          ;; interpret label as symbol/abbreviation
          (rtn_transduce_traverse label networkname newnode tape stack)))))

(defun rtn_transduce_pop (tape stack)
  (if (and (null stack) (null (car tape)))
    (throw 'rtn (cadr tape))
    (if (not (null stack))
      (rtn_transduce_next (caar stack) (cadar stack) tape (cdr stack)))))

(defun rtn_transduce_push (label networkname newnode tape stack)
  (dolist (initialnode (initial_nodes (get_network label)))
    (rtn_transduce_next label initialnode tape
      (cons
        (list networkname newnode)
        stack))))

(defun rtn_transduce_traverse (label networkname newnode tape stack)
  (dolist (newtape (rtn_transduce_move label tape))
    (rtn_transduce_next networkname newnode newtape stack)))

(defun rtn_transduce (networkname tape)
  (catch
    'rtn
    (dolist (initialnode (initial_nodes (get_network networkname)))
      (rtn_transduce_next networkname initialnode (list tape ()) ()))))
```

```
;;; plan.lsp [Chapter 10] Simple generation of illocutionary act plans
```

```lisp
(uses 'bckinfer)
(uses 'tunify)

(defvar operators)

(setq operators '(
  ( (request _speaker _addressee _act)
    ((can_do _addressee _act) (channel _speaker _addressee))
    ((want _speaker (request _speaker _addressee _act)))
    ((believe _addressee (want _speaker _act))))

  ( (cause_to_want _agent1 _agent2 _act)
    ((can_do _agent2 _act) (believe _agent2 (want _agent1 _act)))
    ()
    ((want _agent2 _act)))

  ( (move _agent _source _destination)
    ((at _agent _source))
    ((want _agent (move _agent _source _destination)))
    ((at _agent _destination)))

  ( (inform _speaker _addressee _proposition)
    (_proposition (channel _speaker _addressee))
    ((want _speaker (inform _speaker _addressee _proposition)))
    ((believe _addressee (believe _speaker _proposition))))

  ( (inform_ref _speaker _addressee _predicate)
    ((knows_ref _speaker _predicate) (channel _speaker _addressee))
    ((want _speaker (inform_ref _speaker _addressee _predicate)))
    ((knows_told_ref _addressee _speaker _predicate)))

  ( (convince_ref _speaker _addressee _predicate)
    ((knows_told_ref _addressee _speaker _predicate))
    ()
    ((knows_ref _addressee _predicate)))

  ( (convince _speaker _addressee _proposition)
    ((believe _addressee (believe _speaker _proposition)))
    ()
    ((believe _addressee _proposition)))))

;;; predicates for which there is universal knowledge

(defvar universal_knowledge)

(setq universal_knowledge '(channel at can_do knows_ref))

;;; The main function to call
;;; It assumes that the initial world model is in the variable
;;; infrules, as required for lib bckinfer.
;;; Note that facts recorded in infrules are interpreted
;;; outside all belief spaces, so that, for instance,
;;; beliefs of the planning agent need to be explicitly
;;; stated as such. On the other hand, goals presented to
;;; plan are assumed to be interpreted in the planning
;;; agent's belief space. For example, for the goal (at John inroom)
;;; the planner actually tries to satisfy
;;; (believe agent (at John inroom))
```

```
(defun plan (agent goals)
  (catch 'plan
    (do ((maxdepth 0 (1+ maxdepth))) ((equal maxdepth 10))
      ;; maxdepth limits the number of actions allowed in a
      ;; possible plan. Increasing maxdepth by 1 each time
      ;; results in a kind of breadth-first search
      (print (list 'trying 'depth maxdepth))
      (plan_next agent goals nil empty_subst 0 maxdepth))))


(defun plan_next (agent goals actions currentsubst depth maxdepth)
  (if (null goals)
    (throw 'plan (apply_subst currentsubst actions))
    (if (> depth maxdepth)
      nil
      (let ((goal (apply_subst currentsubst (car goals))) (othergoals (cdr goals)))
        (if (and
              (equal (car goal) 'believe)
              (consp (caddr goal))
              (member (caaddr goal) universal_knowledge))
          ;; (believe X (Y.Z)), Y universally known
          ;; -adopt (Y.Z) as a goal
          (plan_next agent (cons (caddr goal) othergoals) actions currentsubst depth maxdepth)
          (if (equal (car goal) 'can_do)
            (try_to_achieve_can_do agent goal othergoals actions currentsubst depth maxdepth)
            ;; (can_do X Y)
            ;; -find the can_do component of action Y and
            ;; -adopt them as goals
            (progn
              ;; the next two cases check for the goal being a want or belief
              ;; of the planning agent. Since the wanter or believer specified
              ;; in the goal may not be uninstantiated, we have to consider
              ;; other possible wanters/believers as well as the planner
              (try_planners_own agent goal othergoals actions currentsubst depth maxdepth)
              ;; now look for instances of the goal in the database,
              ;; taking the point of view of the planning agent
              (try_already_true agent goal othergoals actions currentsubst depth maxdepth)
              ;; even if one instance of a goal is already true,
              ;; there may be other instances that are achievable
              (try_to_make_true agent goal othergoals actions currentsubst depth maxdepth))))))))


;;; Try to enable X to do action Y. Look up the can_do preconditions
;;; for this action and introduce them as planning goals


(defun try_to_achieve_can_do (agent goal goals actions currentsubst depth maxdepth)
  (dolist (operator operators)
    (let* (
      (o (rename operator))
      (subst (termunify (caddr goal) (car o))))
      (if subst
        (plan_next agent (append (cadr o) goals) actions (compose_substs subst currentsubst) depth maxdepth)))))
```

```
;;; Check for the goal being a want or belief
;;; of the planning agent. Since the wanter or believer specified
;;; in the goal may not be uninstantiated, we have to consider
;;; other possible wanters/believers as well as the planner

(defun try_planners_own (agent goal goals actions currentsubst depth maxdepth)
  (if (and (equal (car goal) 'want) (termunify agent (cadr goal)))
    ;; (want X Y), X could be agent
    ;; - goal immediately satisfied
    (plan_next agent goals actions (compose_substs (termunify agent (cadr goal)) currentsubst) depth maxdepth)
    (if (and (equal (car goal) 'believe) (termunify agent (cadr goal)))
      ;; (believe X Y), Y could be agent
      ;; - goal immediately satisfied
      (plan_next agent goals actions (compose_substs (termunify agent (cadr goal)) currentsubst) depth maxdepth))))

;;; try to match the goal against a fact already known to be true

(defun try_already_true (agent goal goals actions currentsubst depth maxdepth)
  (let ((dbgoal
          (if (member (car goal) universal_knowledge)
            goal
            (list 'believe agent goal))))
    (dolist (subst (back_infer dbgoal))
      (plan_next agent goals actions (compose_substs subst currentsubst) depth maxdepth))))

;;; see what actions might achieve a given goal, and add their preconditions
;;; to the list of goals

(defun try_to_make_true (agent goal goals actions currentsubst depth maxdepth)
  (dolist (operator operators)
    (let ((o (rename operator)))
      (dolist (e (cadddr o)) ; the effects of the operator
        (let ((subst (termunify goal e)))
          (if subst
            (plan_next agent (append (cadr o) (caddr o))
              (cons (car o) actions)
              (compose_substs subst currentsubst)
              (1 + depth) maxdepth)))))))
```

```
;;; predict.lsp [Chapter 10] Prediction by plausible inference rules
```

```
(uses 'subst)
(uses 'bckinfer)

;;; predict is given a list of assertions (possibly containing
;;; variables) and attempts to predict them simultaneously
```

```lisp
(defun predict (assertions)
  (let
    ((substs (back_infer_all assertions)))
    (if (and (null substs) (ground assertions))
      (progn
        (print '(assertions not predicted but unambiguous))
        (dolist (ass assertions)
          (setq infrules (cons (list ass) infrules))))
      (if (equal (length substs) 1)
        (progn
          (print '(assertions uniquely predicted))
          (print (apply_subst (car substs) assertions)))
        (if (null substs)
          (progn
            (print '(assertions ambiguous but no prediction))
            (dolist (ass assertions)
              (setq infrules (cons (list ass) infrules))))
          (progn
            (print '(assertions ambiguous and multiple predictions))
            (dolist (subst substs)
              (print (apply_subst subst assertions)))))))))

;;; example inference rules

(setq infrules
  '(((church (church_of _x)) (town _x))
    ((see people _x) (famous _x) (object _x))
    ((object _x) (spire _x))
    ((spire (spire_of _x)) (church _x))))
```

```lisp
;;; presupp.lsp [Chapter 10] Presupposition grammar and inference rules
```

```lisp
(defvar rules)
(defvar lexical_rules)
(defvar infrules)

(uses 'dagunify)

(setq rules
  '((Rule (IMP -> V NP PP)
      (IMP cat) = IMP
      (V cat) = V
      (NP cat) = NP
      (PP cat) = PP
      (V p) = (PP p)
      (V arg1) = (NP referent)
      (V arg2) = (PP arg1)
      (IMP sem) = (V sem)
      (IMP pre connective) = and
      (IMP pre prop1) = (V pre)
      (IMP pre prop2 connective) = and
      (IMP pre prop2 prop1) = (NP pre)
      (IMP pre prop2 prop2) = (PP np_pre))
```

```
(Rule (NP -> DET N)
   (NP cat) = NP
   (DET cat) = DET
   (N cat) = N
   (NP pre) = (N pre)
   (NP referent) = (N referent))
(Rule (NP1 -> NP2 PP)
   (NP1 cat) = NP
   (NP2 cat) = NP
   (PP cat) = PP
   (NP1 referent) = (NP2 referent)
   (NP1 referent) = (PP arg0)
   (NP1 pre connective) = and
   (NP1 pre prop1) = (NP2 pre)
   (NP1 pre prop2 connective) = and
   (NP1 pre prop2 prop1) = (PP p_pre)
   (NP1 pre prop2 prop2) = (PP np_pre))
(Rule (PP -> P NP)
   (PP cat) = PP
   (P cat) = P
   (NP cat) = NP
   (PP arg0) = (P arg0)
   (PP arg1) = (NP referent)
   (PP arg1) = (P arg1)
   (PP p) = (P p)
   (PP np_pre) = (NP pre)
   (PP p_pre) = (P pre))))


(setq lexical_rules
 '((Word (in)
    (cat) = P
    (p) = in
    (pre predicate) = in
    (pre arg0) = (arg0)
    (pre arg1) = (arg1))
   (Word (on)
    (cat) = P
    (p) = on
    (pre predicate) = on
    (pre arg0) = (arg0)
    (pre arg1) = (arg1))
   (Word (to)
    (cat) = P
    (p) = to
    (pre predicate) = true)
   (Word (fix)
    (cat) = V
    (sem predicate) = fix
    (sem arg1) = (arg1)
    (sem arg2) = (arg2)
    (pre predicate) = manipulate
    (pre arg0) = (arg1))
```

```
(Word (put)
  (cat) = V
  (p) = in
  (sem predicate) = put_in
  (sem arg1) = (arg1)
  (sem arg2) = (arg2)
  (pre predicate) = fit_in
  (pre arg0) = (arg1)
  (pre arg1) = (arg2))
(Word (put)
  (cat) = V
  (p) = on
  (sem predicate) = put_on
  (sem arg1) = (arg1)
  (sem arg2) = (arg2)
  (pre predicate) = fit_on
  (pre arg0) = (arg1)
  (pre arg1) = (arg2))
(Word (box)
  (cat) = N
  (pre predicate) = box
  (pre arg0) = (referent))
(Word (screw)
  (cat) = N
  (pre predicate) = screw
  (pre arg0) = (referent))
(Word (washer)
  (cat) = N
  (pre predicate) = washer
  (pre arg0) = (referent))
(Word (hole)
  (cat) = N
  (pre predicate) = hole
  (pre arg0) = (referent))
(Word (the)
  (cat) = DET)
(Word (it)
  (pre predicate) = true
  (cat) = NP)))


(defun category (d subst)
  (list
    (find_feature_value 'pre d subst)
    (find_feature_value 'sem d subst)))



(defun tree (cat subtrees)
  cat)



;;; inference rules
```

```
(setq infrules
 '(((manipulate _x) (screw _x))
   ((manipulate _x) (washer _x))
   ((fit_in washer1 hole1))
   ((fit_in screw2 hole1))
   ((fit_in _x box1) (screw _x))
   ((fit_in _x box1) (washer _x))
   ((fit_on _x _y) (washer _x))
   ((on washer1 screw1))
   ((screw screw1))
   ((screw screw2))
   ((washer washer1))
   ((hole hole1))
   ((box box1))
   ((true _x))))
```

```
;;; randfgen.lsp [Chapter 7] Random generation of sentences from a PATR grammar
```

```
(uses 'lisppatr)

(defvar current_substitution)
(defvar rules)
(defvar lexical_rules)

(defun generate (dag)
  (if (atom dag)
    (list dag)
    (let ((rs (matching_rules dag)))
      (if (null rs)
        (throw 'generate nil)
        (let ((subst_rhs (lhs_match dag (oneof rs))))
          (setq current_substitution
            (compose_substs current_substitution (car subst_rhs)))
          (generate_all (cadr subst_rhs)))))))

(defun generate_all (body)
  (if (null body)
    '()
    (append
      (generate (apply_subst current_substitution (car body)))
      (generate_all (cdr body)))))

(defun oneof (list)
  ;; randomly returns one of the given list
  (nth (random (length list)) list))

(defun matching_rules (dag)
  (let ((results ()))
    (dolist (rule rules)
      (let ((subst_rhs (lhs_match dag rule)))
        (if (car subst_rhs)
          (setq results (cons rule results)))))
```

```
  (dolist (rule lexical_rules)
    (let ((subst_rhs (lhs_match dag rule)))
      (if (car subst_rhs)
        (setq results (cons rule results)))))
    results))

(defun g (description)
  (setq current_substitution empty_subst)
  (catch 'generate
    (generate description)))
```

```
;;; randftre.lsp [Chapter 7] Random generation of trees from a PATR grammar

(uses 'randfgen)

(defun generate (dag)
  (if (atom dag)
    dag
    (let ((rs (matching_rules dag)))
      (if (null rs)
        (throw 'generate nil)
        (let ((subst_rhs (lhs_match dag (oneof rs))))
          (setq current_substitution
            (compose_substs current_substitution (car subst_rhs)))
          (cons
            (category dag current_substitution)
            (generate_all (cadr subst_rhs))))))))

(defun generate_all (body)
  (if (null body)
    '()
    (cons
      (generate (apply_subst current_substitution (car body)))
      (generate_all (cdr body)))))
```

```
;;; randgen.lsp [Chapter 4] Random generation from a CF-PSG

(defvar rules)

(defun generate (description)
  (if (atom description)
    (list description)
    (let ((rs (matching_rules description)))
      (if (null rs)
        (error "Cannot generate description")
        (generate_all (cdr (oneof rs)))))))
```

```
(defun oneof (list)
  ;; randomly returns one of the given list
  (nth (random (length list)) list))

(defun generate_all (body)
  (if (null body)
    '()
    (append
      (generate (car body))
      (generate_all (cdr body)))))

(defun matching_rules (description)
  (let ((results ()))
    (dolist (rule rules results)
      (if (unify description (car rule))
        (setq results (cons rule results))))))

(defun unify (x y)
  (equal x y))
```

```
;;;; randtree.lsp [Chapter 4] Random generation of parse trees from a CF-PSG

(defvar rules)

(defun generate (description)
  (if (atom description)
    description
    (let ((rs (matching_rules description)))
      (if (null rs)
        (error "Cannot generate from description ~S" description)
        (cons
          (category description)
          (generate_all (cdr (oneof rs))))))))

(defun generate_all (body)
  (if (null body)
    '()
    (cons
      (generate (car body))
      (generate_all (cdr body)))))

(defun category (description)
  (car description))

(defun matching_rules (description)
  (let ((results ()))
    (dolist (rule rules results)
      (if (unify description (car rule))
        (setq results (cons rule results))))))

(defun unify (x y)
  (equal x y))
```

```
(defun oneof (list)
  ;; randomly returns one of the given list
  (nth (random (length list)) list))
```

```
;;;; rtnrecog.lsp [Chapter 3] Recognition using RTNs
```

```
(uses 'finite)
(uses 'fstape)
(defvar networks)

(defun rtn_recognize (networkname tape)
  (catch
    'rtn
    (dolist (initialnode (initial_nodes (get_network networkname)))
      (rtn_recognize_next networkname initialnode tape ()))
    nil))

(defun get_network (name)
  (cadr (assoc name networks)))

(defun rtn_recognize_next (networkname node tape stack)
  (if (member node (final_nodes (get_network networkname)))
      (rtn_recognize_pop tape stack))
  (dolist (transition (transitions (get_network networkname)))
    (if (equal (trans_node transition) node)
        (let ((label (trans_label transition))
              (newnode (trans_newnode transition)))
          (if (get_network label)
              ;; interpret label as network name
              (rtn_recognize_push label networkname newnode tape stack))
              ;; interpret label as symbol/abbreviation
              (rtn_recognize_traverse label networkname newnode tape stack)))))

(defun rtn_recognize_traverse (label networkname newnode tape stack)
  (dolist (newtape (rtn_recognize_move label tape))
    (rtn_recognize_next networkname newnode newtape stack)))

(defun rtn_recognize_pop (tape stack)
  (if (and (null stack) (null tape))
      (throw 'rtn t)
      (if (not (null stack))  ; not finished
          (rtn_recognize_next
            (caar stack)      ; stacked networkname
            (cadar stack)     ; stacked node name
            tape
            (cdr stack)))))

(defun rtn_recognize_push (label networkname newnode tape stack)
  (dolist (initialnode (initial_nodes (get_network label)))
    (rtn_recognize_next label initialnode tape
      (cons
        (list networkname newnode)
        stack))))
```

```
(defun rtn_recognize_move (label tape)
  (recognize_move label tape))
```

```
;;; scripts.lsp [Chapter 10] Script matching
```

```
;;; the global variable scripts holds the list of scripts

;;; Example value:

(defvar scripts)

(setq scripts
  '(
    ((auto_buy _Customer _Auto1 _Auto2 _Driver _Garage)
     (goes _Customer _Garage)
     (test_drives _Customer _Auto1)
     (orders _Customer _Auto2 _Driver)
     (delivers _Driver _Auto2 _Customer)
     (drives _Customer _Auto2))

    ((hat_buy _Customer _Hat _Assistant _Store)
     (goes _Customer _Store)
     (tries_on _Customer _Hat)
     (buys _Customer _Hat _Assistant)
     (delivers _Assistant _Hat _Customer)
     (wears _Customer _Hat))))

(uses 'subst)
(uses 'tunify)

;;; script_match is given a list of propositions, for example
;;;    ((tries_on fred hat7) (wears _x _y))
;;; It tries to match them in the order given to the
;;; expectations expressed in a script

(defun script_match (story)
  (dolist (script scripts nil)
    (let ((predictions (cdr script)))
      (let (
        (substs (predict_all_ways predictions story empty_subst)))
        (if substs
          (return (apply_subst (car substs) script)))))))

;;; test to see whether a list of predictions can be matched with a story.
;;; For each possible way, a corresponding substitution is returned

(defun predict_all_ways (predictions story current_subst)
  (if (null story)
    (list current_subst)
```

```
(let ((event (car story)) (successes ()))
   (do (
       (restpredictions (cdr predictions) (cdr restpredictions))
       (predict (car predictions) (car restpredictions)))
      ((null predict) successes)
      (let ((subst (termunify event predict)))
       (if subst
         (setq successes
           (append
             (predict_all_ways
               (apply_subst subst restpredictions)
               (apply_subst subst (cdr story))
               (compose_substs subst current_subst))
             successes)))))))
```

```
;;; subst.lsp [Chapter 7] Substitution utilities
```

```
;;;; Procedures and constants provided:
;;;
;;; empty_subst (a substitution)
;;; (lookup_subst item substitution) returns an item
;;; (add_subst variable item substitution) returns a substitution
;;; (apply_subst substitution structure) returns a newstructure
;;; (compose_substs substitution substitution) returns a substitution
;;;
;;; (isvar item) returns t/nil
;;; (rename item) returns a newitem
;;; (newvar) returns a variable
;;; (ground item) returns t/nil
;;;
;;; operations on variable symbols

(defun isvar (x)
  (and
    (symbolp x)
    (equal (char (symbol-name x) 0) # \_)))
    ;; EQ not guaranteed to work with characters

(defun ground (term)
  (if (isvar term)
    nil
    (if (listp term)
      (dolist (x term t)
        (if (ground x)
          t
          (return nil)))
      t)))
```

```lisp
;;; renames an arbitrary list structure
;;; sublist which satisfies isvar is assumed to denote a variable

(defvar rename_assoc)

(defun rename (list)
  (setq rename_assoc nil)
  (ren list))

(defun ren (list)
  (if (isvar list)
    (rename_var list)
    (if (listp list)
      (mapcar #'ren list)
      list)))

(defun rename_var (v)
  (let
    ((freshvar (cadr (assoc v rename_assoc))))
    (if freshvar
      freshvar
      (progn
        (setq freshvar (newvar))
        (setq rename_assoc (cons (list v freshvar) rename_assoc))
        freshvar))))

;;; generate a new variable

(defun newvar ()
  (gensym "_"))

;;; operations on substitutions

;;; empty_subst is represented as a list containing nil, rather than nil,
;;; in order that nil can be used to represent 'false'
(defparameter empty_subst '(()))

(defun lookup_subst (value substitution)
  (if (and (isvar value) (assoc value substitution))
    (lookup_subst
      (cadr (assoc value substitution))
      substitution)
    value))

(defun add_subst (var value substitution)
  (cons (list var value) substitution))

(defun compose_substs (s1 s2)
  (append s1 s2))

;;; apply a substitution to an
;;; arbitrary list structure

(defun apply_subst (subst item)
  (let ((realitem (lookup_subst item subst)))
    (if (listp realitem)
      (apply_subst_to_list subst realitem)
      realitem)))
```

```
(defun apply_subst_to_list (subst list)
  (if (null list)
    '()
    (cons
      (apply_subst subst (car list))
      (apply_subst_to_list subst (cdr list)))))
```

;;; subsumes.lsp [Chapter 7] Subsumption for DAGs

```
;;; does the first subsume the second?
;;; This function attempts to construct a substitution which
;;; when applied to the first structure gives the second.
;;; This is put in var_map. var_map is used to hold values for
;;; some variables in the first structure. These are the only
;;; substitutions that can be made for these variables.
;;; The code here will not always correctly handle remainders
;;; when the first dag contains a variable that only occurs once
;;; and the second has no entry for the relevant feature

(uses 'dagunify)

(defvar var_map)

(defun subsumes (dag1 dag2)
  (setq var_map nil)
  (subsumes1 dag1 dag2))

(defun subsumes1 (dag1 dag2)
  (if (equal dag1 dag2)
    t
    (if (and (isvar dag1) (assoc dag1 var_map))
      (same_dag dag2 (cadr (assoc dag1 var_map)))
      (if (isvar dag1)
        (progn
          (setq var_map (cons (list dag1 dag2) var_map))
          t)
        (if (and (consp dag1) (consp dag2))
          (do
            ((d1 dag1) (d2 dag2))
            ((or (not d2) (isvar d1)) (and d2 (subsumes1 d1 d2)))
            (let ((fpair (car d1)))
              (if (equal (car fpair) '&)
                (setq d1 (cadr fpair))
                (progn
                  (setq d1 (cdr d1))
                  (setq d2 (find_and_remove fpair d2))))))
          nil)))))

(defun same_dag (dag1 dag2)
  (equal (unify dag1 dag2) empty_subst))
```

```
;;; Given a pair (feature val),
;;; find the value of feature in dag, checking that it is subsumed by
;;; val. If so, return the remainder of dag. Otherwise return nil.

(defun find_and_remove (fpair dag)
  (if (consp dag)
    (let ((value (assoc (car fpair) dag)))
      (if value
        (and
          (subsumes1 (cadr fpair) (cadr value))
          (delete_feature_entry (car fpair) dag))
        ;; dag must have a continuation entry
        (let ((rest (cadar (last dag))) (first (butlast dag)))
          (if (isvar rest)
            ;; feature in the first has no analogue in the second, but
            ;; the second is open. this will only work if the feature
            ;; value in the first is a variable which only occurs once.
            (and
              (subsumes1 (cadr fpair) (newvar))
              dag)   ;; INCORRECT
            (let ((rest1 (find_and_remove fpair rest)))
              (and
                rest1
                (append first rest1)))))))
    nil))

;;; delete the entry for a given feature in a dag
;;; (guaranteed to come before the continuation entry)

(defun delete_feature_entry (feature dag)
  (if (equal feature (caar dag))
    (cdr dag)
    (cons (car dag) (delete_feature_entry feature (cdr dag)))))
```

```
;;; tdparse.lsp [Chapter 5] Top-down parser for a CF-PSG
```

```
(defun find_trees (goal string)
  ;; returns a list of (parse_tree remaining_string) pairs
  (if (listp goal)                                   ; a category
    (let ((results ()))
      (dolist (rule rules)
        (if (equal goal (car rule))
          (dolist (treelist_remainder (find_subtrees (cdr rule) string))
            (setq results
              (cons
                (list
                  (cons (car goal) (car treelist_remainder))  ; parse tree
                  (cadr treelist_remainder))                  ; remainder
                results)))))
      results)
    (if (equal goal (car string))                    ; a terminal
      (list (list goal (cdr string))))))
```

```
(defun find_subtrees (goals string)
  ;; returns list of (list_of_daughter_trees string_remainder)
  (if (null goals)
    (list (list '() string))
    (let ((results ()))
      (dolist (tree_rem (find_trees (car goals) string))
        ;; find parses of first goal
        (dolist (trees_rem (find_subtrees (cdr goals) (cadr tree_rem)))
          (setq results
            (cons
              (list
                (cons (car tree_rem) (car trees_rem))    ; tree
                (cadr trees_rem))                        ; remainder
              results))))
      results)))

(defun parse (goal string)
  (let ((results ()))
    (dolist (tree_rem (find_trees goal string) results)
      (if (null (cadr tree_rem))                          ; if uses the whole string
        (setq results (cons (car tree_rem) results))))))
```

```
;;; tdrecog.lsp [Chapter 5] Top-down recognition for a CF-PSG
```

```
(defun next (goals string)
  (if (and (null goals) (null string))
    (print '(yes))
    (if (listp (car goals))
      (dolist (rule rules)
        (if (equal (car goals) (car rule))
          (next (append (cdr rule) (cdr goals)) string)))
      (if (equal (car goals) (car string))
        (next (cdr goals) (cdr string))))))
```

```
;;; termify.lsp [Chapter 7] Translation from DAGs to terms
```

```
;;;; This program assumes that a set of 'rules' for how to
;;;; do the translation is specified in the global variable
;;;; dag_patterns
;;;; It will not work with dags that have shared remainders
;;;; An example legal value for dag_patterns is the following:
;;;;
```

```
;;; (setq dag_patterns
;;; '((predicate arg0 arg1)
;;;   (predicate arg0)
;;;   (predicate)
;;;   (conj prop1 prop2)
;;;   (action arg0 arg1)
;;;   ((cat VP) ? meaning ? presupp)
;;;   ((cat V) ? subcat ? preposition ? object1 ? object2 ? meaning ? presupp)
;;;   ((cat PP) ? preposition ? subject ? object ? ppresupp ? objpresupp)
;;;   ((cat NP) ? presupp ? referent)
;;;   ((cat N) ? presupp ? referent)
;;;   ((cat P) ? root ? presupp ? subject ? object)
;;;   ((cat D))
;;;   ((cat Pron))))
;;;
;;; Each rule (single line above) specifies the positions which features
;;; are to be assigned in the term representation. For instance,
;;;   (predicate arg0 arg1)
;;; indicates that the predicate value comes first (will be the
;;; function symbol), the arg0 value next and the arg1 value last.
;;; No other features will be given positions if this rule is used.
;;; termify_dag goes through the rules in sequence, until it finds
;;; one that will apply to the dag it is given. It then constructs
;;; a term as directed by that rule, calling termify_dag recursively
;;; on any category-valued features
;;;
;;; The elements in the rules are to be interpreted as follows.
;;; Each element provides a condition that the dag may satisfy
;;; and a specification of what value is to be put in the
;;; corresponding position in the term
;;;
;;; <simple feature name> -in order for the rule to apply, the dag
;;;                        MUST explicitly mention this feature.
;;;                        The value used is the termify_dag of
;;;                        the feature value.
;;; ? <feature name>      -the dag need not explicitly mention this
;;;                        feature. The value used is the termify_dag
;;;                        of the value in the dag, if there is one,
;;;                        or a new variable otherwise.
;;; * <constant>          -the constant value is to be put in this
;;;                        position in the term.
;;; (<name> <value>)      -the rule only applies if the dag specifies
;;;                        exactly this value for this feature. In
;;;                        this case, the value used is the value

(uses 'dagunify)
(uses 'subsumes)
(uses 'tunify)
(uses 'tsubsume)

(defvar dag_patterns)

(defun termify_dag (dag)
  (if (consp dag)
    (catch 'got_it
      (dolist (patt dag_patterns)
```

```lisp
         (do
           ((remaining patt) (result nil) (failed nil))
           ((or (null remaining) failed)
            (if failed
                 nil
                 (throw 'got_it (reverse result))))
            (if (equal (car remaining) '*)
               (progn
                  (setq result (cons (cadr remaining) result))
                  (setq remaining (cddr remaining)))
               (if (equal (car remaining) '?)
                 (let
                   ((val
                      (find_feature_value (cadr remaining) dag empty_subst)))
                   (setq result
                     (cons
                       (if (equal val 'ANY)
                         (newvar)
                         (termify_dag val))
                       result))
                   (setq remaining (cddr remaining)))
                 (if (consp (car remaining))
                   (let
                     ((val
                        (find_feature_value (caar remaining) dag empty_subst)))
                     (if (equal val (cadar remaining))
                       (progn
                         (setq result (cons (termify_dag val) result))
                         (setq remaining (cdr remaining)))
                       (setq failed t)))
                   (let
                     ((val
                        (find_feature_value (car remaining) dag empty_subst)))
                     (if (equal val 'ANY)
                       (setq failed t)
                       (progn
                         (setq result (cons (termify_dag val) result))
                         (setq remaining (cdr remaining)))))))))
        (error "No termify rule matches dag ~S" dag))
      dag))
```

```lisp
;;; tsubsume.lsp [Chapter 7] Subsumption for term
```

```lisp
(defvar var_map)

(defun termsubsumes (t1 t2)
  (setq var_map nil)
  (tersubs1 t1 t2))
```

```
(defun tersubs1 (t1 t2)
  (if (equal t1 t2)
    t
    (if (isvar t1)
      (if (assoc t1 var_map)
        (equal (cadr (assoc t1 var_map)) t2)
        (progn
          (setq var_map
            (cons (list t1 t2) var_map))
          t))
      (if (and (consp t1) (consp t2) (equal (length t1) (length t2)))
        (tersubs_list t1 t2)
        nil)))))
(defun tersubs_list (t1 t2) ; lists assumed same length
  (if (null t1)
    t
    (and
      (tersubs1 (car t1) (car t2))
      (tersubs_list (cdr t1) (cdr t2)))))
```

```
;;; tunify.lsp [Chapter 7] Term unification
```

```
(uses 'subst)

(defun termunify (term1 term2)
  (termunify1 term1 term2 empty_subst))

(defun termunify1 (term1 term2 subst)
  (let (
    (realterm1 (lookup_subst term1 subst))
    (realterm2 (lookup_subst term2 subst)))
    (if (equal realterm1 realterm2)
      subst
      (if (isvar realterm2)
        (add_subst realterm2 realterm1 subst)
        (if (isvar realterm1)
          (add_subst realterm1 realterm2 subst)
          (if (and
              (consp realterm1) (consp realterm2)
              (equal (length realterm1) (length realterm2)))
            (termunify_lists realterm1 realterm2 subst)
            nil))))))
(defun termunify_lists (list1 list2 subst) ; lists assumed same length
  (if (null list1)
    subst
    (let ((newsubst (termunify1 (car list1) (car list2) subst)))
      (if newsubst
        (termunify_lists (cdr list1) (cdr list2) newsubst)
        nil))))
```

SOLUTIONS TO SELECTED EXERCISES

Chapter 2

2.13 *Hint*: Use trace on recognize_next to spot when a state in the search space keeps repeating. Look to see which node in the network this state involves and reorder the arcs coming from this node so that another one is chosen first.

2.15 A solution to this exercise is presented in lib bubrecog.

2.16 *Hint*: Include in the representation of a state in the search space the list of nodes that have been visited previously. Thus, redefine recognize_next to be of the form:

```
(defun recognize_next (node tape network visited_previously)
    ...
```

When recognize_next is called recursively, the recursive call needs to be given a list that is the same as the original call, except that the current node is added to the front. When a final state is encountered, an appropriate list of nodes can be returned, instead of true. It does not matter if the list of nodes visited comes out in reverse order.

2.25 *Hint*: For your network to 'remember' the first character and to produce it at the end of the second tape, the nodes that a traversal passes through must be different for each possible value of the first character. Thus, the network will consist of many pieces of network like the following:

```
From    1 to 212 by a_h
From 212 to 213 by ^_^
From 213 to    2 by h_a
```

2.28 A solution to this exercise is presented in lib fstgen.

2.29 Here is a sketch of how one might argue. Imagine an FSTN that can recognize precisely the strings in the language $a^n b^n$. Since this network can accept any number of initial as but the network itself only has a finite number of nodes, there must be at least one cycle in the network that accepts a sequence of m as, where m is greater than 0. Moreover, for any n sufficiently large, the recognition of $a^n b^n$ must involve the traversal of such a cycle. Let N be such a value and M be the length of one such cycle that is traversed. Then there is a traversal of the network that is just like the traversal for $a^N b^N$, except that the cycle is traversed one more time. This traversal accepts the string $a^{N+M} b^N$, which is not in the desired language. This contradicts the original assumption. Therefore, such an FSTN cannot exist.

Chapter 3

3.4 *Hint*: You need to argue that at each stage a selected state only leads to a finite number of next states and that it is not possible for a state to lead to a state that leads to a state, and so on indefinitely. Therefore, if a given state is not immediately selected, then it will be nevertheless eventually selected, even if you have to wait until all the other alternatives, and the states that follow from them, have been exhausted.

3.12 A solution to this exercise is presented in lib pdtransd.

3.13 *Hint*: A string is of the form $a^n b^n$ if it is empty or if it consists of an a, followed by a string of this form, followed by a b.

3.14 If there is no VP network, then it is not possible for networks to talk about VPs as constituents. For instance, it is hard to express the fact that VPs can be conjoined ('took over the company and sacked the directors') and that certain verbs subcategorize for VPs ('threatened to take over the company').

3.16 *Hint*: To associate the right NP with the right 'hole', it is necessary for the HOLD register to be a stack. The only element that can be used to fill a hole is then the last element that was 'pushed' on to the register. This ensures that, in the second example, Hanni is seen to have erased the tape, rather than the man. Previous tests for ensuring that the HOLD register is empty in various places now have to be appropriately modified.

3.17 The extended ATN is presented in lib atnarcs2.

Chapter 4

4.2 *Hint*: For a rule like A → B C D, you can introduce arcs like the following in a network named A:

```
Initial 1
Final 10
From 1 to  2 by B
From 2 to  3 by C
From 3 to 10 by D
```

Where there are multiple rules for a category A, you simply add together the nodes and arcs from the individual rules. For elegance, you could conflate together all the initial nodes, as well as all the final nodes.

4.4 *Hint*: Here is one possible approach. You will need to create a new category for each cycle in a network. The rules for this category consist of one rule that corresponds to going round the cycle and one rule that has an empty RHS. For each path through a network (from an initial node to a final node) that does not go round a cycle, you can create a rule for the category named by the network, simply spelling out the sequence of arc labels encountered. Finally, wherever such a path goes through a node that is on a cycle, you need to splice into the rule an occurrence of the category created to represent that cycle. This procedure, while correct, does not result in optimal rule sets.

4.8 *Hint*: Does the grammar allow a whole sentence to be topicalized, with the remaining S/S being simply the empty string?

4.12 *Hint*: Consider VPs like 'I handed Dr Chan donations' and 'I bet Dr Chan thousands patients had recovered'.

4.13 *Hint*: If a mother category has a non-0 slash, how many of the daughters will also have a non-0 slash?

4.20 *Hint*: You will need to introduce rules rather like the following:

```
NP → Det N S
  <S slash> = NP
```

4.23 A solution to this exercise is presented in lib featexp.

Chapter 5

5.2   *Hint*: This problem is described in Hopcroft and Ullman (1979, Section 4.4). The basic idea is, first of all, to determine the set of categories that can be realized by the empty string (the 'nullable' categories). Any category that has a rule with an empty RHS is obviously a nullable category. Similarly, any category with a rule, all of whose RHS categories are nullable, is nullable. Secondly, the new grammar is constructed out of all the rules with non-empty RHSs that can be derived by deleting zero or more nullable categories from the RHS of rules in the original grammar.

5.5   A solution to this exercise is presented in lib buparse1.

5.6   A solution to this exercise is presented in lib buparse2.

5.7   *Hint*: The basic idea is to replace a pair of rules like $A \to AB$ and $A \to C$ by the rules $A \to CZ$, $Z \to$ and $Z \to BZ$. Variations on this theme can eliminate rules of the form $A \to AB...$, but will not handle indirect left recursion in cases like $A \to BC$ and $B \to AD$. Aho and Ullman (1972, Vol.1, Section 2.4.4) present a general algorithm.

Chapter 6

6.1   Here is probably the simplest way to change lib tdparse to use a WFST. Whenever the procedure find_trees produces a result, it also adds a new element of the form:

> ((goal string) list_of_results)

to the value of a global variable wfst. This variable now serves as a primitive WFST, recording the successful results of previous parsing attempts (even though it uses a representation that does not facilitate rapid retrieval by indexing on the position in the input). The start of find_trees now needs to be altered to consult this table:

```
(defun find_trees (goal string)
  ;; returns a list of (parse_tree remaining_string) pairs
  (let ((results (cadr(assoc (list goal string) wfst :test #'equal))))
    (if results
      results
      (if (listp goal)     ; a category
        ...
```

6.3 If the grammar contains ε-productions, then the WFST graph needs to include arcs that start and finish at the same point in the input, that is, it needs to allow certain simple cycles.

6.7 *Hint*: If the grammar has the rule A → A, as well as other rules for A, then it assigns infinitely many different analyses to any phrase of type A. If a chart parser, as described, considers edges to be different if they include different parse trees, then it should get into an infinite loop with such a grammar. A similar problem will arise with A → B A if B can be realized as the empty string. It could be argued that natural language grammars are not (should not be?) of this form. Otherwise, one solution might be to run a chart recognizer and then, somehow, reconstruct as many different parse trees as are needed.

Chapter 7

7.9 *Hint*: You will find that the program sometimes seems to get involved in a very long computation without returning an answer in reasonable time. Use trace to see what sorts of phrases it is trying to generate. Having found out when the problem arises, use the interactive version of oneof to help the program avoid these problems. On the basis of the sentences that you can then generate, comment on the deficiencies of the grammar.

7.10 A solution to this exercise is presented in lib randftre.

7.14 Consult Shieber (1985c).

7.18 *Hint*: One way is to encode in sequence the restrictions that a verb makes on the phrases that follow it and then the restrictions it makes on its subject. Thus, the following entry:

```
Lexeme persuade:
    <cat> = V
    <subcat first cat> = NP
    <subcat first case> = non_subject
    <subcat rest first cat> = VP
    <subcat rest rest first cat> = NP
    <subcat rest rest first case> = subject
    <subcat rest rest rest> = NIL.
```

encodes the fact that 'persuade' requires a non-subject NP and a VP to follow it, and that 'persuade' requires a subject NP to come before it. Here are two rules that make use of such a representation:

```
Rule
  VP → V:
    <VP subcat> = <V subcat>.

Rule
  VP1 → VP2 X:
    <VP2 subcat first> = X
    <VP1 subcat> = <VP2 subcat rest>.
```

7.21 A solution to this exercise is presented in lib lexicon.

Chapter 8

8.2 Here are some of the rules that you might employ:

```
Rule
  number → less_than_1000.
Rule
  number → less_than_1000 thousand less_than_1000.
Rule
  less_than_1000 → digit hundred.

Word two: <cat> = digit.
Word thousand: <cat> = thousand.
```

and here is part of one possible interpretation procedure:

```
(defun interpret_number (tree)
  (if (equal (length tree) 2)          ; (number (less_than_1000 ...))
    (interpret_less_than_1000 (nth 1 tree))
    (if (equal (length tree) 4)        ; (number ... thousand ...)
      (+
        (* (interpret_less_than_1000 (nth 1 tree)) 1000)
        (interpret_less_than_1000 (nth 3 tree)))
      ...
```

8.3 Of course, the shape of your program will depend on the output language that you choose. If you choose English (using the grammar above), then part of the program might look like the following:

```
(defun generate_number (tree)
  (if (<= (length tree) 3)
    (list 'number (generate_less_than_1000 tree))
    (let ((thousands (butlast tree 3)) (htu (nthcdr (-(length tree) 3) tree)))
      (list
        'number
        (generate_less_than_1000 thousands)
        '(thousand thousand)
        (generate_less_than_1000 htu)))))
```

Chapter 9

9.1   *Hint*: Here is the value of dag_patterns that you will need:

```
((predicate ? arg0 ? arg1 ? arg2)
 (connective prop1 prop2)
 ((cat IMP) ? sem ? pre)
 ((cat V) ? subcat ? p ? arg1 ? arg2 ? sem ? pre)
 ((cat PP) ? p ? arg0 ? arg1 ? p_pre ? np_pre)
 ((cat NP) ? pre ? referent)
 ((cat N) ? pre ? referent)
 ((cat P) ? p ? pre ? arg0 ? arg1)
 ((cat DET)))
```

9.4   A solution to this sort of problem is discussed in S. J. Kaplan (1983).

9.9   Here are the inference rules for the grammar corresponding to Grammar1 of Chapter 4:

```
(((S _s1 _s3) (NP _s1 _s2) (VP _s2 _s3))
 ((VP _s1 _s3) (V _s1 _s2) (NP _s2 _s3))
 ((VP _s1 _s2) (V _s1 _s2))
 ((NP (Dr (Chan _s)) _s))
 ((NP (nurses _s) _s))
 ((NP (MediCenter _s) _s))
 ((NP (patients _s) _s))
 ((V (died _s) _s))
 ((V (employed _s) _s)))
```

With these rules, try doing the following:

```
(dolist (x (back_infer '(S _s ()))) (print (apply_subst x '_s)))
```

9.10   Here is how the above inference rules could be modified to build parse trees:

```
(((S (S _nptree _vptree) _s1 _s3) (NP _nptree _s1 _s2) (VP _vptree _s2 _s3))
 ((VP (VP _vtree _nptree) _s1 _s3) (V _vtree _s1 _s2) (NP _nptree _s2 _s3))
 ((VP (VP _vtree) _s1 _s2) (V _vtree _s1 _s2))
 ((NP (NP Dr Chan) (Dr (Chan _s)) _s))
 ((NP (NP nurses) (nurses _s) _s))
 ((NP (NP MediCenter) (MediCenter _s) _s))
 ((NP (NP patients) (patients _s) _s))
 ((V (V died) (died _s) _s))
 ((V (V employed) (employed _s) _s)))
```

With these rules, try doing the following:

```
(dolist (x (back_infer '(S _s (Dr (Chan (employed (nurses ())))))))
   (print (apply_subst x '_s)))
```

Chapter 10

10.13 For the first example, here are the inference rules and the desired call to plan:

```
(((channel sue alan))
 ((at alan inside))
 ((at sue inside)))

(plan 'sue '((at alan outside)))
```

Here are the same for the new example:

```
(((channel sue alan))
 ((channel alan sue))
 ((channel alan ann))
 ((channel ann alan))
 ((knows_ref ann combination)))

(plan 'sue '((knows_ref sue combination)))
```

BIBLIOGRAPHY

Ahlswede, Thomas E. (1985). A tool kit for lexicon building. *ACL Proceedings, 23rd Annual Meeting*, 268–76.

Aho, Alfred V. (1968). Indexed grammars – an extension of context-free grammars. *Journal of the ACM*, **15**, 647–71.

Aho, Alfred V. and Ullman, Jeffrey D. (1972). *The Theory of Parsing, Translation, and Compiling*. Prentice-Hall: Englewood Cliffs, NJ.

Aho, Alfred V. and Ullman, Jeffrey D. (1977). *Principles of Compiler Design*. Addison-Wesley: Reading, MA.

Aho, Alfred V., Hopcroft, John E. and Ullman, Jeffrey D. (1982). *Data Structures and Algorithms*. Addison Wesley: Reading, MA.

Alam, Yukiko Sasaki (1983). A two-level morphological analysis of Japanese. *Texas Linguistic Forum*, **22**, 229–52.

Allen, James F. (1983). Recognizing intentions from natural language utterances. In *Computational Models of Discourse* (Michael Brady and Robert C. Berwick, eds.), pp. 107–66, MIT Press: Cambridge, MA.

Allen, James (1987). *Natural Language Understanding*. Benjamin Cummings: Menlo Park.

Allen, James F. and Perrault, C. Raymond (1980). Analyzing intention in utterances. *Artificial Intelligence*, **15**, 143–78. Reprinted in *Readings in Natural Language Processing* (Barbara J. Grosz, Karen Sparck Jones and Bonnie Lynn Webber, eds.), pp. 441–58, Morgan Kaufmann: Los Altos, 1986.

Alshawi, Hiyan (1987). *Memory and Context for Language Interpretation*. Cambridge University Press: Cambridge.

Alshawi, Hiyan, Boguraev, Branimir K. and Briscoe, Edward J. (1985). Towards a dictionary support environment for real time parsing. *ACL Proceedings, Second European Conference, 171–8.*

Appelt, Douglas E. (1985). *Planning English Sentences*. Cambridge University Press: Cambridge.

Ballard, Bruce W. and Jones, Mark A. (1987). Computational linguistics. In *Encyclopaedia of Artificial Intelligence* (Stuart C. Shapiro, ed.) pp. 133–51, Wiley: New York.

Barnett, Brigitte, Lehmann, Hubert and Zoeppritz, Magdalena (1986). A word database for natural language processing. *COLING-86*, 435–40.

Barr, Avron and Feigenbaum, Edward A. eds. (1981). *The Handbook of Artificial Intelligence*, 1. William Kaufmann: Palo Alto.

Barton, Edward, G. Jr., Berwick, Robert C. and Sven Ristad, Eric (1987). *Computational Complexity and Natural Language*. MIT Press: Cambridge, MA.

Bartsch, Renate (1987). Frame representations and discourse representations. *Theoretical Linguistics*, **14**, 65–117.

Barwise, Jon (1981). Some computational aspects of situation semantics. *ACL Proceedings, 19th Annual Meeting*, 109–11.

Barwise, Jon and Perry, John (1983). *Situations and Attitudes*. MIT Press: Cambridge, MA.

Bates, Madeleine (1978). The theory and practice of ATN grammars. In *Natural Language Communication with Computers* (L. Bolc, ed.), pp. 191–259, Springer Verlag: Berlin.

Bear, John (1988). Morphology with two-level rules and negative rule features. *COLING-88*, 28–31.

Beierle, Christoph and Pletat, Udo (1988). Feature graphs and abstract data types: a unifying approach. *COLING-88*, 40–5.

Blåberg, Olli (1985). A two-level description of Swedish. In *Computational Morphosyntax: Report on Research 1981–1984* (Fred Karlsson, ed.), pp. 43–62, University of Helsinki, Helsinki.

Black, Alan, Ritchie, Graeme, Pulman, Stephen G. and Russell, Graham (1987). Formalisms for morphographemic description. *ACL Proceedings, Third European Conference*, 11–18.

Blank, Glenn D. (1985). A new kind of finite-state automation: register vector grammar. *IJCAI-85*, **2**, 749–55.

Bobrow, Danny G. and Fraser J. Bruce (1969). An augmented state transition network analysis procedure. *IJCAI-69*, 557–67.

Boguraev, Branimir K., Carter, David and Briscoe, Edward J. (1987a). A multi-purpose interface to an on-line dictionary. *ACL Proceedings, Third European Conference*, 63–9.

Boguraev, Branimir K., Briscoe, Edward J., Carroll, John, Carter, David and Grover, Claire (1987b). The derivation of grammatically indexed lexicon from the Longman Dictionary of Contemporary English. *ACL Proceedings, 25th Annual Meeting*, 193–200.

Bolc, Leonard, ed. (1980). *Natural Language Question Answering Systems*. Hanser: Munich.

Bouma, Gosse (1988). Modifiers and specifiers in categorial unification grammar. *Linguistics*, **26**, 21–46.

Brachman, Ronald J. and Levesque, Hector J. (1985). *Readings in Knowledge Representation*. Morgan Kaufmann: Los Altos.

Brachman, Ronald J. and Schmolze, J. (1985). An overview of the KL-ONE knowledge representation system. *Cognitive Science*, **9**, 171–216.

Briscoe, Edward J. and Boguraev, Branimir K. (1988). *Computational Lexicography for Natural Language Processing*. Longman/Wiley: London/New York.

Brodda, Benny (1986). BetaText: an event driven text processing and text analyzing system. *COLING-86*, 421–2.

Bruce, Bertram C. and Moser, M.G. (1987). Case grammar. In *Encyclopaedia of Artificial Intelligence* (Stuart C. Shapiro, ed.), pp. 333–9, Wiley: New York.

Bundy, Alan (1983). *The Computer Modelling of Mathematical Reasoning*. Academic Press: London.

Bunt, Harry C. (1984). The resolution of quantificational ambiguities in the TENDUM computational linguistics research system. *COLING-84*, 130–3.

Calder, Jonathan, Klein, Ewan and Zeevat, Henk (1988). Unification Categorial Grammar: a concise, extendable grammar for natural language processing. *COLING-88*, 83–6.

Calzolari, Nicoletta and Picchi, Eugenio (1988). Acquisition of semantic information from an on-line dictionary. *COLING-88*, 87–92.

Carden, Guy (1983). The non-finite-state-ness of the word formation component. *Linguistic Inquiry*, **14**, 537–41.

Carlson, Lauri and Linden, Krister (1987). Unification as a grammatical tool. *Nordic Journal of Linguistics*, **10**, 111–36.

Carson, Julie (1988). Unification and transduction in computational phonology. *COLING-88*, 106–11.

Cercone, Nick, Krause, Max and Boates, John (1983). Minimal and almost minimal perfect hash function search with application to natural language lexicon design. *Computers and Mathematics with Applications*, **9**, 215–31.

Charniak, Eugene (1973). Jack and Jane in search of a theory of knowledge. In *Readings in Natural Language Processing* (Barbara J. Grosz, Karen Sparck Jones and Bonnie Lynn Webber, eds.), pp. 331–7, Morgan Kaufmann: Los Altos, 1986.

Charniak, Eugene (1983). A parser with something for everyone. In *Parsing Natural Language* (Margaret King, ed.), pp. 117–49, Academic Press: London.

Charniak, Eugene and Goldman, Robert (1988). A logic for semantic interpretation. *ACL Proceedings, 26th Annual Meeting*, 87–94.

Charniak, Eugene and McDermott, Drew V. (1985). *Introduction to Artificial Intelligence*. Addison-Wesley: Reading, MA.

Charniak, Eugene, Riesbeck, Christopher K. and McDermott, Drew V. (1980). *Artificial Intelligence Programming*. Lawrence Erlbaum: Hillsdale.

Choffrut, Christian and Culik, Karel, II (1983). Properties of finite and pushdown transducers. *SIAM Journal of Computing*, **12**, 300–15.

Church, Kenneth W. (1983a). A finite-state parser for use in speech recognition. *ACL Proceedings, 21st Annual Meeting*, 91–7.

Church, Kenneth W. (1983b). *Phrase Structure Parsing: A Method for Taking Advantage of Allophonic Constraints*. MIT PhD Dissertation, Indiana University Linguistics Club, Bloomington.

Church, Kenneth W. and Patil, Ramesh (1982). Coping with syntactic ambiguity or how to put the block in the box on the table. *American Journal of Computational Linguistics*, **8**, 139–49.

Cohen, Philip R. (1984). Referring as requesting. *COLING-84*, 207–11.

Cohen, Philip R. and Levesque, Hector J. (1985). Speech acts and rationality. *ACL Proceedings, 23rd Annual Meeting*, 49–60.

Cohen, Philip R. and Perrault, C. Raymond (1979). Elements of a plan-based theory of speech acts. In *Readings in Natural Language Processing* (Barbara J. Grosz, Karen Sparck Jones and Bonnie Lynn Webber, eds.) pp. 423–40, Morgan Kaufmann: Los Altos, 1986.

Colmerauer, Alain (1978). Metamorphosis grammars. In *Natural Language Communication with Computers* (L. Bolc, ed.), pp. 133–89, Springer Verlag: Berlin.

Conway, M.E. (1963). Design of a separable transition-diagram compiler. *Communications of the ACM*, **6**, 396–408.

Cooper, Robin (1983). *Quantification and Syntactic Theory*. Reidel: Dordrecht.

Cooper, Robin (1987). Meaning representation in Montague grammar and situation semantics. *Computational Intelligence*, **3**, 35–44.

Cullingford, Richard E. (1981). SAM. In *Readings in Natural Language Processing* (Barbara J. Grosz, Karen Sparck Jones and Bonnie Lynn Webber, eds.), pp. 627–49, Morgan Kaufmann: Los Altos, 1986.

Culy, Christopher (1985). The complexity of the vocabulary of Bambara. *Linguistics and Philosophy* **8**, 345–51.

Daelemans, Walter M. P. (1987). A tool for the automatic creation, extension and updating of lexical knowledge bases. *ACL Proceedings, Third European Conference*, 70–4.

Dahlgren, Kathleen (1988). *Naive Semantics for Natural Language Understanding*. Kluwer: Boston, 1988.

Daly, R. T. (1974). *Applications of the Mathematical Theory of Linguistics*. Mouton: The Hague.

De Smedt, Koenraad (1984). Using object-oriented knowledge-representation techniques in morphology and syntax programming. *ECAI-84*, 181–4.

Domenig, Marc and Shann, Patrick (1986). Towards a dedicated database management system for dictionaries. *COLING-86*, 91–6.

Dowty, David R., Wall, Robert and Peters, P. Stanley (1981). *Introduction to Montague Semantics*. Reidel: Dordrecht.

Dowty, David R., Karttunen, Lauri and Zwicky, Arnold M. eds. (1985). *Natural Language Parsing*. Cambridge University Press: Cambridge.

Dyer, Michael G., Cullingford, Richard E. and S. Alvarado (1987). Scripts. In *Encyclopaedia of Artificial Intelligence* (Stuart C. Shapiro, ed.), pp. 980–94, Wiley: New York.

Earley, Jay (1970). An efficient context-free parsing algorithm. *Communications of the ACM*, **14**, 453–60. Reprinted in *Readings in Natural Language Processing* (Barbara J. Grosz, Karen Sparck Jones and Bonnie Lynn Webber, eds.), pp. 25–33, Morgan Kaufmann: Los Altos, 1986.

Ejerhed, Eva (1982). The processing of unbounded dependencies in Swedish. In *Readings on Unbounded Dependencies in Scandinavian Languages* (Elisabet Engdahl and Eva Ejerhed, eds.), pp. 99–149, Almqvist & Wiksell: Stockholm.

Ejerhed, Eva and Church, Kenneth W. (1983). Finite state parsing. In *Papers from the Seventh Scandinavian Conference of Linguistics* (Fred Karlsson, ed.), pp. 410–32, University of Helsinki: Helsinki.

Engdahl, Elisabet (1986). *Constituent Questions*. Reidel: Dordrecht.

Etherington, David W. (1988). *Reasoning with Incomplete Information*. Pitman/ Morgan Kaufmann: London/Los Altos.

Evans, David A. (1981). A situation semantics approach to the analysis of speech acts. *ACL Proceedings, 19th Annual Meeting*, 113–6.

Evans, David A. and Katz, Sandra (1986). A practical lexicon for constrained NLP. In *ESCOL'86 Proceedings of the Third Eastern States Conference on Linguistics* (Fred Marshall, Ann Miller and Zheng-sheng Zhang, eds.), pp. 151–62, Ohio State University: Columbus.

Evans, David A. and Scott, Dana S. (1986). Concepts as procedures. In *ESCOL'86 Proceedings of the Third Eastern States Conference on Linguistics* (Fred Marshall, Ann Miller and Zheng-sheng Zhang, eds.), pp. 533–43, Ohio State University: Columbus.

Evans, R. and Gazdar, G. (1989a). Inference in DATR. *ACL Proceedings, Fourth European Conference*.

Evans, R. and Gazdar, G. (1989b). The semantics of DATR. In *Proceedings of AISB89* (Tony Cohn, ed.). London: Pitman.

Evens, Martha W. (1988). *Relational Models of the Lexicon: Representing Knowledge in Semantic Networks*. Cambridge University Press: Cambridge.

Evey, R. James (1963). Application of pushdown-store machines. In *Proceedings of the 1963 Fall Joint Computer Conference*, pp. 215–27, AFIPS Press: Montvale, NJ.

Fenstad, Jens Erik, Halvorsen, Per-Kristian, Langholm, Tore and van Benthem, Johan (1987). *Situations, Language and Logic*. Reidel: Dordrecht.

Fillmore, Charles J. (1968). The case for case. In *Universals in Linguistic Theory* (Emmon Bach and Robert Harms, eds.), pp. 1–88, Holt, Rinehart & Winston: New York.

Flickinger, Daniel P., Pollard, Carl J. and Wasow, Thomas (1985). Structure-sharing in lexical representation. *ACL Proceedings, 23rd Annual Meeting*, 262–7.

Frazier, Lyn and Fodor, Janet D. (1978). The sausage machine: a new two stage parsing model. *Cognition*, **6**, 291–325.

Friedman, Joyce, Moran, Douglas B. and Warren, David S. (1978a). An interpretation system for Montague grammar. *American Journal of Computational Linguistics*, **5**, Microfiche 74.

Friedman, Joyce, Moran, Douglas B. and Warren, David S. (1978b). Explicit finite intensional Models for PTQ. *American Journal of Computational Linguistics*, **5**, Microfiche 74.

Frisch, Alan M. (1986). Parsing with restricted quantification: an initial demonstration. *Computational Intelligence*, **2**, 142–50.

Gajek, Oliver, Beck, Hanno T., Elder, Diane and Whittemore, Greg (1983). KIMMO Lisp implementation. *Texas Linguistic Forum*, **22**, 187–202.

Gallaire, H. and Minker, Jack (1978). *Logic and Databases*. Plenum: New York.

Gallier, Jean H. (1986). *Logic for Computer Science*. Harper & Row: New York.

Gärdenfors, Peter (1987). *Generalized Quantifiers*. Reidel: Dordrecht.

Garnham, Alan (1983). What's wrong with story grammars? *Cognition*, **15**, 145–54.

Gazdar, Gerald (1985). Review article: finite state morphology. *Linguistics*, **23**, 597–607.

Gazdar, Gerald (1987). Linguistic applications of default inheritance mechanisms. In *Linguistic Theory & Computer Applications* (Peter Whitelock, Mary McGee Wood, Harold L. Somers, Rod L. Johnson and Paul Bennett, eds.), pp. 37–67, Academic Press: London.

Gazdar, Gerald (1988). Applicability of indexed grammars to natural languages. In *Natural Language Parsing and Linguistic Theories* (U. Reyle and C. Rohrer, eds.), pp. 69–94, D. Reidel: Dordrecht.

Gazdar, Gerald and Pullum, Geoffrey K. (1985). Computationally relevant properties of natural languages and their grammars. *New Generation Computing*, **3**, 273–306.

Gazdar, Gerald, Klein, Ewan, Pullum, Geoffrey and Sag, Ivan (1985). *Generalized Phrase Structure Grammar*. Blackwell: Oxford.

Gazdar, Gerald, Franz, Alex, Osborne, Karen and Evans, Roger (1987). *Natural Language Processing in the 1980s: A Bibliography*. University of Chicago Press: Chicago.

Gazdar, Gerald, Pullum, Geoffrey K., Carpenter, Robert, Klein, Ewan, Hukari, Thomas E. and Levine, Robert D. (1988). Category structures. *Computational Linguistics*, **14**, 1–19.

Genesereth, Michael R. and Nilsson, Nils J. (1987). *Logical Foundations of Artificial Intelligence*. Morgan Kaufmann: Los Altos.

Gersting, Judith L. (1982). *Mathematical Structures for Computer Science*. W.H. Freeman: San Francisco.

Gibbon, Dafydd (1987). Finite state processing of tone systems. *ACL Proceedings, Third European Conference*, 291–7.

Ginsberg, Matthew L. (1987). *Readings in Nonmonotonic Reasoning*. Morgan Kaufmann: Los Altos.

Gold, E. Mark (1967). Language identification in the limit. *Information and Control*, **10**, 447–74.

Görz, Günther (1981). GLP: a general linguistic processor. *IJCAI-81*, **1**, 429–31.

Görz, Günther (1982). Applying a chart parser to speech understanding. *ECAI-82*, 257–8.

Görz, Günther and Paulus, Dietrich (1988). A finite state approach to German verb morphology. *COLING-88*, 212–5.

Gray, Peter (1984). *Logic, Algebra and Databases*. Ellis Horwood: Chichester.

Grishman, Ralph (1986). *Computational Linguistics: An Introduction*. Cambridge University Press: Cambridge.

Groenendijk, Jeroen A.G. and Stokhof, Martin B.J. (1984). *Studies on the semantics of questions and the pragmatics of answers*. University of Amsterdam: Amsterdam.

Grosz, Barbara J. (1977). The representation and use of focus in dialogue understanding. PhD dissertation, University of California at Berkeley.

Grosz, Barbara J. and Sidner, Candace L. (1986). Attentions, intentions, and the structure of discourse. *Computational Linguistics*, **12**, 175–204.

Grosz, Barbara J., Sparck Jones, Karen and Webber, Bonnie Lynn eds. (1986). *Readings in Natural Language Processing*. Morgan Kaufmann: Los Altos.

Grosz, Barbara J., Appelt, Douglas E., Martin, Paul A. and Pereira, Fernando C.N. (1987). TEAM: An experiment in the design of transportable natural-language interfaces. *Artificial Intelligence*, **32** 173–243.

Guida, Giovanni and Mauri, Giancarlo (1986). Evaluation of natural language processing systems: issues and approaches. *Proceedings of the IEEE*, **74**(7), 1026–35.

Gunji, Takao (1987). *Japanese Phrase Structure Grammar*. Reidel: Dordrecht.

Haas, Andrew (1987). Parallel parsing for unification grammars. *IJCAI-87*, **2**, 615–8.

Haddock, Nicholas J. (1987). Incremental interpretation and combinatory categorial grammar. *IJCAI-87*, **2**, 661–3.

Haddock, Nicholas, Klein, Ewan and Morrill, Glyn eds. (1987). *Categorial Gram mar, Unification Grammar and Parsing*. Centre for Cognitive Science Edinburgh.

Hajicôvá, Eva and Sgall, Petr (1985). Towards an automatic identification of topic and focus. *ACL Proceedings, Second European Conference*, 263–7.

Hankamer, Jorge (1986). Finite state morphology and left to right phonology. In *Proceedings of the Fifth West Coast Conference on Formal Linguistics* (Mary Dalrymple, Jeffrey Goldberg, Kristin Hanson, Michael Inman, Chris Pinon and Stephen Wechsler, eds.), pp. 29–34, Stanford Linguistics Association: Stanford.

Harel, David (1987). Statecharts: a visual formalism for complex systems. *Science of Computer Programming*, **8**, 231–74.

Hawkins, John A. (1978). *Definiteness and Indefiniteness*. Croom Helm/ Humanities Press: London/Atlantic Highlands, NJ.

Heidorn, George E. (1982). Experience with an easily computed metric for ranking alternative parses. *ACL Proceedings, 20th Annual Meeting*, 82–4.

Hellwig, Peter (1986). Dependency unification grammar. *COLING-86*, 195–8.

Hendrix, Gary G. (1975). Expanding the utility of semantic networks through partitioning. *IJCAI-75*, 115–21.

Heny, Frank (1981). *Ambiguities in Intensional Contexts*. Reidel: Dordrecht.

Hess, Michael (1987). Descriptional anaphora in discourse representation theory. *ACL Proceedings, Third European Conference*, 148–55.

Hinrichs, Erhard W. (1986). A compositional semantics for directional modifiers – locative case reopened. *COLING-86*, 347–9.

Hinrichs, Erhard W. (1987). A compositional semantics of temporal expressions in English. *ACL Proceedings, 25th Annual Meeting*, 8–15.

Hirst, Graeme (1983). A foundation for semantic interpretation. *ACL Proceedings, 21st Annual Meeting*, 64–73.

Hirst, Graeme (1986). *Semantic Interpretation and the Resolution of Ambiguity*. Cambridge University Press: Cambridge.

Hobbs, Jerry R. (1983). An improper treatment of quantification in ordinary English. *ACL Proceedings, 21st Annual Meeting*, 57–63.

Hobbs, Jerry and Rosenschein, Stanley (1978). Making computational sense of Montague's intensional logic. *Artificial Intelligence*, **9**, 287–306.

Hobbs, Jerry R. and Shieber, Stuart M. (1987). An algorithm for generating quantifier scopings. *Computational Linguistics*, **13**, 47–63.

Hofstadter, Douglas R. (1979). *Gödel, Escher, Bach: An Eternal Golden Braid*. Basic Books: New York.

Hopcroft, John and Ullman, Jeffrey (1979). *Introduction to Automata Theory, Languages, and Computation*. Addison-Wesley: Reading, MA.

Horrocks, Geoffrey (1987). *Generative Grammar*. Longman: London.

Horton, Diane L. and Hirst, Graeme (1988). Presuppositions as beliefs. *COL-ING-88*, 255–60.

Houghton, George (1989). *A Computational Model of Discourse Production*. Ablex, Norwood: New Jersey.

Hurum, Sven O. (1988). Handling scope ambiguities in English. *ACL Proceedings, Second Conference on Applied Natural Language Processing*, 58–65.

Hurum, Sven O. and Schubert, Lenhart K. (1986). Two types of quantifier scoping. *Proceedings of the 6th Canadian Conference on Artificial Intelligence*, 39–43.

Hutchins, W. John (1986). *Machine Translation: Past, Present, Future*. Ellis Horwood/Wiley: Chichester/New York.

Huybregts, Riny (1985). The weak inadequacy of context-free phrase structure grammar. In *Van Periferie naar Kern* (Gier de Haan, Mieke Trommelen and Wim Zonneveld, eds.), pp. 81–99, Foris: Dordrecht.

Isoda, Michio, Aiso, Hideo, Kamibayashi, Noriyuki and Matsunaga, Yoshifumi (1986). Model for lexical knowledge base. *COLING-86*, 451–3.

Israel, David J. (1983). A prolegomenon to situation semantics. *ACL Proceedings, 21st Annual Meeting*, 28–37.

Jacobs, Paul and Zernik, Uri (1988). Acquiring lexical knowledge from text: a case study. *AAAI-88*, 739–44.

Johnson, C. Douglas (1972). *Formal Aspects of Phonological Description*. Mouton: The Hague.

Johnson, Mark (1988). *Attribute-Value Logic and the Theory of Grammar*. CSLI Lecture Notes No. 14, Chicago University Press: Chicago.

Johnson, Mark and Klein, Ewan (1986). Discourse, anaphora and parsing *COL-ING-86*, 669–75.

Johnson, Rod L. (1983). Parsing with transition networks. In *Parsing Natural Language* (Margaret King, ed.), pp. 59–72, Academic Press: London.

Johnson, Tim (1985). *Natural Language Computing: the Commercial Implications*. Ovum: London.

Johnson-Laird, Philip N. (1983). *Mental Models*. Cambridge University Press: Cambridge.

Joshi, Aravind K. (1987). Phrase structure grammar. In *Encyclopaedia of Artificial Intelligence* (Stuart C. Shapiro, ed.), pp. 344–51, Wiley: New York.

Joshi, Aravind K., Webber, Bonnie Lynn and Sag, Ivan A. eds. (1981). *Elements of Discourse Understanding*. Cambridge University Press: Cambridge.

Kamp, Hans (1981). A theory of truth and semantic representation. In *Formal Methods in the Study of Language* (J.A.G. Groenendijk, T.M.V. Janssen and M.B.J. Stokhof, eds.), pp. 277–322, Mathematical Centre Tracts 135: Amsterdam.

Kaplan, Ronald M. (1972). Augmented transition networks as psychological models of sentence comprehension. *Artificial Intelligence*, **3**, 77–100.

Kaplan, Ronald M. (1973). A general syntactic processor. In *Natural Language Processing* (Randall Rustin, ed.), pp. 193–241, Algorithmics Press: New York.

Kaplan, Ronald M. and Bresnan, Joan (1982). Lexical functional grammar: A formal system for grammatical representation. In *The Mental Representation of Grammatical Relations* (Joan Bresnan, ed.), pp. 173–281, MIT Press: Cambridge MA.

Kaplan, S. Jerrold (1983). Cooperative responses from a portable natural language database query system. In *Computational Models of Discourse* (Michael Brady and Robert C. Berwick, eds.) pp. 167–208, MIT Press: Cambridge, MA.

Karttunen, Lauri (1983). KIMMO: a general morphological processor. *Texas Linguistic Forum*, **22**, 165–86.

Karttunen, Lauri (1984). Features and values. *COLING-84*, 28–33.

Karttunen, Lauri (1986). D-PATR: a development environment for unification-based grammars. *COLING–86*, 74–80.

Karttunen, Lauri and Kay, Martin (1985). Structure sharing with binary trees. *ACL Proceedings, 23rd Annual Meeting*, 133–6.

Karttunen, Lauri and Wittenburg, Kent (1983). A two-level morphological analysis of English. *Texas Linguistic Forum*, **22**, 217–28.

Kasper, Robert (1987). A unification method for disjunctive feature descriptions. *ACL Proceedings, 25th Annual Meeting*, 235–42.

Kasper, Robert and Rounds, Williams (1986). A logical semantics for feature structures. *ACL Proceedings, 24th Annual Meeting, 257–66.*

Kataja, Laura and Koskenniemi, Kimmo (1988). Finite-state description of Semitic morphology: a case study of ancient Accadian. *COLING-88*, 313–5.

Katz, Jerrold J. and Fodor, Jerry A. (1963). The structure of a semantic theory. *Language*, **39**, 170–210.

Kay, Martin (1973). The MIND system. In *Natural Language Processing* (Randall Rustin, ed.), pp. 155–88, Algorithmics Press: New York.

Kay, Martin (1979). Functional grammar. In *Proceedings of the Fifth Annual Meeting of the Berkeley Linguistics Society* (Christina Chiarello *et al.*, eds.) pp. 142–58.

Kay, Martin (1980). Algorithm schemata and data structures in syntactic processing. In *Readings in Natural Language Processing* (Barbara J. Grosz, Karen Sparck Jones and Bonnie Lynn Webber, eds.), pp. 35–70, Morgan Kaufmann: Los Altos, 1986.

Kay, Martin (1983). When meta-rules are not meta-rules. In *Automatic Natural Language Parsing* (Karen Sparck Jones and Yorick A. Wilks, eds.), pp. 94–116, Ellis Horwood/Wiley: Chichester/New York.

Kay, Martin (1984). Computational linguistics = generalized unification + applied graph theory. *Proceedings of the Fifth Biennial Conference of the Canadian Society for Computational Studies of Intelligence*, 1–5.

Kay, Martin (1985a). Parsing in functional unification grammar. In *Natural Language Parsing* (David R. Dowty, Lauri Karttunen and Arnold M. Zwicky, eds.), pp. 251–78, Cambridge University Press: Cambridge.

Kay, Martin (1985b). Unification in grammar. In *Natural Language Understanding and Logic Programming* (Veronica Dahl and Patrick Saint-Dizier, eds.), pp. 233–40, North-Holland: Amsterdam.

Kay, Martin (1987). Nonconcatenative finite-state morphology. *ACL Proceedings, Third European Conference*, 2–10.

Keller, William R. (1988), Nested Cooper storage: the proper treatment of quantification in ordinary noun phrases. In *Natural Language Parsing and Linguistic Theories* (U. Reyle and C. Rohrer, eds.), pp. 432–47, D. Reidel: Dordrecht.

Khan, Robert (1983). A two-level morphological analysis of Rumanian. *Texas Linguistic Forum*, **22**, 253–70.

Khan, Robert, Liu, Jocelyn S., Ito, Tatsuo and Shuldberg, Kelly (1983). KIMMO user's manual. *Texas Linguistic Forum*, **22**, 203–15.

Kilbury, James (1985). Chart parsing and the Earley algorithm. In *Kontextfreie Syntaxen und verwandte Systeme* (Ursula Klenk, ed.), Max Niemeyer: Tübingen.

Kimball, John P. (1973). Seven principles of surface structure parsing in natural language. *Cognition*, **2**, 15–47.

King, Margaret (1987). The prospects of machine translation. In *Advances in Artificial Intelligence* (Ben du Boulay, David Hogg and Luc Steels, eds.), pp. 437–48, North-Holland: Amsterdam.

Klein, Ewan and van Benthem, Johan eds. (1987). *Categories, Polymorphism and Unification*. CCS/ILLI: Edinburgh/Amsterdam.

Koskenniemi, Kimmo (1983a). *Two-level morphology: a general computational model for word-form recognition and production*. University of Helsinki: Helsinki.

Koskenniemi, Kimmo (1983b). Two-level model for morphological analysis. *IJCAI-83*, 683–5.

Koskenniemi, Kimmo (1984). A general computational model for word-form recognition and production. *COLING-84*, 178–81.

Koskenniemi, Kimmo and Church, Kenneth W. (1988). Complexity, two-level morphology and Finnish. *COLING-88*, 335–40.

Langendoen, D. Terence (1981). The generative capacity of word-formation components. *Linguistic Inquiry*, **12**, 320–2.

Langendoen, D. Terence and Langsam, Yedidyah (1984). The representation of constituent structures for finite-state parsing. *COLING-84*, 24–7.

Leech, Geoffrey N. (1983). *Principles of Pragmatics*. Longmans: London and New York.

Lehnert, Wendy G. (1988). Knowledge-based natural language understanding. In *Exploring Artificial Intelligence* (Howard E. Shrobe, ed.), pp. 83–131, Morgan Kaufmann, San Mateo.

Lespérance, Yves (1986). Toward a computational interpretation of situation semantics. *Computational Intelligence*, **2**, 9–27.

Levinson, Stephen C. (1981). The essential inadequacies of speech act models of dialogue. In *Possibilities and Limitations of Pragmatics* (H. Parret, M. Sbisa and J. Verschueren, eds.) pp. 473–92, John Benjamins: Amsterdam.

Levinson, Stephen C. (1983). *Pragmatics*. Cambridge University Press: Cambridge.

Lewis, Philip M., II and Stearns, Richard E. (1968). Syntax-directed transduction. *Journal of the ACM*, **15**, 465–88.

Lindstedt, Jouko (1984). A two-level description of Old Church Slavonic morphology. *Scando-Slavica*, **30**, 165–89.

Lun, S. (1983). A two-level morphological analysis of French. *Texas Linguistic Forum*, **22**, 271–8.

Lynch, William C. and Pierson, H.L. (1968). A finite state transducer model for compiler lexical scanners. *Proceedings of the IFIP Congress (Information Processing 68)*, 448–55, Edinburgh, Scotland, August 1968.

Lyons, John (1977). *Semantics 1 & 2*. Cambridge University Press: London and New York.

Maier, David (1983). *The Theory of Relational Databases*. Computer Science Press: Rockville, MD.

Main, Michael G. and Benson, David B. (1983). Denotational semantics for 'natural' language question-answering programs. *American Journal of Computational Linguistics*, **9**, 11–21.

Mann, William C. (1983). An overview of the Nigel text generation grammar. *ACL Proceedings, 21st Annual Meeting*, 79–84.

Marcus, Mitchell P. (1980). *A Theory of Syntactic Recognition for Natural Language*. MIT Press: Cambridge, MA.

Martin, William A., Church, Kenneth W. and Patil, Ramesh S. (1987). Preliminary analysis of a breadth-first parsing algorithm: theoretical and experimental results. In *Natural Language Parsing Systems* (Leonard Bolc, ed.), pp. 267–328, Springer: Berlin.

McCawley, James D. (1968). The role of semantics in grammar. In *Universals in Linguistic Theory* (Emmon Bach and Robert Harms, eds). pp. 125–69, Holt, Rinehart & Winston: New York.

McCawley, James D. (1970). Semantic representation. In *Cognition: A Multiple View* (Paul M. Garvin, ed.) pp. 227–47, Spartan Books: New York.

McDermott, Drew (1978). Tarskian semantics, or no notation without denotation. In *Readings in Natural Language Processing* (Barbara J. Grosz, Karen Sparck Jones and Bonnie Lynn Webber, eds.), pp. 167–9, Morgan Kaufmann: Los Altos, 1986.

McDonald, David D. (1983). Natural language generation as a computational problem: an introduction. In *Computational Models of Discourse* (Michael Brady and Robert C. Berwick, eds.), pp. 209–65, MIT Press: Cambridge, MA.

McKeown, Kathleen R. (1985). *Text Generation: Using Discourse Strategies and Focus Constraints to Generate Natural Language Text*. Cambridge University Press: Cambridge.

Mellish, Christopher S. (1983). Incremental semantic interpretation in a modular parsing system. In *Automatic Natural Language Parsing* (Karen Sparck Jones and Yorick A. Wilks, eds.), pp. 148–55, Ellis Horwood/Wiley: Chichester/New York.

Mellish, Christopher S. (1985). *Computer Interpretation of Natural Language Descriptions*. Ellis Horwood/Wiley: Chichester/New York.

Mellish, Christopher S. (1988). Implementing systemic classification by unification. *Computational Linguistics*, **14**, 40–51.

Mercer, Robert E. (1988). Solving some persistent presupposition problems. *COLING-88*, 420–5.

Mercer, Robert E. and Reiter, Raymond (1982). The representations of presuppositions using defaults. *Proceedings of the Fourth Biennial Conference of the Canadian Society for Computational Studies of Intelligence*, 103–7.

Mercer, Robert E. and Rosenberg, Richard S. (1984). Generating corrective answers by computing presuppositions of answers, not of questions, or mind your P's, not Q's. *Proceedings of the Fifth Biennial Conference of the Canadian Society for Computational Studies of Intelligence*, 16–19.

Meya, Montserrat (1987). Morphological analysis of Spanish for retrieval. *Literary & Linguistic Computing*, **2**, 166–70.

Milne, Robert W. (1982). Predicting garden path sentences. *Cognitive Science*, **6**, 349–73.

Minker, Jack (1988). *Deductive Databases and Logic Programming*. Morgan Kaufmann: Los Altos.

Minsky, Marvin (1981). A framework for representing knowledge. In *Mind Design* (John Haugeland, ed.), pp. 95–128, MIT Press: Cambridge.

Mitton, Roger (1986). A partial dictionary of English in computer-usable form. *Literary & Linguistic Computing*, **1**, 214–5.

Montague, Richard (1974). *Formal Philosophy*. Yale University Press: New Haven.

Moortgat, Michael (1988). *Categorial Investigations: Logical and Linguistic Aspects of the Lambek Calculus*. Foris: Dordrecht.

Moran, Douglas B. (1982). The representation of inconsistent information in a dynamic model-theoretic semantics. *ACL Proceedings, 20th Annual Meeting*, 16–18.

Moran, Douglas B. (1988). Quantifier scoping in the SRI core language engine. *ACL Proceedings, 26th Annual Meeting*, 33–40.

Moshier, M. Drew and Rounds, William C. (1987). A logic for partially specified data structures. *Conference Record of the Fourteenth ACM Symposium on Principles of Programming Languages*, pp. 156–67, Munich, West Germany.

Mukai, Kuniaki and Yasukawa, Hideki (1985). Complex indeterminates in PROLOG and its application to discourse models. *New Generation Computing*, **3**, 441–66.

Nakashima, Hideyuki, Suzuki, Hiroyuki, Halvorsen, Per-Kristian and Peters, P. Stanley (1988). Towards a computational interpretation of situation theory. *Future Generations Computer Systems*, **3**.

Nakazawa, Tsuneko, Neher, Laura and Hinrichs, Erhard W. (1988). Unification with disjunctive and negative values for GPSG grammars. *ECAI-88*, 467–72.

Neff, Mary S., Byrd, Roy J. and Rizk, Omneya A. (1988). Creating and querying hierarchical lexical data bases. *ACL Proceedings, Second Conference on Applied Natural Language Processing*, 84–92.

Neuhaus, H. Joachim (1986). Lexical database design: the Shakespeare dictionary model. *COLING-86*, 441–4.

Nilsson, Nils J. (1980). *Problem Solving Methods in Artificial Intelligence*. Tioga: Palo Alto.

Nozohoor-Farshi, R. (1987). Context-freeness of the language accepted by Marcus' Parser. *ACL Proceedings, 25th Annual Meeting*, 117–22.

Nutter, Jane T. (1987). Default reasoning. In *Encyclopaedia of Artificial Intelligence* (Stuart C. Shapiro, ed.), pp. 840–8, Wiley: New York.

Pareschi, Remo and Steedman, Mark J. (1987). A lazy way to chart-parse with categorial grammars. *ACL Proceedings, 25th Annual Meeting*, 81–8.

Partee, Barbara H. (1970). Opacity, coreference, and pronouns. *Synthese*, **21**, 359–85.

Partee, Barbara H. (1984). Compositionality. In *Varieties of Formal Syntax, Proceedings of the 4th Amsterdam Colloquium, September 1982* (Fred Landman and Frank Veltman, eds.), pp. 281–311, Foris: Dordrecht.

Pearl, Judea (1984). *Heuristics: Intelligent Search Strategies for Computer Problem Solving*. Addison-Wesley: Reading, MA.

Pelletier, Francis J. and Schubert, Lenhart K. (1984). Two theories for computing the logical form of mass expressions. *COLING-84*, 108–11.

Pereira, Fernando C.N. (1985). A structure-sharing representation for unification-based grammar formalisms. *ACL Proceedings, 23rd Annual Meeting*, 137–44.

Pereira, Fernando C.N. and Shieber, Stuart M. (1984). The semantics of grammar formalisms seen as computer languages. *COLING-84*, 123–9.

Pereira, Fernando C.N. and Warren, David H.D. (1980). Definite clause grammars for language analysis – a survey of the formalism and a comparison with augmented transition networks. *Artificial Intelligence*, **13**, 231–78. Reprinted in *Readings in Natural Language Processing* (Barbara J. Grosz, Karen Sparck Jones and Bonnie Lynn Webber, eds.), pp. 101–24, Morgan Kaufmann: Los Altos, 1986.

Pereira, Fernando C.N., Gazdar, Gerald, Pulman, Stephen G., Joshi, Aravind K. and Kay, Martin (1987). Unification and the new grammatism (panel). *TINLAP-3*, 32–55.

Perlis, Donald (1987). Nonmonotonic reasoning. In *Encyclopaedia of Artificial Intelligence* (Stuart C. Shapiro, ed.), pp. 849–53, Wiley: New York.

Perrault, C. Raymond (1984). On the mathematical properties of linguistic theories. *Computational Linguistics*, **10**, 3–4, 165–76.

Perrott, D.V. (1951). *Swahili*. Hodder & Stoughton: Sevenoaks.

Petrick, Stanley R. (1987). Parsing. In *Encyclopaedia of Artificial Intelligence* (Stuart C. Shapiro, ed.), pp. 687–96, Wiley: New York.

Pinkal, Manfred (1986). Definite noun phrases and the semantics of discourse. *COLING-86*, 368–73.

Pollard, Carl and Sag, Ivan A. (1988). *An Information-Based Approach to Syntax and Semantics: Volume 1 Fundamentals*. CSLI Lecture Notes No. 13, Chicago University Press: Chicago.

Power, Richard (1979). The organisation of purposeful dialogues. *Linguistics*, **17**, 107–52.

Power, Richard and Longuet-Higgins, H. Christopher (1978). Learning to count: a computational model of language acquisition. *Proceedings of the Royal Society, Series B*, **200**, 391–417.

Pullum, Geoffrey K. (1983). Context-freeness and the computer processing of human languages. *ACL Proceedings, 21st Annual Meeting*, 1–6.

Pullum, Geoffrey K. (1984a). On two recent attempts to show that English is not a CFL. *Computational Linguistics*, **10**(3–4), 182–6.

Pullum, Geoffrey K. (1984b). Syntactic and semantic parsability. *COLING-84*, 112–22.

Pullum, Geoffrey K. (1987). Natural language interfaces and strategic computing. *AI & Society*, **1**, 47–58.

Pullum, Geoffrey K. and Gazdar, Gerald (1982). Natural languages and context-free languages. *Linguistics & Philosophy*, **4**, 471–504.

Pulman, Stephen G. (1983). Generalized phrase structure grammar, Earley's algorithm, and the minimisation of recursion. In *Automatic Natural Language Parsing* (Karen Sparck Jones and Yorick A. Wilks, eds.), pp. 117–31, Ellis Horwood/Wiley: Chichester/New York.

Pulman, Stephen G. (1986). Grammars, parsers, and memory limitations. *Language and Cognitive Processes*, **1**, 197–225.

Ramsay, Allan (1985). Effective parsing with generalized phrase structure grammar. *ACL Proceedings, Second European Conference*, 57–61.

Ramsay, Allan (1988). *Formal Methods in Artificial Intelligence*. Cambridge University Press: Cambridge.

Raphael, Bertram (1976). *The Thinking Computer: Mind Inside Matter*. W.H. Freeman: San Francisco.

Reape, Mike and Thompson, Henry S. (1988). Parallel intersection and serial composition of finite state transducers. *COLING-88*, 535–9.

Reyle, Uwe (1985). Grammatical functions, discourse, referents, and quantification. *IJCAI-85*, **2**, 829–31.

Rich, Elaine (1983). *Artificial Intelligence*. McGraw-Hill: New York, NY.

Riesbeck, Christopher K. (1986). From conceptual analyzer to direct memory access parsing: An overview. In *Advances in Cognitive Science 1* (Noel E. Sharkey, ed.), pp. 236–58, Ellis Horwood/Wiley: Chichester/New York.

Ritchie, Graeme D. (1983a). The implementation of a PIDGIN interpreter. In *Automatic Natural Language Parsing* (Karen Sparck Jones and Yorick A. Wilks, eds.), pp. 69–80, Ellis Horwood/Wiley: Chichester/New York.

Ritchie, Graeme D. (1983b). Semantics in parsing. In *Parsing Natural Language* (Margaret King, ed.), pp. 199–217, Academic Press: London.

Ritchie, Graeme D. (1984). Simulating a Turing machine using functional unification grammar. *ECAI-84*, 127–36.

Ritchie, Graeme D. (1985). Simulating a Turing machine using functional unification grammar. In *Advances in Artificial Intelligence* (Tim O'Shea, ed.), pp. 285–94, North-Holland: Amsterdam.

Ritchie, Graeme D. (1986). The computational complexity of sentence derivation in functional unification grammar. *COLING-86*, 584–6.

Ritchie, Graeme D. (1987). The lexicon. In *Linguistic Theory and Computer Applications* (Peter Whitelock, Mary McGee Wood, Harold L. Somers, Rod L. Johnson and Paul Bennett, eds.), pp. 225–56, Academic Press: London.

Ritchie, Graeme D. and Thompson, Henry S. (1984). Natural language processing. In *Artificial Intelligence: Tools, Techniques, and Applications* (Tim O'Shea and Marc Eisenstadt, eds.), pp. 358–88, Harper & Row: New York.

Robinson, J.A. (1965). A machine-oriented logic based on the resolution principle. *Journal of the ACM*, **12**, 23–41.

Rosenschein, Stanley J. and Shieber, Stuart M. (1982). Translating English into logical form. *ACL Proceedings, 20th Annual Meeting*, 1–8.

Russell, Graham J., Pulman, Stephen G., Ritchie, Graeme D. and Black, Alan W. (1986). A dictionary and morphological analyser for English. *COLING-86*, 277–9.

Sågvall Hein, Anna (1987). Parsing by means of Uppsala Chart Processor (UCP). In *Natural Language Parsing Systems* (Leonard Bolc, ed.), pp. 203–66, Springer: Berlin.

Saint-Dizier, Patrick (1985). Handling quantifier scoping ambiguities in a semantic representation of natural language sentences. In *Natural Language Understanding and Logic Programming* (Veronica Dahl and Patrick Saint-Dizier, eds.), pp. 49–63, North-Holland: Amsterdam.

Sampson, Geoffrey (1983a). Context-free parsing and the adequacy of context-free grammars. In *Parsing Natural Language* (Margaret King, ed.), pp. 151–70, Academic Press: London.

Sampson, Geoffrey (1983b). Deterministic parsing. In *Parsing Natural Language* (Margaret King, ed.), pp. 91–116, Academic Press: London.

Sanamrad, Mohammad Ali, Wada, Koichi and Matsumoto, Haruya (1987). A hardware syntactic analysis processor. *IEEE Micro*, **7**, 73–80.

Scha, Remko J.H., Bruce, Bertram C. and Polanyi, Livia (1987). Discourse understanding. In *Encyclopaedia of Artificial Intelligence* (Stuart C. Shapiro, ed.), pp. 233–45, Wiley: New York.

Schank, Roger C. (1972). Conceptual dependency: a theory of natural language understanding. *Cognitive Psychology*, **3**, 552–631.

Schank, Roger C. and Abelson, Robert (1977). *Scripts, Plans, Goals and Understanding*. Lawrence Erlbaum and Associates: Hillsdale, NJ.

Schank, Roger C. and Rieger, Charles J., III (1974). Inference and the computer understanding of natural language. *Artificial Intelligence*, **5**, 373–412.

Schank, Roger C. and Riesbeck, Christopher K. eds. (1981). *Inside Computer Understanding: Five Programs plus Miniatures*. Erlbaum: Hillsdale.

Schubert, Lenhart K. (1986). Are there preference trade-offs in attachment decisions? *AAAI-86*, **1**, 601–5.

Schubert, Lenhart K. and Pelletier, Francis J. (1982). From English to logic: context-free computation of 'conventional' logical translation. *American Journal of Computational Linguistics*, **8**, 27–44. Reprinted in *Readings in Natural Language Processing* (Barbara J. Grosz, Karen Sparck Jones and Bonnie Lynn Webber, eds.), pp. 293–311, Morgan Kaufmann: Los Altos, 1986.

Schwartz, Steven C. (1987). *Applied Natural Language Processing*. Petrocelli: Princeton, NJ.

Sedgewick, Robert (1983). *Algorithms*. Addison-Wesley, Reading, MA.

Selfridge, Mallory (1986). A computer model of child language learning. *Artificial Intelligence*, **29**(2), 171–216.

Sells, Peter (1985). *Lectures on Contemporary Syntactic Theories*. CSLI Lecture Notes No. 3, Chicago University Press: Chicago.

Shapiro, Stuart C. (1987). *Encyclopaedia of Artificial Intelligence*. Wiley: New York.

Sheil, Beau A. (1976). Observations on context free parsing. *Statistical Methods in Linguistics*, 71–109.

Shieber, Stuart M. (1983). Sentence disambiguation by a shift-reduce parsing technique. *IJCAI-83*, 699–703.

Shieber, Stuart M. (1985a). Criteria for designing computer facilities for linguistic analysis. *Linguistics*, **23**, 189–211.

Shieber, Stuart M. (1985b). Evidence against the non-context-freeness of natural language. *Linguistics and Philosophy*, **8**, 333–43.

Shieber, Stuart M. (1985c). Using restriction to extend parsing algorithms for complex-feature-based formalisms. *ACL Proceedings, 23rd Annual Meeting*, 145–52.

Shieber, Stuart M. (1986a). *An Introduction to Unification-Based Approaches to Grammar*. Chicago University Press: Chicago.

Shieber, Stuart M. (1986b). A simple reconstruction of GPSG. *COLING-86*, pp. 211–5.

Shieber, Stuart M. (1987). Separating linguistic analyses from linguistic theories. In *Linguistic Theory & Computer Applications* (Peter Whitelock, Mary McGee Wood, Harold L. Somers, Rod L. Johnson and Paul Bennett, eds.), pp. 1–36, Academic Press: London.

Shieber, Stuart M. (1988). A uniform architecture for parsing and generation. *COLING-88*, 614–9.

Slack, Jon M. (1986). Distributed memory: a basis for chart parsing. *COLING-86*, 476–81.

Slocum, Jonathan (1985). A survey of machine translation: its history, current status, and future prospects. *Computational Linguistics*, **11**, 1–17.

Smith, Brian C. (1982). Linguistic and computational semantics. *ACL Proceedings, 20th Annual Meeting*, 9–15.

Sondheimer, Norman K., Weischedel, Ralph M. and Bobrow, Robert J. (1984). Semantic interpretation using KL-ONE. *COLING–84*, 101–7.

Sparck Jones, Karen (1983). So what about parsing compound nouns? In *Automatic Natural Language Parsing* (Karen Sparck Jones and Yorick A. Wilks, eds.), pp. 164–8, Ellis Horwood/Wiley: Chichester/New York.

Sparck Jones, Karen and Wilks, Yorick A. eds. (1983). *Automatic Natural Language Parsing*. Ellis Horwood/Wiley: Chichester/New York.

Steel, Sam and De Roeck, Anne N. (1987). Bidirectional chart parsing. In *Advances in Artificial Intelligence (Proceedings of AISB-87)* (Christopher S. Mellish and John Hallam, eds.), pp. 223–35, Wiley: Chichester.

Steele, Guy L., Jr. (1984). *Common Lisp: The Language*. Digital Press.

Sugimura, Ryoichi (1986). Japanese honorifics and situation semantics. *COL-ING-86*, 507–10.

Tait, John I. (1983). Semantic parsing and syntactic constraints (mark IV). In *Automatic Natural Language Parsing* (Karen Sparck Jones and Yorick A. Wilks, eds.), pp. 169–77, Ellis Horwood/Wiley: Chichester/New York.

Tennant, Harry R. (1981). *Natural Language Processing*. Petrocelli: New York.

Thomason, Richmond H. (1972). A semantic theory of sortal incorrectness. *Journal of Philosophical Logic*, **1**, 209–58.

Thompson, Henry S. (1981). Chart parsing and rule schemata in PSG. *ACL Proceedings, 19th Annual Meeting*, 167–72.

Thompson, Henry S. (1983). MCHART: a flexible, modular chart parsing system. *AAAI-83*, 408–10.

Thompson, Henry S. (1985). Speech transcription: an incremental, interactive approach. In *Advances in Artificial Intelligence* (Tim O'Shea, ed.), pp. 267–74, North-Holland: Amsterdam.

Thompson, Henry S. and Ritchie, Graeme D. (1984). Implementing natural language parsers. In *Artificial Intelligence: Tools, Techniques, and Applications* (Tim O'Shea and Marc Eisenstadt, eds.), pp. 245–300, Harper & Row: New York.

Thorne, James, Bratley, P. and Dewar, Hamish (1968). The syntactic analysis of English by machine. In *Machine Intelligence 3* (Donald Michie, ed.), Elsevier: New York.

Tomita, Masaru (1984). LR parsers for natural languages. *COLING-84*, 354–7.

Tomita, Masaru (1986). *Efficient Parsing for Natural Language: A Fast Algorithm for Practical Systems*. Kluwer: Boston.

Touretzky, David S. (1984). *LISP: A Gentle Introduction to Symbolic Computation*. Harper & Row: New York.

Touretzky, David S. (1986). *The Mathematics of Inheritance Systems*. Pitman/Morgan Kaufmann: London/Los Altos.

Touretzky, David S. (1987). Inheritance hierarchy. In *Encyclopaedia of Artificial Intelligence* (Stuart C. Shapiro, ed.), pp. 422–31, Wiley: New York.

Trost, Harald and Buchberger, Ernst (1986). Towards the automatic acquisition of lexical data. *COLING-86*, 387–9.

Tsujii, Jun-ichi (1986). Future directions of machine translation. *COLING–86*, 655–68.

Ullman, Jeffrey D. (1982). *Principles of Database Systems*. Computer Science Press: Rockville, MD.

Uszkoreit, Hans (1986). Categorial unification grammar. *COLING-86*, 187–94.

van Benthem, Johan and ter Meulen, Alice (1985). *Generalized quantifiers in natural language*. Foris: Dordrecht.

van der Sandt, Rob A. (1988). *Context and Presupposition*. Croom Helm: London.

Wada, Hajime and Asher, Nicholas (1986). BUILDRS: an implementation of DR theory and LFG. *COLING-86*, 540–5.

Wahlster, Wolfgang (1986). The role of natural language in advanced knowledge-based systems. In *Artificial Intelligence and Man–Machine Systems* (H. Winter, ed.), pp. 62–83, Springer: Heidelberg.

Waltz, David L. and Pollack, Jordan B. (1984). Massively parallel parsing: a strongly interactive model of natural language interpretation. *Cognitive Science*, **9**(1), 51–74.

Warren, David S. and Friedman, Joyce (1982). Using semantics in non-context-free parsing of Montague grammar. *American Journal of Computational Linguistics*, **8**, 123–38.

Webber, Bonnie Lynn (1987). Question answering. In *Encyclopaedia of Artificial Intelligence* (Stuart C. Shapiro, ed.), pp. 814–22, Wiley: New York.

Wehrli, Eric (1985). Design and implementation of a lexical data base. *ACL Proceedings, Second European Conference*, 146–53.

Weischedel, Ralph M. and Sondheimer, Norman K. (1983). Meta-rules as a basis for processing ill-formed output. *American Journal of Computational Linguistics*, **9**(3–4), 161–77.

Weizenbaum, Joseph (1966). ELIZA – a computer program for the study of natural language communication between man and machine. *Communications of the ACM*, **9**(1), 36–45.

Whorf, Benjamin L. (1940). Linguistics as an exact science. *Technology Review*, **43**, 61–3, 80–3.

Wilensky, Robert (1983). *Planning and Understanding*. Addison-Wesley: New York.

Wilensky, Robert (1986). Points: a theory of the structure of stories in memory. In *Readings in Natural Language Processing* (Barbara J. Grosz, Karen Sparck Jones and Bonnie Lynn Webber, eds.), pp. 459–73, Morgan Kaufmann: Los Altos, 1986.

Wilks, Yorick (1975). A preferential, pattern-seeking, semantics for natural language inference. *Artificial Intelligence*, **6**, 53–74.

Wilks, Yorick (1977). Good and bad arguments about semantic primitives. *Communication & Cognition*, **8**, 201–19.

Wilks, Yorick (1985). Right attachment and preference semantics. *ACL Proceedings, Second European Conference*, 89–92.

Wilks, Yorick (1987). Primitives. In *Encyclopaedia of Artificial Intelligence* (Stuart C. Shapiro, ed.), pp. 759–61, Wiley: New York.

Winograd, Terry (1972). *Understanding Natural Language*. Academic Press: New York.

Winograd, Terry (1983). *Language as a Cognitive Process: Syntax*. Addison-Wesley: Reading, MA.

Winograd, Terry and Flores, Fernando (1986). *Understanding Computers and Cognition*. Ablex, Norwood.

Winston, Patrick H. (1984). *Artificial Intelligence* 2nd edn. Addison-Wesley: Reading, MA.

Winston, Patrick H. and Horn, Berthold K.P. (1989). *Lisp* 3rd edn. Addison-Wesley: Reading, MA.

Wiren, Mats (1987). A comparison of rule-invocation strategies in context-free chart parsing. *ACL Proceedings, Third European Conference*, 226–35.

Wittenburg, Kent (1986). A parser for portable NL interfaces using graph-unification-based grammars. *AAAI-86*, **2**, 1053–8.

Wood, Derek (1987). *The Theory of Computation*. Harper & Row: New York.

Woods, William A. (1968). Procedural semantics for a question–answering machine. *AFIPS Conference Proceedings*, **33**, 457–71.

Woods, William A. (1970). Transition network grammars for natural language analysis. *Communications of the ACM*, **13**, 591–6. Reprinted in *Readings in Natural Language Processing* (Barbara J. Grosz, Karen Sparck Jones and Bonnie Lynn Webber, eds.), pp. 71–87, Morgan Kaufmann, Los Altos, 1986.

Woods, William A. (1973). Progress in natural language understanding: an application to lunar geology. *AFIPS Conference Proceedings*, **42**, 441–50.

Woods, William A. (1978). Semantics and quantification in natural language question answering. In *Readings in Natural Language Processing* (Barbara J. Grosz, Karen Sparck Jones and Bonnie Lynn Webber, eds.), pp. 205–48, Morgan Kaufmann: Los Altos, 1986.

Woods, William A. (1980). Cascaded ATN grammars. *American Journal of Computational Linguistics*, **6**, 1–12.

Woods, William A. (1981). Procedural semantics as a theory of meaning. In *Elements of Discourse Understanding* (Aravind K. Joshi, Bonnie Lynn Webber and Ivan Sag, eds.), pp. 300–34, Cambridge University Press: Cambridge.

Woods, William A. (1987). Augmented transition network grammar. In *Encyclopaedia of Artificial Intelligence* (Stuart C. Shapiro, ed.), pp. 323–33, Wiley: New York.

Wos, Larry, Overbeek, Ross A., Lusk, Ewing L. and Boyle, James (1984). *Automated Reasoning: Introduction and Applications*. Prentice-Hall, Englewood Cliffs, NJ.

Wroblewski, David (1987). Nondestructive graph unification. *AAAI-87*, 582–9.

Yngve, Victor H. (1958). A programming language for mechanical translation. *Mechanical Translation*, **5**, 25–41.

Younger, David H. (1967). Recognition and parsing of context-free languages in time n^3. *Information and Control*, **10**, 189–208.

Yuasa, Taiichi (1988). *Common Lisp Drill*. Academic Press: New York.

Yuasa, Taiichi and Hagiya, Masami (1987). *Introduction to Common Lisp*. Academic Press: New York.

Zeevat, Henk (1988). Combining categorial grammar and unification. In *Natural Language Parsing and Linguistic Theories* (U. Reyle and C. Rohrer, eds.), pp. 202–29, D. Reidel: Dordrecht.

NAME INDEX

General Index